THE HUMAN INSIDE

Discover who you were before the world told you who to become

RAFAEL ANDRADE

The Human Inside
Discover who you were before the world told you who to become

Copyright © 2025 by Rafael Andrade

All rights reserved.
No part of this publication may be reproduced, distributed, or transmitted in any form or by any means, including photocopying, recording, or other electronic or mechanical methods, without the prior written permission of the author, except in the case of brief quotations embodied in critical reviews and certain other noncommercial uses permitted by copyright law.

For permission requests, contact the author at:
info@thehuman-inside.com
www.thehuman-inside.com

ISBN: 978-1-83556-510-0 Paperback
ISBN: 978-1-83556-511-7 Hardcover
ISBN: 978-1-83556-512-4 Ebook

Disclaimer:
This book is intended to provide personal insights, reflections, and guidance for self-discovery based on the author's experiences and research. It is offered for informational and inspirational purposes only. It is not intended to be a substitute for professional psychological, medical, spiritual, or financial advice, diagnosis, or treatment. Readers are encouraged to seek the advice of qualified professionals for any specific concerns or issues. The author and publisher disclaim any liability, loss, or risk, personal or otherwise, which is incurred as a consequence, directly or indirectly, of the use and application of any of the contents of this book.

Credits:
Editing: Rafael Andrade & John Mullahy
Printed in the United States of America
First Edition

"We should every night call ourselves to an account: What infirmity have I mastered today? What passions opposed? What temptation resisted? What virtue acquired? Our vices will abate of themselves if they be brought every day to the shrift."

Seneca

To my beloved children Maya, Nico, and Tino,

May you always remember the profound truth in Marcus Aurelius's words:

"These are the characteristics of the rational soul: self-awareness, self-examination, and self-determination. It reaps its own harvest... It succeeds in its own purpose..."

May your lives be a testament to profound self-observation of the world around you, diligent scrutiny of the universe inside you, and the power of conscious adaptation. In this, you will discover that much of what appears beyond your grasp is, in fact, within your control, leading you to a life of authentic flourishing.

I am so incredibly fortunate to be your father.

I love you and I am so proud of you.

ACKNOWLEDGEMENT

The Human Inside emerged from a journey of personal inquiry that began with a pivotal conversation in 1992 with Father Douglas Bailey. In that exchange, he shared a profound insight: feelings and emotions are 100% changeable through deliberate and disciplined action. More importantly, I learned that how we see others reveals more about who we are than who they are. Father Bailey, thank you for planting the seed that began my process of questioning everything – including my thoughts, feelings and emotions. That mindset opened me to countless conversations that would shape my understanding and transform me into the person capable of writing this book.

I am eternally grateful to my parents, Rufina and Rafael, who provided the foundation for everything that followed. Mamá, thank you for embodying selfless devotion as you protected, provided for, guided, and cared for me and my sisters. You were the perfect example of unconditional love in action. My sisters and I became the humans we are today because of your sacrifice and dedication. I love you and miss you deeply. Papá, you exemplified what it means to serve others above oneself. As a tireless physician, you consistently placed your patients' well-being ahead of monetary gain, embodying the Hippocratic oath better than anyone I have ever known. Through both of you, I learned the true meaning of hard work, dedication, and lifelong learning. My journey of self-observation was only possible because of the solid foundation you provided.

To my family, especially my children Maya, Nico and Tino and my sisters Pili and Mili – thank you for your unwavering love and support throughout my life journey. You continue to be a source of inspiration and motivation for me.

Special recognition and gratitude goes to several individuals who directly influenced this work:

- Ivan Guerra, for the long hours of deep intellectual discussions, and the books, papers, and articles you shared with me that inspired the ideas in this book.
- Dr. Scott Sherr, for teaching me the principles of precision medicine and inspiring me to observe my body and thoughts more deeply.

- John Mullahy, for the great Aristotelian conversations that helped me expand my mind beyond science.
- Todd Sampson & Liz Sampson, for sharing your tools and experience in the world of book publishing. You were so generous with your time during a time I truly needed support. Thank you.
- Felipe Navarrete, for listening to my ideas, for encouraging me to create The Human Inside Mentoring Program and for being my first client. Thank you for your vote of confidence.
- Wayne Alleyne, for your friendship and support and for agreeing to listen to my mentoring program and providing feedback. That feedback led to the development of this book.
- Juan Santos, for supporting me with the podcast, the accelerator office space and for being a great friend.
- David Zambrano, thank you for your friendship and support. You are the example of a true friend.
- Monique Bergh, your love and support during such a difficult time in both of our lives cannot be explained with words. Thank you for believing in me. I love you.

I am grateful to all my teachers during my undergraduate and graduate studies. Some of you served as examples to follow, others as warnings to heed. Both were equally important and necessary in the path toward mindful growth. I extend the same gratitude to my mentors during my corporate years, who enabled me to travel the world and collaborate with exceptional professionals across 51 countries. This global perspective on the human condition proved instrumental in developing the insights contained within these pages.

A Note on Technology and Integrity

In pursuing scientific accuracy and trustworthiness for "The Human Inside," I embraced modern technological tools, including generative AI, as powerful assistants to enhance precision and efficiency — never as substitutes for human insight and research. AI supported this work in three specific ways:

- **Citation Verification:** Ensuring meticulous cross-referencing and proper formatting of academic sources, maintaining rigorous scholarly standards throughout.
- **Research Enhancement:** When initial peer-reviewed sources needed expansion, AI helped identify complementary academic research, broadening the factual foundation for key arguments.

- **Manuscript Polish:** Following extensive human editing, AI tools assisted with final reviews of flow, consistency, grammar, and readability.

Every insight, argument, and conclusion in this book has been rigorously reviewed, verified, and approved by me. I take full responsibility for all content and its accuracy. The integration of AI served solely to strengthen the integrity and presentation of human-driven research and insights, ensuring you receive the most precise and reliable information possible. I am not an expert in any domain presented in this book, nor I would ever pretend to be. I am simply a student of science who has chosen to live a scientifically and spiritually examined life. As such, I respectfully request your help in keeping this work factual, accurate and current. If you find any errors, misquotes or inconsistencies, or if you simply want to share newer information, please send me an email at admin@thehumaninside.com. I will do my best to publish any relevant updates on my webpage and any future editions.

The ideas within these pages represent decades of personal inquiry, professional experience, and careful study of the latest scientific understanding of human consciousness and potential. Every principle in this book has directly or indirectly impacted my life in a positive way. It is my hope is that they serve you as powerfully as the journey of discovering them has served me.

CONTENTS

Foreword..15

Introduction: The Best of Times?...................................17

PART 1: FOUNDATIONS FOR THE HUMAN INSIDE

Chapter 1. Our Evolutionary Heritage................................. 25
    An Environment Suitable for Life........................... 26
    From single cells to complex beings 28
    The Journey to Becoming Human 30
    Chapter 1 Summary: Key Insights........................... .37

Chapter 2. The Human Brain: A Masterpiece of Evolution............. 41
    What made us so different? 42
    Fire as an Evolutionary Catalyst............................ 43
    The Neuroenergetic Trade-Off 45
    The Metabolic Revolution 48
    What is the human brain for?................................ .51
    An Ancient brain in a modern world...................... 57
    The Foundations of Consciousness...................... 59
    Implications for Modern Living 62
    Chapter 2 Summary: Key Insights 65

Chapter 3. The Predictive Brain 67
    The Unfinished Miracle: Why Humans Are Born Helpless 68
    The Prediction Machine: How Our Brain Really Works 70
    Neuroplasticity: The Brain That Changes Itself.................. 76

The Human Mind. 81

How Language Shapes the Human Mind 89

Chapter 3 Summary: Key Insights 93

PART 1 CONCLUSION: Connecting Evolution, Brain, and Mind . 95

PART 2: CONSTRUCTING REALITY

Chapter 4. Multiple Dimensions of Reality 99

What is "Real"? 100

Neuroscience and the Constructed Self / Reality 101

When Timeless Insight Converges with Contemporary Discovery . . 105

Western Philosophy's Prescient Insights on Reality 107

Eastern Wisdom: The Beauty of Inner Investigation 112

Quantum Physics: When Science Meets Mystery 122

Converging Insights: Ancient Wisdom, Modern Science, and the Nature of Reality 128

Chapter 4 Summary: Key Insights 130

Chapter 5. The Bayesian Brain... 133

The Bayesian Model of Reality 134

The Paradox of Human Statistical Reasoning. 138

Is Reality a Hallucination? 149

Applying Bayesian Thinking to Everyday Life 162

The Reality Of Belief: A Scientific Perspective 167

Truth and Identity: Who You Are vs. What You Believe 175

Chapter 5 Summary: Key Insights 181

Chapter 6. Truth, Social Reality and Collective Illusions................ 183

When Individual Minds Create Shared Illusions 184

Understanding Truth in a World of Constructed Realities. 191

A Scientific Foundation: Objective Truths 193

Subjective Truths: When Objective Science is Not Enough 195
  Pragmatic Truths – What Works in Practice 197
  Living in a world of objective and subjective truths 199
  Ancient Wisdom and Modern Application. 203
  Truth in the Digital Age: New Challenges and Opportunities 208
  Chapter 6 Summary: Key Insights 215

Chapter 7. The Embodied Mind 217
  Our Second Brain: Our Gut's Role in Reality Perception 218
  Sleep Deficit and Reality Processing 226
  Stress, Inflammation, and Cognitive Performance. 231
  Chapter 7 Summary: Key Insights 235

PART 2 CONCLUSIONS: Toward A Unified Model Of Reality ...239

PART 3: A PRACTICAL TRANSFORMATION

Chapter 8. The Art of Self Scrutiny 245
  Developing Balanced Self-Awareness for Authentic Growth 246
  Metacognition 254
  Chapter 8 Summary: Key Insights 262

Chapter 9. COMMUNICATING BETTER 265
  Beyond Information Exchange: The Multi-Dimensional Nature of
  Communication. 266
  Learning from Ancient Argumentation Wisdom 268
  Internal Communication: Dialoguing with Yourself 275
  Advanced Interpersonal Communication Skills 277
  A Practical Framework for Communication Improvement 287
  Communication Across Worldviews. 289
  Advanced Techniques: Productive Concession and Strategic Patience
 290

Technology and the Evolution of Human Communication 292

Chapter 9 Summary: Key Insights 294

Chapter 10. Your Daily Practice: The 39-Minute Journey............297

The Science of Sustainable Change: Why 39 Minutes Works. 298

The 39-Minute Journey: Your Daily Practice 300

Adapting Your Journey: Flexibility, Assessment, and Growth 303

Chapter 10 Summary: Key Insights 306

CONCLUSION: Reclaiming the Human Inside............................309

Synthesis of Key Insights 309

Bridging Ancient Wisdom and Modern Science. 312

Living Authentically in a Complex World 314

A Path Forward 317

Final Reflections: Returning to the Human Inside 320

Appendix..323

Creating a Generic and Structured Personal Development Plan. . . .323

A Practical 24-Week Communication Development Program. 324

7-Day Communication Starter Program. 327

References..329

Books. 329

Journal Articles. 336

Other Articles 347

Online Videos 351

Websites/Webpages 351

Index 349

LIST OF TABLES

Table 1 – Key Hominin Milestones 35
Table 2 – Comparative Neuroanatomical and Morphological Data for Select Primate Brains. 46
Table 3 – The Human Nervous System – High-Level 51
Table 4 – Summary of Default Mode Network Functions. 102
Table 5 – Parallels between Plato's Allegory of the Cave and Neuroscience 108
Table 6 – Parallels Shared by Hinduism, Buddhism, and Modern Science 119
Table 7 – Examples of Our Hidden Statistical Skills 139
Table 8 – Examples of Explicit Human Statistical Struggles 142
Table 9 – Examples of Perceptual Phenomena 151
Table 10 – Traditional vs Bayesian Learning principles 166
Table 11 – Four Column Technique 174
Table 12 – Examples of Pluralistic Ignorance 186
Table 13 – Practical Strategies for Information Consumption 214
Table 14 – The Human Nervous System Expanded 219
Table 15 – Example of Our Brain's Nutritional Needs. 222
Table 16 – How the Brain Benefits from Omega-3, B Complex and Iron . 222
Table 17 – Examples of Inflammatory and Anti-inflammatory Foods   224
Table 18 – Acute vs Chronic Stress Effects 231
Table 19 – Self-Criticism vs Self-Comparison 247
Table 20 – Components of Evidence-Based Confidence 248
Table 21 – Examples of Self-Assessment Biases 250
Table 22 – Troubleshooting Common Metacognitive Obstacles. . . .258
Table 23 – Examples Personal Development Philosophy Components 260

Table 24 – Some Common Communication Failures.. 267
Table 25 – Argumentation in Ancient Greece vs Today.. 269
Table 26 – Components of Ethos. 272
Table 27 – Components of Pathos 273
Table 28 – Components of Logos 273
Table 29 – Examples of Useful Emotional Language Terms. 276
Table 30 – Example of Sustainable Growth Cycle.. 299
Table 31 – The 50-40-10 Rule 300

FOREWORD

Why does our brain work the way it does? How has it evolved? Could we think differently? Those are some of the questions my good friend Rafael Andrade considers in his first book "The Human Inside." And I'm so proud of this worthy accomplishment. I've known Mr. Andrade since we were seniors in high school. I gravitated toward him then because his curiosity was as commanding as his voice was calm. Behind his big, bright smile and kind demeanor was a preternatural drive. America wasn't his first country, English wasn't his first language. But he thrived here because he chose to. I've enjoyed his many well-crafted oral stories since then, and I welcome you to enjoy this well-written one now.

With facts, figures, tables and numbers sandwiched between compelling narrative and tight bullet points, "The Human Inside" offers historical, philosophical, and scientific support for our thought processes. Using information culled from his podcasts and his independent research, Mr. Andrade examines the brain under a microscope and takes us on an evolutionary tour de force of our senses and thoughts. He discusses how our single-celled simple ancestors preferred not to become extinct, but rather to adapt, survive, and become the complex multi-celled organisms we are today. He explains how we discern what's real from what's imaginary, why we respond the way we do to certain stimuli, and how our development from primates to human beings has shaped our mindset. He also notes that with practice and focus we could overcome some negative evolutionary baggage, think more positively, and become healthier in the process.

"The Human Inside" shines as bright as Mr. Andrade's smile because he takes complex terms and concepts about the brain and how we think and simplifies them. He shows us what he knows while not expecting us to accept his points blindly. He doesn't always answer some of the questions he poses. And he questions some of the answers he provides. He writes Socratically instead of didactically, and that works well because it encourages the reader to return to this book regularly as a resource. Enjoy the ride!

John Mullahy

August 7, 2025

INTRODUCTION: THE BEST OF TIMES?

In a recent conversation, a friend of mine told me that "we live in the best of times". This was an interesting comment and one that I had to process. In fact, for me, this simple statement opened up a profound inquiry into what it means to be human in the 21st century. You see, in some ways, we seem to be doing better than ever in our history as a species. Evidence shows that we live longer than in years past, have more access to education, and millions engage in daily acts of charity toward those in need. In general terms, it is a great time to be alive; in fact, there is no other time in history where I would rather be. At least according to the **World Health Organization (WHO)**, we have reasons to believe that we are living in the best of times. Here is an excerpt of their 2022 report, which can be found at https://www.who.int/news/item/20-05-2022-world-health-statistics-2022

> "Global life expectancy at birth had increased from 66.8 years in 2000 to 73.3 years in 2019, and healthy life expectancy increased from 58.3 years to 63.7 years. This was largely due to gains in maternal and child health, and to major investments and improvements in communicable disease programmes, such as HIV, tuberculosis and malaria. But the 2020 data shows how service disruptions contributed to an increase in deaths from tuberculosis and malaria between 2019 and 2020.
>
> Prior to the pandemic, there had also been encouraging trends globally in the reduction of child stunting, alcohol consumption and tobacco use, as well as in increased access to safely managed drinking water, safely managed sanitation, basic hygiene, and clean fuels and technologies for cooking.
>
> These advances had been partly underpinned by a doubling in global spending on health between 2000 and 2019, reaching 9.8% of global gross domestic product. But approximately 80% of that spending occurred in high-income countries, the bulk of it (about 70%) coming from government budgets. In low-income countries, out-of-pocket spending was the main source of health expenditure (44%), followed by external aid (29%)."

However, while we may live in "the best of times" we are far from being our best. Given the amount of wealth available globally, our collective well-being should be significantly better. According to Oxfam's 2022 report, the world's ten richest men more than doubled their wealth during the pandemic while 99% of humanity experienced worsened socioeconomic circumstances. The wealthiest 1% own more than 45% of global wealth, while nearly half the world's population survives on less than $5.50 daily. Tens of millions worldwide are living lives that are far from great (at least from a health and well-being perspective).

Although statistics in general can be useful, I find it difficult to use the data to discern well-being when it comes to the human condition and overall health. Global statistics, while impressive, often mask individual suffering and the vast variations in quality of life both between and within countries. Averages tell us little about any single person's lived experience. When it comes to well-being, I gravitate toward more basic and direct questions: how are you doing? How are you feeling? Is it possible that you are not living your best life in "the best of times"? Could you feel better? Could you DO better? Of course you can DO better…of course we can. But how? How do we DO better?

To DO better, we need greater awareness of both the world around us and the universe inside of us. We must find ways to understand ourselves better before we try to understand the people and situations around us. Understanding how our brain and biology function is the key to unlocking our potential for improvement. This awareness and understanding can help us become better versions of ourselves through continuous observation and action. In the past, concepts like awareness and self-awareness were studied subjectively. However, thanks to advancements in technology, behavioral science, and research techniques, scientists have learned more about the human brain in the last 30 years than in all previous centuries. This helps us understand ourselves and others better than ever before. I believe that before understanding ourselves in a traditional way, we must first consider understanding how our brains evolved and how we think they work according to current peer-reviewed science.

Traditional biology tells us that the human brain receives inputs from our senses, processes information from those inputs, and then acts. As mammals, we evaluate the outcome of such actions to determine if the actions were successful or not. Some refer to this as a direct mapping from sensory input to action, and we can see this in everyday life (i.e., reflexively pulling back after unexpectedly touching something hot). In his book "**A Thousand Brains**", **Jeff Hawkins** tells us that this type of response occurs in the spinal cord, but that the neocortex <u>does not</u> operate like the spinal cord. The neocortex is the part of our brain responsible for what we consider intelligence and where most of what we call "thinking" takes place.

However, the fact that thinking takes place in the brain doesn't mean the brain evolved specifically for thinking. This may seem like a petty point, but it is essential to understanding ourselves. In her book "**7½ Lessons About the Brain**", **Dr. Lisa Feldman Barrett** explains that the brain's primary purpose is NOT thinking. She tells us that the brain's most important job is managing allostasis, managing our energy budget by predicting our energy needs before they arise, using past experiences to determine how to move through this world efficiently and survive. Rather than pure reaction, this fundamental predictive function shapes everything from our simplest movements to our most complex social interpretations, serving as our brain's core strategy for survival and efficiency.

To manage the body's energy budget, our brain constantly processes information and learns **a model of the world** around and within us. In his book, Hawkins articulates that learning extends beyond formal education, including how objects behave and how a door or an app opens and closes. We learn where objects are located in the world, and we learn concepts like politics, ethics, language, and mathematics. While genes may determine basic functions like eating and responses to pain, everything we know is learned. Hawkins teaches us that all this information is not just stored and piled up in the brain as facts but instead is organized in a way that reflects the structure of the world and everything in it. In other words, the brain creates a model of the world it senses, and through this model, the brain can consolidate interdependent sensory inputs into a singular experience. This model helps us understand why identical sensory inputs lead to distinct **beliefs and conclusions**. Two people can witness the exact same political speech and come away with completely different interpretations - one seeing inspiration, the other seeing manipulation - because their brain's prior models filter the incoming sensory data differently.

What makes this particularly fascinating is not that the brain models the world around us and how we fit in it, but that **the model is predictive and is constantly and forever being refined.** According to Dr. Shamil Chandaria, Senior Research Fellow at the Center for Eudaimonia and Human Flourishing at Imperial College London, the brain's primary function is to reduce environmental uncertainty. In other words, the brain must reduce prediction errors about its anticipated environment. In a conversation with Sam Harris on the "Making Sense" podcast, Dr. Chandaria describes the brain as a hierarchical predictive processing entity that receives data from our senses at one end, while maintaining an existing model of the world that was built by our prior experiences at the other end. The brain then creates a model based on sensory data, compares it to the prior model already created, and calculates an error. Based on this error, the prior model can be adjusted and become the current model until new sensorial data arrives to be considered and compared. This leads to a fundamental concept central to this book: The brain continually predicts what exists in the environment based on prior experiences and new sensory data. In practical terms, this means that when we're driving and see a yellow light, our brain instantly predicts multiple outcomes based on our speed, distance to the intersection, and past experiences with yellow lights. These rapid predictions largely determine our decision to stop or continue, most of which happen below conscious awareness.

The model of the world the brain creates not only includes the physical things we see and recognize, but also includes everything about us. The model includes what **we believe, what we think is good or bad, what we consider attractive, what we may think is common sense, and concepts like democracy, capitalism, fashion, leadership, etc**. Engaging in a daily process that helps us construct a better version of ourselves today requires continuous self-scrutiny and self-observation, followed by learning and corresponding corrective actions. If we choose to live the same life we have always lived, with identical or similar sensory inputs, ideas, and experiences, the brain's processing of that data will yield minimal or no errors when compared to the existing model. And that would leave us stuck with past models. This is precisely how some of us become "stuck in our ways"; we simply stop challenging and questioning ourselves and our beliefs. But there's good news. Suppose we start or resume challenging the model in our brains with new sensory data, ideas, experiences, and paradigms. In that case, our brain will engage in a phenomenal updating process that is relatively new in the world of modern science.

In their book "**Brain Wash**," **Drs. David and Austin Perlmutter** teach us that our brains use neurotransmitters and hormones to transfer and modify messages across the brain and body. These molecules work together to drive feelings of joy, anger, bliss, hunger, lust, and desire." As these molecules do their work, connections in our brain become stronger or weaker **as a function of the activities we choose to engage or not engage in**. This process is central to one of the most important discoveries in neuroscience: neuroplasticity. To say that the brain is plastic means that it can reorganize itself by forming new connections or strengthening existing ones. It means the brain is pliable, impressionable, and moldable. **Dr. Michael Merzenich**, a pioneer in the field of neuroplasticity, explains this concept as follows:

> "Experience coupled with attention leads to physical changes in the structure and future functioning of the nervous system. This leaves us with a clear physiological fact: moment by moment, we choose and sculpt how our ever-changing minds will work. We choose who we will be in the very next moment in a very real sense, and these choices are left embossed in physical form in our material selves."

This is both powerful and sobering because neuroplasticity can help or hurt us. Every time we engage in a new experience, the brain changes itself to accommodate this new experience. And the more we engage in any activity, the stronger the connections needed to perform that activity become. This is true whether the activity is good or bad for you. If we engage in activities rooted in negativity or fear, our brains will be rewired to respond to these negative and fear-driven states.

Research shows that spending just 30 minutes daily scrolling through negative social media content increases activity in the amygdala (the brain's fear center) and decreases activity in the prefrontal cortex (the area responsible for rational thinking), physically reshaping neural connections toward anxiety and reactivity.

Conversely, positive neuroplasticity can be cultivated through specific practices. For example, studies have shown that after 8 weeks of daily meditation (for at least 10 minutes per day), gray matter density can increase in regions associated with self-awareness and compassion. For example, learning a new language or musical instrument creates new neural pathways that enhance cognitive flexibility. Even simple practices such as keeping a gratitude journal for five minutes each evening can strengthen positive neural circuits over time.

Why does this matter to you in your everyday life? Here is why:

1. The brain manages our energy budget through prediction and past experiences.
2. The brain then creates a model of the world, verifies it, and constantly updates it through sensory data from our chosen experiences.
3. The quality of experiences and information we expose ourselves to is used to verify and update that model.
4. If we fill our lives with experiences and mental narratives that merely validate existing models, we will continue to live within the limitations and biases of that model, we will become stuck, and we will end up blaming external factors for what we feel and experience. This is neuroplasticity working against us.
5. If we fill our lives with experiences and mental experiments that challenge our biases, if we read challenging literature, and if we safely challenge our bodies with physical activity, we will upgrade our model, re-framing our worldview and taking full advantage of neuroplasticity.

I understand you might be skeptical about your ability to change, especially if past attempts have proven difficult. Many believe that after a certain age, we become "set in our ways" and significant personal change becomes impossible. However, the scientific evidence for neuroplasticity throughout the lifespan is overwhelming. Research has shown that even in our 80s and 90s, the brain maintains its ability to form new connections and pathways. The key is not age but rather consistent practice and the right approach.

As you consider embarking on this journey of self-improvement, I invite you to reflect on these questions:

- What models or beliefs about yourself might be limiting your potential now?
- When was the last time you intentionally exposed yourself to ideas that challenged your existing worldview?
- What small daily practice could you begin tomorrow to create positive neuroplastic changes in your brain?

Do you want to become a better version of yourself every day? Then you may enjoy the rest of this book. But be prepared. What is seen cannot be unseen, and there are no shortcuts. The work must be done, and it must be done daily. In the words often attributed to **Sheryl Sandberg**, former COO of Meta Platforms (formerly Facebook):

> *"We cannot change what we are not aware of, and once we are aware, we cannot help but change."*

I agree with Ms. Sandberg, and science tells us that it doesn't matter how old we are; we can always improve by updating our model of the world. This book will attempt to offer not just information, but a pathway to transformation; a science-based pathway to consciously reshape your brain's model of reality and, in doing so, reshape your experience of life itself.

PART 1

FOUNDATIONS FOR THE HUMAN INSIDE

CHAPTER 1
OUR EVOLUTIONARY HERITAGE

"Evolution is very slow, but societal change isn't"

Think about this scenario for a moment:

Maria sits in her car, stuck in traffic, feeling her stress levels rise as she watches the clock. She will be late for an important meeting and feels overwhelmed by the endless stream of notifications, texts, and emails on her smartphone. Her heart races, muscles tense up, and stress hormones flood her system.

But here is what's fascinating: these are the same biological responses her ancestors experienced hundreds of thousands of years ago when facing predators in the African savannah. These are the same neural circuits, the same chemical cascade, the same ancient alarm system, just triggered by different circumstances. Maria doesn't know it, but she's experiencing the profound mismatch between her evolutionary heritage and modern life. Her brain, shaped by millions of years of survival challenges, can't distinguish between a traffic jam and an approaching predator. Both represent obstacles to her goals; therefore, both trigger the same emergency response system.

This is the human condition in the 21st century: We're extraordinary beings carrying ancient wisdom in our cells, yet we often feel disconnected from both our evolutionary past and our authentic selves. We've become so focused on who we think we should be (or who we've been told we should be) that we've lost touch with who we actually are beneath all that conditioning.

To reclaim that authentic self, we need to understand our origins. Not just our personal history or cultural background, but the epic 4.5-billion-year journey that created the remarkable being now reading these words. This isn't just fascinating science, it's practical wisdom. When we understand our evolutionary heritage, we begin to see why we react the way we do, why certain things feel difficult or natural, and how to work with our nature rather than against it.

Let's explore the remarkable journey from the first life forms to modern human consciousness, discovering how our brains evolved not for happiness or even accuracy, but for survival. We'll examine the pivotal role of fire and cooking in human brain development and understand why our roughly 2-million-year-old neural architecture still shapes every moment of our contemporary experience.

An Environment Suitable for Life

Imagine Earth 4.5 billion years ago: a hostile, alien world that would instantly kill anything we consider life today. The atmosphere was a toxic cocktail of carbon dioxide (CO_2), methane (CH_4), ammonia (NH_3), and water vapor (H_2O). There was virtually no free oxygen. The surface was bombarded by radiation that would fry any unprotected organism in seconds. This planet did not have an ecosystem suitable for life as we know it. Yet somehow, in this hostile environment, something extraordinary began to stir.

For the next billion years, this young Earth went through severe transformations. In his book **"How the World Really Works"** Environmental Scientist **Vaclav Smil** tells us the history of life on earth is a history of energy conversions. He explains that around 3.5 billion years ago, a new form of life emerged: single-cell microbes. These bacteria couldn't think, move purposefully, or see. Instead, they drifted aimlessly through Earth's early seas. However, these simple organisms could convert one form of energy into another, which is how they accessed the nutrients they needed to survive and reproduce. Today, we call these ancient organisms **Cyanobacteria**, and they were one of the first organisms to perform the energy conversion that today we call **Oxygenic Photosynthesis**.

Cyanobacteria played a crucial role in shaping the Earth's atmosphere. Using sunlight, water (H_2O), and carbon dioxide (CO_2), they produced glucose (a sugar) for energy and released oxygen (O_2) as a byproduct:

$$6CO_2 + 6H_2O + light \rightarrow C_6H_{12}O_6 + 6O_2$$

This process continued for another billion years. Then, around 2.4 billion years ago, cyanobacteria began releasing significant amounts of oxygen into Earth's oceans and atmosphere. At first, oxygen reacted with dissolved iron in the oceans, forming iron oxides that settled as banded iron formations. This prevented the buildup of atmospheric oxygen, but not for long. Once the iron was depleted, oxygen started accumulating in the atmosphere, leading to what is called the Great Oxygenation Event (GOE), which led to a shift from an anoxic (oxygen-free) environment to an oxic (oxygen-rich) atmosphere. This rise in oxygen levels was toxic to many anaerobic (oxygen-intolerant) organisms, leading to their mass extinction in what is sometimes called the 'Oxygen Catastrophe' or 'Oxygen Crisis'. While devastating for these early life forms, this dramatic planetary transformation paved the way for aerobic (oxygen-dependent) life. Furthermore, it is during this oxygenation event that some oxygen molecules combined to form ozone (O_3) in the upper atmosphere, creating the ozone layer, which protects the Earth's surface from harmful ultraviolet (UV) radiation.

Why Does This Matter to Your Daily Life?

The Great Oxygenation Event teaches us something profound about change:

- Crisis creates opportunity: What seems destructive often enables new possibilities
- Systems adapt or perish: When environments change dramatically, only flexible beings survive.
- Patience with process: Meaningful transformation happens over extended time scales.
- Collective impact: Individual actions (like cyanobacteria producing oxygen) can reshape entire worlds

Bottom Line: When you face major life changes, job loss, relationship ending, health challenges, remember that evolutionary history shows us that disruption often precedes breakthrough. Your ability to adapt is literally in your DNA.

This process of destruction, enabling new creation (which repeated through evolutionary history), helped transform the earth by contributing to the formation of an atmosphere with enough oxygen to support life as we know it. In essence, these primitive microscopic organisms were the architects of Earth's breathable atmosphere, setting the stage for the evolution of diverse life forms, including humans. Understanding this principle helps us navigate the inevitable disruptions in our modern lives with greater wisdom and resilience.

From single cells to complex beings

Although cyanobacteria played a crucial role in enabling the evolution of humans and other life forms by transforming Earth's environment, it was not a direct role. Humans and all other complex life forms have an evolutionary lineage that can be traced back to common ancestors that existed billions of years ago, and cyanobacteria set the stage for that evolution. Cyanobacteria are thought to be the ancestors of **chloroplasts** in plants and algae. This occurred through a process called **endosymbiosis**, in which a larger host cell engulfed cyanobacteria-like organisms and formed a mutually beneficial relationship.

The new oxygen-rich atmosphere allowed for the evolution of **aerobic respiration**, which is substantially more efficient than anaerobic processes. This energy efficiency was critical for the evolution of **eukaryotic cells**, which became the building blocks of all complex life, including humans. Over billions of years, eukaryotic cells evolved into larger, more complex, and energy-demanding multicellular organisms. This progression from single-celled organisms to multicellular life required numerous evolutionary innovations, including cell specialization, tissue formation, and the development of internal systems for energy distribution. Eventually, these evolutionary processes led to the emergence of early animals with primitive nervous systems and digestive tracts.

One of these more complex organisms were **Chordates**, which were organisms with a dorsal nerve cord. Popular chordates include the **Amphioxi** or **Amphioxuses** (singular: Amphioxus, also known as lancelets). Amphioxi appeared approximately 600 million years ago, and they belong to the subphylum **Cephalochordata**, a group within the phylum **Chordata**. Amphioxi are important because they are **basal chordates**, meaning they represent a primitive lineage within the chordates. They provide insights into the early evolution of chordates, serving as a model organism for studying the transition from invertebrates to vertebrates. Amphioxi share many features with vertebrates but lack complex structures such as a braincase (cranium) or vertebral column, distinguishing them from vertebrates.

Something to consider:

Billions of years of biological innovation transformed what was once poisonous deadly air into the life-giving air that now fills your lungs and powers your brain.

Destruction became creation. Crisis became opportunity. This pattern defined evolution and human growth for billions of years to come.

Every breath you take connects you to those ancient microorganisms.

Most experts in this field agree that the amphioxi eventually gave rise to vertebrates, including fish. Modern amphioxus, commonly known as **lancelets**, still exist today, providing a living window into our deep evolutionary past. Take the **European lancelet, *Branchiostoma lanceolatum***, for instance. This small, translucent marine invertebrate, often found burrowed in shallow coastal sands, perfectly embodies the basic chordate body plan that prefigured all vertebrates. These creatures, whether *Branchiostoma* or other lancelet species, demonstrate how simple neural organization can coordinate basic behaviors like swimming, feeding, and avoiding predators. Their nervous system, while primitive by human standards, established the fundamental architecture upon which all subsequent vertebrate brains would build. What's remarkable is that these ancient innovations continue to shape our experience today. The spinal reflexes that make us pull our hand away from a hot stove operate through the same basic neural pathways that first evolved in our chordate ancestors hundreds of millions of years ago.

As evolution continued its never-ending process, it went through fascinating changes that led to creatures that can be found in the fossil record. Here is a high-level summary of how many experts think hundreds of millions of years of evolution, driven by genetic variation, natural selection, and changing environmental conditions, led from cyanobacteria to our species today:

1. Cyanobacteria – around 3.5 billion years ago
2. Amphioxi – around 600 million years ago
3. Auroralumina Attenboroughii (first known predator) – around 560 million years ago
4. Haikouichthys (first known fish) – around 530 million years ago
5. Elginerpeton (first known amphibian) – around 370 million years ago
6. Hylonomus (first known reptile) – around 315 million years ago
7. Morganucodontids (first known mammal) around 200 million years ago
8. First known monkeys – around 55 million years ago
9. Australopithecus (walked upright, but great tree climber) – around 3 million years ago
10. Homo Habilis (new tools and bigger brains) – around 2.3 million years ago
11. Homo Erectus (domestication of fire) – around 2 million years ago

12. Homo Naledi (mosaic of primitive and derived features) – around 335 - 236 thousand years ago

13. Neanderthals and Denisovans – around 400 - 40 thousand years ago

14. Homo Sapiens – from around 250 thousand years ago to the present.

The journey from bacteria to humans wasn't a straight line – it was a series of revolutionary breakthroughs, each one seeming impossible until it happened. Understanding these transitions helps explain why human growth often feels difficult yet ultimately transformative.

The Journey to Becoming Human

The path from those first bacteria to us contains an almost incomprehensible story of innovation, adaptation, and survival. Each transition required not just genetic mutations but environmental pressures that favored certain traits over others. Every creature in our lineage faced the ultimate test: adapt or disappear. That we exist means an unbroken chain of our ancestors successfully met that challenge for the past 3.5 billion years. The survivors weren't necessarily the strongest, but those who best adapted to their changing circumstances. Consider what this means: Every single one of our ancestors, from ancient microbes to early mammals to human tribes, lived long enough to reproduce. Not one of them died before passing on their genes. We are the product of the greatest success story in the history of life on Earth.

These adaptations led to physiological changes, which over time led to behavioral changes that eventually began to separate us from the other mammals around us. And what makes the human chapter of this story unique is that our lineage developed something unprecedented somewhere along the way: The ability to understand our own evolutionary journey. We're not just a product of evolution; we are evolution that is constantly becoming conscious of itself.

At this point, it is very important to take a moment to address a common and unfortunate misconception about evolution: the continued existence of primates alongside humans. The question "If we evolved from primates, why are there still primates around?" reflects a fundamental misunderstanding of how evolutionary processes operate. You may ask, Why is this of any relevance? Recall the premise of the introduction: "we live in the best of times, yet we are far from being our best." I believe one of the possible reasons we are not our best is that we don't truly understand who we are as a species. It turns out that who we are today, why we think the way we do, and why we do the things we do have everything to do with our evolutionary lineage. So, let's see why this is of utmost relevance.

We Didn't Evolve From Modern Primates; We Share a Common Ancestor

Based on our current scientific understanding, evolution does not operate as a linear progression (like a ladder where one species transforms into another, and the "old" species disappears), but rather as a branching process resembling a tree. Humans did not evolve from modern chimpanzees, gorillas, or any other living primate species. Instead, humans and all other contemporary primates share a **common ancestor** that existed approximately 6 to 7 million years ago. This ancestral species was neither human nor chimpanzee, but an ape-like creature from which multiple lineages diverged. This evolutionary "tree of life" exhibits the following elements:

- **The Branches:**

    From that common primate ancestor, different populations faced different environmental pressures, developed different mutations, and underwent natural selection along various paths. These paths led to new species, much like branches growing off a main trunk.

- **Divergence (Speciation):**

    Over vast spans of time, these separate populations accumulated enough genetic differences that they could no longer interbreed, leading to the formation of new, distinct species. This process is called **speciation**. One branch led to the lineage that eventually included humans, while other branches led to the lineages of chimpanzees, gorillas, and other primates we see today.

- **No "Replacement":**

    There's no inherent evolutionary rule that says when a new species evolves, its closely related ancestral or sister species must disappear. If a species (like the common ancestor) splits into two or more distinct descendant species, and if those descendant species continue to thrive in their respective environments, there's no reason why they can't coexist.

    Charles Darwin's fundamental insight was that evolution occurs through natural selection, a process whereby individuals possessing advantageous traits demonstrate higher rates of survival and reproduction. This mechanism operates through four essential components:

- Variation among individuals within populations,
- Inheritance of traits from parents to offspring,

- Differential selection pressure favoring certain traits, and
- Sufficient time for changes to accumulate across generations

Modern evolutionary synthesis has enhanced this understanding by incorporating molecular genetics, revealing that evolutionary change occurs at the DNA level through mutations that provide the raw material for natural selection, genetic drift, and gene flow.

Using this as a premise, it is not difficult to see how modern humans and modern primates adapted to different ecological niches and lifestyles:

- **Humans** evolved to thrive in open savanna environments, developing bipedalism, advanced tool use, and complex communication, leading to our unique cognitive abilities.
- **Chimpanzees and gorillas**, for example, remained largely adapted to forest environments, with adaptations for climbing, different diets, and social structures optimized for their habitats.

Because they occupy different environmental roles and have different survival strategies, they are not directly competing for the exact same resources in the exact same way, allowing them to continue to exist alongside each other.

Something to consider:

Imagine your family tree. You and your cousin share a common grandparent. You didn't evolve from your cousin; you both descended from the same grandparent, and then your family lines branched off. If you were to trace back your lineage beyond your grandparent for 1000 years, you would easily see the multitude of branches in that tree and all those far-removed cousins.

Evidence Supporting Common Ancestry

The scientific evidence for evolutionary common ancestry derives from multiple independent disciplines, creating a robust framework of support:

- The fossil record provides direct historical evidence of organismal change over millions of years, with transitional forms such as Australopithecus afarensis demonstrating characteristics intermediate between apes and humans.
- Advanced radiometric dating techniques establish accurate chronological sequences that align with evolutionary predictions.
- Genetic evidence offers perhaps the most compelling support for common ancestry. Humans share about 98-99% of their DNA with

chimpanzees, including not only functional genes but also non-coding regions. More significantly, humans and other primates share identical pseudogenes and endogenous retroviruses in the same genomic locations, a pattern virtually impossible to explain except through inheritance from a common ancestor. The fusion of two ancestral chromosomes to form human chromosome 2, evidenced by telomeric sequences in the chromosome's center and remnants of a second centromere, provides direct physical evidence of shared evolutionary history.

- Comparative anatomy reveals homologous structures across species, such as the pentadactyl limb pattern found in human arms, bat wings, whale flippers, and mammalian legs. These structural similarities, despite functional differences, indicate descent from common ancestors. Vestigial structures in humans, including the coccyx, wisdom teeth, and appendix, represent evolutionary remnants of ancestral features.

- Embryological evidence demonstrates that vertebrate embryos, including humans, exhibit striking developmental similarities during early stages, developing structures like gill slits and tails that may later disappear or be repurposed. These shared developmental patterns reflect common ancestral genetic programs.

Modern molecular techniques enable real-time observation of these evolutionary processes. Molecular clock analyses, which estimate divergence times based on mutation rates, consistently align with fossil evidence for human-primate split dates. Direct observation of evolution includes documented cases of antibiotic resistance development in bacterial populations, speciation events in laboratory fruit fly populations, and rapid adaptive changes in natural populations such as Darwin's finches following environmental perturbations.

Convergent evolution, where unrelated species independently develop similar adaptations to comparable environmental challenges, provides additional evidence for natural selection's explanatory power. Familiar examples include the morphological similarities between dolphins and sharks, both adapted for efficient aquatic locomotion, and the independent evolution of camera-type eyes in vertebrates and cephalopods.

Why Does This Matter to Your Daily Life?

Grasping evolution correctly changes how you see yourself and others:

- You didn't evolve FROM apes: You share common ancestors with other primates (like sharing a great-great-grandparent with your cousin).

- Evolution continues: You're not a "finished product" but part of an ongoing process.

- All life is connected: Every living thing shares common ancestry, you are literally related to every organism on Earth.
- Diversity is strength: Different "branches" of evolution solve survival challenges in different ways.

Bottom Line: Humility and Wonder are key. You're simultaneously utterly unique (no being exactly like you has ever existed) and deeply connected (sharing DNA with all life). This paradox (special yet connected) is at the heart of authentic human identity.

Addressing scientific misconceptions and broader scientific significance

The characterization of evolution as "just a theory" reflects a misunderstanding of scientific terminology. In scientific usage, **a theory** represents a well-substantiated explanation supported by extensive empirical evidence, comparable to the theory of gravity or germ theory of disease. The fact that organisms have changed over time (evolution) is supported by the theoretical framework explaining the mechanisms responsible for these changes (evolutionary theory).

Evolution does not imply directional progress toward predetermined goals. Contemporary species, including humans, represent different solutions to environmental challenges rather than stages in a hierarchical progression. Bacterial species that have persisted for billions of years demonstrate remarkable evolutionary success, emphasizing that evolutionary fitness relates to environmental adaptation rather than anthropocentric notions of advancement.

Why is this important? Understanding evolutionary principles provides essential insights across multiple disciplines:

- In medicine, evolutionary theory explains the presence of vestigial organs, predicts pathogen behavior, and informs treatment strategies.
- Agricultural applications include crop and livestock improvement through selective breeding programs that harness evolutionary principles.
- Conservation biology relies on evolutionary understanding to maintain genetic diversity and predict species responses to environmental change.

The convergence of evidence from paleontology, molecular biology, comparative anatomy, embryology, and biogeography creates an overwhelming case for evolutionary common ancestry. This interdisciplinary support establishes evolution as one of the most robustly supported theories in science, providing a unifying framework for <u>understanding biological diversity and the relationships among all living organisms</u>.

Aside from all this wonderful science, the Theory of Evolution delivers a much more important and humbling lesson:

We humans are not the "pinnacle" of evolution... all we are is one successful branch among many on the vast, intricate, and interdependent tree of life.

The milestones of our hominin ancestors

With that background now under our belts, we can briefly explore our hominin species by summarizing key features most relevant to our direct lineage and understanding of human evolution.

Table 1 – Key Hominin Milestones

Feature	Australopithecus	Homo Habilis	Homo Erectus	Homo Naledi	Neanderthals / Denisovans	Homo Sapiens (Modern)
Approx. Dates	~4 mya to 2 mya	~2.4 mya to 1.4 mya	~1.9 mya to 100 kya	~335 kya to 236 kya	~400 kya to 40 kya	~300 kya - present
Key Locations	East/ South Africa	East/ South Africa	Africa, Asia, Europe	South Africa (Rising Star)	Europe, Asia	Africa, then Global
Approx. Brain Size	~400 cc to 550 cc	~500 cc to 650 cc	~750 cc to 1250 cc	~465 cc to 610 cc	~1200 cc to 1750 cc	~1200 cc to 1600 cc
Key Features/ Innovations	Bipedalism, Tree Climbing	Simple Stone Tools (Oldowan)	Controlled Fire, More Complex Tools (Acheulean), Migration out of Africa	Mosaic Features (Small Brain, Modern Hands / Feet)	Complex Tools (Mousterian), Hunting, Potential Symbolic Behavior, Interbreeding	Complex Language, Art, Symbolic Thought, Agriculture

In the table above, "mya" means millions of years ago, "kya" means thousands of years ago, and "cc" means cubic centimeters

The inclusion of Homo Naledi is particularly significant because it demonstrates the complexity of human evolution during the Middle Pleistocene. Discovered in the **Rising Star Cave** system in South Africa and announced in 2015, Homo Naledi presents a fascinating mosaic of traits.

Despite its small brain size (465 - 610 cc, comparable to australopithecines and much smaller than modern humans), it possessed Homo-like features, including hands capable of tool use and feet adapted for efficient bipedal locomotion. Surprisingly, despite its primitive features, Homo Naledi lived between 335,000 and 236,000 years ago, making it a contemporary of more advanced hominins, including potentially early Homo Sapiens.

While the discovery of Homo Naledi and its anatomical characteristics are widely accepted by the scientific community, recent claims about its behavioral capabilities have generated significant controversy. In 2023, researchers suggested that Homo Naledi may have engaged in complex behaviors such as intentional burial of the dead, creation of rock engravings, and use of fire. However, these claims have been met with substantial skepticism within the paleoanthropological community, with many experts arguing that the evidence presented is insufficient to support such interpretations. The current scientific consensus does not support the attribution of these advanced symbolic behaviors to Homo Naledi based on available evidence.

Furthermore, the inclusion of Neanderthals and Denisovans is particularly important, as recent genetic evidence shows they contributed significantly to modern human DNA. Denisovans, discovered only in 2010, left genetic traces especially in populations in Asia and Oceania, with some indigenous Papuans having up to 6% Denisovan DNA. This evidence, along with the discovery of Homo Naledi, reinforces that human evolution was not a simple linear progression but rather a complex branching process with multiple hominin species coexisting and potentially interacting at various points in our evolutionary history.

Why Does This Matter to Your Daily Life?

Right now, you carry the legacy of millions of years of successful adaptation:

- Your craving for sweet and fatty foods: Survival traits from when calories were scarce.
- Your fight-or-flight response: Instant threat detection that kept ancestors alive.
- Your need for social connection: Isolation meant death in ancestral environments.
- Your pattern-recognition abilities: Spotting dangers and opportunities faster than conscious thought.
- Your capacity for learning: The ultimate survival advantage in changing environments.

Bottom Line: You are not "broken" when you struggle with modern challenges, you are human. Your reactions make perfect sense given your evolutionary heritage.

As we trace this evolutionary timeline, it's crucial to understand that our knowledge of human origins continues to evolve. Science is not a destination but a continuous observation, discovery, and refinement process. The dates and transitions presented here represent our current best understanding, based on available evidence and peer-reviewed research. However, new discoveries frequently emerge that add nuance to or sometimes significantly revise our understanding of human evolution. This dynamic nature of scientific knowledge doesn't invalidate our current understanding; rather, it demonstrates the rigorous, self-correcting nature of scientific inquiry.

Chapter 1 Summary: Key Insights

The 4.5-billion-year journey from hostile planet to human consciousness reveals the fundamental principles of energy conversion and adaptation that still govern your daily experience. Understanding this heritage provides both humility and empowerment, humility about our place in the vast web of life, and empowerment about our extraordinary capabilities.

Charles Darwin's insight was that evolution occurs through natural selection, a process where individuals with advantageous traits are more likely to survive and reproduce. This happens through four key components: variation (individuals differ), inheritance (traits pass to offspring), selection (some traits improve survival), and time (changes accumulate over generations).

Today's understanding of evolution combines Darwin's original theory with modern genetics, revealing that evolution occurs at the molecular level through changes in DNA. Mutations provide the raw material for evolution, while genetic drift, gene flow, and natural selection shape how these changes spread through populations.

The human lineage split from our closest relatives around 6-7 million years ago in Africa. Key evolutionary developments included bipedalism (walking upright), brain enlargement, tool use, and complex language. These adaptations were responses to changing environments, particularly the expansion of grasslands in Africa.

Addressing Common Misconceptions

Evolution is often misunderstood as "just a theory." In scientific terminology, a theory is a well-substantiated explanation supported by extensive evidence, like the theory of gravity or germ theory of disease. The "fact" of evolution (that life forms have changed over time) is supported by the "theory" of evolution (the mechanisms explaining how it occurs).

Evolution also doesn't imply progress toward a goal. Humans aren't "more evolved" than other species; we're differently evolved. A bacterial species that has survived and thrived for billions of years is incredibly successful in evolutionary terms.

The Broader Significance

Understanding evolution provides crucial insights into medicine (why we have vestigial organs, how diseases spread), agriculture (crop and livestock breeding), conservation (maintaining genetic diversity), and our place in the natural world. It explains both the unity of life (that all organisms share common ancestry) and its diversity (that millions of species adapted to countless ecological niches).

The evidence for evolution from common ancestry is overwhelming and comes from multiple independent sources that all point to the same conclusion. This convergence of evidence from fossils, genetics, anatomy, development, and biogeography makes evolution one of science's most strongly supported theories, providing a unifying framework for understanding all biology.

Why does this matter in our daily lives? Understanding your evolutionary heritage isn't just fascinating, it's practical and necessary:

- **Crisis Enables Creation:**

    From the Oxygen Catastrophe to human challenges, disruption often precedes breakthrough, a pattern that applies to personal growth as much as planetary evolution.

- **Adaptation is Your Superpower:**

    Our ancestors survived every possible challenge for billions of years; their adaptability lives in our cells and can be consciously cultivated.

- **We are Connected to All Life:**

    Understanding our common ancestry creates both scientific humility and practical wisdom about our interdependence and cooperation.

- **Ancient Responses, Modern Triggers:**

    Our stress responses, social needs, and survival instincts made perfect sense in ancestral environments and can be understood and worked with in contemporary life.

- **Evolution Continues:**

    We are not a finished product but an active participant in the ongoing story of life becoming more conscious and capable.

Understanding our evolutionary inheritance creates the foundation for something even more remarkable: exploring how this ancient biological system created the most complex structure in the known universe: our brain. The journey from bacterial energy conversion to human consciousness reveals why our mind works the way it does and how we can optimize its extraordinary capabilities.

CHAPTER 2
THE HUMAN BRAIN: A MASTERPIECE OF EVOLUTION

"The brain did not evolve to see the world the way it is. The brain evolved to see the world the way it was useful to see it... in the past"

Picture this scene:

Two million years ago, in what is now Kenya, a small group of our ancestors huddles around flickering flames as darkness falls. A species has learned to control fire for the first time in Earth's history. For millions of years before this moment, all energy conversion happened inside living cells. Every creature on Earth, from bacteria to our ape-like ancestors, had to unlock nutrients through purely internal, metabolic processes.

These early humans don't know they've just triggered the most important breakthrough in brain evolution, one that would transform a clever ape into a conscious, self-aware human being. They are cooking, and that meat smells different (richer, more appealing), and something extraordinary is happening with those extra calories that will fuel larger brains. Those larger brains will develop language, art, and eventually the capacity for self-reflection. The creatures staring into those flames will evolve into the being now reading these words, wondering about the nature of their own mind.

The fascinating part about this story is that our brain today still operates on the same fundamental principles as it did for those fire-gazing ancestors. Our brain is still primarily concerned with energy management, still making predictions based on past experience, still optimized for survival rather than happiness or even accuracy. Understanding this ancient heritage is crucial because it explains why modern life feels so challenging.

We're trying to navigate 21st-century complexity with a neural architecture that evolved for a much simpler world. The good news? Once we understand how our brain actually works, we can learn to work with it rather than against it.

Let's explore the remarkable journey from those first controlled flames to the three-pound universe now inside your skull.

What made us so different?

About two million years ago, everything changed. Our ancestors, clever primates who looked somewhat like us but thought very differently from us, made a discovery that would separate us forever from every other species on Earth. They discovered the first **Extrasomatic** use of energy: the conversion of energy outside the body. Extrasomatic processes represent the external adaptations and innovations (like tools or technology) that extend human capabilities beyond the body's biological limitations. Some examples of extrasomatic processes include using tools to accomplish tasks or regulate temperature. This distinction between somatic (internal) and extrasomatic (external) energy use is fundamental to understanding what made humans unique among all species on Earth.

This might not sound revolutionary, but think about it: all other creatures on the planet were limited by what their bodies could do internally. Lions had to rely on their teeth and claws. Birds were constrained by their wing strength. Even our closest cousins, the chimpanzees, could only work with what their muscles and digestive systems could provide.

But our ancestors discovered something unprecedented: They could convert energy outside their bodies to accomplish goals impossible through biology alone. Of the various forms of extrasomatic conversion, there is one that stands out above all: **the domestication of fire**. Fire converts the chemical energy of plant matter, be it wood or peat, into thermal energy and light. Mastery of fire is one of the most significant milestones in human evolution, as it enabled early hominins to harness energy from an external source to transform themselves and their environment, to improve survival, and to enhance cultural development. The earliest evidence we know of fire use dates to around **2 million years ago**, with more definitive evidence appearing around **1 million years ago.** The Homo Erectus are believed to be the first to control and use fire. Here are some of the ways fire changed our ancestors:

1. **Cooking**

    - Fire allowed early humans to cook food, which made indigestible foods edible and digestible foods easier to chew and quicker to digest.
    - Cooking also unlocked more calories and nutrients, supporting the growth of larger brains.
    - Cooking food reduced the need for large, energy-demanding digestive systems, possibly contributing to the smaller guts and larger brains of later hominins.

2. **Warmth**

    - Fire provided warmth, allowing early humans to survive and reproduce in colder climates and expand their geographic range.

3. **Protection**

    - Fire helped ward off predators, especially at night, giving early humans a sense of safety and security.

4. **Toolmaking**

    - Fire was later used to improve the effectiveness of tools, such as hardening wooden spears or shaping stone tools.

5. **Social Focus**

    - Fire became a focal point for social interaction, fostering communication and cooperation within groups.

After fire, and later in the evolutionary path, humans began using other forms of external energy sources. Humans domesticated animals for labor, harnessed wind for sailing, and used water for grinding grain. Although interesting, these other forms of extrasomatic energy conversion are the topic for another book. For now, we will focus on cooking with fire because, as we will see in the next section, it is the one process that many believe dramatically changed the course of our physiological evolution.

Fire as an Evolutionary Catalyst

Our brain is the most complex structure in the known universe and a marvel of evolution. It contains roughly 86 billion neurons, 85 billion other cells, and over 100 trillion connections. This is truly remarkable, but why did our brains grow so dramatically? Why do we think, communicate, and behave differently from our closest relatives? Many researchers agree that the answer lies in a simple discovery that changed everything: the controlled use of fire and cooking.

Let's walk through a fascinating detective story in science: How cooking made us who we are.

According to **Richard Wrangham**, professor of evolutionary biology at Harvard, if we go back three million years, our ancestors looked a lot like us, but not quite. They were capable of walking upright, but they were also great tree climbers. They were the size of chimpanzees, and their bellies and facial features were like those of modern apes. These were the Australopithecines, and their brains were not much larger than that of a modern-day chimpanzee. Fast forward around 700 thousand years, and a new species appears: the Habilines. Habilines were the same size as Australopithecines, with long arms and jutting faces. However, they figured out how to make stone tools, and their brains were almost twice as big as those of living non-human apes. By about 1.9 million years ago, some of these Habilines evolved into Homo Erectus.

In his book **Catching Fire**, professor Wrangham tells us:

> "Homo erectus looked much more like us than any prior species. They are considered to have walked and run as fluently as we do today. Their various descendants, including the Neanderthals more than a million years later, all exhibited the same form and stature."

Although the Homo Erectus had larger brains than the Habilines, they still had smaller brains and lower foreheads than modern humans. Wrangham suggests that the two-step evolutionary process that helped Australopithecines evolve into Habilines, and then Habilines into Homo Erectus (which was hundreds of thousands of years apart), could not be driven by the same cause. He tells us that MEAT EATING can account for the first transition. It was the addition of meat to their diet of vegetables, fruits, and nuts that transformed the chimp-looking Australopithecines into the tool-making, bigger-brained Habilines. As far as we know, this was the first major transition from an ape-like brain to a more human-like one.

But what about the second transition? Although we have focused so far on the changes that led to our modern brain, the entire anatomy of our ancestors was being affected in parallel. For instance, in the second transition the Homo Erectus ended up with smaller jaws, smaller teeth, and a smaller gut than their ancestors, all while having a bigger brain. How did this happen? As we read in the previous section, many believe cooking played an important role. But how did changing our diet from raw to cooked food enable our ancestors to experience such physiological changes? To provide an answer to this question, we will rely on the contributions to the field of comparative neuroanatomy from **Dr Suzana Herculano-Houzel** from Vanderbilt University.

Why Does This Matter to Your Daily Life?

Your brain's evolutionary history explains some puzzling aspects of modern life:

- **Why you crave cooked food:** Your digestive system evolved specifically for cooked food over 2 million years ago.
- **Why raw food diets feel difficult:** You're fighting millions of years of evolution.
- **Why you feel energized by warm, cooked meals:** Your brain associates cooking with the energy abundance that made human civilization possible.
- **Why gathering around food feels so important:** Shared cooking created the social bonds that define humanity.

Bottom Line: Understanding your brain's relationship with food isn't just about nutrition, it's also about honoring the evolutionary breakthrough that made you human.

The Neuroenergetic Trade-Off

Comparative neuroanatomy provides us with a powerful lens we can use to explore the evolution of the brain and behavior across the animal kingdom. By comparing the structural organization and cellular composition of brains from different species, researchers aim to understand the principles governing brain design, the neural basis of cognitive abilities, and the evolutionary pressures that have shaped nervous systems. Today, we consistently find three key metrics in many comparative neuroanatomical studies:

1. **Neuron Count**:

    Neurons are widely considered the fundamental information-processing units of the brain. Quantifying the number of neurons, particularly within specific brain regions like the cerebral cortex, offers a potential proxy for computational capacity and cognitive potential. However, the relationship is complex and debated.

2. **Brain Mass**:

    Absolute and relative brain mass have long been used as indicators of neural investment. While a larger brain does not automatically equate to higher intelligence, brain mass provides a fundamental anatomical measure.

3. **Body Mass**:

    The size of an animal's body is intrinsically linked to the size and metabolic demands of its brain. Understanding the relationship between brain mass and body mass (allometry) is crucial for interpreting evolutionary trends and testing hypotheses about energetic constraints on brain evolution.

    The following table shows a basic comparative neuroanatomy analysis between humans and some of our closest living relatives:

- **Humans (*Homo sapiens*)**:

    Primates are characterized by exceptionally large brains relative to body size and complex cognitive abilities.

- **Chimpanzees (*Pan troglodytes*)**:

    Humans' closest living relatives provide a crucial point of comparison within the primate lineage.

- **Gorillas (*Gorilla gorilla*)**:

    The largest living primates exhibit significant sexual dimorphism, providing another key comparison point among great apes.

- **Orangutans (*Pongo pygmaeus*)**:

    Another great ape species, known for their arboreal lifestyle and distinct evolutionary path within the Hominidae family.

Table 2 – Comparative Neuroanatomical and Morphological Data for Select Primate Brains

Species	Avg Total Neuron Count	Avg Brain Mass	Avg Body Mass	Notes
Human (*Homo sapiens*)	~86 billion	~1.35 kg	~70 kg	<ul><li>Neuron count debated (~67 to 99 billion range suggested)</li><li>~16 billion cortical neurons</li><li>Significant body mass variation globally</li></ul>

Chimpanzee (Pan troglodytes)	~28 billion	~0.39 kg	Male: ~40 to 70 kg Female: 27 to 50 kg	• Cortical neuron count ~6 to 7.4 billion • Total neuron count ~1/3 human
Gorilla (Gorilla gorilla)	~33 billion	~0.49 kg	Male ~170 kg Female: ~85 kg	• Cortical neuron count ~9 billion • Conforms to primate scaling rules
Orangutan (Pongo pygmaeus)	~30 billion	~0.40 kg	Male: ~88 kg Female: ~38 kg	• Cortical neuron count ~9 billion • Total neuron count estimated based on primate scaling rules

Note: All values are approximate averages and subject to significant intra-species variation and sexual dimorphism.

    This table clearly shows that while humans have the largest brain mass and highest total and cortical neuron counts, all four species adhere to the same fundamental primate brain scaling rules. Gorillas and orangutans, despite having body masses that can significantly exceed humans (especially males), possess brains that are only about one-third the mass of human brains and contain substantially fewer total and cortical neurons. Chimpanzees follow this pattern, with brain mass and neuron counts roughly one-third of human values. This comparative framework leads us to what can be called the "metabolic constraint hypothesis," which is the next step toward answering the question of how cooking food played a key role in our brain's evolution.

    A central tenet of the metabolic constraint hypothesis is that brain tissue, particularly neurons, is energetically expensive to maintain. Research suggests that the average metabolic cost per neuron is remarkably constant across different mammalian species, estimated at approximately <u>6 kcal per day per billion neurons</u>. Interestingly, this cost appears to be independent of neuronal size, meaning that, on average, larger neurons do not necessarily consume proportionally more energy than smaller ones. This linearity implies that the total energy budget required by a brain is primarily a function of its total number of neurons. If accurate, the constancy of this cost across species provides a basis for modeling the energetic impact of adding neurons during evolution.

Why Does This Matter to Your Daily Life?

Right now, consider the following as you read this:

- Your brain is using approximately 20% of your total energy, despite being only about 2% of your body weight.
- If you're tired, it's harder to think clearly because your brain is literally running out of fuel.
- When you're hungry, decision-making becomes more difficult because your brain prioritizes finding food over complex reasoning.
- After eating, you might feel mentally sharper because your brain has fresh glucose to work with.

Bottom Line: Notice how your thinking changes throughout the day based on your energy levels. Your ancestors' energy trade-offs are still playing out in your daily experience.

The Metabolic Revolution

Research reveals that primate brains exhibit distinct scaling rules compared to other mammals. Primate brain mass scales close to linear as a function of the number of neurons. This means that as primate brains get larger, they add neurons proportionally, maintaining a relatively consistent overall neuronal density. This efficient packing allows primates to accommodate more neurons within a given brain volume compared to what would be expected based on scaling rules from other mammals, like rodents, for example.

Based on the high cost of neurons and primate scaling rules, Herculano-Houzel and colleagues proposed that diet imposed a significant constraint on primate brain evolution. The hypothesis stipulates that primates relying on a diet of raw foods face a metabolic ceiling due to two primary factors:

1. **Time Limitation**:

    - Foraging for and consuming sufficient quantities of raw food is time-consuming.
    - Gorillas, for instance, may spend 8 hours or more per day feeding.
    - There is a practical limit to how many hours per day can be dedicated to feeding.

2. **Low Caloric Yield**:

    - Raw foods generally provide fewer net calories than cooked foods because more energy is spent in digestion; thus, nutrient absorption may be less efficient.

These factors create an energetic trade-off: the limited daily energy intake must be allocated between maintaining a given body mass and fueling the energetically demanding brain (i.e., its total number of neurons). Using mathematical models based on estimated energy intake per hour of feeding and the estimated cost per neuron, researchers calculated the viable combinations of body size and neuron number sustainable for a given number of daily feeding hours on a raw diet. These calculations suggest a strict upper limit, arguing that great apes, despite their large bodies, could not evolve significantly larger brains without either reducing body size or finding a more energy-efficient diet. In other words, the time and energy constraints of a raw diet severely limit the simultaneous expansion of both body size and neuron number in primates.

The hypothesis proposes that the invention of cooking was the key evolutionary development that allowed our ancestors to overcome the metabolic limitations that other primates faced. Cooking allows the digestive process to begin outside our body by making hard and stringy roots digestible and poisonous roots or herbs safe to eat. Cooking creates new tastes and reduces spoilage. But cooking also does something that is far more important and relevant to this discussion: <u>it increases the amount of energy our bodies obtain from food by approximately 30% when compared to raw food</u>. It is that extra energy that this hypothesis argues gave our ancestors a biological advantage and a larger brain than any other primate. This metabolic trade-off is crucial: As our digestive systems became smaller and more efficient with cooked food, more energy could be invested in supporting a larger, more neuron-dense brain without necessitating a reduction in body size, ultimately leading to the ~86 billion neurons in modern humans – a number seemingly unaffordable on a raw primate diet.

This perspective reframes cooking from a purely cultural advancement to a profound biological catalyst that fundamentally altered human energy budgets and enabled our unique evolutionary path. However, just like every other hypothesis in the scientific world, the cooking hypothesis is not universally accepted as the sole explanation for human brain expansion. Some researchers and alternative hypotheses suggest that the timeline of widespread, controlled cooking may not perfectly align with the earliest significant jumps in hominin brain volume. Instead, as **Leslie Aiello and Peter Wheeler** proposed with their "expensive tissue hypothesis," the need to fuel a larger brain required an energetic trade-off, which could have been met by an initial shift to a higher-quality diet rich in nutrient-dense raw foods like meat, marrow, and tubers. Furthermore, non-thermal food processing techniques, such as pounding or cutting, could have enhanced digestibility even before the regular use of fire.

More recently, **Kelsey Bryant, Corinna Hansen, and Erin Hecht** have proposed that the accidental or intentional fermentation of cached foods could have pre-digested nutrients, making them more bioavailable and reducing the energetic burden on the digestive system, potentially serving as an early, unappreciated driver of brain expansion.

Beyond dietary factors, the increasing demands of navigating complex social structures, developing sophisticated tool technologies, and adapting to variable environments are also considered powerful selective pressures that favored greater cognitive capacity and brain size. For instance, later in this chapter, we will introduce **Robin Dunbar's** "social brain hypothesis," which suggests that the challenges of managing larger and more intricate social groups drove the need for larger, more complex brains. Ultimately, the evolution of our remarkable brains was likely not driven by a single factor, but rather a dynamic interplay of these diverse and interconnected biological, technological, and social adaptations, each contributing to the unique trajectory of human development.

Time will tell if the cooking hypothesis stands, or if new peer-reviewed research improves on it. Regardless, this discussion highlights something that most scientists would agree with: While our human brain adheres to the same fundamental primate brain-scaling rules, its **uniquely large number of neurons for a given body size** is what sets it apart. Our body and brain size ratio can be easily explained via metabolic consumption calculations, and cooking directly or indirectly enabled this evolutionary process.

Wrangham tells us that this was just the beginning. Once our ancestors had that extra energy, they reproduced better, and their bodies responded by biologically adapting to cooked food. Their anatomy, physiology, and psychology changed, leading them to change the environment and the societies they lived in. Once our ancestors didn't have to chew for long hours per day, they had time to use those extra neurons to observe the world and themselves. That led to language, agriculture, and the world we see today. In short, scientific data support that we have a human brain partly because of fire and cooking.

Something to consider:

The human brain's evolution wasn't just about getting bigger; it was about becoming more efficient at extracting energy from the environment. This principle applies to personal development: growth often requires finding ways to get more value from our existing resources rather than simply working harder.

Now that we understand how fire gave us the energy budget for larger brains, let's explore what those brains actually do. The answer might be surprising, and it surprised scientists who spent decades thinking about the brain incorrectly.

What is the human brain for?

Popular culture often portrays the brain as a biological computer designed for thinking, reasoning, and problem-solving. While these are certainly important functions, we know the brain is far more than that. Before we dive into how the brain interprets our senses and regulates our bodily functions, it is important to have a high-level understanding of the entire human nervous system and how the brain fits into it:

Table 3 – The Human Nervous System – High-Level

Central Nervous System (CNS)	Brain
	Spinal Cord
	Retina, optic nerve, olfactory nerves and olfactory epithelium.
Peripheral Nervous System (PNS) - *consists of all nerve tissue outside the brain and the spinal cord*	**Somatic Nervous System (SoNS)** - *controls voluntary movements (motor neurons to skeletal muscles) and carries sensory information*
	Autonomic Nervous System (ANS) - *controls involuntary functions like heart rate, digestion, breathing*

The brain is the body's control center and part of the **Central Nervous System (CNS)**. Some scientists define the CNS as the brain and the spinal cord. At the same time, others also include the retina, optic nerve, olfactory nerves, and olfactory epithelium, because they connect directly with the brain without any intermediate nerve fibers.

The human brain interprets the senses and controls movement, breathing, temperature, hunger, and every process that regulates our body. However, our current brain wasn't always this way, and understanding what the brain is *for* vs what it can do requires looking beyond these functions to its fundamental organizing principles.

Beyond the thinking machine

As we learned in the previous section, our amphioxus ancestors were small wormlike creatures with nervous systems that only had sensing cells directly connected to movement cells. They did not need a complex brain because life was simple: They swam in the water with very basic movements and ate whatever happened to drift into their mouths. They didn't have senses, so they couldn't see, hear, taste, or smell. This simple arrangement worked well until predators arose. The group of neurons that were responsible for movement evolved into what today is the spinal cord, and a cluster of cells appeared at one end of the body to control new and necessary functions. This cluster is the predecessor of the brain stem. This development took place during the Cambrian period, when predators developed better and faster movement to catch and eat prey, while the prey developed better ways to sense the environment so they could evade these predators. In her book **7 ½ Lessons About the Brain**, Dr Lisa Feldman Barrett explains this elegantly:

> "Once creatures could sense at a distance and make more sophisticated movements, evolution favored those who performed those tasks efficiently. If they chased a meal but moved too slowly, something else caught the meal and ate it first. If they burned up energy fleeing from a potential threat that never arrived, they wasted resources that they might have needed later."

Basically, survival became not only a function of new sensory or motor skills but also a function of energy budgeting and predicting the future based on past experiences. Feldman Barrett tells us that a creature that prepared its movement before the predator struck was more likely to survive than a creature that merely reacted to a predator's move. This process of energy budgeting helps us automatically predict and prepare to meet the body's needs before they arise.

Fast forward a few million years, and now we have creatures with all kinds of new and complex internal systems – cardiovascular systems, immune systems, more advanced digestive systems, and so on. With this complexity, these organisms needed more than a simple cluster of cells to manage all these processes. They needed a brain. As evolution worked its magic, previous clusters of brain cells were NOT replaced with new ones. Feldman Barrett teaches us that as the brain grew, regions expanded and subdivided to redistribute their responsibilities. This segregating and integrating among brain regions created a more complex brain that can control larger and more complex bodies. In other words, our brain does NOT have multiple layers on top of each other as the triune model alludes. In this popular but incorrect model, our brain has three layers:

1. The reptilian or survival brain;
2. The mammalian or limbic brain, and
3. The neocortex or rational brain.

Today, we know this model inaccurately represents the organization of our human brain. We now understand that we have ONE brain that, over time, has reorganized and redistributed itself to meet the new needs of an evolving body. We are lucky to live in an era of continuous and rapid scientific advancement that provides us with valuable knowledge on this topic. In fact, by the time this book is published, there will be more information and knowledge I wish I could've included. In the next chapter, we will explore additional research that will help us understand our human brain and how it helps us construct the reality we perceive.

Now that we have a basic background, we can try to address the question "What is the human brain for?" This might surprise you, but it is not for thinking, not for rationality, not for emotions, nor creativity, imagination, compassion, nor empathy. Feldman Barrett tells us:

> "The brain's most important job is to manage <u>Allostasis</u>; that is to manage our energy budget by predicting our energy needs before they arise, using past experiences so we can move through this world efficiently and survive."

Allostasis can be seen in everyday life. For example, when we're about to exercise, our brain anticipates the increased energy demand and begins to raise our heart rate and respiration before we start moving. When we see food, our brain triggers digestive processes in preparation for eating. When we enter a social situation, our brain predicts the energy needed for interaction and adjusts our alertness accordingly.

These predictive processes happen constantly, mostly below our level of conscious awareness, and they're essential for efficient functioning in a complex world. The brain is constantly integrating information about our body's internal state with our external environment, continuously updating its predictions based on past experiences. This predictive regulation forms the foundation for virtually all brain functions, including perception, emotion, learning, and decision-making.

However, there is one specific, yet basic reason why the brain engages in this constant predictive regulation: to produce adaptable and complex movements, because movement is the only way to affect the external environment. Even the world inside our bodies depends on movement: blood flow, breathing, digestion, hormonal flow, cellular respiration, the list goes on and on. Motion is important and essential, and, at the most fundamental level, all of this is done with a simple evolutionary goal: Successful Reproduction; to pass our genes to the next generation.

How do we think the human brain works?

If we ask neuroscientists around the world HOW the human brain works, they will likely agree that despite knowing more than ever before, we still have much to discover. So, what do we know? We know our brain constantly processes information and learns a model of the world around us. In his book **A Thousand Brains**, **Jeff Hawkins** tells us that learning is not just relegated to what we are taught in school:

1. We learn how objects behave: from how a door opens and closes to how to operate a smartphone app.
2. We learn where objects are located in the world.
3. We learn abstract concepts such as government, compassion, and mathematics while acquiring tens of thousands of words.
4. While our genes may determine basic functions such as eating and pain response, everything else we know is learned.

We will dive into much more detail on the brain's predictive nature in the next chapter. For now, know that, as a prediction machine, the human brain is constantly doing at least the following actions:

- **Constant Forecasting**: Your brain generates millions of predictions every second.
- **Energy Conservation**: Prediction is more efficient than reaction.
- **Survival Focus**: Accuracy matters less than staying alive and reproducing.
- **Pattern Recognition**: Past experiences guide future predictions.

Usually, at this point in the conversation, people start questioning whether the idea that the brain is a predictive entity is real or imaginary. In these situations, I find that math and real-world examples can help. Let's use an example some of you might relate to: Baseball. Whether you are a fan of the sport or not, it is common knowledge that hitting a high-speed fastball thrown at you requires very special skills. What most people are not aware of is that hitting a high-speed fastball is a classic example used to illustrate why the brain *must* operate as a predictive organ rather than a reactive one. The physics and neurobiology involved don't allow enough time for a simple stimulus-response process. Here's the science behind that statement:

- The Physics of the Fastball:

  - **Speed:** A Major League fastball travels between 90 to 100+ mph. Let's use 95 mph (~139 ft/sec).
  - **Distance:** On average, pitchers release the ball about 55 feet from the batter.
  - **Flight Time:** Time = Distance/Speed. So, 55 ft / 139 ft/sec ≈ **0.396 sec**, or about **400 milliseconds (ms)**.

- The Limits of Human Reaction (The Reactive Bottleneck):

- **Visual Processing:** Light from the ball hits the retina, is converted to neural signals, and travels to the visual cortex for processing. This time is at least **~100 ms**.
- **Decision Making:** Identify pitch type, trajectory, speed, and decide *whether* to swing and *where* to swing. This process takes at least another **~75 to 100 ms**.
- **Motor Command Transmission:** A signal must travel from the brain down the spinal cord and out to the relevant muscles in the torso, arms, and legs. This takes about **~25 to 50 ms**.
- **Muscle Activation & Swing Initiation:** Muscles need time to contract and begin the physical motion of the swing (latency). This adds another **~50 to 100 ms**.
- **Total "Reaction" Time:** Just adding these minimums gets us to **250 ms** *before the physical swing even properly starts*.

- **Swing Execution:** The physical act of swinging the bat from initiation to the point of contact takes around **150-200 ms**.

The Problem: If batters wait until they process the ball's initial flight path (100 to 150 ms into the flight) before starting the reactive sequence (another 250 to 350ms minimum before the swing starts), the ball would be in the catcher's mitt before their bat is near the hitting zone. The total time needed for reaction + swing execution (> 400 ms) exceeds the ball's total flight time (~400 ms).

The Predictive Solution: Successful batters don't wait to see the ball clearly. They can't wait that long. They use predictive cues, the pitcher's arm angle, release point, and body mechanics, to begin their swing based on predictions about where the ball will be, not where it is. Hitting a fastball is a remarkable feat that illustrates the predictive nature of the brain. It relies on rapidly processing subtle cues, leveraging vast stores of experience to make accurate predictions, and initiating complex actions proactively based on those predictions. A purely reactive system, bound by the inherent delays in neural processing and muscle activation, would simply be too slow to succeed in this game.

Not a fan of baseball? No problem. Here are some day-to-day examples that, if observed thoroughly, can help us realize our brain's truly predictive nature:

1. **Morning Predictions**: Before getting out of bed, notice what your brain predicts about the day ahead.
2. **Traffic Predictions**: Observe how you anticipate other people's movements while driving or walking.

3. **Social Predictions**: In conversations, notice how you predict what others will say.
4. **Evening Review**: Reflect on which predictions were accurate and which weren't.

Reflection Questions:

- How often do you react to your predictions rather than actual events?
- What patterns do you notice in your prediction accuracy?
- How might improving your predictions improve your daily experience?

The human brain is indeed a predictive machine. Every decision we make, from what to eat for breakfast to whether to trust a new acquaintance, reflects our brain's attempt to efficiently manage our biological resources by a prediction process that uses past information to maximize energy efficiency and survival.

Why Does This Matter to Your Daily Life?

Your brain's primary job is managing your energy budget. Here's how this matters in daily life:

- Morning routine: Your brain predicts your energy needs and prepares your body before you're even awake.
- Social interactions: You unconsciously predict how much energy different people will require and adjust accordingly.
- Decision fatigue: After many decisions, your brain conserves energy by defaulting to easier choices.
- Comfort seeking: When stressed, you crave familiar foods and activities because they require less predictive energy.

Bottom Line: When you're tired, stressed, or overwhelmed, you're not necessarily being lazy: Your brain is doing exactly what it evolved to do: conserve energy for survival.

Understanding our brain's evolutionary purpose isn't just fascinating – it's practical. When we know what our brain is actually optimized for, we can work with its natural tendencies rather than fighting against them.

An Ancient brain in a modern world

Our brains reached their current organizational structure about 12,000 to 13,000 years ago, which was around the beginning of the first Agricultural Revolution. From an evolutionary perspective, this is incredibly recent: it is the equivalent of the last second of a 24-hour day. Yet in this brief moment, our environments have changed more dramatically than in the previous millions of years of human evolution.

Our human brain developed long ago to survive in an environment dramatically different from today's world. In a 2021 paper, researchers **Marcia Ponce de León and Christoph Zollikofer from the University of Zurich** tell us the modern human brain emerged 1.5 to 1.7 million years ago. Those brains had organizational features typical of modern humans: frontal lobe areas responsible for planning and executing complex patterns of thought, action, and language.

That our human brains today are not much different from the brains of our ancestors 120 centuries ago should raise some flags in your modern brain. Why should this matter to you? Because evolution proceeds very SLOW when compared with societal change:

> *The human brain does not instantaneously create new areas of cognition to address emerging social challenges.*

To process the modern social media and globalization world, our brain must use the organizational and cognitive functions that evolved for an entirely different environment. This evolutionary mismatch creates specific challenges in modern life.

For example, our brains evolved a "negativity bias" that gave preferential attention to potential threats - crucial for survival when predators were common, but problematic in today's media environment, where it drives us toward consuming negative news and social media content. This example is just one of several potential mismatch challenges we experience due to the fact that our brain uses hardware that is tens of thousands of years old to process and manage new social problems. Here are some additional examples (we kept negativity bias for completeness):

- **Negativity Bias**: This evolved to detect threats, now triggered by news media and social comparison.
- **Social Group Size**: This evolved for tribes of 50-150, but it is now navigating global networks.
- **Food Scarcity Responses**: This evolved for unpredictable food supply, but it is now facing abundance (comparatively speaking with regard to life 12,000+ years ago).

- **Immediate vs. Long-term**: This evolved for immediate survival, but it now requires long-term planning.

Consider the following example:

> When we lose our temper during an argument, why do we experience increased heart rate, red face, sweaty palms, stress hormone release, muscle tension, and/or other physiological reactions? Are you aware that these physiological reactions are either identical or at least very close to those our ancestors experienced when facing physical threats? Are we in danger? Are you in danger? Are you experiencing the same type of danger they were thousands of years ago? No, yet our brain interprets threats to our beliefs or identity as survival threats, activating ancient defensive systems <u>even when no physical danger exists</u>.

> Most of us don't have to worry about the things that our ancestors worried about daily in order to survive. Yet, for all intents and purposes, we have the same brain. So, what happens? Our brain adapts to the best of its ability and tries to keep us safe so that we can live another day and pass down our genes. What doesn't happen is the brain does NOT create new areas of cognition on the fly to deal with new social problems. Instead, we become prepared for fight, flight, freeze, or fawn.

We must be fully aware of this if we intend for our ancient brain and its predictive model to deliver optimal outcomes in today's modern world. Our brain uses old hardware to construct a comprehensive representation of reality, based on prior experiences, to anticipate or predict future outcomes. It integrates past knowledge and encounters with the ever-changing stream of new sensory inputs, seamlessly constructing a comprehensive representation of reality and shaping existing models. This predictive prowess manifests across many cognitive domains, from the most straightforward act of recognizing a familiar face to the more complex task of deciphering intricate patterns within groups of people. Here are some practical areas where this level of self-observation may be of use:

1. **Stress Management**:

    Recognize when ancient threat-detection systems are responding to modern, non-physical challenges

2. **Decision Making**:

    Understand how evolutionary biases influence our choices

3. **Social Interaction**:

    Appreciate how group dynamics reflect ancient survival strategies

4. **Learning and Growth**:

   Leverage neuroplasticity to adapt ancient brains to modern demands

Understanding our evolutionary heritage isn't just intellectually interesting; it's practically essential for navigating modern life effectively. When we recognize that our brains evolved for environments dramatically different from today's world, we can become diligent observers of ourselves to work with our biology rather than against it. We can begin our path to better self-awareness.

The Foundations of Consciousness

The journey from simple energy conversion in ancient bacteria to human self-awareness represents one of the most remarkable developments in the history of life on Earth. Yet this consciousness didn't emerge suddenly; it developed gradually and carefully through millions of years of incremental innovations. The timeline that shows the evolution from survival to self-awareness can be summarized as follows:

- **Basic Sensation**: Simple organisms detecting light, chemicals, and touch.
- **Nervous System Integration**: Coordinating multiple sensory inputs.
- **Memory Formation**: Learning from past experiences.
- **Pattern Recognition**: Identifying recurring environmental features.
- **Predictive Modeling**: Anticipating future events.
- **Self-Recognition**: Distinguishing self from environment.
- **Abstract Thought**: Manipulating concepts independent of immediate experience.

Each level built upon previous developments, creating increasingly sophisticated forms of awareness. Human consciousness represents the current pinnacle of this evolutionary process, but we're still fundamentally biological creatures operating through ancient neural mechanisms. We may be capable of abstract thought, art, complex math, and many other wonderful things; however, our biology is still as fundamental and primitive as that of our ancestors thousands of years ago. Being aware of this gives us the opportunity to become less reactive to the incessant stimuli we receive in this modern world.

The Social Brain Hypothesis - How Social Complexity Shaped Human Intelligence

Anthropologist **Robin Dunbar's** groundbreaking Social Brain Hypothesis fundamentally challenges traditional assumptions about human cognitive evolution. Rather than viewing intelligence as primarily an adaptation to environmental challenges like tool use, hunting, or navigation, Dunbar proposes that human intelligence evolved principally to navigate the intricate web of complex social relationships that characterize human societies. This revolutionary perspective suggests that our remarkably large brains function essentially as sophisticated social processing systems, finely tuned through millions of years of evolution to track relationships, monitor alliances, manage reputations, and understand the subtle dynamics that govern group behavior.

The hypothesis emerges from a compelling observation: Across primate species, brain size correlates more strongly with social group size than ecological factors. This relationship, known as Dunbar's number, suggests that humans can maintain stable social relationships with about 150 individuals. This figure appears remarkably consistent across hunter-gatherer societies, military units, and even modern social networks.

The Architecture of Social Cognition

The social cognitive demands that shaped human intelligence are extraordinarily sophisticated and multifaceted:

- **Theory of Mind**:

    This represents perhaps the most fundamental of these capabilities - the profound ability to understand that other individuals possess their own unique perspectives, beliefs, desires, and intentions that may differ dramatically from our own. This cognitive breakthrough allows humans to predict behavior, manipulate outcomes, and engage in the complex dance of social interaction that defines human relationships.

- **Reputation Management:**

    This constitutes another critical dimension of social intelligence, requiring individuals to constantly monitor and strategically influence how others perceive them across multiple social contexts. This involves not only managing one's own reputation but also tracking the reputations of others within the group, creating a complex matrix of social standing that influences everything from mating opportunities to resource access.

- **Coalition Building:**

    This demands the ability to form, maintain, and strategically dissolve alliances based on shifting interests and circumstances. Humans must navigate temporary partnerships, long-term friendships, family loyalties, and professional relationships while constantly recalibrating these connections as social landscapes evolve.

- **Deception Detection:**

    This requires sophisticated pattern recognition and emotional intelligence to identify when others aren't being truthful, while simultaneously managing one's own strategic disclosure of information. This creates an evolutionary arms race between deceptive capabilities and detection mechanisms that has profoundly shaped human psychology.

- **Cultural Learning**

    This involves the complex acquisition of group-specific knowledge, skills, customs, and values that define social membership and identity. Unlike simple imitation, cultural learning requires understanding the social significance of behaviors and adapting them appropriately to different contexts and relationships.

Psychological Implications and Human Nature

This social focus provides elegant explanations for numerous features of human psychology that appear puzzling when viewed through a purely individualistic lens. Our intense preoccupation with social status reflects the critical importance of hierarchical position in ancestral environments where status directly influenced access to resources, mates, and survival opportunities. The profound human tendency to conform to group norms demonstrates the adaptive value of social cohesion and the dangers of ostracism in small, interdependent communities.

Perhaps most remarkably, the Social Brain Hypothesis illuminates our extraordinary capacity for both unprecedented cooperation and devastating competition. Humans can work together in massive coordinated efforts involving millions of individuals, yet we can also engage in sophisticated forms of social manipulation and conflict. This dual nature reflects the complex social environment in which our ancestors evolved - one requiring both intense cooperation within groups and fierce competition between groups.

The hypothesis also explains our remarkable sensitivity to social rejection, our sophisticated capacity for empathy and emotional contagion, and our unique ability to engage in complex forms of communication that convey not just information but also social signals about relationships, status, and group membership. These capabilities represent profound adaptations to the social world that ultimately shaped not just human intelligence, but the very essence of what it means to be human.

Implications for Modern Living

Understanding our evolutionary heritage represents a profound shift in how we approach personal development and well-being. Rather than viewing ourselves as prisoners of our biological past, this knowledge empowers us to work more intelligently and compassionately with our inherited neural architecture. The key insight is that we need not fight against our fundamental nature; rather, we can create environments, habits, and practices that align harmoniously with how our brains actually function after millions of years of evolutionary refinement.

This approach acknowledges that our modern brains are essentially ancient operating systems running contemporary software. Our neural circuits evolved in vastly different environments - small hunter-gatherer groups facing immediate physical threats and operating within tight-knit social networks. Yet these same brains must now navigate urban environments, digital communication, abstract careers, and global information streams. By understanding these evolutionary mismatches, we can design our lives to work with, rather than against, our biological inheritance. Below are some basic principles that could be useful:

Honor Your Energy Budget: The Economics of Mental Resources

Your brain is constantly managing limited resources. Despite representing about 2% to 3% of our body weight, our brain consumes 20% to 25% of our total daily energy expenditure. This remarkable energy demand reflects the brain's role as a sophisticated prediction and decision-making machine that operates continuously, even during sleep. However, this energy budget is not unlimited, and different cognitive functions draw from shared resource pools in ways that create important practical implications for daily life.

Willpower, attention, and decision-making capacity function more like muscles than we typically realize - they can become fatigued through use and require recovery time to operate at peak efficiency. Research in cognitive psychology demonstrates that these mental resources operate according to principles similar to physical energy: they can be depleted through overuse, strengthened through appropriate training, and restored through rest and recovery.

The phenomenon of "decision fatigue" illustrates this principle dramatically. Studies show that judges make harsher sentencing decisions later in the day when their decision-making resources are depleted, and that people make progressively poorer choices as they face more decisions throughout the day. This isn't a character flaw, but a fundamental feature of how our brains manage limited cognitive resources.

Practical Application: Schedule important decisions for times when your mental energy is highest (typically morning for most people), and create systems that reduce the number of trivial decisions you need to make daily.

Leverage Prediction Mechanisms: Harnessing Our Brain's Forecasting Systems

Our brain operates as a sophisticated prediction machine, constantly generating forecasts about what will happen next based on past experiences and current context. This incessant predictive processing occurs largely below conscious awareness but profoundly influences your emotions, behaviors, and decision-making processes. These predictions shape not only what we notice in our environment but also how we interpret ambiguous situations and what actions we choose to take.

The brain's prediction system evolved to help our ancestors anticipate threats, opportunities, and social dynamics in environments where accurate forecasting could mean the difference between survival and death. In modern contexts, these same predictive mechanisms continue to operate, but we can become more conscious collaborators in this process rather than mostly passive recipients of automatic predictions.

Understanding prediction mechanisms also reveals why preparation and mental rehearsal are so powerful. When you explicitly consider potential scenarios and your responses to them, you're essentially training your brain's predictive systems to generate more accurate and useful forecasts in real situations.

Practical Application: Before entering challenging situations, explicitly consider what you expect to happen and what you'll do if those expectations aren't met.

Satisfy Social Needs Consciously: Designing Modern Connections for Ancient Brains

Our brain evolved within the context of small, stable social groups where every individual knew every other individual personally, relationships were multifaceted and enduring, and social connection was a matter of survival. These evolutionary pressures created neural circuits that crave deep social bonds, seek consistent social feedback, and experience genuine distress when social needs remain unmet.

Modern life often fails to satisfy these fundamental social needs in healthy ways. We may have hundreds of social media connections, but lack intimate friendships. We may interact with dozens of people daily, but feel profoundly lonely. We may have access to constant communication, but struggle to find meaningful conversation. This mismatch between our evolved social needs and contemporary social structures contributes to widespread feelings of isolation, anxiety, and depression.

The quality of our social connections has profound impacts on physical health, mental well-being, and cognitive function. Research consistently demonstrates that strong social relationships are among the most powerful predictors of happiness, longevity, and resilience. However, building and maintaining these connections requires intentional effort in environments that don't naturally facilitate them.

Practical Application: Prioritize deep relationships over numerous shallow connections, and create regular opportunities for meaningful social interaction.

Respect the Negativity Bias: Working Skillfully with Threat Detection Systems

Our brain's negativity bias represents one of evolution's most successful survival strategies. Our ancestors who paid careful attention to potential threats (the rustle in the bushes, the subtle signs of social disapproval, the possibility of resource scarcity) were more likely to survive and reproduce than those who maintained a consistently optimistic outlook. <u>This bias manifests as a tendency to notice, remember, and be influenced more strongly by negative information than positive information</u>.

While this negativity bias served our ancestors exceptionally well in environments filled with immediate physical dangers, it can create significant challenges in modern contexts where most threats are abstract, distant, or greatly exaggerated by media coverage. The same neural circuits that helped detect genuine threats now respond to work emails, news headlines, and social-media posts as if they represented immediate dangers to our survival.

The intent here is not to eliminate negativity bias but to understand it as it serves important functions even in modern life. Let's work more skillfully with this bias, recognizing when it's providing useful information versus when it's creating unnecessary suffering or poor decision-making.

Practical Application: Consciously balance negative information consumption with positive experiences, and practice gratitude to counteract the brain's natural negativity bias.

Chapter 2 Summary: Key Insights

The journey from controlled fire to human consciousness reveals something profound: Our remarkable brain exists not because evolution "intended" to create a thinking machine, but because our ancestors solved an energy problem in a way that accidentally created the most complex structure in the known universe. Here are some essential takeaways

1. **Energy is Fundamental**:

    Life is about efficient energy conversion and management from ancient bacteria to modern brains. Our brain's 20% energy demand explains why thinking is literally exhausting and why good nutrition directly impacts mental performance.

2. **Cooking Made Us Human**:

    The mastery of fire provided the extra calories necessary for large, energy-intensive brains.

3. **Prediction over Reaction**:

    Your brain's main job isn't thinking; it's predicting future needs and preparing appropriate responses.

4. **Ancient Brains, Modern Challenges**:

    Our neural architecture evolved for environments very different from today's, creating both opportunities and challenges. Again, understanding that we're running Stone Age software on Digital-Age problems creates compassion for our struggles and wisdom for our solutions.

5. **Consciousness is Embodied**:

    Self-awareness emerges from biological processes and remains fundamentally connected to our physical being.

6. **Social Architecture**: Our "social brain" evolved to navigate complex relationships, explaining why social rejection hurts physically and why community feels essential.

7. **Survival, Not Happiness**: Our brain evolved for survival efficiency, not for happiness or even accuracy, which explains why modern life often feels challenging.

Reflection Questions:

1. How does understanding your evolutionary heritage change your perspective on daily challenges?
2. What aspects of modern life most conflict with your evolutionary programming?
3. How can you create environments that better support your ancient brain's functioning?
4. What would change if you treated your mental energy as carefully as you treat your financial resources?

Understanding why our brain evolved the way it did sets the foundation for exploring how it actually works in creating our moment-to-moment experience. While evolution explains the hardware, we need to understand the operating system: the sophisticated predictive processes that construct our reality from moment to moment.

In the next chapter, we'll dive deep into the mechanisms of prediction, examining how our brain doesn't just react to the world but actively creates our experience of it. We'll explore the revolutionary concept of neuroplasticity and discover how understanding your brain as a prediction machine can transform how we approach learning, relationships, and personal growth.

The journey from evolutionary biology to practical neuroscience will reveal that we are not a passive recipient of experience but an active participant in creating our reality. This realization opens up extraordinary possibilities for conscious development and authentic living.

CHAPTER 3
THE PREDICTIVE BRAIN

Prediction is NOT something the brain does every now and then; it is an intrinsic property that never stops and it serves an essential role in learning"

Helen is walking to her car after a late dinner when she hears footsteps behind her.

Instantly, without conscious thought, her brain launches into action: analyzing the rhythm of the steps, comparing them to thousands of stored patterns, and predicting whether they represent a threat. Her heart rate increases, her muscles tense, and she shifts her purse to her other arm, all before she turns around to see a jogger with earbuds passing by harmlessly.

What just happened in Helen's brain represents one of the most remarkable discoveries in modern neuroscience: our brain is a predictive organ, not a reactive organ. It's constantly predicting what will happen next, constructing reality moment by moment, and preparing our bodies accordingly. In the split second before Helen saw the jogger, her brain had already run through dozens of scenarios, accessed memories from her entire life, and prepared multiple response options to the footsteps she heard.

This isn't a special talent Helen has developed. It's the fundamental operating system of human consciousness. Right now, as you read these words, your brain is generating thousands of predictions per second about everything from the next word in this sentence to whether that sound you just heard deserves your attention. Understanding our brain as a prediction machine changes everything. It explains why anxiety often feels worse than actual events, why we can "sense" someone's mood before they speak, and why breaking habits feels so difficult. However, it also reveals how we can work with our brain's predictive nature to create the experiences we want rather than being unconsciously controlled by automatic patterns.

The evolutionary heritage we explored in the previous chapters explains why we have brains capable of such sophisticated processing. Now we'll discover how (according to the latest scientific peer-reviewed data) this remarkable three-pound universe creates and influences our experience of reality through an intricate convergence of prediction, comparison, and continuous updating.

We'll journey into the mechanisms of consciousness itself, exploring how our "unfinished" brain learns to model the world, how neuroplasticity allows continuous adaptation, and how our mind extends far beyond the boundaries of our skull. We'll discover that what we call "thinking" emerges from processes far more complex and interconnected than most people realize.

But first, we need to understand how we became such a sophisticated prediction machine in the first place. The answer begins with one of the most vulnerable starts in the animal kingdom.

The Unfinished Miracle: Why Humans Are Born Helpless

If alien scientists studied Earth's mammals, they'd probably conclude that humans have evolved the worst survival strategy. Consider the evidence:

- A baby horse? It walks within hours, and runs within days.

  A human baby? It is completely helpless for months; it can't even hold up its own head.

- A baby dolphin? It swims and hunts within weeks.

  A human baby? It takes a year just to walk and three years to speak coherently.

- A baby elephant? It follows the herd and finds food almost immediately.

  A human baby? It requires intensive care for at least a decade.

By almost any measure, human babies seem like an evolutionary disaster. We're born too early, develop too slowly, and demand too much parental investment. Any sensible alien would predict our species would become extinct within a generation. We inherently know that those aliens would be wrong in their assessment, but why? In his book **The Brain – The Story of You**, **David Eagleman** tells us that this apparent disadvantage is actually our greatest strength and a limitation for the other mammals. He tells us that humans are born "unfinished," but with incredible potential. What looks like helplessness is limitless possibilities.

Baby animals develop quickly because their brains are wired according to preprogrammed routines, but that preparedness comes at the expense of flexibility. To shed light on this concept, let's explore the following example:

> Imagine a hippo suddenly appearing on the Arctic Tundra. This poor hippo would struggle to adapt and probably perish quickly because its brain and body are optimized for African river environments. Arriving with a pre-arranged brain works well in a specific ecosystem but proves maladaptive in different environments.

> Humans, on the other hand, can thrive in many diverse ecosystems. Humans can survive in the Arctic and develop sophisticated technologies and cultural practices that make such environments livable. This is because instead of arriving fully preprogrammed, humans arrive unfinished, which allows the <u>human brain to be shaped by the details of life experiences</u>. Eagleman states that:

> *"At birth, a baby's neurons are disparate and unconnected, and in the first two years of life they begin connecting up extremely rapidly as they take in sensory information. By the age of two, a child has over one hundred trillion connections (or synapses), which is double the number an adult has, and far more than it needs."*

The brain then begins a strategy of neural pruning, which leads to the removal of 50% of the synapses. Basically, <u>synapses stimulated by experiences are strengthened, and unused synapses are weakened and eventually eliminated</u>. Imagine a forest with many trails. If only a few of those trails are walked over time, the rest will eventually be overgrown and disappear.

This might seem like a loss, but it's actually a gain: a sophisticated optimization process. Like a sculptor removing excess marble to reveal a statue, your brain eliminates unused connections while strengthening those that prove useful.

The Neural Pruning Process:

1. **Overproduction**: Initial neural connections in babies exceed adult levels.
2. **Experience-Dependent Shaping**: Our frequently used connections strengthen.
3. **Pruning**: Our unused connections are eliminated.
4. **Myelination**: Important pathways become faster and more efficient.

5. **Ongoing Refinement**: The process continues throughout our lives at varying rates.

Eagleman tells us that the process of becoming who you are is defined by eliminating the possibilities that were already present. He says:

> *"You become who you are not because of what grows in your brain... but because of what is removed."*

As we grow and develop, we engage in this perpetual dance of being shaped by our environment while also shaping the environment around us, and our ever-evolving brain is at the center of that dance. Our day-to-day activity becomes the direct result of the experiences and interactions that fill our waking hours. Our brain makes sense of our environment by processing sensory data and making decisions for us before we are even aware of them.

Why Does This Matter to Your Daily Life?

Your brain's extended development period creates lifelong superpowers:

- Incredible adaptability: Unlike animals with "finished" brains, you can thrive in environments your ancestors never imagined.
- Cultural transmission: You can learn from your own experience and from the accumulated wisdom of all humanity.
- Continuous learning: Your neural plasticity means you can rewire your brain throughout life.
- Creative problem-solving: Your "unfinished" brain can generate novel solutions and not just follow preprogrammed responses.

Bottom Line: When you feel frustrated by how long it takes to learn new skills, remember: this "inefficiency" is what makes you human. Your brain trades speed for ultimate flexibility.

This vulnerable beginning, being born "unfinished," created the foundation for something extraordinary: a brain that remains changeable throughout life. But how does this plastic brain actually create our moment-to-moment experience?

The Prediction Machine: How Our Brain Really Works

For decades, scientists compared the brain to a computer: information comes in through your senses, gets processed by neural circuits, and produces thoughts and actions as output. Input → Processing → Output. Simple, logical, and wrong. Here's what actually happens:

- Right now, your brain is generating a constant stream of predictions about what you'll see, hear, and feel in the next few seconds.
- When sensory information arrives, your brain doesn't passively process it; <u>it compares it to what it expected</u>.
- If the information matches your prediction, your brain barely notices.
- If it doesn't match, that's when you become consciously aware.

Think about driving a familiar route home. You can arrive with almost no memory of the journey because your brain predicted every turn, every traffic light, every landmark so accurately that nothing surprised it enough to require conscious attention. But if construction forces an unexpected detour, suddenly you're fully alert because your predictions failed. This is prediction error in action, the gap between what your brain expected and what actually happened. Your entire conscious experience is built from these moments when reality surprises your predictions and expectations. This represents a paradigm shift in neuroscience: from viewing the brain as a reactive system to understanding it as a proactive prediction engine.

Beyond the computer metaphor

It is widely accepted in the scientific community that our brain creates a MODEL of the world it perceives. This model includes the outside world as well as the world inside our bodies, and through this model, the brain can consolidate interdependent sensory inputs into a singular experience. This model-building process is central to what neuroscientists call predictive processing theory.

According to this theory, the brain doesn't passively receive sensory information; instead, it actively predicts what it expects to sense based on its internal model and then compares these predictions with actual sensory input. When there's a mismatch between prediction and "reality" (prediction error), the brain updates its model. This constant cycle of prediction, comparison, and updating is how we learn and adapt to our environment. It also explains why identical sensory inputs can lead to distinct beliefs and conclusions in different people. This is because we're all working with different predictive models based on our unique experiences. But what makes this very interesting and challenging for us is not that the brain models the world around us, but that this predictive model is forever being tuned. In the third chapter of his book "**A Thousand Brains**", Jeff Hawkins tells us that:

> "Prediction is NOT something the brain does every now and then; it is an intrinsic property that never stops and it serves an essential role in learning. When the brain predictions are verified, that means the brain's model of the world is accurate, while a mis-prediction cause

you to attend to the error and update the model. When we are born, our brain knows almost nothing. It doesn't know any words, what buildings are like, or how a computer works. At birth, the brain is structured to see, hear and learn, but it doesn't know what it will see, hear or learn. Through experience it learns a rich and complicated model of the world."

This aligns with the predictive processing framework developed by researchers like **Andy Clark**, **Jakob Hohwy**, and **Anil Seth**, which has gained substantial empirical support over the past two decades. These models allow prediction, which is far more metabolically efficient than pure reaction, as the brain can prepare appropriate responses before stimuli fully unfold.

The predictive brain theory is supported by extensive neuroimaging evidence showing that brain activity often precedes conscious awareness of stimuli, with neural patterns associated with preparing actions detectable even before people report being aware of their decisions. This phenomenon, which has sparked extensive debate about the nature of conscious will, strongly suggests that the brain is constantly running predictive simulations rather than merely responding to incoming data.

What Your Brain Models

Our brain's modeling system operates across multiple domains simultaneously, creating an integrated understanding of our world:

- **Physical Objects**:

    How doors open, how chairs support weight, and how apps respond to touch. These models incorporate physics-based understanding; our brain automatically calculates trajectories when we throw a ball, anticipates the weight distribution when we pick up an object, and predicts resistance when we push against surfaces.

- **Spatial Relationships**:

    Where objects exist relative to each other and to us. The hippocampus and associated structures maintain cognitive maps that extend beyond simple navigation, encoding complex spatial hierarchies and relationships that allow us to mentally navigate environments even when not physically present.

- **Temporal Patterns**:

    When events typically occur and how long processes take. Our circadian rhythms, learned through repeated exposure, help predict daily cycles. Our brain also models longer temporal patterns – seasonal changes, social rhythms, and personal behavioral patterns that unfold over weeks or months.

- **Social Dynamics**:

    How people typically behave in various contexts. This includes theory of mind capabilities, allowing us to model others' mental states, intentions, and likely behaviors. Research in social neuroscience shows that regions like the medial prefrontal cortex and temporal-parietal junction are crucial for these social predictions.

- **Abstract Concepts**:

    Justice, democracy, love, mathematics, and creativity. These complex conceptual models allow us to navigate abstract reasoning, moral decision-making, and creative problem-solving by drawing analogies and applying learned patterns to novel situations.

- **Personal Identity**:

    Our capabilities, limitations, values, and role in various contexts. This metacognitive modeling allows us to predict our own performance, emotional responses, and behavioral tendencies across different situations.

The Model-Building Process

The brain's model-building follows a sophisticated iterative process supported by multiple neural systems:

1. **Initial Exposure**:

    Encountering new information or experiences activates attention networks that determine what information is worth modeling. The novelty detection system, involving structures like the locus coeruleus, helps prioritize unexpected or potentially important stimuli.

2. **Pattern Recognition**:

    We identify recurring features or relationships through both supervised and unsupervised learning mechanisms. The brain automatically extracts statistical regularities from experience, even without conscious effort or intention.

3. **Model Construction**:

    We create internal representations of how things work through the formation of new neural connections and the strengthening of existing pathways. This involves both bottom-up sensory integration and top-down conceptual organization.

4. **Prediction Generation**:

   We use models to anticipate future events by running forward simulations. The prefrontal cortex plays a crucial role in generating these predictions and evaluating their likelihood.

5. **Error Detection**:

   We compare predictions with actual outcomes through specialized error-detection circuits. When predictions fail, this generates prediction error signals that propagate throughout the brain's hierarchical structure.

6. **Model Updating**:

   We refine representations based on prediction errors through processes similar to machine learning algorithms. The strength of this updating depends on factors like the magnitude of the error, the confidence in the original prediction, and the perceived reliability of the new information.

Predictive Processing in Action

Every moment of consciousness involves this predictive process operating at multiple levels simultaneously. When you reach for a coffee cup, your brain predicts its weight, temperature, and texture before your hand makes contact. This prediction involves integration across sensory modalities: visual information about the cup's size and material, tactile memories of similar objects, and motor predictions about the required grip strength and movement trajectory.

When we enter a familiar room, our brain fills in details beyond our current visual field based on memory models. This predictive filling-in is so seamless that we're typically unaware it's happening. Research on "change blindness" demonstrates how extensively our conscious experience depends on these predictions rather than actual sensory input. Change blindness is a phenomenon of visual perception where a change in a visual stimulus goes unnoticed by the observer. The fundamental principles of this research demonstrate that our visual system does not create a complete, detailed, and continuous representation of the world. Instead, it relies on focused attention to process information. Experiments show that people often fail to detect even large changes when a brief visual disruption (like a blank screen or an eye blink) is introduced between two images.

The research suggests that we form a "gist" or a schematic representation of a scene and that attention acts like a spotlight; if a change occurs outside of this focused attention, we are "blind" to it. This has led to the conclusion that a detailed memory of the visual world is not a prerequisite for navigating it, and that our perception is much more selective and fragile than we intuitively believe. The research has been extended to real-world scenarios, such as missing a conversation partner swap or failing to see a car in one's periphery, highlighting the practical implications of these cognitive limitations. Here are a few classic and compelling examples you can watch:

- **The "Flicker" Paradigm:** This is the most common type of change blindness video. An original image and an altered image are shown one after another with a brief blank screen in between, making it surprisingly difficult to spot the change. Here is an example: https://www.youtube.com/watch?v=vJG698U2Mvo
- **Real-World Scenarios:** Some videos demonstrate change blindness in real-world settings, such as a person giving directions to a stranger who is then swapped out with a different person behind a large object. This video from NOVA demonstrates this effect: https://youtu.be/VkrrVozZR2c?si=kWAF3TG2V-ZZZ8QN
- **Gradual Changes:** There are also videos that demonstrate how changes can go unnoticed when they happen slowly and gradually over time, rather than with a sudden visual disruption. This gradual change video shows this effect: https://youtu.be/EARtANyz98Q?si=nZkKq7Hrva423u3M

Something to consider:

Stop reading for a moment and look around your environment. Notice how much you "know" about objects you're not directly looking at: the weight of objects, the texture of surfaces, the likely contents of containers. This knowledge comes from your brain's predictive models, not from current sensory input. Your confidence in these predictions reflects the reliability your brain has learned to associate with similar past experiences.

The brain processes predictions through a hierarchical structure where different levels handle different types of information:

- **Lower Levels**:

    To process basic sensory features like edges, colors, sounds, and textures. These levels generate predictions about immediate sensory input and detect basic prediction errors when sensory data doesn't match expectations.

- **Middle Levels**:

    To recognize objects, faces, words, and more complex patterns. These levels integrate information across sensory modalities and temporal sequences to identify meaningful units in the environment.

- **Higher Levels**:

    To understand contexts, meanings, implications, and abstract relationships. These levels generate predictions about complex scenarios, social situations, and conceptual relationships that may unfold over extended time periods.

- **Top-Down Influence**:

    Higher levels continuously send predictions downward, influencing what lower levels "see" and how they interpret ambiguous sensory information. This top-down flow is as important as bottom-up sensory processing.

- **Bottom-Up Correction**:

    When sensory data strongly contradict predictions, error signals propagate upward through the hierarchy, forcing higher levels to update their models and generate new predictions.

This enhanced awareness of our brain's predictive processes can improve decision-making, reduce anxiety about uncertainty, and help us recognize when our mental models may need updating based on new evidence.

Neuroplasticity: The Brain That Changes Itself

Remember the old saying, "*You can't teach an old dog new tricks*"? I do, and for most of the 20th century, neuroscientists agreed, at least about human brains. They believed our brain was essentially fixed by adulthood, like a computer with unchangeable hardware. This belief made sense from their perspective:

- Brain injuries often seemed permanent.
- Personality traits appeared stable.
- Learning new skills became harder with age.
- We are born with a certain number of neurons that seem to decline with age.
- The evidence seemed clear: adult brains don't change.

Those neuroscientists couldn't have been more wrong. In their book **Brain Wash**, **Dr David and Austin Perlmutter** teach us that:

> *"Our brains use neurotransmitters and hormones to transfer and modify messages across the brain and body. Neurotransmitters and hormones are molecules that work together driving feelings of joy, anger, bliss, hunger, lust and desire. These molecules are affected and influenced by food, sleep, physical movement and interactions with the environment and other people. They are also affected by stress, feelings of gratitude, empathy and compassion."*

As these molecules operate, neural connections strengthen or weaken depending on the activities we engage in. This process underlies one of neuroscience's most important discoveries: neuroplasticity. The concept of neuroplasticity was first introduced by **William James** in 1890, and decades later, **Jerzy Konorski** coined the term "neural plasticity." Neuroplasticity refers to the brain's ability to reorganize by forming new connections or strengthening existing ones throughout our lives in response to learning, experience, or injury. It enables the brain to change and adapt to intrinsic or extrinsic stimuli by reorganizing its structure, function, or connections, resulting in physiological and morphological modifications. The brain remains pliable, impressionable, and moldable throughout life. **Dr. Michael Merzenich**, a pioneer in neuroplasticity research, explains:

> *"Experience coupled with attention leads to physical changes in the structure and future functioning of the nervous system. This leaves us with a clear physiological fact: moment by moment we chose and sculpt how our ever-changing minds will work. We choose who we will be in the very next moment in a very real sense, and these choices are left embossed in physical form in our material selves."*

Neuroplasticity plays a crucial role in developing and maintaining brain function, including learning and memory, as well as in recovery from brain injury and adaptation to environmental changes. This adaptability occurs through several mechanisms:

1. **Structural changes**:

    This includes formation of new neurons in specific brain regions (neurogenesis), creation of new synapses (synaptogenesis), and alterations in the complexity of neural branching patterns.

2. **Functional changes**:

    This involves strengthening or weakening of existing connections through processes like long-term potentiation (LTP) and long-term depression (LTD).

3. **Network reorganization**:

This concerns shifts in how large-scale brain networks communicate and coordinate activity.

Studies have explored the temporal patterns of neuroplastic changes and their implications for learning and recovery from brain injury. A landmark 2006 study by **Eleanor Maguire, Katherine Woollett, and Hugo Spiers,** demonstrating neuroplasticity in action, was conducted with London taxi drivers. Researchers found that the hippocampi (brain regions crucial for spatial memory) of experienced taxi drivers were significantly larger than those of control subjects, particularly in the posterior region. Moreover, the size of this brain region correlated with the amount of time spent as a taxi driver, suggesting that the intensive spatial navigation demands of memorizing London's complex street layout physically reshaped their brains. This research provides compelling evidence that specific activities can cause measurable structural changes in the adult human brain, even without genetic predisposition.

In a 2023 paper titled *"Exploring the Role of Neuroplasticity in Development, Aging, and Neurodegeneration,"* **Patricia Marzola, Thayza Meizer,** and colleagues explore how our aging brain changes and the significance of neuroplasticity in maintaining cognitive function later in life. Here is an excerpt of the paper:

> *"Neurodevelopmental exposures, numerous lifestyle factors, acute neurological processes (such as stroke and TBI), and neurodegenerative processes (such as AD and PD) can all disrupt neuroplasticity, leading to impairments in motor skills, affective behaviors, and cognitive function. Nevertheless, recent studies have highlighted the brain's ability to compensate for these impairments through processes involving neural reorganization, which consists of recruiting other brain regions and neuronal circuits to compensate for the damaged ones. Psychological traits, such as personality, motivation, and attention, also play a significant role in neuroplasticity mechanisms. For instance, individuals with high levels of motivation have been shown to exhibit greater neuroplasticity than those with low levels of motivation."*

Studies like this one do not necessarily confirm the specific claim of neuroplastic changes occurring in coordinated waves across different brain regions; however, they underscore the complexity and temporal dynamics of neuroplasticity in the brain.

What's important and exciting is that scientific understanding of neuroplasticity is continually evolving, and new mechanisms are regularly being discovered. For instance, while in the past scientists viewed cognition, emotion, bodily regulation, and motor control as separate modules, today, neuroscientists tell us that these functions are deeply integrated through the dynamic interaction of large-scale brain networks. Today, we know that emotion and cognition are interdependent processes that constantly influence each other. Emotions shape attention, perception, memory, and decision-making, while cognitive processes like appraisal and regulation modulate emotional responses. These functions emerge from overlapping brain networks spanning both cortical and subcortical regions. The brain achieves this integration through the dynamic interplay of several key networks:

- **The Salience Network** detects biologically relevant stimuli (both internal and external) and helps direct attention and switch between other networks.
- **The Default Mode Network** contributes to self-reference, memory, future planning, and internal modeling.
- **The Executive Control Network** supports goal-directed behavior, working memory, and cognitive control.

These networks continuously reconfigure based on current needs and context, allowing the brain to integrate information across domains and prioritize processing appropriately.

Here's what this means practically: The brain you have right now differs from the brain you had when you started reading this chapter. Every new concept you've encountered has created physical changes in your neural networks. You're not just learning about neuroplasticity, you're experiencing it.

Implications for Personal Development

From a behavioral point of view, neuroplasticity delivers a powerful and sobering message: <u>it can either work to our advantage or completely against us</u>. Every time we engage in a new experience, the brain changes itself to accommodate this new experience, and the more we engage in any activity, the stronger the connections needed to perform that activity become. **And this is true whether the activity is something good for us or bad for us**, as Drs. Perlmutter state in their book, if we choose to engage in activities that bombard us with negativity or provoke a sense of fear, our brains will be rewired to respond to this negativity and fear-driven state. His holiness the **Dalai Lama** perhaps says it best:

"The brain we develop reflects the life we lead."

This understanding of neuroplasticity has profound practical implications for our daily lives. Here are some ways you can apply this knowledge:

1. **Deliberate Practice**:

   When learning a new skill, focused, consistent practice strengthens neural pathways. Whether learning an instrument, a language, or a sport, regular practice with attention to improvement creates lasting brain changes.

2. **Environmental Enrichment**:

   Exposing yourself to novel, stimulating environments promotes neuroplasticity. Travel, explore new hobbies, or simply take different routes to familiar destinations to create new neural connections.

3. **Mindfulness Meditation**:

   Regular meditation has been shown to increase gray matter density in brain regions associated with learning, memory, and emotional regulation (after 8 weeks of practice). Even brief daily sessions can promote positive neuroplastic changes.

4. **Physical Exercise**:

   Regular aerobic exercise increases brain-derived neurotrophic factor (BDNF) levels, which promotes neuroplasticity and the growth of new neurons, particularly in the hippocampus.

5. **Sleep Optimization**:

   Quality sleep is essential for consolidating learning and memory. The brain strengthens important neural connections during deep sleep while pruning less important ones.

6. **Social Connection**:

   Meaningful social interactions stimulate multiple brain regions and promote positive neuroplastic changes. Regular social engagement is associated with cognitive resilience and reduced risk of dementia.

7. **Nutrition**:

   Certain nutrients, particularly omega-3 fatty acids, antioxidants, and flavonoids, support neuroplasticity. A Mediterranean-style diet has been associated with better brain health and cognitive function.

Why Does This Matter to Your Daily Life?

Right now, neuroplasticity is working either for you or against you:

Working FOR you when you:

- Practice new skills with focused attention and engage in regular physical exercise
- Challenge yourself with novel experiences and get adequate sleep
- Maintain social connections and meaningful relationships

Working AGAINST you when you:

- Repeat negative thought patterns and consume excessive stress-inducing media
- Engage in mindless, automatic behaviors and neglect sleep and physical health
- Isolate yourself from growth opportunities

Bottom Line: Every moment, you're sculpting your future brain. What kind of neural architecture are you building today?

As we process this information and move on to the next section, there is an important key insight to keep in mind: <u>specific skill matters less than the process of deliberately challenging our brain with focused attention over time</u>. Our remarkable, plastic, predictive brain doesn't operate in isolation. As we'll discover, our mind extends far beyond our skull, incorporating our body, environment, and relationships into its cognitive processes.

The Human Mind

Before we delve into the concept of the human mind, it's important to establish a clear distinction between the brain and the mind. While the brain is a physical, biological organ composed of neurons, blood vessels, and supporting cells, the mind is a more abstract concept referring to our conscious experiences, thoughts, feelings, and sense of self. This distinction will help us better understand the unique qualities of human cognition.

What is The Human Mind?

There is no easy answer to this question. If you go online searching for the definition, you might end up as confused as I did. This is because some of the available literature uses the terms mind, brain, and consciousness interchangeably. But that can't possibly be the case. For one, we know that the brain is a biological entity, and the mind isn't. On the other hand, there is an ongoing scientific and philosophical debate on the "hard problem of consciousness", and most leaders in this field define clear boundaries between the brain, the mind, and consciousness. So then, what is the human mind?

Let's start with the basics. Merriam-Webster dictionary defines the mind as

> "The element or complex of elements in an individual that feels, perceives, thinks, wills, and especially reasons."

Great! Good start, but we are still left with more questions than answers; For example, what is an element in this context?

Dan Siegel (professor of Psychiatry at UCLA) has been studying the human mind for a few decades now. In his book **Mindsight,** Siegel states that the human mind is a process. He says the mind is

> "A Relational and Embodied process that regulates the flow of energy and information."

How interesting. It's a process we can feel and that our biology is in tune with. It's also a process that manages energy consumption from information and interprets information from metabolic processes.

Alan Jassanoff (professor of biological engineering at MIT) takes a similar approach in his book **The Biological Mind.** He states that

> "Our minds are the product of complex interactions between our biological brain, our physical bodies and the environment around us."

This is a great step. Dr Siegel and Dr Jassanoff's definitions are concise, helpful, and actionable. In summary:

- The Mind is a series of interactions; an ongoing process, not a thing.
- This ongoing process doesn't take place in our brains alone, but instead continuously through our entire biology.
- This continuous biological process is observable and changeable.

These are not the only definitions of the Human Mind, but they are definitions that leave me with a workable foundation for my day-to-day life.

How does the Human Mind work?

To attempt to understand how the human mind works, it makes sense to first understand where possible boundaries are. In their revolutionary 1998 paper, **Andy Clark** and **David Chalmers** ask that very question:

> "Where does the mind end and the rest of the world begin?"

At first glance, this might seem like a simple question, but it is far from it. In the article "**Do we have minds of our own?**" **Meghan O'Gieblyn** tells us that thinkers like Descartes and Galileo had to dismiss the mind to do science. They concluded that things like intention, agency, purpose, love, and meaning must be secondary qualities, inexplicable within the framework of materialism. This approach contributed to a world divided into two camps: mind and matter. This dualistic approach was essential for the development of the many technological advancements we enjoy today, as it works well for understanding the material world. But it doesn't address the immaterial world. In fact, this approach created a radical disconnect between what many consider essential to being human and what can be measured.

Although dualism is still supported today by some, there is compelling research supporting alternate viewpoints. In her book **The Extended Mind**, **Annie Murphy Paul** tells us that the mind is not only everywhere in our bodies but also in our environment and relationships. Murphy Paul tells us that:

"Our culture insists that the brain is the sole locus of thinking, a cordoned-off space where cognition happens. This book argues otherwise: it holds that the mind constructs our thought processes from the resources available outside the brain. These resources include the feelings and movements of our bodies; the physical spaces in which we learn and work; and the other minds with which we interact – our classmates, colleagues, teachers, supervisors, friends."

Murphy Paul draws upon research from neuroscientists, cognitive scientists, and psychologists to illustrate how artists, scientists, and authors have used various forms of "mental extensions" throughout history. This includes the role of interoception, which represents knowledge derived from bodily sensations, and the unconscious mimicry of facial expressions and postures during face-to-face interactions, which informs one's own emotional construction.

Today, our minds have become entangled with technology and are impacted by the myriad of data captured by our senses. In the 1970s, **Horace Barlow** found out that a single photon hitting the retina can trigger three neural actions. Today, according to **Dr Jassanoff**, this means that at any given moment, 40 percent of our cortex is dedicated to processing information from our senses. A large portion of this data is processed subconsciously, where patterns are noticed, and our body alerts us of such patterns through sensations generated in our organs, bones, and muscles. Does this sound familiar? Have you heard of the gut feeling?

The Mind-Body Connection

Take a moment to think about that question from Clark and Chalmers: *"Where does the mind end and the rest of the world begins?"* Most of us would say our mind exists in our head or maybe is inside our brain. However, we know from "The Extended Mind" book that our cognitive processes routinely extend beyond our brains to include the environment and other minds. However, we also know that the mind can extend internally to our bodies. Our body isn't just a vehicle for our brain; it's an integral part of our thinking system and embodied knowledge. Part of the process of understanding how our brains and minds work involves the crucial realization that they do NOT work in isolation, but instead are deeply interwoven with the rest of our body processes.

Consider this moment: As you read these words, you're simultaneously processing the text, monitoring your emotional response, sensing your physical comfort, and unconsciously tracking sounds around you. Your "mind" includes not just your brain's activity but signals from your gut, your heart (which sends more signals to your brain than it receives), and even your social environment (other people's emotions literally influence your neural activity). This is consistent with research by leading microbiologists and gastroenterologists globally. Their work increasingly reveals that our cognitive processes extend beyond the brain to include our entire body, particularly the gut-brain axis with its 500 million neurons. Because of these processes, this gut-brain axis has been referred to as "the second brain". But it is not only microbiologists and gastroenterologists who are looking at this information seriously. This has now received the attention of mental health specialists as well. A 2020 publication by **Bastiaanssen et al.** in the *Harvard Review of Psychiatry* states that:

> *"The gut contains the largest number of neurons in the body, after the brain. In recent years, it has become clear that the gut microbiome is in communication with the brain, through the gut-brain axis."*

The paper further concludes that generally, people with depression have a less diverse gut microbiome, with higher levels of bacteria associated with inflammation, and decreased levels of bacteria associated with anti-inflammation. What's particularly striking is that approximately 90% of serotonin, a neurotransmitter crucial for mood regulation, is produced in the gut, not the brain. This finding dramatically illustrates the bidirectional relationship between our gut microbiome and mental health and helps explain why digestive issues often accompany psychological disorders. In other words, disruptions to the gut microbiome can trigger reactions in the body that may affect psychological, behavioral, and neurological health. I guess the old saying "you are what you eat" goes far beyond what you can see in the mirror: What you eat actually impacts what you think and how you think.

Scientists are discovering that thinking happens not just in our heads but throughout our entire biological and social system. Our mind isn't a thing; it's a process that emerges from the dynamic interaction between our brain, body, and world. We'll explore this 'second brain' in more detail in Chapter 7, but for now, it's important to understand that thinking involves our whole biological system, not just the organ in our skull.

Interoception: Our Inner Sense

In the previous section, we introduced the term "Interoception" as our ability to sense and interpret our internal bodily states. By becoming aware of our internal bodily signals, we truly add a sixth sense to our traditional five senses, opening the door to crucial information for decision-making, emotional regulation, and self-awareness. The profound connection between our internal bodily sensations and our mental life has been illuminated by neuroscientists. **Antonio Damasio's** work on the "somatic marker hypothesis," for instance, established how the brain's representation of bodily states (a form of interoception) is critical for emotional experience and sound decision-making. Building on such foundations, contemporary research by **Sarah Garfinkel** and her collaborators has rigorously shown that individuals with higher interoceptive accuracy (the objective ability to detect internal signals like heartbeats) tend to exhibit greater emotional intelligence, make more effective decisions, and demonstrate better mental health outcomes. Such interoceptive signals include:

- **Cardiovascular Awareness**:

    Heart rate and rhythm variations signal emotional states, stress levels, and autonomic nervous system activity. Heart rate variability, in particular, has been linked to cognitive flexibility and emotional regulation capacity.

- **Respiratory Sensations**:

    Breathing patterns both reflect and influence anxiety, attention, and cognitive performance. Controlled breathing practices have been shown to enhance prefrontal cortex function and emotional regulation.

- **Digestive Processes**:

    Gut feelings may represent genuine physiological information about safety, threat, or optimal choices based on past experience and current metabolic needs.

- **Muscular and Postural Awareness**:

    Muscle tension and postural changes signal emotional states, which can influence cognitive processing through embodied cognition mechanisms.

- **Thermoregulatory Signals**:

    Temperature regulation and circulation patterns affect alertness, comfort, and cognitive performance.

- **Hormonal and Energy Fluctuations**:

    Energy levels reflect circadian rhythms, metabolic states, and hormonal cycles, all of which significantly influence cognitive capacity and emotional regulation.

Environmental Cognition

Our physical environment profoundly shapes our thinking processes through mechanisms documented in environmental psychology, architecture research, and cognitive science. This extends far beyond obvious factors like noise and lighting to include subtle but measurable influences on creativity, attention, memory, and problem-solving abilities. Research in environmental psychology has identified specific ways that physical spaces influence mental processes:

- **Ceiling Height Effects**:

    Studies by **Joan Meyers-Levy and Rui (Juliet) Zhu** (2007) demonstrate that higher ceilings (10+ feet) promote abstract thinking, creative ideation, and freedom-oriented thoughts, while lower ceilings (8 feet or less) enhance focus on details, systematic processing, and constraint-oriented thinking. This occurs because ceiling height unconsciously activates concepts of freedom versus constraint.

- **Color Psychology**:

    Controlled experiments show that blue environments promote creative thinking and innovation by encouraging an exploratory mindset, while red environments enhance attention to detail and careful processing by triggering vigilant attention. Green environments support sustained attention and reduce mental fatigue through attention restoration mechanisms.

- **Natural Elements**:

Research by environmental psychologist **Roger Ulrich** and others demonstrates that views of nature improve attention restoration, stress recovery, and cognitive performance. Even brief exposure to natural scenes can restore directed attention capacity after mental fatigue, while exposure to urban environments without natural elements can exacerbate cognitive depletion.

- **Spatial Organization**:

    Organized environments support systematic thinking, goal pursuit, and conventional problem-solving approaches. However, research by **Kathleen Vohs** suggests that moderately disorderly environments can actually promote creativity and novel thinking by encouraging people to break free from conventional approaches and explore new possibilities.

This is indeed an interesting concept that gives us a different perspective on the human mind. If the mind uses the external environment to construct thoughts, then how much of that is conscious vs unconscious? And what are the potential consequences? In a paper titled "**Quantifying The Influence of Climate in Human Conflict**" published in the journal Science, researchers **Solomon Hsiang, Marshall Burke,** and **Edward Miguel** from Princeton and the University of California-Berkeley reported that <u>even a slight temperature difference can dramatically influence incidences of violence and aggression</u>. Hsiang, Burke, and Miguel analyzed 60 studies from archaeology, criminology, economics, and psychology that have explored connections between weather and violence in various parts of the world from about 10,000 BCE to the present day. Princeton's **Morgan Kelly** summarized their findings as follows:

> *"They found that while climate is not the sole or primary cause of violence, it undeniably exacerbates existing social and interpersonal tension in all societies, regardless of wealth or stability. They found that 1 standard-deviation shift – the amount of change from the local norm – in heat or rainfall boosts the risk of a riot, civil war or ethnic conflict by an average of 14 percent. There is a 4 percent chance of a similarly sized upward creep in heat or rain sparking person-on-person violence such as rape, murder and assault. The researchers report that climate-change models predict an average of 2 to 4 standard-deviation shifts in global climate conditions by 2050."*

This is as eye-opening as it is concerning. Although we may be good at noticing large temperature changes, we're not good at identifying subtle temperature changes. Well, we think we don't notice, but our subconscious mind does notice. Hsiang cited studies of police officers with firearms. He found that room temperature changes during police exercises influenced how much they fired their guns. If their research is correct, an Earth that is expected to warm by 2 degrees Celsius by 2050 could experience more human conflict.

In addition to our living and working spaces, modern technology and cultural tools represent perhaps the most obvious examples of how we extend our minds and influence the way we interact with others and with ourselves:

- **External Memory Systems**:

    Smartphones, cloud storage, and digital tools have fundamentally altered how we encode, store, and retrieve information. Research shows that people are increasingly relying on "Google effects" or "digital amnesia" – the tendency to forget information we believe will be available electronically. This represents a genuine cognitive adaptation where external memory systems become integrated into our thinking processes.

- **Computational Aids**:

    Calculators, GPS systems, and specialized apps augment cognitive abilities by offloading specific computational tasks. Studies of GPS use show that while these tools enhance navigation efficiency, they may also reduce spatial memory development and hippocampal engagement, suggesting complex trade-offs in extended cognition.

- **Visualization and Modeling Tools**:

    Maps, diagrams, scientific models, and virtual reality systems support spatial and conceptual reasoning by making abstract relationships visible and manipulable. Research in science education shows that external representations can dramatically improve learning and problem-solving in complex domains.

- **Cultural Symbol Systems**:

    Language, mathematical notation, musical notation, and other symbolic systems fundamentally shape thought by providing cognitive tools for organizing and manipulating concepts (**Lev Vygotsky**, 1986; **Alan Blackwell**, 2004). Indeed, contemporary research, notably by **Lera Boroditsky** and **Stephen Levinson**, demonstrates that different languages influence cognition in measurable ways, robustly supporting the Sapir-Whorf hypothesis in its weaker forms. This hypothesis posits that the structure of a language influences or even determines the ways in which its speakers conceptualize the world. While its stronger, deterministic version is largely discredited, the weaker version, which suggests that language *influences* rather than *determines* thought, is widely supported by empirical evidence.

So far, this makes sense. The human mind takes inputs from our body, senses, and the environment, and uses all that information to create and update a model of the world we perceive. But that's not all. The mind also takes inputs from other minds. According to **Richard Brodie's** book "**Virus of the Mind**," human minds influence each other through the creation and proliferation of memes. In his book, Brodie uses Richard Dawkins' definition of meme as

> *"a unit of information in a mind whose existence influences events such that more copies of itself get created in other minds."*

This concept of memes has evolved dramatically in the digital age. Consider the ALS Ice Bucket Challenge of 2014, which spread rapidly across social media platforms and raised over $115 million for ALS research. This modern meme demonstrates how ideas can now propagate globally at unprecedented speeds, influencing behavior and creating tangible, real-world impacts. Digital technology has accelerated and amplified the transmission of memes, making the interconnection between minds more immediate and far-reaching than ever before.

Our ancestors began this process when they started asking questions deeper than 'where is the food?', 'Who should I mate with?' or 'How do I hide from danger?' They started asking questions like 'where do we come from?', 'What should we do?', and 'Why are we here?' They answered these questions with fiction and myths that eventually became ideas and memes. This is where the inner workings of our human mind began the ongoing process of changing ourselves and the world around us. This leads us to the next section, as none of this could've taken place without a key feature of the human condition: complex language.

How Language Shapes the Human Mind

We've covered some of the beautiful evolutionary background of how we came to have a brain and a mind based on current scientific peer-reviewed information. But our ancestors did not populate the earth in one language or one culture; they came up with diverse languages and cultural traits, which makes a huge difference in how we observe the world and ourselves. It turns out that understanding complex concepts (like What is the Human Mind?) unfolds differently depending on which language we speak. In fact, the word or concept of mind may not even exist in other languages. Let's take a brief look at the evolution of language in homo sapiens.

In his book **Sapiens**, historian **Yuval Noah Harari** tells us that somewhere between 70,000 and 30,000 years ago, our ancestors (Homo Sapiens) started doing some very special things. They built boats, oil lamps, bows and arrows, and needles to sow warm clothing. Some researchers believe that these unprecedented accomplishments were the product of a revolution in Sapien's cognitive abilities. However, there are a few theories for how and why this revolution took place; one of the most accepted ones is that a mutation in at least one gene (**FOXP2**) led to, among other things, the development of language in homo sapiens. This finding adds nuance to our understanding of language evolution and raises questions about the cognitive abilities of our evolutionary cousins.

This is not to say that we are the only species with language, as we know that many other mammals communicate through language. It seems the difference between our evolutionary path and that of other mammals is that our language became increasingly complex, and that is in part due to the shape of our vocal tract: our mouth, tongue, and throat. According to **Dr. Ray Jackendoff** from the Linguistic Society of America, it wasn't until about 100,000 years ago that hominid vocal tracts began to permit the modern range of speech sounds. This does not mean that language began there, but it certainly suggests that this ability to communicate through more complex sounds played a role in the cognitive revolution.

In a paper titled "**Why Language is All Thumbs**", **Chip Walter** states that:

> *"A mind capable of language is also a self-aware mind."*

What does this mean? It means that at some point our mind became capable of complex language, complex pattern recognition, and complex thought. It means that a Human Mind can create physical objects like tools, cars, and cities, but can also create ideas like religion, democracy, and money. A human mind is "self-aware" because it is a mind that thinks about thinking.

So why do we have a human mind? It's hard to say, but research shows that we may not have one without complex language. Perhaps **Terrence McKenna** was onto something when he mused on the deep connection between language and consciousness, suggesting that:

> *"Our mind is somehow a co-creator in the process of reality through acts of language."*

In his book "**Naming the Mind**" psychologist **Kurt Danziger** shares the work of linguistic scholar **I.A. Richards** in the 1930s in China. Richards noticed that the work of Chinese philosopher **Meng Tzu** presented a coherent body of psychological concepts that had no modern or Western equivalents. He states that Chinese concepts that linguistically translate to the word "mind" do not represent what we mean by the word mind. He states:

"Chinese thinking often gives no attention to distinctions which for western minds are so traditional and so firmly established in thought and language; we forget that these distinctions have been made and maintained as part of one tradition of thinking, and that another tradition of thinking might neither find use for them nor be able to admit them."

This linguistic diversity extends to how different cultures conceptualize thought itself. Let's consider the following examples:

- The Pirahã people of the Amazon have a language that lacks number words beyond 'one,' 'two,' and 'many.' Research by linguist **Daniel Everett** (in collaboration with cognitive scientists **Peter Gordon** and **Michael Frank)** shows that this correlates with their different conceptualization of quantity: They perform differently on numerical tasks compared to speakers of languages with extensive number systems. This suggests that language doesn't just express thought but can fundamentally shape how we think about basic concepts like quantity.

- Consider color perception: Russian speakers, who have distinct words for light blue (goluboy) and dark blue (siniy), can distinguish between these shades faster than English speakers who use one word for both. The Russian speakers' language gives their brains more precise prediction categories for visual processing.

- Some languages have no words for "past" and "future," only different degrees of present experience. Speakers of these languages show different neural activation patterns when thinking about time compared to English speakers.

So, this begs a very important question that has been debated extensively: *Does the mind depend on language or does language depend on the mind?* Both perspectives can and have been explored:

Language depends on the human mind:

- The mind's cognitive capacities had to exist first to create and process language.
- We can think in non-linguistic ways (through images, emotions, abstract concepts).
- Pre-linguistic infants and animals show clear signs of thinking and problem-solving.

- The brain's neural architecture provides the foundation for language ability.

The mind depends on language:

- Language shapes how we think and perceive reality (linguistic relativity).
- Complex abstract thinking seems to require linguistic structures.
- Our inner monologue uses language to process thoughts.
- Language provides the tools for higher-order reasoning and metacognition.

A probably more encompassing approach is to conclude that the relationship between the human mind and language is bidirectional and mutually reinforcing:

- The mind's basic cognitive abilities evolved first, enabling the development of language.
- But once language emerged, it dramatically enhanced our mental capabilities.
- Language and mind then co-evolved, each driving the development of the other.
- Modern human consciousness seems to involve both linguistic and non-linguistic elements.

This bidirectional relationship is more like how a river both shapes its banks and is also shaped by them - it's impossible to separate cause from effect. Language shapes our thoughts, giving us new ways to conceptualize and understand the world, while our minds continuously reshape and evolve language to express new ideas and experiences. The difficulty of defining the mind's boundaries is especially apt because language itself often defies clear boundaries - it's not just spoken or written words. Still, it includes gesture, expression, and even the way we organize our thoughts internally. This dynamic relationship might explain why human consciousness and language seem to have co-evolved so rapidly. Each advancement in one domain would have catalyzed development in the other, creating a powerful feedback loop that helped drive human cognitive evolution.

Why Does This Matter to Your Daily Life?

The words you regularly use create the categories your brain uses for prediction. Expanding your vocabulary, especially for emotions, sensations, and relationships, expands your capacity for conscious experience.

Bottom Line: Instead of saying you feel "bad," get more specific. Are you disappointed? Frustrated? Overwhelmed? Anxious? Verbal precision helps your brain make better predictions about your needs

What's your perspective on this? Have you noticed ways that language shapes your own thinking? Here is something to consider: A human mind is capable of complex language AND is self-aware. The level of awareness is a function of:

1. The richness of the vocabulary in the language or <u>languages we choose to speak.</u>
2. The richness of the environment we choose to live in, and
3. The richness of the relationships we choose to have with others and ourselves.

Growing up, we do not have much of a say in the development of our vocabulary, environment, and relationships. Although they are not predetermined genetically, they are certainly predetermined by our caretakers and society. However, as we get older and become more independent, we do have a say in how rich our vocabulary, environment, relationships, and experiences can be.

Chapter 3 Summary: Key Insights

Our brain's predictive nature (shaped by extended development, enhanced by neuroplasticity, and extended throughout our embodied mind) creates both our greatest challenges and opportunities. Understanding these processes transforms us from a passive recipient of experience to an active participant in creating our reality. Here are some important takeaways:

1. **Born for Possibilities**:

    Our "helpless" beginning created maximum flexibility. Human brains remain adaptable throughout life, not only allowing continuous learning and growth.

2. **Prediction over Reaction**:

    Our brain constantly generates predictions about future events, and our experience largely consists of these predictions rather than raw sensory data. This ongoing predictive capability, combined with neuroplasticity, allows us to continuously adapt and learn from our environment.

3. **Mind Extends Beyond Brain**:

   Our cognitive processes include our body, environment, and social relationships, not just neural activity. This understanding has profound implications for how we approach learning, decision-making, and personal growth.

4. **Language as Architecture**:

   The words we use create the prediction categories our brain relies on; expanding our vocabulary expands our conscious experience.

5. **Lifelong Changeability:**

   Neuroplasticity means we can literally rewire our brains throughout life through focused attention and deliberate practice.

   Recognizing these key takeaways allows us to more consciously shape our experiences and, consequently, our neural pathways. It also shows that the quality of experiences we expose ourselves to MATTERS. So, what will you do with this insight? Will you fill your life with negative fear-based mental narratives that validate a potentially detrimental model of the world? Or will you expose yourself and update your model with new positive, challenging, and enriching experiences? Science tells us that regardless of age, we can always update and refine how our brains model and respond to the world.

   Understanding our brain as a changeable prediction machine raises a profound question:

   If our experience is actively constructed rather than passively received, what can we know for certain about reality itself?

   The answer will take us on a journey through ancient wisdom and cutting-edge science, revealing how multiple traditions have grappled with the fundamental nature of reality and existence.

PART 1 CONCLUSION: CONNECTING EVOLUTION, BRAIN, AND MIND

As we've explored the interrelated concepts of our environment, brain, and mind, several connecting threads emerge that weave these ideas into a cohesive framework. Our evolutionary journey from single-celled organisms to complex, self-aware beings has been shaped by our environment - particularly through the transformative discoveries of fire and cooking that enabled our large, energy-hungry brains to develop. These brains, in turn, created predictive models of the world that allowed us to adapt to diverse environments far beyond what our genetic programming alone could achieve.

Our minds emerged from this biological foundation but extended beyond it, incorporating our bodies, environments, tools, and relationships with others. This extended mind gives us the remarkable ability to question not just our surroundings but our very selves - to think about thinking. Through language and culture, we've developed diverse ways of understanding ourselves and the environment, and we have drastically changed over time.

The key insight connecting these concepts is adaptability. Just as our species adapted to changing environments through both biological and cultural evolution, our individual brains continuously adapt through neuroplasticity, and our minds adapt through learning and experience. This adaptability is both our greatest strength and our greatest challenge. It allows us to thrive in environments from tropical jungles to arctic tundra, to develop technologies that extend our capabilities far beyond our biological limitations, and to create meaning in a universe that offers no inherent purpose.

The connections between our environment, brain, and mind help us gain not just scientific knowledge but practical wisdom. We learn that growth requires both stability and change, both certainty and doubt, both objective facts and subjective meaning. We also learn that the journey of human understanding is never complete - like our brains themselves, it is a process of continuous adaptation and discovery.

The journey from truth frameworks to ancient-modern convergence will reveal that the most profound insights often emerge when rigorous scientific investigation meets contemplative wisdom, creating possibilities for understanding that neither approach achieves alone. These foundational insights into our evolutionary heritage, brain function, and the nature of the mind now prepare us to explore the profound ways in which we actively construct our experience of reality, the subject of Part 2.

PART 2

CONSTRUCTING REALITY

CHAPTER 4
MULTIPLE DIMENSIONS OF REALITY

"We don't just passively perceive the world, we actively generate it. The world we experience comes as much, if not more, from the inside out as from the outside in."
Anil Seth

David stares at his smartphone screen, scrolling through social media at 2 am. The blue light tricks his brain into thinking it's daytime. The carefully curated posts create a false sense of what "normal" life looks like. The algorithm feeds him content designed to trigger emotional reactions, not inform rational decisions. Within minutes, his stress levels spike, his sleep hormones shut down, and his perception of reality becomes distorted by a device designed to capture his attention, not serve his well-being.

Meanwhile, 2,500 years ago, a young prince named Siddhartha sat under a tree, examining his own mind with nothing but careful attention and systematic inquiry. Through pure observation, he discovered that what he had always taken for "reality" – his thoughts, emotions, and perceptions – was actually a constantly changing construction of his consciousness. This insight was so profound that it became the foundation of Buddhism and influenced billions of lives across centuries.

David and Siddhartha are separated by millennia and lived in vastly different societies, yet they grappled with the same fundamental question: What is real? How do we distinguish between accurate perception and convincing illusion? How do we navigate a world where our experience is actively constructed by forces we barely understand? Our perception of what is real shapes how we interact with the world, make decisions, and find meaning in our existence. Is reality something we passively perceive, or something more complex? Although we still may not have a definitive answer to this question, thanks to advancements in technology, we certainly have interesting approaches to the question.

Today, neuroscientists using brain scanners are discovering what contemplatives found through inner investigation: Reality as we experience it is not a simple reflection of what exists "out there" but an active construction happening inside our consciousness. Ancient wisdom and cutting-edge science are converging on a revolutionary understanding of human experience. More specifically, the overlap between neuroscience and philosophy has evolved from minimal interaction to a deep, dynamic, and often formalized interdisciplinary relationship. Neuroscience provides empirical data and constraints that ground philosophical theories, while philosophy offers conceptual clarification, ethical frameworks, identifies key questions, and critically analyzes neuroscientific methods and interpretations. Many of the most profound questions about the mind, consciousness, self, knowledge, and ethics (e.g., free will, the nature of self, ethics of neurotechnology) are now actively investigated in a synergistic way by researchers working across both fields.

This convergence isn't just intellectually fascinating, it's practically essential. <u>In an age of so-called "fake news," virtual reality, social media manipulation, and information overload, understanding how your mind constructs reality has become a survival skill.</u> The insights we'll explore help you distinguish between useful models of reality and harmful illusions.

Let's journey through the remarkable intersection where timeless wisdom meets contemporary discovery.

What is "Real"?

From recent neuroscientific research, we know that what we experience as "reality" is fundamentally a construction of our brain. Everything we perceive - sights, sounds, textures, even our sense of self - is processed and interpreted by different neural networks. Consider reading this book as an example: Light bouncing off the book hits our retinas, which then become electrical signals that are sent to our brain. The brain then compares those electrical signals with stored memories, predicts what comes next, and then creates the seamless experience we call "reading". The brain fills in blind spots, corrects for motion, and makes countless unconscious adjustments. Even color itself doesn't exist in the external world - it's our brain's way of representing different wavelengths of light. The "voice" you might hear as you silently read is a construction of your auditory system, even though no sound is being made.

Here's the startling truth: Our nervous system actively constructs everything we experience (the weight of this book, the temperature of the air, even our sense of "self"). We do not passively receive reality like a video camera records a scene. Rather than passively receiving information, our brain actively generates predictions about what it expects to perceive and then updates these predictions based on sensory input. This means our experience of reality is partly constructed from our prior expectations and beliefs; indeed, it's not a direct readout of the external world but a dynamic, **partly constructed representation** shaped by these expectations and constantly updated by sensory input.

The question then becomes: If our experience of reality is constructed by our brains, what constitutes "real?" We might consider the following levels:

- The physical world of particles and energy exists independently of our perception.
- The shared social reality we construct through language and collective agreement.
- The subjective reality of our conscious experience.

Each of these could be considered "real" in different ways. The physical world follows consistent laws we can study scientifically. Our shared social reality, while constructed, has genuine causal power in shaping human behavior and experience. And our subjective experience, while personal, is undeniably real to us as conscious beings. This reminds me of a quote popularized some time ago by **Anaïs Nin**:

> "We don't see things as they are, we see them as we are."

The fact that we are actively creating our experience moment by moment is NOT philosophical speculation; it's demonstrable neuroscience. But what makes it truly fascinating is that this same insight has been discovered independently by contemplatives, physicists, and philosophers across cultures and centuries. Somehow, using very different methods, they've all arrived at the same conclusion about the nature of human experience.

What does this convergence tell us? And more importantly, what does it mean for how you live your daily life?

Neuroscience and the Constructed Self / Reality

In our earlier discussion on neuroplasticity, we introduced the **Default Mode Network (DMN)** as a key brain area active during states of rest and self-referential thinking. This network is possibly the most important brain system we've never heard of and appears to construct something we take for granted: our sense of being a continuous, coherent "self."

Think about it: We wake up each morning feeling like the "same person" who went to sleep, despite our brain having been "offline" for hours and billions of our cells having been replaced. How does this sense of continuity happen when everything about us is constantly changing? The answer lies in our brain's remarkable storytelling ability. The Default Mode Network weaves together memories, sensations, thoughts, and emotions into a coherent narrative called "you." It's like having a film editor constantly creating a movie of our life, making millions of cuts and edits to create the illusion of a smooth, continuous experience. The DMN functions are summarized in the table below:

Table 4 – Summary of Default Mode Network Functions

DMN Function	Definition
Autobiographical Memory	Constructing personal narrative from past experiences
Future Planning	Imagining possible scenarios and outcomes
Moral Decision Making	Evaluating actions according to personal values
Theory of Mind	Understanding others' mental states and intentions
Self-Referential Processing	Maintaining sense of continuous personal identity

Its discovery represents a significant contribution to neuroscience's understanding of our inner world. Interestingly, this neuroscientific understanding of the DMN's role in constructing the "self" finds striking resonance with ancient wisdom traditions, particularly those from the East, which have long explored the nature of the ego and the concept of "no-self" (Anatta in Buddhism) or the illusory nature of the individual self (Maya in Hinduism). Buddhist psychology's analysis of the "self-grasping mind" remarkably parallels current DMN research:

- Both describe a mental process that creates the sense of solid, continuous selfhood.
- Both recognize this process as the source of much psychological suffering.

- Both offer practices for reducing identification with this constructed self.
- Both point toward states of consciousness with reduced self-referential processing.

The concept of reality as a brain-generated model is deeply rooted in the brain's fundamental purpose: **survival**. Recall Lisa Feldman Barrett's argument: The brain's primary job is managing the body's energy budget by constantly predicting needs based on past experiences to ensure efficient biological regulation. This forms the very foundation of the brain's reality-modeling process:

Our brains build a reality that is useful for survival, and not necessarily a perfectly objective mirror of the external world

This constructive process is largely unconscious, leading to what philosophers call **"naive realism"** – the intuitive belief that we perceive the world directly and objectively as it is. We aren't aware of the intricate neural computations underlying our perceptions; we simply experience the seamless, resulting model as reality itself.

However, as we will learn in the next chapter, multiple perceptual illusions compellingly demonstrate the constructed nature of our experience. Consider the **blind spot** in our visual field (where the optic nerve connects to the retina) – it contains no photoreceptors. Yet, we don't perceive a hole because the brain automatically fills this gap based on surrounding visual information. Similarly, the brain creates a stable image despite our eyes' constant, rapid **saccadic movements**, seamlessly filling in information during these shifts. These examples vividly illustrate how much of what we perceive as a continuous, stable reality is, in fact, a sophisticated construction of our brains.

In the section titled *The Prediction Machine: How Your Brain Really Works* we briefly introduced research on "change blindness." Recall how extensively our conscious experience depends on predictions rather than actual sensory input, which further underscores the limitations of our visual attention and awareness. Research in this area shows that people often fail to notice significant changes introduced into a visual scene, even when they are large and seemingly obvious once pointed out. Our subjective impression of seeing a rich, detailed, and continuous visual world is somewhat illusory; our brains prioritize what changes in a scene and process details only when specifically attended to.

Recent research strongly reinforces this perspective. A 2018 study in *Trends in Cognitive Sciences* by **Floris de Lange**, **Micha Heilbron**, and **Peter Kok** found that visual perception is shaped by expectations even at the earliest stages of visual processing. Similarly, a 2020 study by **Georg Keller** and **Thomas Mrsic-Flogel** demonstrated that even in the absence of sensory input, the brain generates patterns of activity resembling actual perception, supporting the idea that perception involves active generation rather than passive reception.

This neuroscientific perspective offers fascinating and profound parallels with both Eastern philosophical concepts like **Maya** (the illusory nature of perceived reality) and Western traditions like **Kant's distinction between the phenomenal world** (as we experience it) and the **noumenal world** (the "thing-in-itself" we can never fully know). It highlights that the human mind is not a passive receiver but an active participant in shaping its own reality. Moreover, neuroscience can now offer scientific validation on how practices like meditation give us the opportunity to forgo some of the negative burdens of a purely self-referential ego. For example, research by **Judson Brewer** and **Richard Davidson** has shown that experienced meditators can:

- **Reduce DMN activity** – leading to less self-referential processing during meditation and daily life
- **Increase present moment awareness** – leading to greater activation of attention networks
- **Improve emotional regulation** – leading to a better balance between emotion and cognition networks
- **Enhanced compassion** – leading to increased activity in empathy and care-giving networks

Why Does This Matter to Your Daily Life?

Understanding that your brain constructs reality explains everyday mysteries:

- Optical illusions: Our brain fills in gaps and makes predictions that can be fooled.
- People remembering the same event differently: Each brain constructs the experience uniquely based on attention, emotions, and prior beliefs.
- Why changing perspectives feels difficult: We're not just changing opinions – we're rewiring the neural networks that construct your reality.
- Why meditation feels profound: We observe the construction process rather than being lost in it.

Bottom Line: When we disagree with someone, remember that we're not just seeing different facts, we're experiencing different constructions of reality. This creates space for curiosity instead of conflict.

These are only a handful of examples that show how modern neuroscience is essentially validating what contemplatives discovered through careful inner investigation: the "self" you feel so certain about is actually a dynamic construction project happening in your brain every moment.

When Timeless Insight Converges with Contemporary Discovery

Philosophers have made great contributions to the concept of reality for thousands of years. In fact, it is well known that these contributions are still quite useful to us today, even though the world today is dramatically different from it was back then. However, the correlation between some of these philosophical insights and modern scientific understanding may even be less recognized. Specifically, we know today that the concept of reality as presented in ancient Eastern philosophy enjoys strong parallels with modern physics and mathematics. In his paper "Concepts of reality in Hinduism and Buddhism from the perspective of a physicist", **Dr Kashyap Vasavada**, Emeritus Professor of Physics, Indiana University-Purdue University Indianapolis (IUPUI) notes conceptual parallels in modern physics, such as quantum physics and cosmology, particularly concerning concepts of ultimate void/emptiness (Shunyata) and ultimate all-encompassing reality (Brahman), and highlights that:

> '... Founding fathers of quantum physics such as Bohr, Schrodinger and Heisenberg were deeply impressed with eastern religious philosophy...'

Niels Bohr was a Danish physicist who made fundamental contributions to understanding the structure of atoms and the early development of quantum mechanics. He and Werner Heisenberg developed the "Copenhagen interpretation" of quantum theory at his institute in Copenhagen. Bohr is recognized as one of the most influential physicists of the 20th Century and received the Nobel Prize in Physics in 1922. With respect to the possible parallels between some ancient wisdoms and his work, Bohr stated that:

> "I go to the Upanishads for questions", "For a parallel to the lesson of atomic theory...[we must turn] to those kinds of epistemological problems with which already thinkers like the Buddha and Lao Tzu have been confronted, when trying to harmonize our position as spectators and actors in the great drama of existence."

Bohr's complementarity principle, which states that objects have complementary properties that cannot be observed simultaneously (like wave-particle duality), parallels the Taoist concept of yin and yang as complementary forces that cannot exist without each other. Just as yin and yang represent seemingly opposite forces that are actually interconnected and interdependent, Bohr's principle suggests that seemingly contradictory properties like waves and particles are complementary aspects of the same reality.

Erwin Schrödinger was an Austrian theoretical physicist who achieved fame for his contributions to quantum mechanics. The philosophical issues raised by his 1935 "Schrödinger's cat" thought experiment (where a cat in a box is simultaneously alive and dead until observed) perhaps remain his best-known legacy. Still, the Schrödinger equation, which he formulated in 1926 to describe the "quantum state" of a system, is his most enduring achievement at a more technical level. It is celebrated as one of the most important achievements in 20th-century physics; it revolutionized quantum mechanics and earned Schrödinger a share in the 1933 Nobel Prize in Physics. Like Bohr, Schrödinger had some interesting things to say regarding ancient wisdom:

> "The unity and continuity of Vedanta are reflected in the unity and continuity of wave mechanics. This is entirely consistent with the Vedanta concept of All in One."; "The plurality that we perceive is only an appearance; it is not real. Vedantic Philosophy ... has sought to clarify it by a number of analogies, one of the most attractive being the many-faceted crystal which, while showing hundreds of little pictures of what is in reality a single existent object, does not really multiply that object..."; "The multiplicity is only apparent. This is the doctrine of the Upanishads. The mystical experience of the union with God regularly leads to this view, unless strong prejudices stand in the West."

Just as the quantum system in Schrödinger's thought experiment conceptually exists in a superposition of states until interaction (often referred to as 'observation') collapses these possibilities into one definite reality, Advaita Vedanta (which Schrödinger references above) suggests that the apparent duality of existence dissolves when one realizes the non-dual nature of Brahman. Both highlight a reality that is not simply 'either/or' until a specific condition (measurement or realization) is met. This connection will be explored further as we delve into the details of quantum mechanics later in this chapter.

Bohr and Schrödinger were intellectual giants in the world of quantum mechanics. The fact that they saw correlations between ancient philosophy and modern science is very interesting and should be explored further. But before this exploration, let's first examine how different philosophical traditions have approached the question of reality.

Western Philosophy's Prescient Insights on Reality

Western Philosophy is full of amazing thinkers who have contributed in one way or another to a lot of the concepts we still use today to approach our daily lives. This section is only intended to highlight a handful of these thinkers and how their teachings correlate with Eastern thinkers and modern science. We will highlight the teachings of Plato, George Berkeley, and Immanuel Kant. Of course, there are many more, but these three thinkers held the concept of reality at the center of their philosophical inquiries, and they approached it in unique ways, reflecting their broader philosophical systems. Below is an overview of their views on reality:

Plato (427–347 BCE): The Realm of Forms

Twenty-four centuries before neuroscientists discovered that perception is actively constructed rather than passively received, Plato proposed a dualistic approach where reality consists of:

- The world of appearances and shadows – the physical world, and
- The world of Forms – true reality.

The imperfect and transient physical world is perceived through our senses and is merely a shadow or copy of a higher, more fundamental, and unchanging reality – the realm or world of Forms or Ideas. In Plato's mind, Forms are perfect, eternal, universal, and unchanging abstract ideas that exist beyond space and time. For example, the Form of a circle exists perfectly, whereas any circle we draw is an imperfect representation.

In his "Allegory of the Cave," Plato describes prisoners who have lived their entire lives chained inside a cave, facing a blank wall. They are only able to see shadows projected on the wall from the objects passing in front of a fire behind them. Unfortunately for the prisoners, they mistake the shadows on the wall for reality. The symbolism here is that <u>humans often confuse sensory experiences with true knowledge or reality</u>. Moreover, Plato suggests that philosophers are like prisoners who are freed from the cave and come to understand that the shadows are not reality, but rather a mere representation of a more fundamental reality. In essence, he used this allegory to illustrate how most humans only perceive shadows of reality rather than true Forms.

Plato's "Allegory of the Cave", from "The Republic," anticipated one of the most important insights of modern cognitive science. Its parallels with modern neuroscience are presented in the table below:

Table 5 – Parallels between Plato's Allegory of the Cave and Neuroscience

Plato's Cave Structure		Modern Neuroscience Parallel	
Prisoners	Humans in ordinary consciousness	Ordinary Consciousness	Brain-constructed experience we take as reality
Chains	Limitations of sensory perception and cultural conditioning	Perceptual Limitations	Cognitive biases and processing constraints
Shadows	The constructed reality we mistake for truth	Predictive Models	The brain's "shadows" that create our experience
Fire	The source of illumination creating the shadows	Neural Activity	The biological "fire" generating conscious experience
Outside World	True reality beyond ordinary perception	Objective Reality	The world as it exists independent of perception
Philosopher	One who escapes the cave and returns to teach others	Scientist / Contemplative	Those who investigate the nature of perception itself

According to Plato, true knowledge comes from understanding the Forms, not from the sensory experience of the physical world. In everyday life, Plato's theory explains why we recognize imperfect instances of concepts like justice or beauty. When we say something is "beautiful" despite its flaws, we're comparing it to an ideal Form of Beauty that exists beyond the physical world. Similarly, when we strive for justice in society, we're attempting to manifest an ideal Form of Justice that transcends any particular legal system.

George Berkeley (1685–1753): Idealism

George Berkeley developed a radical form of idealism, arguing that the physical world exists only as ideas in minds, specifically, in the mind of God and in human minds. In other words, to Berkeley, reality is "mind-dependent". His famous principle was "**esse est percipi**" meaning "to be is to be perceived." According to Berkeley, what we call "matter" has no independent existence; instead, he argued that physical objects only exist as perceptions in minds as collections of ideas or sensations.

Berkeley's idealism was partly motivated by his critique of the concept of "material substance" in philosophers like **John Locke**. Berkeley argued that we never directly experience material substance itself, and that materialism (the belief in an external, independent physical reality) is incoherent because we only ever experience sensory perceptions (color, shape, texture, etc), not matter itself. In other words, according to him, there was no "matter" behind our perceptions - the perceptions themselves are reality. Therefore, he concluded, it is unnecessary and problematic to propose the existence of matter as something distinct from these perceived qualities.

Berkeley's Idealism:

- Physical objects exist only as collections of perceptions.
- Material substance independent of perception is unnecessary and unproven.
- Reality consists of minds and their ideas rather than matter and minds.
- God's perception maintains consistency across individual experiences.

Modern Parallels:

- **In Quantum Measurement**: The role of observation in determining quantum states.
- **In Constructive Perception**: The brain's active creation of perceptual experience.
- **In Intersubjectivity**: Shared reality emerging from collective mental processes.
- **In Information Theory**: Reality as information processing rather than material substance.

Berkeley's ideas might seem abstract, but they relate to common experiences. When you dream, you experience a world that feels real but exists only in your mind. Berkeley would argue that the waking world is similar: it exists as a collection of perceptions in minds, though with more consistency and coherence than dreams because God maintains these perceptions consistently across different minds. His radical proposition that "to be is to be perceived" anticipated modern questions about the role of observation in quantum mechanics and the constructed nature of conscious experience.

Immanuel Kant (1724–1804): The Phenomenal and Noumenal Worlds

Immanuel Kant developed a sophisticated theory that attempted to reconcile empiricism (the view that knowledge comes from sensory experience) with rationalism (the view that reason is the primary source of knowledge). In this philosophy, Kant made two distinctions:

- The **phenomenal world**:

    The reality we perceive and experience through our senses and cognitive faculties, shaped by categories like time, space, and causality.

- The **noumenal world**:

    The reality as it exists independent of human perception, the "thing-in-itself," which we can never fully know.

According to Kant, reality as we experience it is being actively **constructed by the mind** using certain innate categories (such as space, time, and causality). These categories are not features of reality itself but instead are imposed by our minds as a condition for experiencing anything at all. Thus, for Kant, the reality we experience is partly constructed by our minds; although he maintained that there is an objective reality (the noumenon) that exists independently of our perception.

Kant believed we can only know the phenomenal world, not the noumenal world, as our minds impose structures and limitations on sensory input. He maintained that while objective reality exists, we can only know it as filtered through our mental structures. This was his "Copernican Revolution" in philosophy - showing how the mind shapes our reality rather than just passively receiving it. This idea that the mind actively constructs experience is a concept deeply aligned with modern neuroscience's understanding of the brain as a prediction machine.

We experience Kant's distinction between phenomena and noumena whenever we recognize the limitations of our perception. For example, when we see a rainbow, we're experiencing a phenomenon created by the interaction between light, water droplets, and our visual system, not a physical object that exists independently of perception. Similarly, when scientists tell us that solid objects are mostly empty space at the atomic level, we're confronting the difference between how things appear to us and how they might exist independently of our perception.

Something to consider - The Dress That Broke the Internet In 2015:

An image of a dress went viral because people saw it as either blue-black or white-gold. This phenomenon perfectly illustrated Kant's insight: the same sensory input (photons reflecting off pixels) created different experiences based on how individual brains processed the ambiguous lighting information. The dress itself was neither blue-black nor white-gold – it was whatever our neural processing made it appear to be.

The relationship between phenomena and noumena was further expanded by German philosopher **Arthur Schopenhauer**, who was influenced by Kant as well as by Eastern philosophy. Schopenhauer suggested that we cannot penetrate the noumena or "thing-in-itself" from or through the external world. Instead, he proposed that a path "from within" might grant access to the inner nature of reality, given that we ourselves are that reality.

Each thinker provided a unique perspective on reality, ranging from metaphysical idealism (Berkeley) to epistemological frameworks that emphasize the limits of human perception (Plato and Kant). Even though their perspectives were unique, and they lived in very different times, there are some common themes in their approach to reality:

1. All three questioned the reliability of sense perception, but reached different conclusions.
2. They all wrestled with the relationship between mind and reality.
3. Plato and Berkeley appealed to God to help guarantee reality.
4. They all challenged "naive realism" (the view that reality is exactly as we perceive it).

Whether they knew it or not, these philosophers not only gifted us powerful and useful insights, but they also explored the scientific models and interpretations that shape our understanding.

Eastern Wisdom: The Beauty of Inner Investigation

Before we begin to explore a sample of Eastern philosophical traditions, it's worth noting some key similarities and differences between Eastern and Western approaches to reality:

- Western philosophy often emphasizes analytical reasoning, logical argumentation, and individual consciousness.

- Eastern traditions typically focus more on direct experience, non-conceptual awareness, and the transcendence of individual identity.
- Both sets of traditions question the reliability of ordinary perception and seek to understand what lies beyond appearances.

As we'll see, these different starting points often lead to surprisingly similar insights about the constructed nature of our everyday reality and the possibility of accessing deeper truths.

What is "Real" according to Hinduism?

Eastern philosophical traditions have developed their own sophisticated understandings of reality, often emphasizing the illusory nature of the perceived world and the interconnectedness of all things. Originating in Northern India, Hinduism is considered to be one of the world's oldest religions with roots and customs dating back at least 4,000 years. It is a complex and diverse religion that evolved from the Vedic religion and other local traditions.

The Vedas are the most ancient and sacred texts of Hinduism compiled over many centuries (roughly 1500 BCE to 500 BCE). The Vedas are traditionally divided into four main sections, representing different stages of spiritual evolution and approaches to understanding the divine. While the first three sections are a vast collection of hymns, prayers, philosophical treatises, rituals, and material prosperity, the last section, called The **Upanishads,** shift the focus dramatically inward. Aside from being a source of wisdom for Bohr, the Upanishads are the concluding philosophical and spiritual sections of the Vedas, and they deal with the nature of ultimate reality (Brahman), the individual soul or self (Atman), and the relationship between them. Here are some of the core ideas and how they interlace with each other:

Brahman: The Ultimate Reality

Brahman is considered the ultimate reality, that is, the unchanging, infinite, immanent, and transcendent reality that is the divine ground of all beings. It is beyond description and beyond human conceptualization. It is eternal, infinite, and all-pervasive, beyond time, space, and causation, and the source of all existence, consciousness, and bliss. The ancient texts state:

> "That which is imperceptible, ungraspable, without family, without caste, without sight or hearing, without hands or feet, eternal, all-pervading, omnipresent, exceedingly subtle – that is the unchangeable, which the wise perceive as the source of all beings."

Atman: The Self

Atman refers to the individual self or soul. Atman is identical with Brahman, meaning that the individual self is ultimately one with the universal self. This is expressed in the Upanishadic teaching *Tat Tvam Asi* (meaning "You are That") that states that **Atman** and **Brahman** are fundamentally one.

Maya: Illusion or Veil

Maya is a central concept in Hindu philosophy that refers to the illusory nature of the phenomenal world. It is often described as a veil that obscures the true nature of reality and creates the appearance of multiplicity and separateness. Maya is not simply non-existence or unreality. Instead, it causes individuals to perceive the world as separate and distinct, leading to attachment, ignorance, and suffering that is ultimately transcended in the realization of Brahman.

The concept of Maya helps explain why, if Brahman is the only reality, we experience a world of multiplicity and change. According to this view, our ordinary perception of the world as consisting of separate objects and individuals is a product of the Maya illusion that obscures the underlying unity of all existence. In other words, people mistake the transient, material world under Maya for the ultimate reality.

Something to consider:

Consider a mirage in the desert. To a distant traveler it appears to be water on the horizon. This water seems real and may even motivate the traveler to move toward it. However, upon arrival, the traveler approach discovers there is no water, just an optical illusion created by heat waves. Similarly, Maya creates the appearance of separate objects and individuals that seem completely real from our limited perspective, but from the perspective of ultimate reality (Brahman), these distinctions are illusory.

Lila: Divine Play

The concept of Lila or divine play suggests that creation is God's playful self-expression rather than serving any purpose. This explains why Maya exists: reality is a cosmic game or artistic expression of Brahman, not a mistake to be overcome. In this view, the universe is not created out of necessity or for any particular goal, but as a spontaneous expression of divine creativity and joy.

Lila offers a different perspective on why the world of multiplicity exists if Brahman is the only reality. Rather than seeing Maya as a problem or error, Lila suggests that the apparent diversity of the world is a form of divine self-expression, like an artist creating a painting or a child engaged in imaginative play. This concept helps explain why, if Brahman is perfect and complete, creation exists at all, not because Brahman lacks anything, but as an expression of divine abundance and creativity.

Although this summary barely scratches the surface, it shows how profound the Upanishads were. This depth led to various interpretations, particularly regarding the exact nature of Brahman, Atman, the world, and their interrelationships. These interpretations became schools of thought called Vedantas. Although the exact number of Vedantas that arose is still debated, we know is there are six Vedantas that are almost always referred to as the primary ones that have significantly shaped the philosophical landscape of Hinduism. Of these six, **Advaita Vedanta** is the **most widely known and philosophically dominant** school of Vedanta, particularly in academic discourse both within India and globally. Its systematic non-dualistic philosophy, articulated primarily by **Adi Shankara**, has profoundly influenced Indian thought, art, and spirituality. Many modern spiritual teachers and movements, even outside traditional Hinduism, often draw heavily from or are influenced by Advaita's core tenets of oneness. In essence, Advaita Vedanta teaches that:

- The <u>ultimate truth is non-duality</u>: there is only one reality (Brahman).
- Your true self (Atman) is that very Brahman.
- The apparent world and individual existence are Maya, temporary manifestations or illusions.
- Liberation (Moksha) comes from realizing this fundamental oneness.

Advaita Vedanta is a philosophy that calls for rigorous self-inquiry, deep contemplation, and the guidance of a realized teacher to transcend the limitations of the ego and experience the boundless nature of ultimate consciousness. It is important to note that even though it postulates that the physical world and our individual selves are illusions, it doesn't say the world doesn't exist. Instead, it states that <u>it doesn't exist as we typically think it does</u>. It's like mistaking a rope for a snake in dim light - the rope exists, but our perception is mistaken.

Hindu philosophy provides a rich tapestry of approaches to understanding and experiencing reality, from non-dualistic to dualistic perspectives. In traditional Hinduism, reality is ultimately unified in Brahman, the eternal and infinite source of all existence. However, due to Maya, individuals perceive a dualistic world. The goal of human life is to transcend this illusion of Maya, realize the unity of Atman and Brahman, and achieve liberation (moksha). This is attained through sophisticated practices such as meditation, where practitioners claim to experience consciousness as a fundamental rather than a derivative.

What is "Real" according to Buddhism?

Buddhism was originated in the Gangetic plains of Eastern India around 500 BCE, and it was a reaction to the established Hinduism at the time. Buddhism was founded by **Siddhartha Gautama**, a prince who renounced his life of luxury to seek enlightenment. Both religions share some beliefs and practices, such as karma, reincarnation, and the idea of spiritual liberation. However, Buddhism rejects some fundamental Hindu doctrines, such as the existence of a creator God and the concept of a substantial self or soul.

According to some, Buddhist philosophy gives us an even more sophisticated approach to the nature of reality than presented so far. **Dr. Alexander Berzin** is a scholar, translator, and teacher of Tibetan Buddhism, and has served as the Dalai Lama's archivist and occasional interpreter. He teaches us that the Indo-Tibetan Buddhist approach <u>focuses on using logic and reason</u> to analyze how things appear to us. He deconstructs any false appearances that our minds are projecting. Dr Berzin tells us that:

> *"In terms of reality, we all live in what we can say is "true or actual reality," verifiable by scientific method, which Buddhism agrees with. After all, Buddha said not to accept what he taught just on faith, but to examine it like when buying gold. Therefore, in Buddhism, examination and analysis are the supreme methods for discovering and verifying reality. Problems arise when people make up an alternative, false reality and mistake it for what is actually the truth. We can see this happening in the political sphere, but Buddhism looks at this phenomenon on a broader, more universal level."*

When it comes to the concept of reality, Buddhism offers a distinct perspective that shares some elements with Hindu thought but develops them in unique directions. In Buddhism, reality is understood through a nuanced philosophical framework that centers on the nature of existence, suffering, impermanence, and interdependence. The Buddhist view of reality seeks to uncover the truth about life and the world, beyond illusions and misconceptions. Traditional Buddhism emphasizes understanding reality through mindfulness, insight, and wisdom, leading to liberation (Nirvana). The goal is to see reality as it truly is, beyond the illusions created by the mind. Here is a high-level summary of the core teachings on reality in traditional Buddhism:

The Three Marks of Existence

Buddhism identifies three universal characteristics that define *all* phenomena:

- **Anicca (Impermanence) :**
  - Everything is in a constant state of flux. All phenomena (physical and mental) arise, change, and pass away.
  - Nothing in the phenomenal world is permanent or stable.

- **Dukkha (Suffering or Unsatisfactoriness) :**
  - Life is characterized by dissatisfaction and suffering because we cling to things that are impermanent.
  - Even pleasurable experiences are Dukkha because they are transient.

- **Anatta (Non-Self) :**
  - There is no permanent, unchanging self or soul. What we perceive as "self" is a collection of ever-changing physical and mental processes (form, sensation, perception, mental formations, and consciousness), none of which can be identified as a permanent "I" or "mine".

These three characteristics suggest that the world of stable objects and enduring selves we ordinarily perceive and call "real" is fundamentally mistaken. True understanding comes from recognizing the impermanent, unsatisfactory, and selfless nature of all phenomena.

Dependent Origination (Pratitya Samutpada)

Dependent origination is a central principle in Buddhist philosophy that describes how all phenomena arise in dependence on causes and conditions. Nothing exists independently or has a self-nature (Svabhava); rather, everything exists in relation to other things.

The Buddha expressed this principle in the following statement:

"When this exists, that comes to be; with the arising of this, that arises. When this does not exist, that does not come to be; with the cessation of this, that ceases."

Dependent origination implies a radical interconnectedness of all things. It challenges the notion of independent, self-existing entities and suggests that reality is more like a web of relationships than a collection of separate objects. This interdependence means nothing exists independently or in isolation, and this underpins the cycle of **samsara** (birth, death, and rebirth), which explains how suffering arises due to ignorance and craving. It is important to note that the word "ignorance" is used in its original context (simply not knowing) and not in the current popular and often derogatory context.

The Four Noble Truths

The Four Noble Truths constitute the Buddha's basic teaching about the nature of reality and the human condition:

1. **The Truth of Dukkha**: Life involves suffering, dissatisfaction, and stress.
2. **The Truth of the Origin of Dukkha**: Suffering arises from craving and ignorance.
3. **The Truth of the Cessation of Dukkha**: Suffering can be ended by overcoming craving and ignorance.
4. **The Truth of the Path Leading to the Cessation of Dukkha**: There is a path, called The Eightfold Path, that offers a practical guide to transcending suffering and realizing reality as it is.

These truths provide a diagnosis of the human condition and a prescription for addressing it. They suggest that our ordinary experience of reality is characterized by suffering because we misunderstand the nature of things and cling to what is impermanent.

Mind and Perception

Buddhism places great emphasis on the role of the mind in constructing our experience of reality. The first verse of the Dhammapada, a collection of sayings attributed to the Buddha, states:

> "All phenomena are preceded by the mind, led by the mind, created by the mind."

Buddhist psychology identifies various mental factors (cetasika) that color our perception and shape our experience. These include not only cognitive factors but also emotional and volitional ones. Our desires, aversions, preconceptions, and habitual tendencies influence how we perceive reality. Reality as we experience it is shaped by the mind. Our perceptions are filtered through ignorance, attachments, and mental constructs, creating a distorted view of reality.

Through practices like mindfulness and meditation, Buddhism aims to cultivate clear seeing (Vipassana) that penetrates beyond our ordinary, distorted perceptions to the true nature of reality.

The Yogacara School's Contribution

The Yogacara school, also called "Mind-Only" (Cittamatra), developed sophisticated analyses of consciousness that have remarkable parallels with modern neuroscience. This Mahayana Buddhist school developed the concept of the 'Three Natures' (trisvabhava):

- The imagined nature (parikalpita);
- The dependent nature (paratantra), and
- The perfected nature (parinispanna).

This sophisticated framework explains how ordinary perception mistakes conceptual constructs for reality, while acknowledging that these constructs arise dependently on actual phenomena.

The imagined nature refers to our conceptual projections onto reality; we superimpose <u>the labels, categories, and judgments on experience</u>. The dependent nature refers to the way phenomena arise interdependently through causes and conditions. The perfected nature is the true nature of reality when freed from conceptual projections. This three-nature framework provides a nuanced account of how we both construct and can see through our constructed models of reality.

Yogacara also identified eight types of consciousness, including the consciousnesses of the five senses, mind consciousness, afflicted mind consciousness, and store consciousness (alaya-vijnana). The store consciousness, in particular, has interesting parallels with modern neuroscientific concepts of unconscious processing, as it stores all experiences as seeds that later manifest in consciousness.

Nirvana: The Ultimate Truth

Nirvana represents the ultimate goal of Buddhist practice: a state of liberation from suffering and the cycle of rebirth (samsara). It is often described as the cessation of craving, aversion, and ignorance.

Nirvana is not a place or a realm but a realization of the true nature of reality. It involves seeing through the illusions that ordinarily cloud our perception and recognizing the impermanent, unsatisfactory, and selfless nature of all conditioned phenomena.

While Nirvana transcends conceptual understanding, it is sometimes described as the "unconditioned" (asankhata), that which is not subject to dependent origination, not born, not created, not formed. In this sense, it represents the ultimate reality beyond the conditioned world of ordinary experience, free from craving, ignorance, and dualistic notions of self and other.

The Buddhist approach suggests that nothing has inherent, independent existence. Everything is interconnected and exists only in relation to other things. When observed alongside traditional Hinduism, these two Eastern approaches to reality share some common themes:

- Reality as we typically perceive it is, in some sense, illusory.
- True reality lies beyond conceptual thinking.
- The self as we normally think of it is not ultimately real.
- Everything is interconnected and interdependent.
- Direct experience via meditation, rather than intellectual understanding, is the key to grasping reality.

The sophistication of these ancient approaches is remarkable, particularly in how they anticipate modern scientific insights about the constructed nature of perception and the interconnectedness of phenomena. In the table below, we share some of the principles of Hinduism and Buddhism, along with their modern science parallels.

Table 6 – Parallels Shared by Hinduism, Buddhism, and Modern Science

Principle	Definition	Science Parallel	Practical Application
Brahman	The ultimate, undifferentiated reality underlying all phenomena	Quantum field theories describing reality as fundamental energy fields	Recognition that individual consciousness participates in universal consciousness
Atman	The true self, identical with Brahman	The difficulty of locating a fixed "self" within brain activity	Understanding personal identity as process rather than fixed entity
Maya	Illusion that veils underlying unity	How particle-wave duality reveals the constructed nature of our reality	Understanding perception as active construction rather than passive reception
Lila	Divine play rather than purposeful creation	Emergence and self-organization in complex systems	Approaching life with creativity rather than grim necessity

Anicca	Impermanence, everything is constantly changing	Quantum field fluctuations, dynamic nature of matter, neural plasticity and continuous reconstruction of experience	Reducing attachment to fixed outcomes or identities
Pratitya Samutpada	Dependent origination, nothing exists independently	Quantum entanglement and field theories.	Events can't be understood in isolation but only through their relationships with other events.
Anatta	Non-self, No permanent or unchanging self exists	Brains construct narratives of self from distribute processes. The fluid nature of personality.	Free yourself from rigid self-concepts that limit growth
Trisvabhava	Three Natures - Imagined nature, dependent nature and perfected nature	Perception is actively constructed by the brain	Understand how we construct and how to see through our constructed models of reality

These are not the only ancient philosophies that have tried to address the concept of reality. For instance, Chinese Taoism addresses reality in a similar way as Hinduism does. The concept of Brahman is similar to the Taoist concept of the **Dao** (or **Tao**), even though each arises from different cultural and philosophical contexts. Both point towards an ultimate, ineffable, all-pervading reality or principle that is the source and guiding nature of the cosmos. The opening line of the **Tao Te Ching** famously states:

> "The Dao that can be told is not the eternal Dao. The name that can be named is not the eternal name."

In other words, the ultimate reality is fundamentally beyond human language, conceptualization, and description

Why Does This Matter to Your Daily Life?

These philosophical insights offer practical guidance:

From Plato's Cave:

- Question what feels "obviously true" as it might be shadows on the wall

- Be patient with those who see things differently – they might be looking at different shadows
- Stay curious about what lies beyond your current perception

From Buddhism's Impermanence:

- When something feels overwhelming, remember: 'This too shall pass'
- Hold your current identity lightly as you're constantly changing anyway
- Find freedom in recognizing that your problems are constructions, not permanent realities

From Hindu Maya:

- Thoughts and emotions are phenomena arising in consciousness, not absolute truths
- Look for the awareness that notices all experiences but isn't identified with any of them

Bottom Line: Ancient wisdom provides maps for navigating the constructed nature of experience that modern science has confirmed.

Whether it's Hinduism, Buddhism, or Taoism, they all cover this fundamental point: For thousands of years, we have had some level of understanding that what we perceive as "real" might just be a construction in our human minds.

Quantum Physics: When Science Meets Mystery

The dawn of quantum mechanics in the early 20th century ignited intense discussions not only among scientists but also among philosophers and scientists. According to the University of Copenhagen's Niels Bohr Institute page, it was around the mid-1920s when Bohr and his team began formulating the principles of quantum mechanics because the classical atomic model seemed to be in conflict with the general properties of atoms.

Around the same time, Werner Heisenberg and Erwin Schrödinger developed mathematically distinct yet ultimately equivalent theories that described the quantum realm: Heisenberg's "matrix mechanics" often seemed to emphasize particle-like aspects. In contrast, Schrödinger's "wave mechanics" focused on the wave-like description. These profound scientific challenges ultimately led many physicists to converge at Bohr's institute in Copenhagen for collaborative discussions on how to reconcile these seemingly contradictory aspects of nature. Here is an excerpt of what happened according to the Niels Bohr Institute page:

> *"Towards the end of 1927, the differences of opinion converged to a consensus based on Niels Bohr's principle of complementarity, which holds that a physical phenomenon is observed in two different 'complementary' ways depending on the experimental setup. For example, light could sometimes behave like waves and other times like particles. Both images were necessary to obtain a complete description of the phenomenon, even though they excluded each other."*

> *"Niels Bohr argued this radical point of view for the first time at a conference in Italy in late summer 1927 and repeated it at the Solvay Conference a few weeks later. This, which was later called the Copenhagen Interpretation, formed the foundation for the famous debates between Niels Bohr and Albert Einstein at the Solvay Conferences in 1927 and 1930."*

The Copenhagen Interpretation suggests that <u>reality at the quantum level is fundamentally probabilistic</u> and that **physical measurement** plays a crucial role in **actualizing a definite state** from a superposition in the quantum realm. This has profound implications for our understanding of reality, challenging classical notions of determinism and objectivity. A typical Copenhagen Interpretation summary you may find on the web could read as follows:

- Quantum systems do not have definite properties until they are "observed".
- Before "observation," a quantum system is described by a wavefunction, which represents a superposition of all possible states.
- "Observation" collapses the wavefunction into a specific state, making reality inherently probabilistic rather than deterministic.

These fascinating statements, and all their associated implications, changed the world and our reality in ways unforeseen at the time. But, they also created unfortunate amounts of confusion and misinformation when it comes to the nature of reality, especially regarding the term "observation." Understanding this historical context is crucial for a responsible interpretation of quantum insights.

The Measurement-Dependent Nature of Quantum Reality

In 1801, **Thomas Young** performed what is now known as the Young double-slit experiment. This experiment was designed to settle the debate about whether light behaved as a particle (Newton's corpuscular theory) or a wave. Young's focus was on demonstrating **wave interference**, a classical physics phenomenon. His descriptions focused on the physical geometry of the slits, the wavelength of light, and how waves interfere to produce bright and dark fringes. He used terms like "interference fringes," "diffraction," and "superposition of light waves," and he observed the *pattern* that light waves produced on a screen. At the time, there were no quantum concepts yet, as the foundational concepts of quantum mechanics – quantization of energy, wave functions, and superposition - simply didn't exist in physics yet. These ideas emerged much later, in the early 20th century, with **Max Planck**, **Albert Einstein**, **Niels Bohr**, **Werner Heisenberg**, and others.

While Young certainly *observed* the pattern on the screen, his use of the word "observe" would have been in the everyday, classical sense of "to see" or "to detect," not in the loaded quantum sense of "a physical interaction that collapses a wave function." The "observer effect," as it pertains to quantum mechanics (where the act of measurement changes the outcome for individual particles), was a discovery of the 20th century, long after Young's time. Why is this important? Because when we arrive in the quantum world of Bohr, Schrödinger, and Heisenberg, the word observation takes on a meaning different from the context used in Young's experiment. Let's use some of their quotes to dive in:

> *"An independent reality in the ordinary physical sense can neither be ascribed to the phenomena nor to the agencies of observation."*
> **Niels Bohr, from discussions with Albert Einstein.**

> *"...the experiments on atomic events can only be understood as part of a whole, which means that the quantum mechanical description of the experiment refers to the probability of an event and not to the event itself, and this probability changes when we observe it."*
> **Werner Heisenberg, from "Physics and Philosophy" (1958).**

> *"We cannot, however, manage to make do with such old, familiar, and seemingly indispensable terms as 'real' or 'only possible'; we are never in a position to say what really is or what really happens, but we can only say what will be observed in any concrete individual case."*
> **Erwin Schrödinger,**
> **from "Science and the Human Temperament."**

This choice of words, while seemingly innocent at the time (and having a technical meaning within the world of physics), has indeed been a major source of the confusion and misinterpretation we see today. In classical physics, an "observer" was an ideal, detached entity that could measure a system <u>without disturbing it</u>. Even in classical physics, the very act of doing an experiment involves an "observer" (the scientist, or their instruments) interacting with the system. Quantum mechanics then introduced the radical idea that <u>this interaction could *not* be ignored at the quantum scale</u>. The core issue they were grappling with was the **measurement problem**. How does a quantum system, described by a probabilistic wave function existing in a superposition, "choose" a single definite outcome when measured? The "observer" became shorthand for the entire measurement apparatus and the process that led to a definite, classical-like result.

While they were rigorous scientists, these physicists were also deeply philosophical. They recognized that quantum mechanics fundamentally challenged the classical notion of an objective reality existing independently of measurement. The term "observer" underscored this profound epistemological shift — that we cannot talk about the properties of a quantum system *without* reference to the experimental setup that measures it. Bohr, in particular, tried to be careful and often used phrases like "agencies of observation" or "experimental arrangement" to emphasize that the *physical apparatus* and its irreversible interaction were key, not a conscious being. He stressed that quantum mechanics describes phenomena in terms of our interactions with them, rather than describing "things-in-themselves." Despite their attempts at precision, the word "observer" naturally carries connotations of:

- **Consciousness/Sentience:** An observer is a conscious being who sees or perceives in everyday language.
- **Passivity:** "Observing" often implies passive watching, rather than active, physical interaction.
- **Subjectivity:** It can suggest that reality is somehow subjective or dependent on individual minds.

These connotations have proven fertile ground for misinterpretations. Popular science writers, philosophers, and spiritual thinkers latched onto the word "observer" and extrapolated its meaning to fit pre-existing philosophical or spiritual agendas. The nuance of "physical interaction inherent in measurement" got lost in translation to "consciousness creates reality." Yes, the word "observer" was used from the very beginning by the founders of quantum mechanics when discussing the Copenhagen Interpretation. They intended it to refer to the **physical apparatus and the irreversible measurement process**. However, its colloquial meaning has unfortunately led to widespread misinterpretations. With this in mind, we can now present the concept of quantum reality and quantum observation a bit more clearly:

The "reality" of a quantum system fundamentally depends on **how it is physically measured or interacted with** during an experiment, a concept often referred to as "measurement-dependent reality" in the context of the Copenhagen Interpretation.

- **Wave-Particle Duality:** A quantum entity, such as a photon or an electron, does not inherently exist as *only* a wave or *only* a particle. Instead, its behavior manifests as either wave-like (e.g., creating an interference pattern) or particle-like (e.g., being detected at a discrete point), **depending on the specific experimental setup designed to probe it.** The choice of measurement apparatus dictates which aspect of its dual nature is revealed.

- **Complementarity Principle:** This principle states that certain complementary properties of quantum systems (like position and momentum, or wave behavior and particle behavior) cannot be simultaneously known or observed with arbitrary precision. **Measuring one property inevitably influences or precludes the precise knowledge of its complementary counterpart.** You can observe one or the other, but the act of precise measurement for one necessarily disturbs or renders indeterminate the other.

This measurement-dependent nature of quantum reality profoundly challenges the classical notion of an objective, observer-independent physical world. In quantum physics, before a measurement, the state of a system is described by a wave function that mathematically represents a **superposition of all possible states or outcomes**. When a measurement occurs, the wave function is said to "collapse" into a single, definite outcome.

This probabilistic and measurement-dependent aspect of reality led some physicists and philosophers to mistakenly suggest that **consciousness or awareness might play a fundamental, active role in causing the wave function to collapse.** While resonating with certain idealist philosophical traditions, this view is **scientifically inaccurate and a profound misinterpretation of quantum mechanics.**

Quantum mechanics does not require or imply consciousness, knowledge, or sentience in any form to explain wave function collapse. The change in behavior during the scientific process of observation is a direct and unavoidable consequence of the **physical interaction** between the quantum system and the macroscopic measurement apparatus. This interaction (which can either be an energy or a momentum exchange) fundamentally changes the physical conditions of the system, which consequently disturbs its quantum state and fixes a definite outcome. The measurement interactive process changes the physical conditions and thus defines the possible outcomes, entirely without recourse to any conscious observer.

While developing a rigorous scientific framework, the founders of quantum mechanics found themselves confronting a reality that fundamentally defied classical scientific intuition. It was in this intellectual crucible that they turned to ancient wisdom traditions, not for scientific formulas or predictions, but for **alternative conceptual frameworks and epistemological insights** that resonated with their bewildering discoveries. For instance, the **Upanishadic concept of Maya** (that the perceived world is an appearance of a deeper, ultimate reality) offered a philosophical lens through which to view the quantum world's non-deterministic nature and the fact that quantum properties only become definite upon measurement. Similarly, **Buddhist notions of dependent origination and the interconnectedness of all phenomena** found a striking parallel in **quantum entanglement**, where particles, regardless of distance, remain inextricably linked.

Ancient philosophies provided intellectual solace and a conceptual vocabulary that helped these pioneering scientists articulate a reality where **objectivity is not absolute, where observer and observed are interlinked by interaction, and where the fundamental nature of existence is dynamic and relational, rather than static and independently existing.** It wasn't about ancient texts providing scientific answers, but about how profound philosophical insights, achieved through contemplation, could conceptually align with scientific truths revealed through rigorous experimentation thousands of years later.

Something to consider:

Heisenberg's Uncertainty Principle *states that some pairs of physical properties cannot be simultaneously measured with arbitrary precision in quantum systems. For example: the more precisely we measure a particle's position, the more uncertain its momentum becomes, and vice versa*

In classical physics, the future state of a system could, in principle, be precisely predicted given complete knowledge of its current state and the forces acting on it. In quantum physics, even with complete knowledge of a system's current state, we can only predict probabilities of future outcomes, not definite results.

Question: when observing your life, your past, present and future, your relationships, your experiences, have outcomes been completely deterministic (like classical physics) or more probabilistic (like quantum mechanics)?

In the end, it seems that we are still left with questions about what is "real". However, I think it is safe to state that, independent of which approach you prefer, they all tend to converge on the following idea:

> *Reality, as revealed by both quantum physics and neuroscience, is not a simple, passively perceived objective phenomenon, but rather a dynamic interaction between an external world and our methods of inquiry and perception."*

There is no verifiable science (at the time of this publication) that proves that quantum effects at the subatomic level can or do directly influence everyday consciousness or decision-making; the connection between quantum mechanics and consciousness remains highly speculative. But the insights from quantum physics have profound implications beyond the subatomic realm. Just as quantum mechanics revolutionized our understanding of physical reality, modern neuroscience has transformed our understanding of how the brain constructs our experience of reality. Both fields challenge the notion of an objective reality, suggesting instead that what we experience emerges from interactions between external phenomena and our perceptual processes. This parallel is not merely coincidental, as it reflects a deeper truth about the nature of reality that different disciplines are approaching from complementary angles. As we turn to neuroscience, we'll see how the brain's construction of reality mirrors many of the same principles that quantum physics has revealed at the fundamental level of matter.

Why Does This Matter to Your Daily Life?

While quantum effects don't directly influence your daily thoughts, the principles offer valuable perspectives:

- Observer Effect: Your attention can change what you experience (demonstrated in psychology).
- Complementarity: Seemingly opposite things can both be true (like being confident AND humble).
- Uncertainty Principle: You can't know everything precisely, and that's okay.
- Entanglement: You're more connected to others and the environment than classical thinking suggests.

Bottom Line: While quantum effects don't directly influence your thoughts or decisions, they reveal something profound: Reality isn't a collection of solid, independent objects but a dynamic web of possibilities that become actual through interaction. Physical reality is far stranger and more interactive than common sense suggests. This strangeness leaves room for growth, mystery, and transformation in ways that purely mechanical worldviews don't allow.

Converging Insights: Ancient Wisdom, Modern Science, and the Nature of Reality

The journey through ancient philosophical insights, the perplexing revelations of quantum physics, and the modern understanding of the brain's constructive processes reveals a profound convergence on the nature of reality. While their methodologies differ from contemplative inquiry to mathematical rigor and empirical neuroscience, these diverse fields arrive at strikingly similar conclusions:

1. **Reality is Not Simply "Out There":** All three domains challenge naive realism.

    - **Philosophy:** Ancient Eastern traditions (Maya, Anatta) and Western philosophers (Plato's Forms, Berkeley's idealism, Kant's noumena) argue that our everyday perception doesn't reflect ultimate reality directly.

    - **Quantum Physics:** The **measurement-dependent nature of quantum phenomena** demonstrates that fundamental properties don't exist in a definite state independent of interaction; the "observation" (physical measurement) plays an active role in actualizing reality from a probabilistic superposition.

    - **Neuroscience:** The **brain's predictive processing model** reveals that what we experience as "reality" is a sophisticated, active construction based on sensory input, expectations, and the imperative for survival, not a passive, objective readout.

2. **Interconnectedness and Relationality are Fundamental:**

    - **Philosophy:** Concepts like **Dependent Origination** (Buddhism) and the **unity of Brahman/Atman** (Hinduism), along with Taoist **Dao**, emphasize a deep, underlying interconnectedness and interdependence of all things, where nothing exists in isolation.

    - **Quantum Physics:** Quantum entanglement provides a stunning physical manifestation of this interconnectedness, showing that separate particles can remain fundamentally linked regardless of distance, defying classical notions of locality.

    - **Neuroscience:** Our brains constantly integrate vast streams of sensory data and internal states, creating a coherent, unified experience where disparate elements are woven into a relational whole. The "self" itself is understood as an emergent, distributed process, not a fixed, isolated entity.

3. **The Limits of Conceptual Knowledge and the Value of Direct Experience:**

    - **Philosophy:** Many Eastern traditions stress that the ultimate truth transcends conceptual thought and is best approached through **direct, non-conceptual experience** (e.g., meditation for Nirvana/Moksha, Taoist spontaneity). Western thinkers like Kant also highlighted the limits of rational thought in grasping the "thing-in-itself."
    - **Quantum Physics:** The **complementarity principle** and the inherent probabilistic nature of quantum reality demonstrate that we cannot fully grasp all aspects of a quantum system simultaneously or precisely. There are fundamental limits to what we can know about reality through conventional measurement and conceptual frameworks alone.
    - **Neuroscience:** The understanding of how the brain constructs our experience, including our sense of self, opens the door to **neuroplasticity** and the potential for practices like mindfulness to reshape these neural constructions, leading to altered states of perception and well-being. This validates the "inner investigation" advocated by ancient traditions as a means to influence our *experienced* reality.

Indeed, while philosophical traditions and modern physics have provided conceptual frameworks for understanding reality, our physical bodies are the very instruments through which we perceive and construct our model of the world. The ancient wisdom traditions understood this deep connection intuitively; Buddhist mindfulness practices, for instance, recognize how bodily states profoundly influence perception and cognition. Modern neuroscience now allows us to explore these connections with unprecedented precision, revealing how physical factors fundamentally shape our experienced reality. These aren't merely peripheral influences but central components of how humans create meaning from experience. By examining these embodied aspects of reality perception, we gain a more complete understanding of how humans construct their model of the world.

In summary, philosophy, physics, and neuroscience do converge beautifully on the topic of reality: philosophical traditions questioned perception's reliability, quantum physics highlighted the active role of **physical interaction** in actualizing quantum states, and neuroscience models the brain as actively constructing reality through prediction, influenced by evolution's focus on survival rather than objective truth.

These insights offer more than intellectual satisfaction. They provide practical frameworks for understanding consciousness, reality, and human potential that no single discipline achieves alone. They invite us to reconsider the very fabric of existence, not as something static and entirely external, but as a dynamic, interactive, and profoundly mediated experience that we are, in a very real sense, always in the process of generating.

Chapter 4 Summary: Key Insights

The remarkable convergence of neuroscience, philosophy, and physics points toward a revolutionary understanding: reality as you experience it is not a simple reflection of what exists "out there" but an active construction emerging from the interaction between consciousness and world. This insight, discovered through different methods across cultures and centuries, offers both profound wisdom and practical guidance.

1. **Prescient Insights**: Through careful observation and reason, contemplatives and ancient philosophers discovered the same principles of consciousness that modern neuroscience and physics are confirming today via brain imaging.

2. **Active Construction**: Our brain doesn't passively record reality; it actively creates our experience through prediction, interpretation, and continuous updating.

3. **Quantum Parallels**: Quantum mechanics reveals principles about observation, interconnection, and the constructed nature of reality that parallel ancient philosophical insights.

4. **Neuroplasticity Validation**: Scientific research confirms contemplative claims about the possibility of fundamental consciousness transformation through systematic practice.

5. **Practical Liberation**: Understanding reality as construction creates freedom from being unconsciously controlled by automatic perceptions and opens possibilities for conscious participation in experience.

6. **Complementary Methods**: Science and contemplation offer different but equally valid approaches to understanding reality, with synthesis providing enhanced insight.

Having explored how philosophical traditions conceptualize reality and how physical factors can influence our perception, in the next chapter, we turn to a framework that elegantly unites these perspectives: the Bayesian model of reality. This approach provides a mathematical and cognitive framework that aligns with both ancient wisdom traditions and cutting-edge neuroscience. The Bayesian model helps explain not only how we perceive reality but how we continuously update our understanding of it, a process that resonates with both Buddhist notions of impermanence and the quantum understanding of probability. We'll explore why humans often struggle with explicit statistical reasoning despite having brains that are essentially biological Bayesian computers. We'll learn practical methods for working with rather than against your brain's natural inference mechanisms.

By examining reality through this lens, we can build a bridge between seemingly disparate approaches to understanding the nature of existence. This journey from ancient-modern synthesis to Bayesian brain science will reveal how understanding your mind as a prediction machine can transform your approach to learning, decision-making, and personal growth in an uncertain world.

If reality is actively constructed through processes that operate largely below conscious awareness, how can we learn to participate more consciously in this construction? The answer lies in understanding our brain as a sophisticated statistical machine that's constantly updating its beliefs based on evidence, and that operates according to mathematical principles postulated by an 18th-century mathematician whose insights now illuminate the very nature of consciousness itself.

CHAPTER 5
THE BAYESIAN BRAIN

"When beliefs become fused with identity, questioning those beliefs activates the same threat-detection systems as physical danger."

If reality is actively constructed through the interaction of mind and world, as we discovered in Chapter 4, this raises a crucial question: what are the mechanisms by which this construction occurs? The answer lies in understanding our brain as a sophisticated statistical machine that's constantly updating its beliefs based on new evidence. Let's start with an example:

> Sarah stares at her phone, heart racing. Her teenage daughter is coming home from a friend's house an hour late. Her mind immediately jumps to worst-case scenarios: a car accident, an abduction, or something else equally terrible has happened. She can practically see the news headlines, feel the devastation. Every minute that passes confirms her growing certainty that disaster has struck. Then her daughter walks through the door, apologizing casually. She lost track of time and her phone died.
>
> In that instant, Sarah's entire reality shifts. The catastrophic future she was certain was unfolding disappears. Her racing heart begins to slow down, and the terrible scenarios that felt so real moments before now seem almost silly.

What happened in Sarah's brain represents one of the most remarkable discoveries in neuroscience: Our brain doesn't passively receive reality; instead, it actively constructs it, moment by moment, using sophisticated statistical processes that would impress any mathematician.

Sarah's brain was running what scientists call "Bayesian inference," which means that it was constantly generating predictions about what would happen next, updating those predictions based on new evidence, and constructing her experience of reality from these calculations. When her daughter was late, her brain predicted danger based on past experiences and cultural messaging about teenage safety. Each minute without contact strengthened that prediction until it felt like a certain truth. This isn't a special talent Sarah has. It's the fundamental operating system of human consciousness. Today, we understand that our brain is essentially a biological computer running sophisticated Bayesian inference algorithms, continuously updating beliefs based on new evidence in mathematically optimal ways.

Understanding our brain as a prediction machine is essential to becoming better observers of ourselves. It explains why two people can witness the same situation and come away with different interpretations, and why changing our minds can feel so difficult. It also helps us work with our brain's predictive nature to make better decisions, learn more effectively, and navigate uncertainty with greater wisdom. Yet here lies a fascinating paradox: Despite having brains that naturally perform complex statistical reasoning, most people struggle with explicit probability calculations and fall prey to systematic biases when reasoning about uncertainty.

Let's journey into the mathematical principles underlying consciousness itself, discovering how every moment of experience involves sophisticated statistical computations happening below our awareness. We'll explore why humans evolved as intuitive statisticians yet struggle with formal probability. We'll learn practical methods for working with our brain's natural inference mechanisms to transform our approach to learning, decision-making, and personal growth in an uncertain world.

The Bayesian Model of Reality

Here's something that many of us find mind-blowing: Our brain performs more sophisticated statistical calculations in a single day than most people do in their entire lives. Every time we recognize a face, navigate a conversation, or try to learn a musical instrument, we're running complex mathematical processes that would require supercomputers to replicate.

The mathematics underlying these calculations was first described by **Thomas Bayes**, an 18th-century minister and theologian who probably never imagined his theorem would explain elements of human consciousness. Bayes discovered a simple but powerful principle:

> The best way to update our beliefs is to combine what we already know with new evidence, weighing each piece by how reliable it seems.

This Bayesian approach unites philosophical and scientific perspectives, providing a framework for how the brain constructs and updates its model of reality. It aligns very well with ancient wisdom (impermanence) and modern science (probability and predictive processing).

Introduction to Bayes Theorem and Bayesian Thinking

While the mathematical formula might look intimidating, Bayes' theorem describes what our brain does naturally millions of times per day: Updating our beliefs based on new evidence. The theorem states:

$$P(A|B) = [P(B|A) \times P(A)] / P(B)$$

Where:

- *P(A|B) is the posterior probability of A given B*
- *P(B|A) is the likelihood of B given A*
- *P(A) is the prior probability of A*
- *P(B) is the marginal probability of B*

Although the math might seem abstract, what matters is the underlying logic, which we use intuitively. When we encounter new information, our brain automatically goes through this process:

- What did I believe before? (Prior)
- Is there new information to consider? (Evidence)
- If yes, how likely is the new evidence true, based on my prior belief? (Likelihood)
- Should I update my belief based on this new information? (Posterior)

This happens so naturally that we're usually unaware of the sophisticated statistical computation occurring in our brains. Bayes' theorem tells us how to update our belief in a hypothesis (A) when we observe new evidence (B). It combines our prior belief in the hypothesis (A) with the likelihood of observing the new evidence (B) if the hypothesis were true, normalized by the overall probability of observing that evidence (B).

To make this more concrete, let's consider an everyday example: Your Morning Coffee:

1. **Prior Belief**: "My coffee maker usually works fine." (high probability)
2. **New Evidence**: You hear an unusual gurgling sound.
3. **Likelihood Assessment**: "What's the probability of this sound if the machine is working normally?" (low)

4. **Posterior Update**: "There might be something wrong with the coffee maker." (reduced confidence in normal operation)
5. **Action Based on Update**: You investigate the machine before leaving for work.

This entire process, from prior belief through evidence evaluation to updated belief and action, happens almost instantaneously and largely below conscious awareness. At this point, it's important to clarify a common and understandable point of confusion: The word "belief" in a scientific or mathematical context, particularly with Bayesian inference, often carries baggage from everyday usage. It's crucial to distinguish these meanings. Here are two definitions, crafted to clarify the distinction:

- **Definition 1: "Belief" in the Popular/Everyday Sense**

    In popular usage, a **"belief"** typically refers to a conviction or acceptance that something is true, often without definitive proof. These beliefs can be deeply personal, emotionally charged, and frequently derive from cultural, religious, philosophical, or individual experiences. They can range from faith in a divine power to the conviction that a particular political ideology is correct, or even a personal opinion about whether it will rain tomorrow. Crucially, popular beliefs are often resistant to change <u>even in the face of contradictory evidence</u>, and they are not necessarily quantifiable or testable in a rigorous scientific manner.

- **Definition 2: "Belief" in the Context of Bayes' Theorem (Bayesian Beliefs)**

    In the context of Bayes' Theorem and neuroscience's "Bayesian brain" concept, a **"belief"** is a quantifiable probabilistic representation of the brain's internal model of the world. Given all available information, it refers to the brain's assigned probability to the likelihood of a particular situation, hypothesis, or cause. These "beliefs" are not static; they are dynamic, constantly being updated and refined. Specifically:

    - **Prior Beliefs (or Priors):** These are the brain's initial probabilistic expectations about the world *before* receiving new sensory evidence. They are formed through accumulated past experiences, genetic predispositions, and learned associations. In a mathematical sense, a prior belief is a probability distribution representing the brain's current uncertainty about a variable.
    - **Posterior Beliefs (or Posteriors):** These are the updated probabilistic expectations *after* new sensory evidence has been incorporated. Bayes' Theorem provides the mathematical framework

for how priors are combined with new evidence to generate these revised, more informed beliefs.

Therefore, when discussing "beliefs" in a Bayesian framework, we are referring to the brain's continually evolving, quantitative probabilities about the causes and states of its environment, which are refined through an iterative process of prediction and error correction. These are not rigid, unchangeable convictions, but rather flexible, probabilistic hypotheses that are constantly being tested against reality. Later in the book, we will dive into the concept of beliefs from a popular/everyday sense and discuss how they have the ability to mold our present reality.

Prior Beliefs and Updating with New Evidence

Think of our brain as a detective constantly updating its case files. Every morning when we wake up, we have certain expectations about the day ahead: these are our "prior beliefs." Throughout the day, we gather evidence: emails, conversations, and news reports. Our brain automatically weighs this new evidence against what we already believe, updating its predictions for what comes next. This isn't just a metaphor; it's literally how our neural networks process information, following mathematical principles that would make any statistician proud. Here is a bit more detail on the components in belief formation and updating:

1. **Prior Beliefs**:

    These are our existing beliefs or expectations before encountering new evidence. They can come from past experiences, cultural learning, evolutionary predispositions, or previous Bayesian updates.

2. **Likelihood Function**:

    This is the probability of observing the evidence given different possible states of the world. It represents how we expect the world to generate sensory data under different hypotheses.

    When we encounter new evidence, we combine our prior beliefs with the likelihood function to form a posterior belief, an updated probability distribution over possible states of the world.

    This posterior then becomes the prior for future updates, creating a continuous cycle of belief refinement. This process is not just a mathematical abstraction but appears to reflect how the brain actually processes information. Neuroscientific evidence suggests that neural activity patterns are consistent with Bayesian inference, with the brain representing both prior beliefs and likelihood functions in its neural code.

    Practical Example of Bayesian Thinking – Sarah's Brain in Action:

When Sarah's daughter was late, her brain was running this exact process:

- Prior belief: "Teenagers are generally safe when out with friends."
- New evidence: "She's an hour late and not responding to texts."
- Likelihood assessment: "How often does being late + no contact = danger?"
- Updated belief: "Something might be wrong." (anxiety spike)

The remarkable thing is that Sarah's brain did this calculation instantly, below conscious awareness, using millions of data points from her life experience, news exposure, and cultural messaging.

Of note, our brain isn't just using Bayesian inference to update beliefs in certain situations. It's using it to predict what will happen next, all the time, for every single situation. Every moment, we're generating forecasts about:

- What people will say in conversations;
- How our body will feel when we stand up;
- Whether that approaching car will stop at the red light, and
- What emotion will I experience if my plans change?

Most of these predictions are so accurate that we're completely unaware they're happening. We only notice a prediction when it fails: for example, when the car runs the red light, when someone says something unexpected, or when our body feels different than anticipated.

What we have explored so far should shed a very important fact about Bayesian inference: It isn't just about combining priors and evidence but weighting them based on their perceived reliability or *precision*. Strong, reliable sensory data (high precision) will have more influence on updating beliefs than noisy data (low precision), and vice versa for strong or weak priors. Attention plays a key role in modulating this sensory precision, amplifying the weight given to attended sensory evidence compared to prior beliefs.

The Paradox of Human Statistical Reasoning

Remember Sarah from the previous section? Sarah's brain can instantly calculate the probability that her daughter is in danger based on millions of variables (time of day, neighborhood safety, daughter's usual patterns, tone of last conversation). But she probably struggles to figure out whether she should take that car dealer's "best price" seriously or convert from degrees Celsius to Fahrenheit while traveling in Europe.

Table 7 – Examples of Our Hidden Statistical Skills

Some of Our Hidden Statistical Superpowers – Performed Every Day without Conscious Effort	
Face Recognition	Our brain distinguishes our friend from 7 billion other humans using subtle pattern recognition that would challenge the most advanced AI systems.
Language Processing	We understand sarcasm, implied meanings, and context in ways that require incredibly sophisticated probability calculations about what words likely mean given the situation.
Social Prediction	We can sense someone's mood from micro-expressions and predict how they'll react to different conversation topics.
Physical Coordination	Catching a ball requires your brain to calculate trajectory, speed, and timing faster than any computer.

When presented with explicit probability problems, even educated people often make systematic errors. Here are some examples of scenarios where most people would struggle:

- What's the probability of a medical test being wrong?
- How should I interpret polling data?
- What does a 30% chance of rain actually mean?

This paradox that our brains implicitly use sophisticated statistical methods while we explicitly struggle with basic probability reveals important aspects of how our cognitive systems evolved.

Our perceptual systems excel at integrating prior knowledge with new data to form posterior probability distributions, essentially performing complex statistical calculations without conscious awareness. This Bayesian framework helps explain how we navigate uncertainty in our environment with remarkable efficiency in many domains. Let's briefly look at the mathematical evolution that partly sheds light on this paradox.

Mathematics, Statistics, and the Human Condition

It has been said that mathematics is the true universal language. This is probably because mathematics provides consistent, logically sound, and universally applicable frameworks for understanding patterns, structures, and relationships. It transcends cultural and linguistic barriers in a way that spoken languages cannot. The earliest evidence of humankind's engagement with mathematical concepts is found in prehistoric times. Archaeological evidence, such as incised bones like the Lebombo bone (around 35,000 BCE), suggests early attempts at tallying or quantifying time. Geometric patterns on ochre rocks in South Africa date back to around 70,000 BCE. By around 3,000 BCE, a more systematic form of mathematics was available: Egyptians used arithmetic and geometry for land surveying and construction, while Sumerians and Babylonians developed a sophisticated base-60 number system, worked with quadratic equations, and had knowledge of what we now call the Pythagorean theorem. Centuries later (between 600 and 300 BCE) Greeks like **Thales of Miletus**, **Pythagoras,** and **Euclid** led the way in making mathematics a formal, deductive, and abstract discipline.

Between 300 CE and the 17th century, mathematics continued to evolve significantly through contributions from Indian mathematicians (e.g., development of the decimal system, zero), Chinese mathematicians (e.g. development of methods for finding areas and volumes), Islamic scholars during the Golden Age of Islam (e.g., **Al-Khwarizmi** in algebra, c. 780-850 CE), and European mathematicians during the Middle Ages and Renaissance (e.g., **Fibonacci** introducing Hindu-Arabic numerals to Europe, c. 1,202 CE).

Although all this was revolutionary progress, these early explorations lacked a unified theory and systematic methods. The late 16th and 17th centuries were revolutionary, with the development of calculus by Newton and Leibniz, analytic geometry by Descartes, and further advancements in number theory, algebra, and many other fields. Mathematics became increasingly abstract and formalized, especially from the 19th century onwards, with developments in non-Euclidean geometries, abstract algebra, and set theory. The philosophical movement of "formalism" in mathematics, aiming to ground mathematics in rigorous axiomatic systems, gained prominence in the late 19th and early 20th centuries.

Mathematics as a discipline and systematic body of knowledge is thousands of years old and is fundamentally intertwined with human cognition and cultural evolution, representing a defining characteristic of our species. Ancient mathematical thinking predates written language and appears universally across all human cultures, suggesting it emerges from core cognitive capabilities. These capabilities include:

- Pattern recognition;
- Abstract thought;
- Logical reasoning;
- Problem-solving; and
- Symbolic representation.

Beyond its cognitive foundations, mathematics serves as humanity's most effective tool for understanding the universe's underlying structure and laws. This mathematical framework has enabled remarkable technological and scientific progress throughout human history, from basic shelter construction to space exploration. Our inherent tendency to quantify, categorize, and identify order reflects mathematical thinking in everyday cognition.

While not every human becomes an advanced mathematician (just as not everyone becomes a concert pianist, though music is also considered a key human feature), the innate capacity for basic mathematical thinking and the collective human achievement of creating complex mathematical systems are profound testaments to its importance in defining the human experience. It reflects our species' unique ability to move beyond immediate sensory experience to find deeper, abstract structures and use them to understand and shape our reality. But there is a catch: While mathematics is thousands of years old, **statistics as a formal mathematical practice is generally considered to have emerged in the 17th century**, with significant development into a distinct scientific discipline occurring in the late 19th and early 20th centuries.

The earliest roots of statistical thinking can be traced to antiquity. As far back as the 5th century BCE, civilizations like the Athenians were using rudimentary statistical concepts, such as finding the mode (most frequent value) to make estimations. Empires such as the Han Dynasty in China and the Roman Empire systematically collected data on population and resources. Medieval Europe saw practices like the Trial of the Pyx in the 12th century, a form of quality control for coinage that relied on sampling. By the 14th century, cities like Florence were compiling detailed statistical information on demographics and trade. However, the mathematical underpinnings of statistics began to solidify much later.

A significant milestone often cited as a birth point for statistical analysis is **John Graunt's 1662 publication, "Natural and Political Observations Made upon the Bills of Mortality."** Graunt analyzed London's mortality records, identifying patterns and making inferences about population trends, which is a hallmark of statistical practice. Around the same period, concepts like the arithmetic mean, known since antiquity for two values, began to be generalized.

The term "statistics" itself was coined in 1749 by the German scholar **Gottfried Achenwall**, originally referring to the "science of state" or the systematic collection and analysis of data about the country. The true emergence of statistics as a rigorous mathematical discipline took place in the **late 19th and early 20th centuries**. This era saw foundational contributions from pioneers like **Francis Galton** (correlation, regression), **Karl Pearson** (chi-squared test, standard deviation, and the first university statistics department at University College, London in 1911), and **Ronald A. Fisher** (analysis of variance, design of experiments, maximum likelihood). Their work transformed statistics into the powerful tool for data analysis and inference that it is today.

In summary, while statistics is a powerful and sophisticated mathematical science today, its origins as a formal practice and distinct discipline are far more recent when compared to the millennia-long history of mathematics. This leads to a very important question: If mathematics is an essential feature of the human condition, and statistics is a branch of mathematics, why did it take so long for humans to develop formal statistical analysis?

The delayed development of formal statistics compared to other mathematical disciplines can be substantially attributed to how the human brain processes information and approaches reasoning. Our cognitive architecture appears less naturally suited to statistical reasoning than to other forms of mathematical thinking. In evaluating this idea, we can come up with a variety of possible reasons:

1. **Cognitive Biases:**

    A vast body of research in psychology, notably by figures like **Daniel Kahneman** and **Amos Tversky**, has demonstrated that human intuition is often prone to systematic errors when dealing with probabilities and statistical information. We seem to be susceptible to:

    Table 8 – Examples of Explicit Human Statistical Struggles

Base Rate Neglect	Ignoring general statistical information (the base rate) in favor of specific, descriptive information
Conjunction Fallacy	Believing specific scenarios are more likely than general ones.
Anchoring Bias	Over-relying on the first piece of information offered (the anchor) when making decisions.
Gambler's Fallacy	Believing that past independent random events influence future ones.

Availability Heuristics	Overestimating the likelihood of events that are easily recalled, often because they are vivid or recent, rather than statistically frequent.
Representative Heuristics	Judging probabilities based on how much something resembles a stereotype or prototype, rather than on base rates or statistical likelihood.
Difficulty with Randomness	Seeing patterns in random data and struggling with the concept of true randomness.

We will cover some of these examples in more detail later in this chapter. For now, understand that these biases suggest that intuitive, *System 1 thinking* (fast, automatic, implicit, but error-prone) often overrides the more deliberate, analytical *System 2 thinking* (controlled and explicit) required for sound statistical reasoning and accurate evaluations.

2. **Preference for Deterministic Cause-and-Effect:**

   Human brains seem wired to seek clear cause-and-effect relationships. On the other hand, statistics often deal with uncertainty, variability, correlations (which don't always imply causation), and probabilistic outcomes. This inherent uncertainty can be less satisfying or harder to grasp intuitively than a more deterministic mathematical proof or physical law.

3. **Abstraction of Populations and Samples:**

   While early mathematics dealt with tangible quantities or idealized geometric forms, formal statistics requires thinking abstractly about populations, samples, distributions, and the inference from a sample to a larger, unseen whole. This is a higher level of abstraction.

4. **Complexity of Variability:**

   Understanding and quantifying variability is central to statistics. Our everyday experience often focuses on averages or typical cases, and systematically accounting for the full range and nature of variation requires specific tools and a conceptual shift.

Kahneman and Tversky developed a now-famous experiment that demonstrates the conjunction fallacy in human reasoning. The experiment is called "The Linda Problem," and here's what it involves:

Participants are given a description of a woman named Linda: "Linda is 31 years old, single, outspoken, and very bright. She majored in philosophy. As a student, she was deeply concerned with issues of discrimination and social justice and also participated in anti-nuclear demonstrations." They are then asked which statement is more probable:

1. Linda is a bank teller.
2. Linda is a bank teller and is active in the feminist movement.

In their original study, more than 80% of participants chose option 2, demonstrating the erroneous belief that a specific condition (being both a bank teller and a feminist) is more probable than a general one (being just a bank teller). This violates a fundamental rule of probability:

> *"the likelihood of two events occurring together (A and B) cannot be greater than the probability of either event occurring alone."*

This problem illustrates the "representative heuristic," <u>our tendency to judge probabilities based on how much something resembles our mental prototype rather than applying statistical reasoning</u>. The detailed description of Linda makes her seem representative of a feminist, leading people to favor the conjunction even though it's mathematically less probable. As **Stephen Jay Gould** famously commented about his own struggle with this problem: *"a little homunculus in my head continues to jump up and down, shouting at me – 'but she can't just be a bank teller; read the description.'"*

Our brains strongly prefer clear cause-and-effect relationships over the uncertainty and probabilistic thinking central to statistics. Statistics also requires abstract conceptualization of populations, samples, and distributions, moving beyond the more tangible quantities or idealized forms found in early mathematics. Additionally, our cognitive tendency to focus on averages rather than systematically accounting for variability creates another natural barrier.

For completeness, it is only responsible to note that the late emergence of statistics as an independent field is not strictly and solely due to our seeming inability to process statistical reasoning. There are several historical and practical constraints that also contributed to statistics' later emergence:

1. The need for robust, systematically collected data.
2. The prerequisite development of probability theory in the 16th-17th centuries.
3. Reliance on advanced mathematical tools like calculus;
4. Evolving conceptual frameworks in science and society; and
5. The eventual availability of computational aids.

The development of formal statistics thus required not only overcoming inherent cognitive limitations but also the confluence of intellectual, societal, and practical advancements across multiple disciplines and historical periods. Our brains seem more naturally attuned to deterministic logic and tangible quantities than to the nuances of chance, variability, and inference from limited data.

Why Human Brains Struggle with Statistics

The mismatch between implicit statistical competence and explicit probability struggles reflects our evolutionary history and the environments in which human reasoning developed. Here are some contributing factors as to why humans have statistical reasoning difficulties:

- **Evolutionary Environment**

    Our statistical reasoning capabilities evolved in environments where explicit probability calculations were unnecessary. Hunter-gatherer societies required implicit learning of environmental patterns (which foods were safe, which areas held danger) rather than formal statistical analysis. This learning occurred through direct experience and social transmission, not through abstract numerical representations of uncertainty.

    The statistical problems our ancestors faced were embedded in concrete contexts (tracking animal movements, predicting weather patterns, or assessing social dynamics) rather than presented as abstract mathematical problems. Consequently, our cognitive architecture developed specialized systems for intuitive statistical inference in domain-specific contexts rather than domain-general statistical reasoning abilities.

- **Concrete vs. Abstract Thinking**

    Our reasoning systems show a strong preference for concrete, experience-based thinking over abstract statistical reasoning. This manifests in multiple ways:

    - We find anecdotes and individual stories more compelling than statistical summaries.
    - We overweight our personal experiences relative to population-level data.
    - We more easily reason about countable entities than about proportions or percentages.

- **Frequency vs. Probability Format**

    Humans demonstrate significantly improved statistical reasoning when information is presented as "natural frequencies" rather than as probabilities or percentages. This "frequency effect" appears across various domains, including medical diagnosis, risk assessment, and Bayesian reasoning tasks.

    Natural frequencies preserve information about base rates and sample sizes, making the relationship between different statistical quantities more transparent. This format aligns better with how we naturally track and process statistical information in our environment.

- **Emotional Influence**

    - Our statistical reasoning is profoundly influenced by emotional factors. Several mechanisms contribute to this emotional override:
    - **Availability heuristic**: Presented in **Table 8**.
    - **Affect heuristic**: Emotional reactions guide our risk perceptions, often independently of statistical information.
    - **Loss aversion**: We weigh potential losses more heavily than equivalent gains.
    - **Certainty effect**: We overvalue certain outcomes relative to probabilistic ones.

    These emotional influences likely evolved as adaptive shortcuts for rapid decision-making, but they can lead to systematic errors in contexts requiring careful statistical analysis.

- **Cognitive Load and Processing Limitations**

    Statistical reasoning often imposes significant cognitive demands, requiring simultaneous tracking of multiple values and their relationships. Our working memory limitations constrain our ability to perform complex calculations, particularly when problems cannot be easily visualized or mapped onto familiar experiences.

- **Mental Models and Visualization Challenges**

    Many statistical concepts involve complex, abstract relationships that are difficult to visualize mentally. Concepts like conditional probability, statistical independence, or sampling distributions lack intuitive visual representations, making them harder to reason about compared to more concrete physical or spatial relationships.

- **Statistical Education and Methodology**

  Traditional approaches to teaching statistics often emphasize computational procedures over conceptual understanding. This procedural focus can leave individuals with fragmented knowledge that's difficult to apply in novel situations. Additionally, statistical notation and terminology can create unnecessary barriers to understanding core concepts.

- **Cultural and Mathematical Literacy Factors**

  Modern statistical reasoning demands familiarity with mathematical conventions and notational systems that aren't universally accessible. Variations in mathematical education and cultural approaches to quantitative reasoning contribute to differences in statistical thinking abilities across populations.

- **Implications and Modern Challenges**

  The mismatch between our implicit statistical abilities and explicit reasoning capabilities has profound implications in contemporary contexts that require evaluating complex probabilistic information:

  - **Medical Decision-Making**: Understanding diagnostic test results, treatment efficacy statistics, and risk factors requires explicit statistical reasoning that patients and sometimes even healthcare providers struggle with.

  - **Financial Planning**: Evaluating investment risks, understanding compound interest, and planning for an uncertain future test our statistical reasoning abilities.

  - **Climate Change Communication**: Grasping the statistical evidence for climate change and evaluating risk mitigation strategies involves complex probabilistic thinking.

  - **Pandemic Response**: COVID-19 revealed widespread difficulties in understanding concepts like exponential growth, test sensitivity/specificity, and risk assessment.

  This paradox of human statistical reasoning highlights the need for carefully designed information formats, visualization tools, and educational approaches that bridge the gap between our intuitive statistical capacities (and limitations) and the explicit reasoning demands of modern life. Our inherent limitations in explicit statistical reasoning can lead to significant errors in how we understand reality, particularly in modern contexts that require evaluating complex statistical information.

The Human Brain's Built-In Limitations

Despite our brain's remarkable capabilities, our cognitive processes have significant limitations that affect how we perceive and understand reality.

The Myth of Multitasking

While the brain processes many streams of information in parallel, our conscious attention has severe limitations. Contrary to popular belief, humans are generally poor at multitasking, attempting to perform multiple attention-demanding tasks simultaneously.

Research by psychologists **Jason Watson and David Strayer** has shown that only about 2.5% of people can effectively multitask without significant performance decrements. For the vast majority, attempting to multitask leads to slower performance, more errors, and reduced comprehension compared to focusing on one task at a time.

This limitation arises from the bottleneck of attention. While we can process multiple streams of information unconsciously, conscious processing requires attention, which has limited capacity. When we try to attend to multiple tasks simultaneously, attention must switch rapidly between them, leading to performance costs.

The implications for our understanding of reality are significant. We cannot simultaneously attend to all aspects of our environment, so our conscious experience represents a highly selective and limited sample of available information. What we perceive as reality is, in an important sense, what we attend to – and much of what happens around us goes unnoticed.

Cognitive Biases and Heuristics

In the last section, we established that humans rely on numerous mental shortcuts (heuristics) and exhibit systematic biases in perception, judgment, and decision-making. Psychologists have extensively documented how these biases and heuristics shape our experience of reality in profound ways. In addition to examples like availability heuristic and anchoring bias (covered earlier in the chapter), these are popular cognitive biases prevalent in daily life:

- **Confirmation Bias**:

    This is the tendency to search for, interpret, and remember information in a way that confirms our preexisting beliefs while giving less consideration to alternative possibilities.

- **Negativity Bias**:

    This is the tendency to give more weight to negative experiences or information than positive ones.

- **Dunning-Kruger Effect**:

    This is the tendency for people with low ability in a specific area to overestimate their ability, while those with high ability tend to underestimate their competence.

These biases are not mere flaws but adaptive features of cognition that help us make quick decisions with limited information and processing capacity. However, they can lead to systematic distortions in how we perceive and understand reality, particularly in modern contexts that differ from the environments in which these cognitive tendencies evolved. Awareness of these biases requires *metacognition*, which is the ability to reflect on our own thought processes. Developing this self-awareness, as discussed by researchers like **Stephen Fleming**, can help evaluate the reliability of our perceptions and judgments and counter phenomena like the "illusion of explanatory depth" (thinking we know more than we do).

Is Reality a Hallucination?

At least from a Bayesian perspective, we have learned that everything we experience represents our brain's best statistical guess about what's happening based on incomplete sensory information and prior expectations. So, are we hallucinating what we call reality? This question touches on fundamental issues in philosophy of mind, epistemology, and neuroscience. If we approach the topic from a neurological point of view, our experience of reality is entirely constructed by our brains. Everything we perceive (colors, sounds, textures, even time and space) is the product of neural processing. Our brains receive electrochemical signals from our sensory organs and transform them into our conscious experience. In this sense, what we call "reality" may indeed be considered to be a kind of controlled hallucination, in other words, a model created by our minds to help us navigate the world.

However, there are crucial differences between our everyday experience and what we typically call hallucinations:

- Our normal perception is constrained by and responsive to external inputs in a consistent, predictable way.
- These constraints suggest an independent reality that our perceptions attempt to track, even if imperfectly.
- A true hallucination lacks this external constraint, as it's generated entirely internally without corresponding sensory input.

- Furthermore, the shared nature of our experiences suggests something beyond pure hallucination. When multiple people observe the same phenomenon and agree on its basic properties, this points to some objective reality underlying our collective experiences, even if our individual perceptions vary in the details.

So, while our brains indeed construct our experience of reality in ways similar to hallucinations, the consistency, predictability, and shareable nature of these experiences suggest they're anchored to something beyond our individual minds: an external reality that our perceptions approximate rather than purely and entirely invent. As we move forward, to avoid confusion and misunderstandings, we will use the term "controlled hallucination" when referring to our brain's ability to create our version of reality.

Hallucinating Reality from Sensorial Information

Mo Gawdat, former Chief Business Officer for Google X and author of "**Solve for Happy: Engineering Your Path to Joy**," summarizes this perspective, stating that what we call reality might just be the hallucinations we collectively agree upon. Our brain constantly generates predictions or *hypotheses* about the causes of sensory input based on its prior experiences and internal models of the world. What we perceive consciously isn't the raw sensory data itself, but the brain's best guess about what's out there. Sensory input serves primarily to correct or update these predictions when they are wrong (prediction errors). It is because of this feedback loop enabled by sensory information that we say that our perception is like a controlled hallucination. It's not uncontrolled like in psychosis, but rather a constant, active construction generated by the brain and constrained (controlled) by incoming sensory data. This is a leading and well-respected theoretical framework in modern neuroscience for understanding perception, though it's still an area of active research and refinement. Neuroscientist **Beau Lotto** expands on this by telling us that:

> *The brain evolved to see the world not necessarily as it is, but as it was useful to see in the past, continually redefining normality based on learned associations.*

This is really eye-opening given that the world today changes so quickly in front of our eyes; yet, our brain relies heavily on the past to make predictions about the future. In other words, our brains are active builders of our experienced reality based on a useful past.

In his book "**The Case Against Reality: Why Evolution Hid the Truth From our Eyes**" neuroscientist **Donald Hoffman** goes even further by suggesting that our perceptions are not a direct reflection of reality but rather a user interface evolved to guide adaptive behavior. He argues that the reality we perceive is a construction optimized for survival, not necessarily a true representation of an underlying objective reality.

Independent of the nuances between each neuroscientist's approach, there is great consensus in the fact that this predictive process is usually constrained by sensory input, meaning that our "hallucinations" are kept in check by incoming sensory evidence. However, when sensory input is ambiguous, degraded, or absent, the influence of prior beliefs becomes stronger, sometimes **leading to perceptual experiences that diverge significantly from external reality**. This can be observed in various phenomena:

Table 9 – Examples of Perceptual Phenomena

Optical Illusions	Many visual illusions occur because the brain applies prior expectations about lighting, perspective, or object properties that don't match the actual stimulus.
Pareidolia	The tendency to perceive meaningful patterns (like faces) in random or ambiguous stimuli, driven by strong priors for detecting certain high-value patterns. Common examples include perceived images of animals, faces, or objects in cloud formations.
Dreams and Hallucinations	During dreams or psychedelic experiences, the constraint of sensory input is reduced, allowing internally generated predictions to dominate conscious experience.
Phantom Limb Sensations	Amputees often experience sensations from missing limbs because the brain continues to generate predictions about limb position and sensation despite the absence of sensory input.

These phenomena reveal that our experience of reality is fundamentally always a construction; a model generated by the brain based on a combination of sensory input and prior beliefs, with the balance between these factors varying across different states and contexts. Everything we perceive - sights, sounds, textures, even our sense of self - is processed and interpreted by different neural networks. We can see this process very clearly when we explore optical illusions. In the vision process, when light hits our retinas, what we "see" is actually our brain's interpretation of electrical signals. The brain fills in blind spots, corrects for motion, and makes countless unconscious adjustments. Let us explore a few examples:

- **The Illusion of Color:**

    Color itself doesn't exist in the external world. It's our brain's interpretation of different wavelengths of light. For example, a "red" apple appears red because its surface absorbs most wavelengths of light but reflects those corresponding to what we perceive as red. Our retina receives these reflected wavelengths, and the brain then constructs the experience of "redness." Thus, the "red" of the apple is fundamentally a product of our visual system, not an intrinsic property of the apple itself.

- **Figure-Ground Illusions:**

    A figure-ground illusion is an image where it is difficult to discern what the main object is to focus on (the figure) versus what is around this main object (the ground), so our mind switches back and forth trying to make sense of it. When we visually observe the world, we don't see everything at once, as this would be overwhelming to our senses. Instead, the brain works hard to interpret various types of visual images in our field of view, and sometimes these images challenge the way visual information is processed. When this happens, we experience a figure-ground optical illusion. A famous example of this type of illusion is the Rubin vase, where, depending on how you observe it, you may either see two faces in black or a vase in white.

Figure 1 – Rubin Vase Illusion. (Image designed and provided by Freepik - www.freepik.com)

- **Ponzo illusion:**

  The brain is accustomed to perceiving a three-dimensional world in which images higher in the visual field are farther away and therefore larger. The Ponzo illusion consists of two sets of lines: the first set is two straight converging lines on a two-dimensional plane, giving it a sense of depth (resembling a road heading toward a horizon). In contrast, the other set is two parallel lines placed over those converging lines. Upon observation, the higher line appears to be larger than the lower parallel line, when in fact the two lines are the same size.

Figure 2 - Ponzo Illusion.
(Author: Tony Philips, NASA. Image is public domain)

- **Rotating-Snakes Illusion**

  The rotating-snakes illusion was invented in 2003 by **Akiyoshi Kitaoka** of Ritsumeikan University in Japan. This illusion consists of four main circles with specific patterns in them (resembling coiled-up snakes). Upon observation, the circles seem to rotate depending on where you look at the image. Of course, the image is still and has no movement, but that is not what we perceive. **Stephen Macknik** and his colleagues from the Barrow Neurological Institute in Phoenix explain how it works. The team tracked the movement of people's eyes as they gazed at two of these wheels on a computer screen. Their subjects kept a finger pressed on a button, lifting it whenever they seemed to see the wheels move. The researchers found a tight correlation between the onset of the illusion and an involuntary eye movement called microsaccades. It turns out that microsaccades are happening most, if not all, the time; even when we're staring at a still object, our eyes keep moving around. Microsaccades help us compensate for a peculiar property of the eye: if we stare at an object too long, the signals each photoreceptor sends to the brain become weaker. Microsaccades refresh the photoreceptors with a different input, which can end up altering what we visually perceive.

Figure 3 - Rotating Snakes Illusion. ([Creative Commons](#) [CC0 1.0 Universal Public Domain Dedication](#))

This last example of optical illusions is quite interesting because it involves how we perceive motion in the real world. In this rotating-snakes illusion, the microsaccades get in the way of our perception of motion. For instance, if we see a snake slithering along in a desert, we don't have to register an entire image of the snake at one instant, then another image at the next instant, and then compare the location of the two images to figure out that the snake is on the move. Instead, we only have to sense rapidly changing light patterns in neighboring parts of the eyes. If certain neurons in the vision-processing regions of the brain receive a sudden, strong signal from the eye, they register motion. Normally, our eyes can register motion while also performing microsaccades. Our brains can tell the difference between a shift brought on by the movement of an object and one brought on by the movement of our own eyes. But thanks to the strong contrasts and shapes in the Rotating-Snakes Illusion, our brain is "confused," our motion sensors switch on, and we can "see" the snakes moving.

Just as with vision, our auditory system is not a passive receiver of sound waves but an active interpreter, constantly generating predictions and constructing our perception of the auditory world. The brain leverages prior knowledge, context, and expectations to make sense of ambiguous or incomplete acoustic information. When these predictions clash with actual sensory input, or when the input itself is misleading, we experience auditory illusions, highlighting the brain's constructive nature. Here are some prominent examples:

- **The McGurk Effect:**

    This is a powerful demonstration of multisensory integration in perception. When we see a speaker's lips moving to pronounce one sound (e.g., 'ga') while simultaneously hearing a different sound (e.g., 'ba'), our brain often creates a third, entirely different percept (e.g., 'da'). This illusion occurs because the brain attempts to reconcile conflicting visual and auditory information by creating a compromise, demonstrating how visual cues profoundly influence auditory perception. It underscores that what we "hear" is not solely determined by the sound waves entering our ears, but also by the visual context and the brain's top-down processing, trying to form a coherent interpretation. For an example of the McGurk effect, go to https://youtu.be/l_Ql7y5aQqo. In this link, Professor Lawrence Rosenblum from the University of California, Riverside demonstrates and explains this illusion.

- **The Missing-Fundamental Illusion (Virtual Pitch):**

    This illusion (also known as the virtual pitch phenomenon) vividly demonstrates how our auditory system actively constructs what we hear. When we hear a musical note, our brain typically processes its fundamental frequency along with a series of higher harmonics (multiples of the fundamental). However, even if the fundamental frequency is entirely removed, and only its harmonics are played, our brain will still perceive the original, lower pitch of the fundamental. This occurs because the brain infers the missing fundamental from the mathematical relationship between the present harmonics, effectively 'filling in' the missing information to create a coherent perception. For an audio example of this illusion, visit the Auditory Neuroscience webpage on this link: https://auditoryneuroscience.com/pitch/missing-fundamental-stimuli.

- **The Deutsch's Tritone Paradox:**

    Psychologist **Diana Deutsch** discovered this is a fascinating auditory illusion that highlights the interplay of bottom-up sensory processing and top-down cognitive factors, vividly demonstrating how deeply cultural and linguistic experiences can sculpt our auditory perception. When presented without a clear tonal context, the tritone, an interval precisely spanning half an octave (e.g., C to F#), is inherently ambiguous in its pitch height. When a pair of these notes is played, listeners often perceive them as either distinctly ascending or descending. What's remarkable is that this perception remains consistent for an individual but varies significantly across different listeners, frequently correlating with the intonation patterns of their native language. This compellingly suggests that our brains don't just passively receive sound; instead, they actively impose meaning, utilizing learned templates and prior experiences related to pitch and language to interpret ambiguous auditory stimuli. The result is a highly individualized and culturally influenced construction of what we perceive as the "same" sound. To experience the tritone paradox (it is better if done in groups of three or more people), listen to the examples on Diana Deutsch's official website at: https://deutsch.ucsd.edu/psychology/play.php?i=6206

- **The Shepard-Tone Illusion (Auditory Staircase):**

    This illusion, created by cognitive scientist **Roger Shepard**, is an auditory phenomenon where a sequence of specially constructed tones appears to continually ascend or descend in pitch, despite never actually getting higher or lower in absolute frequency. This is achieved by playing several tones separated by octaves simultaneously. Each tone gradually fades in at its peak volume and then fades out, while the next higher (or lower) octave simultaneously fades in, creating a seamless, endless auditory staircase. The brain interprets this careful layering and amplitude modulation as continuous movement in one direction, demonstrating its tendency to construct a coherent, albeit illusory, musical progression. Experience the Shepard-tone illusion by searching online for 'Shepard tone audio' or visiting: https://filmlifestyle.com/what-is-the-shepard-tone/

Sensorial illusions occur far more than we notice on a day-to-day basis. By understanding how our brain processes sensorial information, we begin to clearly see the predictive nature of our ability to perceive reality. This is important as we discuss how we create and process feelings and emotions.

The Construction of Emotional Illusions

Perception, as we've established, is an active process: The brain constantly generates **top-down predictions** and then matches them against incoming sensory information. When sensory input aligns with these predictions, error signals are minimal, and the brain conserves resources by processing primarily unexpected "news." This architecture is highly metabolically efficient, allowing the brain to fluidly navigate a complex world.

However, this efficiency comes with potential drawbacks, as <u>the brain prioritizes maintaining a coherent internal model over perfect external fidelity</u>. This can lead to the **sensory illusions** we discussed in the previous section. In its drive to minimize prediction error, especially when strong prior beliefs are at play or sensory data is ambiguous, the brain tries to "explain away" conflicting information, <u>forcing the input to fit its expectations</u>. Visual illusions often arise when contextual cues or learned assumptions lead the brain to predict certain stimulus configurations, even if actual input is ambiguous. Neuroimaging studies consistently show reduced activity in early sensory areas for predictable stimuli, underscoring how top-down predictions actively "explain away" expected input.

But the brain's predictive machinery isn't limited to traditional sensory inputs. What happens when the "inputs" are not external sights or sounds but are instead internal emotional states and neural pathways? It turns out that the brain applies strikingly similar predictive principles to emotional processing as it does to sensory perception. Both sensory and emotional processing demonstrate a similar hierarchical organization:

- **Sensory pathways**:

    Information flows from specialized receptors through dedicated pathways to primary sensory cortices and higher-order association areas.

- **Emotional pathways**:

    Interoceptive signals (internal bodily sensations) and affective information are processed through limbic and paralimbic structures to higher cortical regions.

Key neural regions involved in emotional/interoceptive processing include:

- **Insula** (particularly anterior insula): It is central to interoceptive awareness and integration of bodily signals into subjective feelings.
- **Anterior Cingulate Cortex (ACC)**: It handles error monitoring and emotional conflict resolution.
- **Amygdala**: It detects and responds to salient stimuli, especially threat-related.
- **Prefrontal Cortex (PFC)**: It addresses emotion regulation and value representation.
- **Hippocampus**: It forms contextual emotional memories.

Today, we have evidence that neural pathways for sensory and affective processing have significant overlap. Early sensory cortical regions show heightened activity when processing affectively charged stimuli compared to neutral ones. The insula serves as a critical hub for integrating sensory, affective, and cognitive information, while the ACC monitors for prediction errors across domains.

This anatomical and functional convergence supports the hypothesis that <u>predictive coding principles may apply similarly across sensory and emotional domains</u>. This establishes the groundwork for "emotional illusions" to arise through mechanisms analogous to those producing sensory illusions. An "emotional illusion" can be conceptualized as a subjective emotional experience that deviates significantly from a veridical representation of an individual's actual internal physiological state, affective condition, or the objective emotional significance of an external situation. Such illusions arise from errors in the brain's predictive processing of interoceptive signals and exteroceptive affective cues. Let's expand briefly on interoceptive signals and exteroceptive affective cues:

Interoceptive signals:

Interoceptive signals can be defined as sensory information arising from **within the body** that informs the brain about the body's internal physiological state. These signals originate from specialized receptors (interoceptors) located throughout the body's internal organs and systems. Examples of interoceptive signals include:

- Heart rates and cardiac rhythms (palpitations, heart pounding);
- Breathing patterns and respiratory sensations (shortness of breath, chest tightness);
- Gut sensations (hunger, nausea, "butterflies in stomach");
- Muscle tension and fatigue;
- Temperature regulation (feeling hot or cold internally);
- Pain and discomfort from internal organs;
- Hormonal fluctuations and their bodily effects;
- Blood pressure changes; and
- Bladder and bowel sensations.

Interoceptive signals can have the following key characteristics:

- They are often diffuse, ambiguous, and less consciously accessible than external sensory information;
- They provide the foundation for many emotional experiences;
- They are processed primarily through the insula and related brain regions, and

- It can be misinterpreted when the brain relies heavily on emotional "priors" to make sense of ambiguous internal sensations.

Exteroceptive Affective Cues

Exteroceptive affective cues can be defined as <u>sensory information from the **external environment** that has acquired emotional significance through learning and experience</u>. These are essentially external stimuli that the brain has learned to associate with emotional outcomes or meanings. Examples of exteroceptive affective cues include:

- Facial expressions of others (smiles, frowns, angry faces);
- Tone of voice and vocal expressions;
- Body language and postures;
- Environmental contexts previously associated with emotions (e.g., a location where something traumatic happened);
- Social situations that trigger emotional responses;
- Visual or auditory stimuli linked to past emotional experiences;
- Cultural symbols or objects with emotional meaning; and
- Contextual cues that signal potential reward or threat.

Exteroceptive affective cues can have the following key characteristics:

- They are processed through regular sensory channels (vision, hearing, etc.) but interpreted for emotional significance;
- Their meaning is largely learned through experience and cultural context;
- They can trigger emotional predictions and responses even when the actual threat/reward is minimal; and
- They often interact with interoceptive signals to create complex emotional experiences

Interoceptive inference is fundamental to understanding emotion generation within predictive processing. The brain actively constructs emotional experiences by predicting, monitoring, and interpreting interoceptive signals. Emotions emerge from the interplay between top-down interoceptive predictions (what the brain expects the body to feel) and bottom-up prediction errors (mismatches between expected and actual bodily feedback). Affective experiences are controlled hallucinations generated through this inferential process. If interoceptive signals are ambiguous (as they often are), the brain relies more heavily on priors, creating conditions for potential misinterpretations or "emotional illusions."

In the predictive brain framework, **emotional illusions** can arise when:

1. **Ambiguous interoceptive signals** (like a racing heart) are misinterpreted based on strong emotional priors (e.g., "racing heart = panic attack" rather than "racing heart = excitement from a desired outcome");

2. **Exteroceptive affective cues** are misread due to biased expectations (e.g., interpreting a neutral facial expression as hostile due to social anxiety); and

3. **Interaction effects** occur when external cues influence how internal sensations are interpreted, or vice versa (e.g., being in a crowded room makes a normal heart rate feel threatening)

The brain constantly tries to <u>create a coherent story from both internal bodily signals and external emotional cues</u>. Still, when this predictive process goes awry (due to strong biases, ambiguous signals, or past trauma), it can generate emotional experiences that don't accurately reflect either the body's actual state or the true emotional significance of the external situation.

Why Does This Matter to Your Daily Life?

When you have a strong emotional reaction, try to understand your brain's predictive processing:

Step 1: Pause and Notice

- What emotion am I experiencing right now?
- How intense is it (1-10 scale)?

Step 2: Identify the Prediction

- What was my brain expecting to happen in this situation?
- What outcome was I predicting?

Step 3: Compare with Reality

- What actually happened?
- How different was reality from my prediction?

Step 4: Update for Next Time

- What can I learn from this prediction error?
- How might I adjust my expectations for similar situations?

Bottom Line: Recognizing when our emotions are responding to predicted threats rather than actual ones is a necessary skill in this modern world.

Research demonstrates that violations of emotional expectations are not merely subjective experiences but play a profound and significant role in shaping our behavior, leaving distinct and measurable neural signatures. In this interesting area, Event-Related Potentials (ERPs) like the **P3b** component are key. The P3b is a prominent positive-going electrical brainwave typically peaking around 300 to 600 milliseconds after a noteworthy event and maximal over central-parietal scalp regions. It serves as a robust indicator of the brain's "context updating" process and precisely tracks **affective-prediction errors**. These errors are the crucial instances when the brain registers a mismatch between an anticipated emotional outcome and the actual emotional experience.

Concurrently, a complex network of distinct brain regions works in concert to process various facets of these emotional expectancy violations, from rapid appraisal by the amygdala to cognitive evaluation within prefrontal areas. These affective prediction errors do not simply register a surprise; instead, they function as potent **teaching signals**. By signaling when our emotional predictions are inaccurate, they drive dynamic learning processes, facilitating the update of our internal models of the world and ultimately leading to adaptive adjustments in our future behavior and decision-making.

If the brain's current emotional state can influence how future prediction errors are processed, then a bidirectional relationship where emotions shape learning, and learning shapes emotions can be created. This dynamic reciprocity explains how "emotional illusions" can become self-reinforcing. By recognizing emotions as actively constructed through predictive inference rather than passive readouts of bodily states, we gain insight into how emotional experiences can sometimes misrepresent reality. This represents a potential paradigm shift in how we understand emotions, moving beyond stimulus-response models to appreciate the active, constructive, and inferential nature of our inner emotional lives.

This statistical paradox presented so far points to a deeper truth: Our brain's predictions are so sophisticated and automatic that we experience them as reality itself, creating a controlled hallucination. But here is the good news: Understanding reality as a constructed, controlled hallucination is liberating, not disturbing. At a minimum, it means:

- We have more influence over our experience than we might think.
- Other people's different perceptions make sense; remember, they're constructing reality differently.

- Changing our predictions can literally change our reality.
- We can learn to work with our brain's constructive processes rather than being unconsciously controlled by them.

Applying Bayesian Thinking to Everyday Life

> *"Strictly speaking it may be said that almost all our knowledge is problematic; and in the small number of things which we are able to know with certainty, even in the mathematical sciences themselves, the principal means of ascertaining truth - induction and analogy - are based on probabilities; so that the entire system of human knowledge is connected with the theory of probability."*
>
> **Pierre-Simon Laplace – French Mathematician, Astronomer and Physicist**

This quote comes from an essay titled "A Philosophical Essay on Probabilities" published by Laplace in 1814. A common modern summary of this quote states that *"all knowledge is probabilistic,"* which beautifully encapsulates the core idea of the Bayesian perspective we have been discussing.

Laplace's statement was revolutionary for its time and laid a foundational stone for modern epistemology (the theory of knowledge) and statistics. Here's what we think he meant:

- **Acknowledging Human Ignorance and Imperfection:**

    Laplace lived in an era of great scientific discovery, often characterized by a belief in absolute determinism. Newton's laws seemed to suggest that if one knew all the initial conditions, one could predict the entire future of the universe. However, Laplace understood that even with the most precise measurements and sophisticated theories, there would always be an irreducible element of uncertainty in our knowledge. <u>Our senses are limited, our instruments imperfect, and the complexity of the world is immense.</u>

- **Probability as the Logic of Uncertainty:**

    For Laplace, probability wasn't just about gambling or games of chance; it was the fundamental tool for reasoning in the face of uncertainty. If we cannot know everything with absolute certainty, then <u>the best we can do is quantify our degree of belief or knowledge</u> about something based on the available evidence. This quantification is precisely what probability theory provides.

- **Induction and Analogy are Probabilistic:**

  Laplace points out that even in disciplines traditionally seen as "certain," like mathematics, the methods by which we extend our knowledge (induction – drawing general conclusions from specific observations; and analogy – inferring new information based on similarities) are inherently probabilistic. We infer future events or unknown properties based on patterns observed in the past, but there's no logical guarantee that those patterns will always hold with 100% certainty. <u>The strength of our inference is a matter of probability</u>.

- **A Unified Framework for Knowledge:**

  Laplace saw probability theory as the overarching framework that connects all human knowledge. From predicting the orbits of planets to assessing the credibility of witnesses, making medical diagnoses, or even philosophical reasoning, he believed that the <u>principles of probability were indispensable for forming rational judgments</u>. It was a universal "calculus of common sense."

- **Subjective vs. Objective Probability (Proto-Bayesianism):**

  Importantly, Laplace's view of probability was largely epistemic or subjective (closer to what we now call Bayesian probability). For him, <u>probability reflected our *state of knowledge* or *ignorance* about an event, rather than an inherent objective property of the world</u> (though he believed in a deterministic universe where a hypothetical omniscient being would know everything with certainty). Since we are not such beings, probability becomes our guide.

In essence, Laplace's idea was that we live in a world where perfect knowledge is unattainable. Therefore, the most rational approach is to embrace this uncertainty and use probability as the framework for understanding, predicting, and making decisions based on the best available, though incomplete, information. This is the spirit that underpins the idea of the "Bayesian brain" and predictive processing we have been discussing so far.

This is wonderful for those who love mathematics and science. However, the average person is trying to be practical and needs to be able to apply complex principles like these in everyday life. At its heart, Bayesian thinking is a structured way to learn from experience and adjust our understanding of the world. It's how our brains often work naturally, but making the process explicit and simple can help us make better, more adaptive decisions. Here are four basic steps you can take to apply Bayesian thinking to everyday situations:

1. **Start with Your Best Guess (Prior Beliefs & Hypotheses):**

   Before you receive new information, what do you already suspect? What are your initial ideas or assumptions about what's going on or why something happened? Think of all the possible explanations, even the less likely ones. This is about being honest with yourself about your starting point and the different "stories" that could explain the situation.

2. **Gather New Information (Evidence):**

   Now, look for facts, observations, or reliable data that relate to your guesses. This is the sensory input from the world — what you see, hear, read, or are told. Critically, actively seek out information, and especially look for things that might challenge your initial ideas, not just confirm them.

3. **Weigh the New Information (Likelihood & Update):**

   This is the core of the update. For each of your initial guesses (hypotheses), ask: "How much does this new information support *or* contradict each of my guesses?"

   - If the new information strongly fits with one guess, that guess becomes much more likely.
   - If the new information makes a guess seem unlikely, the probability of that guess should go down significantly.
   - Weak information should only lead to small adjustments. This process is about being fair with the evidence and letting it shift your understanding proportionally.

4. **Form Your Updated Understanding (Posterior Beliefs & Iteration):**

   After weighing the new information, what's your best, most informed guess now? This new understanding becomes your *new starting point* or "prior belief" for the next round of learning. Real-world problems rarely have a single, immediate answer. You'll continuously gather more information and repeat this process, refining your understanding with each new piece of evidence until you reach a satisfactory conclusion or decision. This acknowledges that our knowledge is rarely 100% certain, but is constantly evolving and probabilistic.

Now let's take this process and use it in a practical example that we can all relate to these days. These days, I tend to stay away from local and global politics because it has become an environment where facts and reason seem to be less welcomed than in previous decades. Precisely because of this, I chose a political example to show how Bayesian thinking can be a valuable tool to make more informed decisions based on evidence:

Using Bayesian thinking to evaluate a candidate's economic plan

Imagine you're an undecided voter, trying to figure out which candidate's economic plan (Candidate A vs. Candidate B) will genuinely create jobs and bring stability. Here's how Bayesian thinking can help you decide:

1. **Start with Your Best Guess (Your "Hunch" or Prior):**

   - Before you've done deep research, you probably have a slight leaning. Maybe you generally like Candidate A's party, or Candidate B's style.
   - This is your **initial hunch** – your starting belief about whose plan is more likely to work. Crucially, you acknowledge it's just a starting point, not a fact. You are open to changing your mind.

2. **Actively Seek Out New Clues (The "Evidence"):**

   - Now, you become a detective. Don't just listen to the candidates; find *diverse, high-quality information*.
   - Candidate A's idea is a big corporate tax cut, promising job growth.
   - Candidate B's idea is a major government investment in infrastructure and green energy, promising direct job creation.
   - The Crucial Clue: You find a report from a *non-partisan economic research group*. This report analyzes similar policies historically. It finds that corporate tax cuts often lead to increased stock buybacks (not always more jobs), while targeted infrastructure investments tend to create jobs more directly and measurably. You also look at **what worked elsewhere**: similar infrastructure programs in other countries (or states) show positive employment, while tax cuts have mixed results.

3. **Weigh the Clues (The Likelihood & Update): How Much Does Each Clue Change Your Hunch?**

   - This is the core of Bayesian thinking: how strongly does each new piece of evidence push you towards one candidate or the other?
   - Candidate A's tax cut proposal might *initially fit* your hunch about their plan.
   - Candidate B's infrastructure plan might *initially fit* your hunch about their plan.
   - But then comes the non-partisan report:
     - This report directly *contradicts* Candidate A's claim about tax cuts creating jobs. This isn't just "different information"; it's

strong disconfirming evidence. Your initial hunch about Candidate A's plan should take a significant hit.

- Conversely, the report strongly *supports* the effectiveness of policies similar to Candidate B's. This is **strong, confirming evidence**, making your belief in Candidate B's plan much stronger.

4. **Form Your Updated Understanding (Posterior Beliefs & Iteration) - Your "New Hunch":**

    - Updated understanding: After weighing everything, your understanding has significantly shifted. You started with a slight lean towards Candidate A, but the evidence (especially the unbiased report) has pushed you firmly towards Candidate B's approach.

    - New starting point: This new, evidence-backed understanding becomes your **updated hunch**. It's not static; it's ready to be refined again if new information emerges.

    - Continued learning: You'll keep watching, reading, and learning, continuously sharpening your view. Each new piece of information will again feed back into this 4-step process, further refining your understanding until you feel confident in your choice for the election. Your "belief" is never static; it's always ready to be updated.

By following these steps, we can move beyond just "feeling" who to support or blindly accepting opinions, and instead build a more robust, evidence-driven understanding of which candidate's policies are more likely to achieve your desired outcomes. Beyond politics, this systematic approach is a powerful and practical tool that can help us improve how we understand and navigate reality in everyday life. In the end, this process is about making decisions based on the best-available evidence while remaining open to new information

Table 10 – Traditional vs Bayesian Learning principles

	Traditional Learning Model
Information Accumulation	Collect facts and skills through repetition.
Right vs Wrong	Focus on correct answers rather than reasoning processes.
Fixed Ability	Believe that intelligence and talent are largely predetermined.
Performance Focus	Success is measured by current achievement levels.

Bayesian Learning Model	
Belief Updating	Continuously revise understanding based on new evidence.
Probabilistic Knowledge	Hold information with appropriate confidence levels.
Growth Mindset	Believe that abilities develop through evidence-based practice.
Process Focus	Success is measured by quality of inference and adaptation.

Applying Bayesian principles can improve decision-making across various domains, from personal health choices to financial decisions to interpersonal relationships. By recognizing the Bayesian nature of our cognitive processes, we can work with rather than against our brain's natural inferential mechanisms.

The Reality Of Belief: A Scientific Perspective

Understanding how beliefs shape human experience has emerged as one of the most important frontiers in cognitive science. Far from being passive reflections of objective reality, beliefs function as active cognitive tools that fundamentally alter how we perceive, interpret, and interact with the world around us. This dynamic relationship between belief and experience has profound implications for personal development, social coordination, and how we construct our reality.

The Nature and Function of Beliefs

What Are Beliefs?

Beliefs can be defined as mental models or cognitive representations that we hold to be true about ourselves, others, and the world (**Schwitzgebel, Eric,** 2024). They range from simple factual beliefs ("I am a human being") to complex worldviews that organize our understanding of reality, including religious, political, or philosophical systems. Beliefs have several key characteristics:

- **Cognitive Content**:

    Beliefs contain propositional content; they are intentional states that can be expressed in the form "I believe that X" (**Fodor, Jerry,** 1987). This representational structure allows beliefs to serve as the building blocks of more complex cognitive processes.

- **Subjective Certainty**:

    Beliefs are held with varying degrees of confidence, from tentative hypotheses to unquestioned assumptions. This graduated certainty reflects the brain's sophisticated probabilistic reasoning systems (**Knill, David & Pouget, Alexandre**, 2004).

- **Emotional Valence**:

    Many beliefs have emotional associations that influence how strongly they are held and how resistant they are to change. The amygdala and other limbic structures integrate emotional significance with cognitive content, creating what researchers call "hot cognition" (**Metcalfe, Janet & Mischel, Walter,** 1999).

- **Interconnectedness**:

    Beliefs typically exist within networks of related beliefs, forming coherent systems that support and reinforce each other, a phenomenon cognitive scientists call a "web of belief" (**Quine, Willard & Ullian, Joe**, 1978). This interconnectedness explains why changing core beliefs often requires addressing entire belief systems.

- **Varying Accessibility**:

    Some beliefs are explicit and readily accessible to conscious awareness, while others remain implicit and influence behavior without conscious recognition. This distinction maps onto dual-process theories that differentiate between the *System 1* and *System 2 thinking* introduced earlier in the chapter. (**Kahneman**, 2011).

- **Neural Foundations of Belief**:

    According to neuroscientist **Rüdiger J. Seitz**, "beliefs are the neuropsychic product of fundamental brain processes that attribute affective meaning to concrete objects and events, enabling individual goal setting, decision making, and maneuvering in the environment." In essence, beliefs emerge from patterns of connectivity and activation across distributed neural networks, and these patterns create predictive models that the brain uses to interpret sensory input and guide behavior. The key brain networks involved in belief processing were introduced in the chapter 3's neuroplasticity section and chapter 4's neuroscience section. For completeness, here they are again:

- **Default Mode Network**: It is associated with self-referential thinking and belief maintenance (**Buckner, Randy,** et al., 2008).
- **Executive Control Networks**: They are involved in belief evaluation and updating (**Miller, Earl & Cohen, Jonathan**, 2001).
- **Salience Network**: It mediates between internal beliefs and external stimuli (**Seeley, William,** et al., 2007).

This distributed neural architecture suggests that beliefs are not stored in discrete locations but emerge from dynamic patterns of network activity that integrate cognitive, emotional, and social information.

Why Humans Form Beliefs

Belief formation serves several adaptive functions that have been crucial for human survival and social coordination:

1. **Prediction and Control**:

   Beliefs allow us to predict future events and exert control over our environment. We can anticipate consequences and adapt our behavior by forming accurate beliefs about cause-and-effect relationships. This predictive function aligns with the brain's fundamental role as a "prediction machine" (**Clark**, 2013; **Friston**, 2010).

2. **Cognitive Efficiency**:

   Beliefs provide mental shortcuts that reduce cognitive load. Rather than reasoning from first principles in every situation, we can rely on established beliefs to guide perception and decision-making (**Tversky & Kahneman**, 1974). This efficiency comes at the cost of potential biases but enables rapid responses in complex environments.

3. **Meaning and Coherence**:

   Beliefs help us construct meaningful narratives that organize our experience and provide a sense of coherence and purpose. This meaning-making function is particularly evident in existential and religious beliefs, which address fundamental questions about identity, mortality, and purpose (**Park, Crystal**, 2010).

4. **Social Coordination**:

   Shared beliefs facilitate social coordination and group cohesion. Common beliefs about values, norms, and reality itself allow humans to cooperate in large-scale social systems, a capacity that may have been crucial for our species' evolutionary success (**Tomasello** et al., 2012).

5. **Identity Formation**:

    Beliefs contribute to both personal and social identity, defining who we are, what groups we belong to, and how we relate to others. This identity function links beliefs to fundamental psychological needs for belonging and self-esteem (**Tajfel, H. & Turner, J.**, 1979).

    These functions highlight that beliefs are not merely passive representations of reality but also <u>active tools</u> that humans can use to navigate physical and social environments.

How Beliefs Shape Our Reality

Perception Filtering

Beliefs act as filters that influence what we perceive and how we interpret sensory information. This filtering occurs through several mechanisms:

- **Selective Attention**:

    Beliefs guide what aspects of our environment capture attention. Information aligning with existing beliefs is more likely to be noticed than contradictory information. We learned in the cognitive biases section that this phenomenon is known as "confirmation bias" (**Nickerson, Raymond**, 1998). Neuroscientifically, this reflects top-down attentional control from prefrontal regions to sensory areas.

- **Interpretation Bias**:

    Ambiguous information is interpreted in ways consistent with existing beliefs. The same event can be perceived very differently by people with different belief systems. This interpretive flexibility demonstrates the constructive nature of perception itself (**Gregory, Richard**, 1970)

- **Memory Encoding and Retrieval**:

    Beliefs influence both what information we encode into memory and what we later recall. Schema theory explains how pre-existing knowledge structures guide memory processes, with belief-consistent information showing enhanced recall (**Bartlett, F.**, 1932; **Alba, J. & Hasher, L.**, 1983).

- **Perceptual Filling-In**:

    When sensory information is incomplete or ambiguous, beliefs guide how the brain reconstructs missing details, <u>often confirming existing</u>

expectations. This process reflects the brain's predictive coding mechanisms (**Rao, Rajesh & Ballard, Dana**, 1999).

These processes create powerful feedback loops in which beliefs shape perception, and filtered perception reinforces those same existing beliefs, a phenomenon known as belief perseverance (**Ross, Lepper** et al., 1975), which is the tendency for beliefs to persist even in the face of contradictory evidence.

Behavioral Influences

Beliefs don't just shape how we perceive reality; they also influence how we act within it, further reinforcing our subjective reality through several mechanisms:

- **Self-Fulfilling Prophecies**:

  Beliefs about ourselves and others can create self-fulfilling prophecies by influencing behavior in ways that produce expected outcomes. Classic research by **Rosenthal, R.** and **Jacobson, L.** (1968) demonstrated this phenomenon in educational settings, where teacher expectations influenced student performance.

- **Behavioral Confirmation** :

  Our beliefs about others can elicit behaviors that confirm those beliefs. If we believe someone is hostile, our defensive behavior may prompt hostile responses that validate the initial belief (**Snyder, M.** et al., 1977).

- **Reality Testing**:

  Beliefs influence what evidence we seek and how we evaluate it. Motivated reasoning leads us to seek information supporting our beliefs while discounting contradictory evidence (**Klayman, J. & Ha, Y.**, 1987).

- **Environmental Selection**:

  Beliefs guide our choices about environments, activities, and social groups, leading us to select contexts that reinforce our existing beliefs and values. This selection process can create "echo chambers" that limit exposure to alternative perspectives (**Pariser, E.**, 2011).

- **Cognitive Dissonance and Belief Maintenance**

  When beliefs conflict with new information or experiences, cognitive dissonance theory explains how people typically resolve this tension by changing their interpretation of events rather than updating core beliefs (**Festinger, L.**, 1957). This resistance to belief change, while sometimes problematic, also provides psychological stability and protects against manipulation.

Through these mechanisms, beliefs can create feedback loops that strengthen over time, sometimes leading to increasingly divergent realities among individuals or groups with different belief systems.

Harnessing Beliefs for Personal Growth

Understanding the powerful role of beliefs in shaping our experience of reality opens possibilities for intentionally cultivating beliefs that promote well-being and personal growth. But more than understanding, we have to be intentional and active examiners and critics of why we believe what we believe. The following are some evidence-based approaches that can be helpful during this process of scrutiny and change of beliefs:

1. **Cognitive Restructuring**:

    Techniques from **Cognitive Behavioral Therapy (CBT)** can help replace limiting beliefs with more adaptive alternatives. This involves identifying distorted thinking patterns, challenging them with evidence, and practicing alternative interpretations (**Beck**, 1976; **Ellis**, 1962). Neuroimaging studies show that cognitive restructuring activates prefrontal regions associated with cognitive control while dampening amygdala reactivity (**Ochsner, K.** & **Gross, J.**, 2005).

2. **Belief Experimentation**:

    Temporarily adopting new beliefs as testable hypotheses can bypass resistance to belief change. This experimental approach can allow gradual belief updating based on direct experience while maintaining psychological safety.

3. **Metacognitive Awareness**:

    Developing awareness of our believing process (i.e., noticing when and how we form and maintain beliefs) can create space for more intentional and useful belief formation. This metacognitive approach draws on research showing that awareness of unconscious or uncontrollable mental processes can reduce the influence of cognitive biases (**Wilson, T.** & **Brekke, N.**, 1994).

4. **Exposure to Diverse Perspectives**:

    Engaging with diverse viewpoints and experiences can highlight the contingent nature of beliefs and can open possibilities for alternative ways of understanding reality. Research on "perspective-taking" shows it can reduce intergroup bias and increase empathy (**Galinsky, A. & Moskowitz, G.**, 2000).

5. **Embodied Belief Change**:

   Beliefs are not purely cognitive but are embodied in physical and emotional responses. Research on embodied cognition suggests that since we learn primarily with our bodies and not just with our brain, practices engaging the body (such as movement, breathwork, or somatic experiencing) can facilitate belief change at deeper levels (**Moyosore, A.**, et al 2022).

6. **Cultivate Growth Mindset:**

   In her book **Mindset**, Psychologist **Carol Dweck's** shares with us the powerful framework of a "growth mindset" we mentioned briefly in the previous section. Dweck tells us that a "fixed mindset" assumes abilities are innate, leading to avoidance of challenges and fear of failure. In contrast, a "growth mindset" sees abilities as developable through effort, embracing challenges, and learning from setbacks. Cultivating a growth mindset (even if challenging) is key to harnessing beliefs for growth. Neuroscience research shows that growth mindset beliefs are associated with increased neural plasticity and learning.

7. **The Four Column Technique – A Practical Application:**

   This is a practical application of well-established psychological theories, aiming to help individuals become more aware of their thought patterns and develop more balanced and realistic perspectives, ultimately leading to improved emotional well-being. While the Four Column Technique itself isn't directly attributed to a single, specific neuroscience publication or scientist, it's scientifically grounded in CBT research and the broader understanding of how thoughts, feelings, and behaviors are interconnected in the brain. While not validated as a specific intervention, it draws on well-established principles of cognitive reappraisal and prefrontal cortex (PFC) function in emotion regulation. The exercise goes as follows:

   1. Identify a limiting belief you hold (e.g., "I'm not creative").
   2. In the first column, write all the evidence that seems to support this belief.
   3. In the second column, write all the evidence that contradicts this belief.
   4. In the third column, write alternative interpretations of the supporting evidence.

5. In the fourth column, formulate a more balanced and empowering belief.

For example, consider the following limiting belief: "I am not creative". The table below shows the four-column technique applied to this limiting belief:

Table 11 – Four Column Technique

Supporting Evidence	Evidence Against	Alternatives	Balanced Belief
My art teacher criticized my work.	I come up with unique solutions at work.	My art teacher had narrow criteria.	I express creatively in many ways.
I can't draw well.	I created a beautiful garden.	Drawing is just one form of creativity.	Even if traditional artistic skills aren't my strength.

It is important to note that the scientific source of the Four Column Technique lies within the empirically supported cognitive behavioral therapy framework (CBT) developed by **Aaron T. Beck** and complemented by the principles of **Rational Emotive Behavior Therapy (REBT)** by **Albert Ellis**.

Regularly examining our beliefs, especially those that are limiting or causing distress, is the first step toward intentional belief cultivation. Questions like "What evidence supports this belief?" and "How is this belief serving me today?" can help identify beliefs that may need updating. However, that belief-change capacity varies among individuals due to factors including personality traits (openness to experience), cognitive flexibility, and neurobiological differences (**DeYoung, C.** et al., 2010). Some core beliefs may be particularly resistant to change due to their centrality to identity and emotional significance. Additionally, not all belief change is beneficial. Stable beliefs provide psychological anchoring and protect against manipulation. The goal should be developing flexibility in belief systems rather than constant belief revision.

In addition to individual differences and limitations, we must also acknowledge that beliefs develop within cultural and social contexts that powerfully shape their content and structure. Cultural neuroscience research reveals that even basic cognitive processes like attention and categorization vary across cultures, reflecting different belief systems about the nature of self and world (**Nisbett, R. & Miyamoto, Y.**, 2005). Understanding these influences helps contextualize individual belief systems within broader social frameworks.

The good news is that moving forward, we will see more peer-reviewed data on this topic because scientific understanding of beliefs has profound implications for education, therapy, organizational change, and social policy. As we develop more sophisticated models of belief formation and change, we can design interventions that promote adaptive believing while respecting individual autonomy and cultural diversity. Future research directions include investigating the neural mechanisms of belief change, developing personalized approaches based on individual differences, and exploring the role of technology in shaping modern belief systems.

Beliefs represent one of the most powerful forces shaping human experience. By understanding their nature, function, and mechanisms of influence, we gain tools for crafting our relationship with reality more intentionally. This understanding reveals that while our experience of reality is indeed constructed through beliefs, this <u>construction process can itself become a tool for growth, well-being, and positive change</u>.

The key insight is not that beliefs are "merely subjective" but that their subjective nature grants us agency in shaping our experience. By consciously cultivating adaptive beliefs while maintaining appropriate flexibility and openness to new information, we can create more empowering and effective ways of navigating both our inner and outer worlds. Maybe then we can live in a reality that acknowledges the constructed nature of our experience while using that understanding to foster growth and well-being.

Truth and Identity:
Who You Are vs. What You Believe

The Belief-Identity Fusion Problem

Understanding beliefs as Bayesian priors reveals why changing them feels so threatening: We're not just updating information but potentially restructuring our sense of self. When beliefs become fused with identity, questioning those beliefs activates the same threat-detection systems as physical danger, making rational evaluation nearly impossible. This fusion creates what psychologist **Dan Kahan** calls "identity-protective cognition," which is our tendency to process information in ways that <u>protect our sense of who we are rather than seeking accuracy</u>. The result is that we often resist updating our beliefs even when presented with compelling evidence, because doing so feels like a fundamental threat to our selfhood.

In the previous section, we introduced research by social psychologist **Leon Festinger** on cognitive dissonance. His work reveals that humans possess a powerful drive for internal consistency that can override commitment to accuracy. <u>When deeply-held beliefs are challenged, the brain's anterior cingulate cortex (the same region activated by physical pain) shows increased activity, explaining why belief challenges can literally hurt</u>. This neurological reality means that belief-identity fusion isn't merely psychological stubbornness but reflects deep-seated survival mechanisms designed to maintain social belonging and self-coherence.

Psychologist **Jonathan Haidt's** research on moral psychology demonstrates that people often make intuitive judgments first, then construct rational justifications afterward. This "motivated reasoning" becomes particularly pronounced when beliefs are tied to identity, leading to what researchers call "biased information processing," which is selectively attending to confirming evidence while dismissing contradictory data regardless of its quality.

Signs of Belief-Identity Fusion

- **Emotional Reactivity to Intellectual Challenges**:

    Feeling personally attacked when beliefs are questioned indicates that the belief has become integrated into your sense of self. Research by psychologist **Tim Kasser** shows that people with secure identity foundations can engage with challenging ideas without experiencing threat. In contrast, those with belief-dependent identities show measurable stress responses to intellectual disagreement.

- **Cognitive Rigidity and Perspective-Taking Deficits**:

    Inability to consider alternative perspectives without emotional distress reflects what cognitive scientists call "cognitive flexibility impairment." Studies using neuroimaging show that when identity-relevant beliefs are challenged, brain regions associated with analytical thinking show decreased activation while emotion-regulation areas work overtime.

- **Social Identity Dependence**:

    Using beliefs as the primary basis for identity, social belonging, and self-worth creates what psychologist **Henri Tajfel** called "social identity theory" dynamics – where group membership becomes more important than truth-seeking (recall Tajfel and Turner's identity formation work introduced in the previous section). This can lead to "tribal epistemology" where truth becomes defined by group consensus rather than evidence.

- **Betrayal Narrative**:

    Treating belief revision as betrayal of fundamental principles reflects what researchers call "psychological reactance," which is the tendency to resist changing beliefs specifically because change feels like surrendering autonomy or admitting error. This creates a psychological trap where learning becomes equated with losing.

- **Existential Anxiety from Uncertainty**:

    Experiencing existential anxiety when certainty is challenged indicates what psychologist **Arie Kruglanski** calls "need for cognitive closure," an individual difference in preference for certainty over ambiguity that can interfere with truth-seeking when taken to extremes.

Healthy Belief-Identity Relationship

Research across psychology, philosophy, and contemplative science reveals characteristics of psychologically healthy relationships between beliefs and identity:

- **Provisional Belief Holding**:

    Maintaining beliefs as provisional tools rather than absolute truths reflects what philosopher **Karl Popper** called "critical rationalism," which is the recognition that all knowledge claims are tentative and subject to revision. Studies by psychologist **Mark Leary** show that intellectual humility (including provisional belief holding) correlates with better learning outcomes and more accurate beliefs.

- **Curiosity Maintenance**:

    Preserving curiosity about alternative perspectives requires the "growth mindset" we introduced in the previous section. Neuroscience research shows that curiosity activates the brain's reward systems, making learning intrinsically motivating rather than threatening.

- **Character-Based Identity**:

    Deriving identity from values and character rather than specific beliefs provides what psychologists call "identity diversification": having multiple sources of self-worth that create resilience when any particular belief system is challenged. Research shows that people with diversified identities demonstrate greater psychological flexibility and lower reactivity to belief challenges.

- **Growth-Oriented Revision**:

    <u>Treating belief revision as growth rather than failure requires reframing cognitive change from loss to gain</u>. Studies in educational psychology show that students who view mistakes and revisions as learning oppor-

tunities demonstrate greater academic achievement and lower anxiety than those who view them as failures.

- **Process-Based Security**:

    Finding security in the process of learning rather than fixed conclusions reflects what contemplative traditions call "beginner's mind" and what psychologists term "tolerance for ambiguity." Research shows that comfort with uncertainty correlates with creativity, problem-solving ability, and psychological well-being.

The Values-Beliefs Distinction

Understanding the difference between values and beliefs provides a crucial framework for maintaining identity coherence while adapting to new evidence and experiences.

Values: The Stable Foundation

Values represent fundamental principles about what matters most to us: compassion, integrity, growth, justice, beauty, and connection. Research on universal values by psychologist **Shalom Schwartz** shows that while value priorities vary across individuals and cultures, core human values remain relatively stable throughout adulthood and provide consistent guidance for major life decisions.

Values operate at what psychologists call the "self-concept" level, meaning they define who we aspire to be rather than what we think about the world. This distinction is crucial because values can remain consistent even as beliefs about how to express those values change dramatically. Neuroscience research shows that value-based decisions activate the brain's reward and meaning-making systems, providing intrinsic motivation and psychological coherence.

Basic Characteristics of Values:

- **Stability**: Provide consistent life direction across changing circumstances.
- **Motivational Power**: Generate energy and commitment for sustained action.
- **Identity Integration**: Become incorporated into the fundamental sense of self.
- **Cross-Situational**: Apply across different domains and contexts.
- **Emotional Resonance**: Connect to deep feelings of meaning and purpose.

Beliefs: The Adaptive Tools

Beliefs represent specific ideas about how the world works or what strategies are most effective: political positions, religious doctrines, and scientific theories, personal approaches to relationships or career. Unlike values, beliefs should ideally remain responsive to evidence, experience, and changing circumstances.

Research on paradigm shifts by philosopher **Thomas Kuhn** reveals that even scientific beliefs (supposedly based purely on evidence) can become entrenched and resistant to change. However, the most effective belief systems maintain what Kuhn called "normal-science" flexibility within paradigms while remaining open to "revolutionary-science" paradigm shifts when evidence accumulates.

Characteristics of Adaptive Beliefs:

- **Responsiveness**: Change appropriately based on new evidence or experience.
- **Pragmatic Focus**: Evaluated based on effectiveness rather than comfort.
- **Specificity**: Address particular situations rather than global worldviews.
- **Evidence-Based**: Grounded in observation, reasoning, and reliable sources.
- **Provisional**: Held with appropriate confidence levels based on available evidence.

We can maintain consistent values while adapting beliefs as we encounter new evidence and experiences. For example, valuing compassion (stable) might lead us to update beliefs about the most effective ways to help others (changeable) based on new research showing that certain interventions produce better outcomes than others.

This integration allows for what psychologist **Albert Bandura** calls "moral agency":

> *Moral Agency: the ability to act consistently with your values while adapting your strategies based on learning and experience.*

Research shows that people who successfully integrate stable values with flexible beliefs demonstrate greater life satisfaction, more effective goal achievement, and lower psychological distress than those who either rigidly maintain all beliefs or frequently change core values.

The relationship between truth-seeking and identity represents one of the most fundamental challenges in human psychology and epistemology.

Research across multiple disciplines reveals that healthy truth-seeking requires what might be called "flexible stability": maintaining a stable foundation of values and character while adapting beliefs and strategies based on evidence and experience.

Successfully navigating truth and identity requires recognizing that our deepest self (values, character, and approach to life) can remain consistent. At the same time, our specific beliefs and strategies evolve based on learning and experience. This represents not a loss of authenticity but its highest expression: being true to our commitment to growth, understanding, and effective action in the world.

The goal is not to eliminate all emotional investment in beliefs, but to invest more deeply in the values and processes that generate beliefs rather than in any particular conclusions. This creates what researchers call "psychological flexibility," which is the ability to adapt thoughts and behaviors to changing circumstances while maintaining connection to what matters most.

Ultimately, the strongest identity foundation comes not from being right about everything, but from being someone who seeks truth with integrity, adapts with wisdom, and acts with compassion. This identity can remain stable and coherent while supporting the intellectual flexibility that both truth-seeking and an ever-changing world require.

Chapter 5 Summary: Key Insights

Our brain operates as a sophisticated Bayesian inference machine, continuously updating beliefs based on new evidence in mathematically optimal ways. Being aware of this process allows us to work with our natural cognitive architecture to make better decisions, learn more effectively, and navigate uncertainty with greater wisdom. Here are some essential takeaways:

1. **Probabilistic Knowledge**:

    All human knowledge is fundamentally probabilistic rather than absolutely certain, and holding beliefs with appropriate confidence levels improves day-to-day decision-making.

2. **Controlled Hallucination**:

    Our experience of reality emerges from Bayesian inference processes that combine prior beliefs with sensory evidence to create our constructed perception of the world.

3. **Individual Processing**:

   While our brain naturally performs sophisticated statistical reasoning, the conscious application of Bayesian principles can enhance our explicit reasoning about uncertainty

4. **Belief as Priors**:

   Our beliefs function as Bayesian priors that profoundly influence how we interpret subsequent experience, making belief examination and updating crucial for growth.

5. **Personal Reality Construction**:

   Learning to appropriately weigh different sources of evidence based on their reliability is key to effective Bayesian reasoning in daily life.

   The Bayesian inference model provides us with practical tools for daily life. The goal here isn't to become a perfect Bayesian reasoner. That's impossible. The goal is to become more aware of our brain's natural inference processes and learn to work with them more skillfully:

1. Decision-Making Framework

   - Identify your priors (current beliefs/assumptions)
   - Gather diverse evidence
   - Weigh evidence by reliability
   - Update beliefs proportionally
   - Remain open to new information

2. Emotional Regulation Strategy

   - Recognize emotions as predictions about future outcomes
   - Distinguish between prediction and reality
   - Update emotional models based on actual results
   - Practice self-compassion during prediction errors

3. Learning Acceleration Method

   - Treat mistakes as valuable prediction errors
   - Actively seek disconfirming evidence
   - Focus on updating models rather than being "right"
   - Embrace uncertainty as information for better predictions

4. Relationship Enhancement Tool

    - Notice assumptions about others' intentions
    - Test social predictions through honest communication
    - Update your models of how relationships work
    - Practice intellectual humility in disagreements

Understanding our brain as a Bayesian inference machine reveals the sophisticated mathematical principles underlying individual consciousness. However, this raises a crucial question: What happens when millions of these individual Bayesian brains interact in complex social networks? In the next chapter, we'll explore how the same predictive processes that construct individual reality can create powerful collective insights, or dangerous shared illusions that can distort our social world.

CHAPTER 6
TRUTH, SOCIAL REALITY AND COLLECTIVE ILLUSIONS

"In a time of deceit telling the truth is a revolutionary act."
Often attributed to George Orwell

Mario scrolls through his social media feed during lunch break, feeling increasingly anxious about the state of the world.

Every post seems to confirm that society is falling apart: crime is skyrocketing, young people are lazy, and "most people" support policies he finds alarming. He feels isolated and concerned, believing he's part of a small minority of reasonable people in a world gone mad.

What Mario doesn't realize is that he's trapped in a collective illusion. Although there is some truth to what he is reading somewhere in the world, in reality, crime rates in his city have been declining for years. Most young people are working harder than previous generations. And surveys show that the majority of people actually share his core values. The problem is that the people who see eye to eye with him are not the ones creating the overwhelming volume of angry content online.

Mario isn't alone in his distorted perception. Across the country, millions of people are experiencing similar false realities, each believing they're isolated voices of reason surrounded by extremism. The loudest, most emotional voices have convinced everyone else that they represent the majority, when they're actually a small but very vocal and active minority.

If our individual brains construct reality through sophisticated Bayesian processes, what happens when millions of these prediction machines interact in complex social networks? The result can be extraordinary collective wisdom, or dangerous shared illusions that feel absolutely real to everyone involved. This is the power of collective illusions, which are shared false beliefs that feel absolutely real because "everyone knows" they're true. These illusions don't require conspiracy or manipulation; <u>they emerge naturally when our individual Bayesian brains interact with information environments designed to amplify engagement rather than accuracy</u>.

Understanding how these illusions form and spread is crucial for navigating our complex world. More importantly, learning to distinguish between reliable knowledge and convincing falsehood has become a survival skill in the digital age.

This chapter explores one of the most crucial challenges of our time: how to navigate truth in a world where reality is actively constructed both individually and collectively. We'll discover how the same cognitive processes that enable learning and adaptation can create persistent false beliefs when they operate at social scales. We'll also develop frameworks for distinguishing between reliable knowledge and convincing illusion – skills that have never been more essential.

The journey ahead reveals why understanding truth requires more than good intentions or critical thinking skills. It demands awareness of how our social nature shapes what we believe, how information technologies amplify both insight and delusion, and how different types of truth serve different purposes in human life.

When Individual Minds Create Shared Illusions

Here's a disturbing thought experiment: What if most of what you believe about "what everyone else thinks" is completely wrong? Research by social psychologist **Todd Rose** reveals this isn't hypothetical; it's happening right now. In study after study, Rose found that people massively misperceive what their fellow citizens actually believe. We think we're surrounded by extremists when most people are actually quite moderate. We assume others support policies we oppose when surveys show broad agreement on core values.

This isn't stupidity or ignorance. It's the result of a simple but powerful mechanism: Our brains use a mental shortcut, assuming the loudest voices we hear most often represent the majority opinion. In Mario's case, the angry political posts that generate the most engagement dominate his feed, creating the illusion that everyone is polarized and hostile.

Bayesian inference doesn't happen in isolation; it occurs within social contexts where collective beliefs shape "shared reality." A shared reality is what happens when this predictive, constructive process extends beyond the individual mind and starts shaping our perception of our social environment. Just as our brains can generate individual sensory and emotional illusions when predictions diverge from objective input, so too can our collective minds coalesce around powerful "collective illusions."

Remember that our brain is essentially a prediction machine, constantly generating forecasts about what will happen next based on past experience and current context. But here's the crucial insight: much of our "past experience" comes not from direct observation but from social learning - what others have told us, what we've read, and what our culture has taught us to expect. This creates a fascinating feedback loop:

> Our individual Bayesian brain uses socially acquired priors to make predictions, while simultaneously contributing to the social environment that shapes others' priors.

When this process works well, it enables collective learning and the accumulation of knowledge across generations. When it goes wrong, it creates shared false realities that can persist for decades or centuries.

What is a Collective Illusion?

The concept of collective illusions builds upon and intersects with several long-standing theories in social psychology that address the dynamics between individual beliefs and group behavior. The general concept originated from the work of American psychologists **Floyd Allport** and **Daniel Katz** in 1931, building upon Allport's earlier discussions in 1924 regarding the "illusion of universality of opinions." Their research observed the following:

- Individuals sometimes hold a mistaken understanding of the values and beliefs of other group members.
- When privately surveyed, individuals would express beliefs that differed from their perceived group norms.
- These private beliefs also diverged from their public actions within the group.
- This misperception often compelled individuals to act contrary to their own beliefs due to a fear of negative group reactions.

Known at the time as "pluralistic ignorance," Allport and Katz's work has experienced renewed interest in social psychology today, with researchers now applying it to modern phenomena from climate change action to social media behavior. As defined in contemporary research, pluralistic ignorance (known today as collective illusion) is a phenomenon in which people mistakenly believe that others predominantly hold an opinion different from their own. The theoretical frameworks for pluralistic ignorance involve a dissonance between people's public actions and their true beliefs. Modern approaches, such as agent-based models, distinguish between internal (private) and external (public) opinions to investigate their manifestation. The degree of uncertainty concerning the population distribution of attitudes significantly influences what individuals learn about the group. Classic examples illustrating pluralistic ignorance include:

Table 12 – Examples of Pluralistic Ignorance

Example	Description
Classroom setting	Students may refrain from asking questions despite being confused, assuming that everyone else understands the material because no one else is speaking up.
Bystander effect	Individuals in emergencies may fail to act, assuming others will intervene, or they may be reluctant to act differently from the group's apparent inaction.
Emperor's new clothes	Fictional yet potent illustration, where townspeople publicly agree with an obvious lie about the emperor's attire due to fear of appearing unintelligent, despite privately seeing the truth.
Racial Segregation in the United States	Pluralistic ignorance has been cited as a factor exacerbating support for racial segregation, stemming from misperceived popular backing.
Alcohol consumption in college campuses	Students often believe their peers are more comfortable with heavy drinking than they truly are, leading to increased participation in such behaviors.
Public concern for climate change	A significant majority of the public may be concerned about climate change but remain silent, erroneously believing they are in the minority with their concern.

In his book **Collective Illusions**, **Todd Rose** confirms that these illusions occur when most people in a group publicly conform to perceived majority opinions that contradict their private beliefs, thus creating a collective hallucination of social realities. According to Rose, these are not merely differences of opinion but profound misrepresentations of the aggregate private beliefs within a social system, representing a deceptive social construct. This shared fiction is implicitly upheld because individuals believe everyone else is upholding it. This phenomenon is deeply rooted in the very same predictive processing mechanisms that shape individual perception: our brains, inherently efficient, rely on "social priors" (predictions about the thoughts, values, and intentions of others) to navigate the complex social landscape.

The core mechanism of collective illusions is a misperception of true majority opinion, leading to decisions contrary to private values and potentially suboptimal collective outcomes. This is all accentuated through modern technology, especially social media, which significantly amplifies these illusions by distorting perceptions of consensus. This ends up creating what Rose calls a "funhouse-of-mirrors" effect, where <u>collective reflection becomes unrecognizable from individual realities</u>. The mechanism operates through a simple but powerful cognitive error:

> *"Humans use a mental shortcut assuming the loudest voices repeated the most are the majority."*

Neuroscientific research reveals this conformity is based on reinforcement learning mechanisms, where neural error-monitoring activity signals <u>the most fundamental social mistake: that of being too different from others</u> (**Klucharev, V.,** et al., 2009). Uncovering these hidden realities requires innovative methodological approaches and fostering environments that encourage authentic expression.

It is wonderful that researchers are investing time and resources to understand this problem, but what can we do to help ourselves? We can begin by understanding the problem at hand. The following sections provide us with a high-level breakdown of how collective illusions sneak up on us and some of the things we can do to not fall prey to them.

Understanding the basic mechanism of collective illusions (mistaking vocal minorities for silent majorities) helps explain why these phenomena are so persistent and difficult to correct. But what makes them truly dangerous is their "self-perpetuating nature."

The Self-Perpetuating Cycle

A critical aspect of collective illusions is their self-perpetuating nature. Rose postulates that all individuals contribute to the creation and maintenance of these illusions. When people publicly conform based on a mistaken belief about the majority's opinion, their public display of conformity inadvertently reinforces that very misperception for others. This establishes a feedback loop where the illusion strengthens itself, even in the absence of malicious intent, thanks in part to that mental shortcut we mentioned earlier: *the loudest voices repeated the most are the majority*. This biological predisposition makes it inherently challenging to dismantle collective illusions, as the very act of individual self-preservation (conforming to a perceived norm) inevitably entrenches the collective deception. Understanding this cycle underscores the necessity for deliberate interventions to break it. Here is a summary of the cycle to be observed and questioned:

1. Vocal minorities express strong opinions publicly.
2. Individuals observe public behavior/expressions.
3. They assume these loud voices represent most people's true beliefs.

4. They conform publicly while maintaining private dissent to avoid seeming different.
5. Their conformity reinforces the illusion for others, as silence is interpreted as agreement.
6. The cycle strengthens over time as people end up believing false narratives about social reality.

Recent neuroscientific studies using fMRI and ERP techniques have identified specific brain mechanisms underlying social conformity, including activation in the rostral cingulate zone and nucleus accumbens when individuals' opinions conflict with perceived group consensus (**Stallen, Mirre** & **Sanfey, Alan**, 2015).

Technological Amplification - The Digital Age Crisis

Social Media as an Accelerant

Modern technology, especially social media, plays a profound role in amplifying collective illusions. What were once rare academic phenomena have exploded and are now everywhere due to the pervasive nature of social media. Social media platforms facilitate a distorted perception of consensus, making it easy for a vocal fringe to end up being perceived as representing a bigger consensus than they do.

This digital environment allows for the rapid dissemination of perceived norms, often by a vocal minority, creating echo chambers where misperceptions are constantly reinforced, and challenging them becomes increasingly difficult. The sheer volume and speed of information, coupled with algorithmic amplification, mean that the "loudest voices" are no longer confined to one's immediate social circle but can represent a global, often artificial, majority. This amplification transforms collective illusions from a localized social phenomenon into a systemic societal threat, impacting democracy, public health, and individual well-being on an unprecedented scale.

Modern research confirms concerns about technology's role in collective illusions, with 66% of U.S. consumers believing that 76% or more of news on social media is biased, and global surveys showing 60% believe news organizations regularly report false stories (Redline Digital, 2024). Social media platforms create perfect conditions for collective illusions through:

- **Algorithmic amplification** of vocal minorities;
- **Echo chambers** that reinforce misperceptions;

- **Bot-driven artificial consensus** (with up to 66% of pandemic misinformation spread by bots); and
- **Rapid viral spread** of false narratives.

Recent data shows that 52% of TikTok users in 2024 regularly get their news there, up from just 22% in 2020, demonstrating social media's growing influence as a news source, especially among younger demographics (Pew Research Center, Short Reads 2024).

The Misinformation Ecosystem

Misinformation can be defined as information that is false or misleading according to the best currently established knowledge. Contemporary studies reveal alarming trends: a 2023 University of Arizona study found that approximately 40% of medical videos on TikTok contained medical misinformation, while vaccine confidence among Americans decreased from April 2021 to October 2023 (Brookings, 2024; Boston University, 2024). This creates a feedback loop where:

- Misinformation spreads rapidly;
- People assume others believe false information;
- They modify their behavior based on perceived consensus, and
- This reinforces the original false narrative.

The current communications landscape has become a fertile breeding ground for misinformation and disinformation campaigns, with a pervasive sense of institutional distrust fueling false narratives. While misinformation is often spread unintentionally, disinformation is spread with the deliberate intent to deceive. In a Harvard Kennedy School study, 14% of those surveyed admitted to knowingly sharing false political information. This new misinformation and disinformation ecosystem demands for more advanced approach to information consumption (Misinformation Review, Harvard Kennedy School, 2023).

The Neurobiology of Social Conformity

We've established that social conformity is the act of aligning one's attitudes, beliefs, and behaviors with group norms. Advanced neuroscientific research has revealed that conformity involves neural signals similar to reinforcement learning, with brain regions like the rostral cingulate zone and nucleus accumbens triggering "prediction error" signals when individual opinions conflict with group consensus. This deep-seated biological predisposition makes collective illusions particularly potent and challenging to overcome, implying that interventions must address not only cognitive misperceptions but also these underlying neural reward and punishment systems associated with social alignment. Here are some key findings of recent scientific research:

- Conformity activates reward/punishment systems in the brain.
- Social influence affects basic perception, not just conscious decision-making.
- Peer presence literally changes brain activity in adolescents.
- The brain processes group disagreement as an "error" requiring correction.

But it doesn't end here. Recent research has also explored conformity in virtual environments. Studies demonstrate that conformity can be elicited by virtual humans and artificial majorities, with the ambiguity of the task influencing the degree of conformity. Increased task difficulty and reduced anonymity within immersive virtual environments have been shown to heighten conformity rates.

Why Does This Matter to Your Daily Life?

Becoming aware of collective illusions is an important step toward improved quality of life. Here are some warning signs you might be experiencing a collective illusion:

Red flags:

- "Everyone knows that..." (but no one has direct experience).
- Strong emotions accompany claims about what "most people" think.
- Dissenting voices are notably absent or dismissed.
- Claims align suspiciously with what you want to believe.
- The only evidence is "common sense" or social media.

Reality check questions:

- Who specifically believes this besides the loudest voices?
- What would I need to see to change my mind?
- Am I confusing "people I hear from" with "most people"?
- Could I explain the opposing view in a way its supporters would recognize?

Bottom Line: We can all fall for collective illusions. It is your responsibility to be aware of them and be prepared to challenge them. Pick one belief you hold about "what most people think" and look for actual data. You might be surprised.

Understanding how collective illusions emerge from our social cognitive architecture reveals a fundamental challenge: If our individual minds construct reality through prediction and inference, and our collective minds can create shared false realities that feel completely convincing, how can we hope to distinguish truth from illusion?

This question becomes even more complex when we realize that truth itself isn't a simple, monolithic concept but comes in different forms that serve different purposes in human life. To navigate our constructed realities wisely, we need frameworks for understanding these different dimensions of truth.

Understanding Truth in a World of Constructed Realities

If our brain constructs reality through predictive processes, as we discovered in the previous chapter, what does it mean to speak of "truth" at all? This isn't merely an academic question; it's one of the most practical challenges we face daily. Every decision we make, from choosing what to believe in the news to determining whom to trust, reflects our relationship with truth.

In our age of information abundance and competing narratives, understanding different approaches to truth isn't an intellectual luxury; it's a survival skill. The same predictive brain that enables consciousness also makes us vulnerable to bias, manipulation, and self-deception. Yet this vulnerability comes with an extraordinary opportunity: <u>by understanding how truth-seeking actually works, we can develop more reliable ways of navigating reality</u>.

Having explored how collective illusions can make false beliefs feel absolutely real, we now turn to a more fundamental question: What is truth, and how can we recognize it amid the noise of competing claims and constructed realities? The concept of truth becomes especially complex when we understand that all human knowledge is filtered through our individual and collective cognitive processes. This doesn't mean truth is purely relative, as some claims about reality are clearly more accurate than others. But it does mean that our approach to truth must account for the constructed nature of human understanding.

A Basic Definition of Truth

The concept of truth is complex and elusive, and has been debated by scholars, scientists, and ordinary people for centuries. This has resulted in many published theories and different categories and types of truth. If we dig into the origins (or etymology) of the word "truth", we find that at least two distinct categories surface right away: On the one hand, the word is associated with fidelity, loyalty, and sincerity; on the other hand, the word is also associated with agreement with fact or reality. We can see this clearly when looking up the word in the dictionary.

According to Merriam Webster dictionary, the first definition of Truth is

> "That which is in accordance with fact or reality."

The second definition in the dictionary states:

> "A fact or belief that is accepted to be true."

And here we have a problem because these definitions are subject to who or what determines what is a fact or what is real, and these can vary as a function of the society's belief system. At the highest level, we can identify two distinct categories of truth:

1. **The Major theories of truth**:

    a. These theories are the ones most people are familiar with, and that is because they come from some of the most popular thinkers in history.

    b. Some of these thinkers include Socrates, Plato, Aristotle, Thomas Aquinas, Baruch Spinoza, Friedrich Hegel, William James, John Dewey, and many others.

3. **The Formal theories of truth**:

    a. These tend to be anchored in logic and mathematics.

    b. The names of the thinkers promoting these theories are not as well-known. Still, they are giants nonetheless: Kurt Gödel, Alan Turing, Alfred Tarski, Bertrand Russell, and Saul Kripke are some of the primary contributors.

A Scientific Foundation: Objective Truths

As I was searching for more actionable definitions of truth, I found the work of **Neil deGrasse Tyson**. Yes, I know, he is an astrophysicist, but it turns out that it may be possible to rely on science to find a consistent and repeatable definition of truth. Instead of using the term Formal Truths, in his book **The Starry Messenger**, deGrasse Tyson uses the term *Objective Scientific Truths* and they rely on logic, evidence, observation, and/or experimentation. deGrasse Tyson states that:

> *"Objective truths are established by repeated experimentation and are NOT later found to be false. There is no need to question whether the earth is round, whether the sun is hot, whether humans and chimps share more than 98% identical DNA, or whether the air we breathe on earth is 78% nitrogen."*

Although my engineering mind tends to relate to this type of approach, I am also cognizant that it does not come without controversy. It has been my experience that some struggle with science and would not rely on it to define truth. Some believe that given enough time, science will contradict itself when it comes to its objective truths. Let's explore an example.

In 1666, 23-year-old **Isaac Newton**, published his Laws of Motion. These laws became undisputed universal truths for the following centuries and set the stage for a revolution of invention and advancement. 200 years later, in 1865, **James Clerk Maxwell** published a set of equations that combined electricity, magnetism, and light into a single phenomenon called "electromagnetism." It didn't take long for scientists to realize that there was something strange with these new equations in how they related to Newton's Laws. Newton's Laws seemed to struggle under very special conditions. It wasn't until **Albert Einstein** that we started making significant progress. Einstein tackled this problem in a very different way from everyone else before him. Recall that he was a patent officer; this means he did NOT have a lab, and at the time, he didn't have access to the type of equipment other scientists had. All he had was access to papers, publications, and his mind. So, he engaged in lots of thought experiments for years, and this eventually led to the very famous and unbelievable useful **Special and General Theories of Relativity** in 1905 and 1915 respectively.

Why am I telling you all this? Because today, many are still confused with this and many similar scientific concepts. Today, we hear people say things like "Newton was wrong, and Einstein corrected him." Others say that this proves that scientific objective truths cannot be considered truths because all it takes is time and new science to disprove the old. That could not be farther from the truth (pun completely intended). In fact, this example demonstrates why we can trust objective scientific truths and showcases the beauty of science and the scientific method:

1. It delivers objective truths, but it doesn't stop there.
2. It then proceeds to question those truths, indefinitely.

3. Nothing and no one is exempt from scientific scrutiny.

Newton's Laws of motion and gravity are still objective truths when gravity has a value inside a specific range. It is because of Newton that we can design and fly airplanes, launch rockets into deep space, build skyscrapers, predict projectile trajectories, and have satellites orbiting Earth. If we drop a ball from the top of a building, Newton's laws will tell us exactly when, where, and how fast the ball will hit the ground below. None of that changed with Einstein. Einstein's laws are objective truths in areas of our known universe beyond where Newton's laws of motion are valid – for example, at the event horizon of a black hole, or at the quantum level.

A concrete example of how both theories work together can be seen in GPS satellites. These satellites orbit at about 20,000 km above Earth and travel at approximately 14,000 km/h. At this altitude and speed, Einstein's theories predict that clocks on the satellites will run about 38 microseconds faster per day than clocks on Earth's surface (due to less gravitational time dilation and more special relativistic time dilation). Without accounting for these relativistic effects, GPS positioning would accumulate errors of about 10 km /day, making the system useless. Engineers must apply both Newton's laws (for basic orbital mechanics) and Einstein's relativistic corrections to make GPS work accurately. This example shows how scientific theories build upon rather than simply replace one another. As deGrasse Tyson states in his book:

> *"The era of modern physics did NOT discard Newton's Laws of motion and gravity. Instead, it described deeper realities of nature, made visible by ever-greater methods and tools of inquiry. Objective truths exist independent of that five–sense perception of reality. With proper tools, they can be verified by anybody, at any time and at any place."*

This approach to scientific truth aligns with philosopher **Karl Popper's** falsifiability criterion, which was introduced in chapter 5. According to Popper, what makes a theory scientific is not that it can be verified by multiple observations, but that it makes predictions that could potentially be shown to be incorrect. This criterion helps distinguish scientific theories from non-scientific claims and emphasizes that scientific knowledge is always provisional and subject to revision in light of new evidence.

We can see that scientists define truth as that which can only be proven via scientific observation. If science is continuously evolving, one could extrapolate that scientific truth is also evolving from one moment to the next. However, the very process of scientific observation, by its nature, involves gathering data in the present which then becomes a record of the past, and forming expectations about future outcomes. This temporal aspect, combined with the continuous evolution of scientific understanding, can lead to the perception that scientific truth itself is constantly shifting.

This dynamic nature of scientific truth, constantly refined by new evidence, can lead some to a relativistic extreme, questioning whether any objective truth can be known. While objective scientific truths excel at helping us understand the physical world, they are not the sole arbiters of human experience, which leads us nicely to the next section. However, sometimes it can be hard to tell the difference between truth and falsehood, especially in situations where there is uncertainty, ambiguity, deception, or bias.

Objective scientific truths provide our most reliable defense against collective illusions. Unlike socially constructed beliefs, scientific truths must withstand rigorous testing that actively seeks to disprove them. The peer-review process, replication requirements, and international collaboration create checks against the social conformity pressures that fuel collective illusions. However, as we've seen with climate change denial and vaccine misinformation, even well-established scientific truths can become entangled in collective illusion processes when they threaten existing beliefs or identity commitments.

So how do we cross this chasm? Not easily. We can count on objective scientific truths to help us understand much of the physical world. This is a great start, but fortunately not enough. This is because we as humans need a lot more than science to operate and coexist, which leads nicely to the next section.

Subjective Truths: When Objective Science is Not Enough

While scientific methods provide our most reliable tools for understanding physical reality, they face fundamental limitations when addressing human experience and meaning. As philosopher **David Hume** observed centuries ago, you cannot derive "ought" from "is." Hume's thought process leads us to a simple, yet powerful element of the human condition: Factual knowledge alone cannot determine values or purpose. Science is valuable and very much needed, but it has its limitations. Here are some examples of both:

Domains Where Science Excels:

- Physical processes and natural laws
- Measurable phenomena and quantifiable relationships
- Predictions about material systems
- Cause-and-effect relationships in controlled conditions

Domains Where Science Has Limitations:

- Questions of meaning and purpose

- Moral and ethical decisions
- Aesthetic judgments and beauty
- Individual life choices and personal values
- Consciousness and subjective experience

Science can tell us how the world works, but not what we should do with that knowledge. It can describe human behavior but not prescribe human values. Understanding these boundaries prevents both scientism (treating science as the only valid knowledge) and anti-intellectualism (rejecting scientific insights about human nature).

The Personal Dimension of Truth

So far, we've seen that some truths can be objective and absolute, meaning that they do not depend on anyone's perspective or opinion. If that is the case, we can also agree that there must be other truths that are relative and **subjective**, meaning they vary according to different contexts, cultures, or beliefs. With this in mind, we could come up with new categories such as logical truths, moral truths, historical truths, artistic truths, etc.

This is precisely the approach that the father of existentialism, Danish philosopher **Søren Kierkegaard,** took as he tackled the problem of truth. Kierkegaard agrees that objective truths for the study of subjects like math, science, and history are relevant and necessary, but argues that objective truths do not shed any light on a person's inner relationship with existence. In his publication "**Concluding Unscientific Postscript,**" he attacks **G.W.F Hegle's** science of logic and argues that at best, objective truths can only provide a severely narrowed perspective that has little to do with one's actual experience of life.

Kierkegaard proposed that truth is subjective, meaning that it depends on the individual's personal commitment and passion. He defined subjective truth as the truth of faith, morality, art, and personal experience. A truth is subjective when it cannot be verified by external evidence and varies with different observers. He argued that subjective truth addressed existential questions of meaning, purpose, and value, and that is more important for human existence, because it involves a personal relationship with a creator and a choice to live authentically. He defined subjective truth as:

> "An objective uncertainty held fast in an appropriation process of the most passionate inwardness."

This means that, according to Kierkegaard, subjective truth is not based on certainty or proof, but on a leap of faith and a passionate commitment to one's beliefs.

It is not hard to find evidence of Kierkegaard's approach in everyday life. In fact, if you turn on your favorite news channel, it may be a long while before you see any objective truths. Subjective truths seem to be at the forefront of most conversations and discussions, and this can be problematic because subjective truths tend to gravitate around one very important human quality – Perception.

We have learned that our brains construct the world we perceive through our senses, and then we use words to communicate, illustrate, and propagate what was perceived and predicted. Following this logic, we can conclude that subjective truths are directly dependent on how individual brains carry out this process of prediction, observation, and perception. In the next chapter, we will learn that how we feel at any given moment in time can also alter the outcomes of this process. Therefore, feelings can alter our perception of what is real, and thus what could be considered truth. So, if perception is reality, and what is real is true, then does each human hold his own version of subjective truths? Maybe, or maybe not. There is a group of philosophers who may be able to help us understand the concept of subjective truth. They are called pragmatists.

Pragmatic Truths – What Works in Practice

Pragmatists emphasize the practical and action-oriented aspects of human thought and experience. They argue that truth is a dynamic and evolving relationship between beliefs and their consequences in day-to-day human practice. To a pragmatist, truth is a function of how well beliefs work for us in:

1. Solving problems;
2. Achieving goals; and
3. Satisfying our needs and desires.

According to pragmatists, truth is relative to human purposes, interests, and contexts, and it can change over time as we learn from our experiences and revise our beliefs accordingly. Pragmatist **Charles Sanders Pierce** proposed that truth is:

"The opinion which is fated to be ultimately agreed to by all who investigate."

Sanders Pierce suggested that truth is the ideal limit of inquiry, the outcome of a process of scientific investigation and rational deliberation that converges on a stable and consistent set of beliefs. Another famous pragmatist, **William James**, defined truth as

"The expedient in the way of our thinking."

James argued that truth is whatever proves useful or beneficial for us in our practical endeavors. He also claimed that truth is not a single or absolute thing, but rather a plural and diverse phenomenon that depends on our perspective and situation.

Pragmatic theories of truth have been criticized by some philosophers for being relativistic, subjective, or anti-realist. However, pragmatists defend their views by arguing that they capture the dynamic and contextual nature of human knowledge and experience better than other theories of truth. In other words, pragmatists state that truth is NOT a fixed and static correspondence between statements and reality. Instead, pragmatists state that truth requires us to test and revise our beliefs based on their practical consequences and usefulness, rather than accepting them dogmatically or uncritically.

In a world of existentialists, pragmatists, rationalists, realists, minimalists, skeptics, pluralists, and many other types of thinkers, where do we end up when it comes to defining subjective truths? Because we are creatures defined by language, we end up with <u>words</u>. But are words really the representation of truth? If something is determined to be truth and put into words afterwards, does it continue to be the truth? As explained previously, truth is a concept that demands constant questioning in the present moment. The minute a concept is put into words, it is stored as memory, becoming part of the past. While this allows for shared understanding, it also captures a snapshot that may need continuous re-evaluation in a constantly changing present. Truth, in this sense, demands constant questioning, in the present moment, rather than rigid adherence to static formulations.

Words attempt to encapsulate what is being perceived. Words and language are tools that have allowed humans to communicate, to survive, and to thrive as a species. They have allowed for the building of an imagined order upon which civilization can exist. Language is one of the key elements that has allowed humans to become the dominant species. Still, what every human must always remember is that truth may exist beyond all of that, beyond perception. To quote the poet **William Blake**:

"If the doors of perception are cleansed, everything would appear to man as it is, infinite."

Instead of experiencing that infiniteness like Blake states, we continuously find ourselves trapped in the confinement of words and the tendency to label everything. Once a label is given to something or to someone, a division is created. Think about all the labels that have been coined throughout time and how they have affected human behavior. All the "isms" are labels that people often use to separate one another. Racism, sexism, capitalism, socialism, atheism, realism, etc., are just easy examples to note. Not only do these labels separate, but this separation can be the first step towards prejudice. Over time, these labels can be repeated and propagated over and over, and eventually become adopted as truths.

We can do better, though. Learning to love, to care for others, and for the world does not come from repeating those words or expressions. It also doesn't come from hanging on to truths just because that is easy or because that's how it has been done in the past. It comes from experiencing the truth of those feelings in the here and now.

Living in a world of objective and subjective truths

At the highest level, our relationship with truth could be understood at least from one of two sides: objective and subjective. This understanding is a direct function of our experience of the world, and that experience is a function of how we perceive that world and how we perceive ourselves in it. This is of crucial importance because that perception takes place inside our brains, and our brains are constantly being changed and shaped by the actions we take, by who we surround ourselves with, and by the content we choose to consume. Therefore, whether they're objective or subjective, the truths that are prevalent in a specific culture will inevitably be permeated into our brain, perception, and experiences.

In today's digital world, this process has been dramatically accelerated and complicated by technology and social media. These platforms don't just passively transmit information; their algorithms actively shape what information we see based on engagement metrics that often favor emotional, divisive content. This creates filter bubbles where our existing beliefs are constantly reinforced while contradictory information is filtered out. The result is increasingly polarized perceptions of truth, where different groups can inhabit entirely different information ecosystems with their own sets of "facts." Understanding this technological mediation of truth is crucial for navigating the modern information landscape.

In a popular TED Talk titled "Science can Answer Moral Questions", **Sam Harris** states that:

> *"There are truths to be known about how human communities flourish whether or not we understand these truths."*

Harris encourages us to use our intellect to evaluate and re-evaluate concepts that may have worked at one time but may no longer work in today's world. In his book **Meditations on First Philosophy**, the famous rationalist **Rene Descartes** proposed that truth is

> "What we can clearly and distinctly perceive."

He suggested that truths are gained without sensory experience, but instead rely on deductive reasoning. In both statements, we can see that truth demands relentless observation and awareness so that we don't fall into the trap of creating present truths with ancient dogma.

Living with Uncertainty

Imagine for a moment that the path of life is like the path that takes you from Jakarta in Indonesia to the top of Mount Everest in Nepal. When you begin that journey on foot, you are south of the equator in tropical humid conditions at sea level, so you collect tools and skills that will allow you to succeed along the way. This trip could look as follows:

1. Traveling on foot west from Jakarta, you will need good shoes, appropriate clothing for a sub-tropical humid climate, and supplies to deal with mosquitoes.

2. Eventually, you will run into the Sunda Strait, which separates the Indonesian Islands of Java and Sumatra, and you will need a boat to cross.

3. Most likely, you will land in Bandar Lampung, which is a coastal city of approximately 1.1 million people in the southern part of Sumatra. Here, you may want to go north toward Burung, which is a coastal town in the South China Sea.

4. The terrain between Bandar Lampung and Burung will be hilly but not too challenging, other than the possible floods (which, as of late, have been more common in the area) and the unforgiving humidity and rain.

5. As you arrive in Burung, once again, you will need a boat to cross the South China Sea and the Singapore Strait to get to Singapore. Singapore is a clean, orderly, and modern metropolis with access to anything you may need.

6. As you leave Singapore, traveling northwest, you will cross Malaysia and a portion of Thailand before getting to Myanmar.

7. Myanmar is a beautiful part of Southeast Asia with rich history and stunning nature. However, you may encounter the side effects of a

70-year-long civil war. There is a chance you will encounter persecution, landmines, bandits, and the opium trade. You will need to be prepared for this just in case.

8. As you keep going north, the terrain becomes mountainous (but not extreme), then flat, and then mountainous again as you approach the border with Bangladesh, where you will have to be prepared to cross several major rivers as you travel north toward the border with India.

9. Once you get to the Indian border, you will need to make some decisions as to where to cross into Nepal. Although Nepal is a beautiful, developing democracy, some areas near the border with India may have higher levels of crime and insecurity.

10. You carry on, and now you are in Nepal! You must be ready for the fact that Nepal is prone to natural disasters such as earthquakes and landslides, and during monsoon season, those landslides easily become floods.

11. Soon after crossing the border into Nepal, you will notice the terrain changing dramatically. Up to this point, you didn't have to worry about your pace as your main concerns would've been hydration (filtered water), comfortable clothing, and staying away from food that could get you sick. Now, however, you need to be aware of altitude sickness.

12. If you keep going, you could eventually reach Everest South Base Camp at 17,598 feet (5,364 meters) above sea level, which would be a great time to evaluate where you came from and where you are going.

As you can see, this trip is no joke. Traveling away from the tropics and into the mountains means that the tools that were once useful earlier in the journey may not only be useless, but in fact, they may get in the way of progress. It requires an open and self-scrutinizing mind to make the appropriate changes at the appropriate time to make this trek work. It would be laughable to you if I told you I was intending to do this trip without ever changing my toolkit and without making any adjustments along the way. Yet, that's how many of us choose to live our lives. We often keep going and charging forward even when the journey has become precarious because we've been carrying tools we can't use, and we are missing new tools we need. When it gets really tough, we may even tell ourselves, "I wouldn't be here without these tools... they have served me well up to now... why change now?"

But guess what? You are resilient, and somehow you made it to Base Camp with the same tools and mindset you had at the beginning of the trip. You feel proud and accomplished, but you are exhausted, your body aches, because you have worked harder than you needed to get there. But your mind is set, and you are strong-willed, so, after resting, you begin the trek from Base Camp to the summit, and you notice people are concerned about you. You see, these people know that if you choose to continue your journey from Base Camp toward the summit, you'll eventually enter what mountaineers call the "death zone" above 26,000 feet (7,925 meters), where the air contains only one-third of the oxygen found at sea level. At this altitude, human survival is measured in hours rather than days. Your tropical clothing and equipment from Jakarta would not just be useless but deadly here. You'll need specialized oxygen tanks, extreme cold-weather gear, ice axes, crampons, and climbing ropes - tools specifically designed for this harsh environment. Without these specific tools and the knowledge to use them properly, reaching the summit would be impossible.

Some of the people coming back from the summit may even stop and share their concern: "*We have been up there... You won't make it with those tools... You need new tools.*" But you are proud of your progress, and you like your bag; in fact, you love your bag of tools and methods. This bag has served you well, and without it, you wouldn't even be at Base Camp. You see the dilemma here? Is it possible to get to the summit with the same tools you left Jakarta? Sure... anything is possible... but it would be highly improbable.

This fictional example might seem ridiculous to you, yet I challenge you to do some self-observation and see if this isn't scarily similar to the way we choose to live our lives. We tend to adopt "truths" early in our lives and stick with them no matter what, without giving ourselves the grace to observe, evaluate, and adapt as we go through life.

The challenge of living with multiple types of truth becomes even more complex in our digitally mediated world. Collective illusions often exploit the boundaries between different truth types:

- **Objective truth distortion**:

    Climate change denial mixes legitimate scientific uncertainty (about specific predictions) with false claims about basic physical processes.

- **Subjective truth manipulation**:

    Political messaging appeals to genuine values (family, security, freedom) while promoting false factual claims.

- **Pragmatic truth confusion**:

    "Alternative facts" work politically in the short term but undermine long-term social trust and decision-making.

Understanding these distinctions helps us navigate information environments designed to blur the boundaries between different types of truth claims. Maybe here is a good time for an exercise that could be helpful when navigating any truth claim you might encounter:

- **Step 1 – Identify the type**

    - Objective – Can this be independently verified?
    - Subjective: Is this about personal meaning or values?
    - Pragmatic: Is this about what works in practice?

- **Step 2 – Apply the right standard**

    - Objective claims – Demand evidence and replication.
    - Subjective claims: Respect differences while sharing your perspective.
    - Pragmatic claims: Test whether they actually work for your goals.

- **Step 3 – Avoid category errors**

    - Don't demand scientific proof for personal values.
    - Don't treat practical strategies as universal truths.
    - Don't dismiss objective facts because you dislike their implications.

Ancient Wisdom and Modern Application

Twenty-five centuries ago, Greek philosopher **Socrates** proposed that truth is something we experience when we live what he called "The Good Life," and that good life comes from the process of examining our lives through the acquisition of knowledge, wisdom, and virtue. He stated that:

> *"The unexamined life is not worth living."*

Socrates' philosophy articulates a principle that has found remarkable validation in contemporary cognitive science and psychology. His approach to truth emphasized continuous questioning rather than fixed conclusions, establishing what philosophers call "epistemic humility" – the recognition that our knowledge is always provisional and subject to revision.

Socrates' method emerged from his famous declaration of knowing nothing except his own ignorance, a stance that modern research shows is psychologically and cognitively advantageous. This intellectual humility correlates with better learning outcomes, more accurate beliefs, and greater openness to evidence that challenges existing views. Unlike the sophists of his time who claimed to possess definitive knowledge, Socrates understood that wisdom begins with recognizing the limitations of our understanding.

The Socratic Method Applied to Personal Truth

The Socratic approach represents what cognitive scientists now call "active open-mindedness" – a thinking style characterized by the willingness to consider evidence against one's beliefs, seek out disconfirming information, and revise conclusions based on new data. Research by psychologist **Jonathan Baron** and others demonstrates that people higher in active open-mindedness make better decisions, hold more accurate beliefs, and show greater intellectual growth over time.

The systematic questioning approach developed by Socrates can be translated into practical cognitive strategies supported by modern research:

1. **Question Assumptions**: What do I believe without evidence?

   This involves identifying implicit beliefs and examining their foundations. Cognitive research shows that most of our beliefs operate below conscious awareness, making this explicit examination crucial for intellectual development.

2. **Examine Origins**: Where did these beliefs come from?

   Understanding the sources of our beliefs (whether from direct experience, cultural transmission, authority figures, or emotional associations) helps evaluate their reliability and identify potential biases.

3. **Test Consistency**: Do my beliefs contradict each other?

   Research on cognitive dissonance shows that identifying and resolving contradictions in our belief systems reduces psychological stress and improves decision-making coherence.

4. **Consider Alternatives**: What other perspectives are possible?

   This involves what psychologist **Adam Grant** calls "perspective-taking," which is the ability to understand how others might reasonably view the same situation differently based on their experiences and values.

5. **Apply to Action**: How do these beliefs influence my behavior?

This connects abstract beliefs to concrete consequences, making belief revision more personally meaningful and increasing motivation for intellectual honesty.

6. **Iterate Continuously**: How might a new experience modify my understanding?

   This establishes beliefs as working hypotheses rather than fixed truths.

Modern Neuroscience Views on Socratic Methodologies

Contemporary research in cognitive neuroscience provides compelling evidence for the benefits of Socratic questioning and intellectual humility. Neuroimaging studies reveal that people who regularly question their assumptions show enhanced activity in the prefrontal cortex, the brain region responsible for executive function, cognitive flexibility, and metacognition.

Research on cognitive flexibility demonstrates that people who regularly question their assumptions show measurable improvements across multiple domains:

- **Enhanced Problem-Solving**:

    The **Remote Associates Test (RAT)** is a test of creative potential developed by **Martha Mednick** in 1962. Studies using RAT and other creativity measures show that individuals trained in questioning techniques demonstrate better performance on novel challenges requiring insight and creative thinking. This occurs because questioning assumptions activates divergent thinking processes and reduces functional fixedness.

- **Reduced Cognitive Rigidity**:

    Psychological research reveals that Socratic questioning practices reduce susceptibility to confirmation bias, the tendency to seek information that confirms existing beliefs while avoiding contradictory evidence. People who practice systematic questioning show less tendency toward black-and-white thinking and greater comfort with ambiguity and uncertainty.

- **Improved Learning**:

    Educational research demonstrates that students taught to question their understanding show faster adaptation to changing circumstances and better transfer of knowledge to new domains. This occurs through enhanced metacognitive awareness (thinking about thinking), which improves learning strategies and error detection.

- **Greater Resilience**:

    Longitudinal studies indicate that individuals who regularly examine their beliefs show better recovery from setbacks and failures. This resilience stems partly from maintaining flexible rather than rigid self-concepts and from developing what psychologist **Martin Seligman** calls "explanatory flexibility" – the ability to generate multiple explanations for events.

Eastern Approaches: Truth Beyond Concepts

We learned in chapter 4 about how Buddhist and Hindu traditions offer sophisticated epistemological approaches that complement Western analytical methods while providing unique insights validated by contemporary contemplative science. Rather than focusing primarily on propositional knowledge (facts about the world that can be stated in language), these traditions emphasize what philosophers call "experiential knowledge" or "acquaintance knowledge," which is direct insight into the nature of experience itself.

Key Eastern Insights About Truth

Eastern contemplative traditions developed sophisticated understandings of what cognitive scientists now call "metacognition", which is awareness of one's own thinking processes, and a topic we dive into in chapter 8. This includes recognition of how conceptual frameworks shape experience, how attention influences perception, and how emotional states affect reasoning. Research on contemplative practices shows that they enhance metacognitive accuracy and reduce what psychologists call <u>"cognitive fusion": the tendency to become overly identified with thoughts and beliefs</u>. In chapter 4, we learned how ancient practices observe reality and how they strongly intersect with modern science. When it comes to the concept of "truth," here is what we can extract from these ancient traditions:

- **Impermanence (Anicca)**:
    - The Buddhist insight that all phenomena are constantly changing challenges the Western tendency to seek permanent, unchanging truths.
    - Modern physics and biology confirm this insight at every scale, from quantum fluctuations to cellular renewal to cosmic evolution.
    - Psychologically speaking, accepting impermanence reduces what researchers call "emotional brittleness," which is the tendency to be devastated when circumstances change unexpectedly.

This recognition of impermanence has practical implications for belief formation and revision. If everything changes, then our beliefs must be provisional and adaptive rather than fixed and permanent. <u>Neuroscientist **Richard Davidson's** research shows that people who understand impermanence at an experiential level demonstrate greater emotional regulation and cognitive flexibility</u>.

- **Interdependence (Pratitya Samutpada)**:

The insight that everything exists in relationship challenges Western tendencies toward atomistic thinking – viewing phenomena as independent entities with fixed properties. Systems theory, ecology, and social psychology all confirm that isolated analysis often misses crucial relational dynamics.

Research in social psychology demonstrates that individual behavior cannot be understood apart from social context, situational factors, and cultural influences. Similarly, cognitive science shows that thinking emerges from the interaction between brain, body, environment, and social relationships rather than occurring in isolation within individual minds.

- **Non-Duality**:

Advanced contemplative traditions point toward experiences where conventional subject-object distinctions dissolve or become transparent. While this might seem mystical, neuroscience research on contemplative states reveals measurable changes in brain networks associated with self-referential processing and the sense of being a separate self.

Studies by neuroscientist **Judson Brewer** and others show that experienced meditators demonstrate reduced activity in the default mode network - brain regions associated with self-referential thinking and mental time travel. This corresponds to reports of expanded awareness and reduced sense of separation from experience.

- **Direct Experience vs. Conceptual Knowledge**:

Eastern traditions distinguish between intellectual understanding and direct, experiential knowledge. Modern cognitive science supports this distinction through research on implicit versus explicit knowledge, procedural versus declarative memory, and embodied versus abstract cognition.

Harvard Medical School neuroscientist **Sara Lazar** published research showing that meditation is associated with changes in brain regions related to attention, interoception, and sensory processing. Her findings suggest that meditation practice can strengthen the brain's capacity for processing direct, non-conceptual information (such as physical sensations and bodily awareness) rather than just abstract thought.

So maybe there is something to be said about the Greek aphorism "Know Thyself." But what does this mean today in the 21st century? As much as we love Greek philosophy, we know the Greeks weren't perfect. We know they harbored ethnic, cultural, and racial prejudice. Similar things could be said about other ancient societies, even though their philosophy is still, to this day, wise and useful. But that is exactly the point here. Ancient truths need NOT to be our truths, but the process ancient philosophers proposed to arrive at truth could still be useful to us today. In other words, maybe truths can manifest themselves on the path of self-knowledge by living an examined life in THIS present moment, not in the past.

Truth in the Digital Age: New Challenges and Opportunities

Mario's smartphone has access to virtually all human knowledge. He can instantly fact-check claims, access primary sources, and connect with experts worldwide. By all logic, he should be better informed than any generation in history. Instead, he feels more confused than ever.

The Information Abundance Problem

Some of us are old enough to remember the following statement: *"When information is available to all, then all of our problems will be solved..."* Well, today we live in an unprecedented era of information availability that fundamentally challenges traditional approaches to truth-seeking and knowledge validation. However, like Mario, many of us are confused and lost. So, what happened? The digital revolution has created what information scientist **Claude Shannon** never anticipated when developing information theory decades ago: a world where the primary limitation is not access to information, but the cognitive capacity to process, evaluate, and synthesize the overwhelming volume of available data.

This phenomenon, which researchers term "information overload" or "choice overload," creates what psychologist **Barry Schwartz** calls "the paradox of choice": where having more options can actually decrease decision-making quality and satisfaction. Applied to truth-seeking, this means that unprecedented access to information can paradoxically make it more difficult to discern truth from falsehood, reliable from unreliable sources, and meaningful signal from distracting noise.

The same digital technologies that provide democratized access to human knowledge also enable the rapid spread of misinformation, the creation of filter bubbles, and the formation of echo chambers. Research by network scientist **Duncan Watts** reveals how digital information networks can amplify both truth and falsehood with equal efficiency, creating what economist **Tyler Cowen** calls "the great stagnation" in our collective ability to distinguish between high-quality and low-quality information.

Neuroscientist **Daniel Levitin's** research on information processing, alongside insights from evolutionary anthropology about how the **human brain prefers social groups of no more than around 150 individuals** (recall Dunbar's number from chapter 2), highlights how our neural architecture struggles to adapt to the overwhelming information demands of digital environments. The constant stream of notifications, updates, and new information creates what researchers call "continuous partial attention," fragmenting our cognitive resources and reducing our capacity for the deep, sustained thinking that effective truth evaluation requires.

Digital Age Truth Challenges

When it comes to truth in the digital age, some of the challenges we are experiencing in today's world can be summarized as follows:

- **Information Overload**:

    The volume of data generated daily exceeds human cognitive processing capacity by orders of magnitude. Research by information scientist **Hal Varian** estimates that we create more information in two days than was created in all human history prior to 2003. This creates an environment where we end up favoring **Daniel Kahneman's** "*System 1 Thinking*". Recall the definition introduced in chapter 5's section on the brain's built-in limitations. In that section, we presented "*System 1*" definition as fast, automatic, but error-prone cognitive thinking, and "*System 2*" as the careful analysis and processing that accurate truth evaluation requires.

    In chapter 5, we also introduced cognitive science research that shows that when faced with information overload, people resort to heuristics (i.e., mental shortcuts) that can lead to systematic errors in judgment. Recall that these include:

    - The availability heuristic: judging probability by ease of mental recall;
    - The representative heuristic: judging based on similarity to mental prototypes; and

- Anchoring bias: over-relying on the first information encountered.

- **Source-Credibility Crisis**:

  The democratization of publishing means that authoritative and non-authoritative sources often appear equally legitimate online. Research by communication scholars like **Miriam Metzger** reveals that people struggle to apply traditional credibility indicators (institutional affiliation, peer review, expertise) in digital environments where these signals may be absent, manipulated, or obscured.

  The proliferation of sophisticated-looking but unreliable sources creates what researchers call "truth decay," a phenomenon identified by political scientist **Jennifer Kavanagh,** where the distinction between opinion and fact becomes increasingly blurred in public discourse. This is exacerbated by the technical sophistication of modern misinformation, which can include fabricated scientific studies, fake expert credentials, and AI-generated content that appears authoritative.

- **Algorithmic Filtering and the Filter Bubble:**

  Social media algorithms and search engines create personalized information environments based on past behavior, geographic location, and inferred preferences. In the section titled "The Reality of Belief" in chapter 5, we introduced research by computer scientist **Eli Pariser** on "filter bubbles". Pariser's work alongside the work of legal scholar **Cass Sunstein** on "echo chambers" shows how these systems can inadvertently narrow exposure to diverse perspectives and challenging information.

- **Confirmation Bias Amplification**:

  Digital environments make it easier than ever to find sources that confirm existing beliefs while avoiding contradictory evidence. Research by psychologist **Raymond Nickerson** shows that confirmation bias (introduced in chapter 5 as the tendency to search for, interpret, and recall information in ways that confirm pre-existing beliefs) is significantly amplified in digital environments where search algorithms and social networks provide unlimited access to confirmatory information.

- **Speed vs. Accuracy Trade-offs**:

  The speed of digital information creates social pressure to form and express opinions quickly rather than engage in careful deliberation. **Daniel Kahneman**'s "Fast Thinking" research, along with studies of social media dynamics, shows that rapid response is often rewarded over thoughtful analysis. Neuroscience research reveals that speed and accuracy often trade off in cognitive processing. The pressure for immediate response can activate what researchers call "hot cognition," thinking influenced by immediate emotional reactions, rather than "cold cognition," which is deliberate, analytical processing more likely to reach accurate conclusions.

Digital Age Truth Opportunities

Careful observation of the world around us shows that whenever there are challenges, there are also opportunities. Here are some of the great opportunities available to us, given the unprecedented access and verification capabilities we currently enjoy:

- **Global Knowledge Access**:

    Digital technologies provide unprecedented access to diverse perspectives, primary sources, and expert knowledge across cultures, languages, and disciplines. Research on digital libraries and open access publishing shows measurable increases in knowledge sharing and cross-pollination of ideas across geographic and institutional boundaries.

- **Real-Time Verification**:

    Modern digital tools enable immediate fact-checking and verification of claims through access to primary sources, databases, and expert networks. Research on fact-checking organizations shows that real-time verification can significantly reduce the spread of misinformation when effectively implemented and widely used.

    Tools like reverse image searches, database queries, and expert verification networks provide unprecedented capability for rapid source verification. However, research shows that these tools <u>are most effective when people are motivated to use them</u> and possess basic digital literacy skills for evaluation and verification.

- **Collaborative Truth-Seeking**:

    Online communities devoted to careful analysis, peer review, and collaborative investigation represent new models for collective truth-seeking. Research on platforms like Wikipedia, scientific collaboration networks, and citizen science projects demonstrates how distributed cognition can sometimes outperform individual expert judgment through aggregation of diverse perspectives and error-correction mechanisms.

Studies by political scientist **Scott Page** on diversity and collective intelligence show that groups with diverse backgrounds and approaches often outperform groups of uniformly high-ability individuals on complex problem-solving tasks.

- **Transparent Methodology**:

    Digital platforms enable unprecedented access to raw data, research methods, and analytical processes, supporting what some researchers call "open science" and "reproducible research." This transparency allows for independent verification, replication attempts, and methodological critique that can improve the reliability of knowledge claims.

- **Cross-Cultural Dialogue**:

    Digital communication enables exposure to truth frameworks, epistemological approaches, and ways of knowing from different cultures and traditions. Research in comparative epistemology shows that different cultures have developed sophisticated but distinct approaches to knowledge validation, reality assessment, and truth evaluation.

    This cross-cultural exposure can reveal the cultural assumptions embedded in any particular approach to truth while providing access to alternative frameworks that may offer complementary insights. However, realizing this opportunity requires overcoming language barriers, cultural biases, and algorithmic filtering that can limit genuine cross-cultural engagement.

The digital age presents unprecedented challenges and opportunities for truth-seeking that require new cognitive skills, social practices, and technological solutions. Research across multiple disciplines reveals several key conclusions about effective truth navigation in digital environments. These conclusions fall into the following categories:

- Cognitive and individual strategies

    - Develop metacognitive awareness
    - Practice intellectual humility
    - Develop information literacy skills

- Social and collective approaches

    - Foster epistemic communities
    - Implement social verification
    - Support institutional solutions

- Technological and systematic solutions
  - Design for truth seeking
  - Leverage Artificial Intelligence thoughtfully
  - Maintain human agency
- Philosophical and practical integrations
  - Embrace epistemic pluralism
  - Balance speed and accuracy
  - Integrate ancient wisdom and modern tools

Every one of these strategies and approaches comes with solid scientific backing. We will dive deeper into each one in the last chapter, when we will provide a practical process that could be of help when addressing the modern world with an ancient brain.

For now, we know that successfully navigating truth in the digital age requires recognizing that information abundance is fundamentally different from information quality. That access to data is not equivalent to access to wisdom. The challenges are significant: Cognitive limitations, systematic biases, algorithmic manipulation, and social pressures all work against careful truth evaluation. However, the opportunities are equally significant: Unprecedented access to diverse perspectives, powerful verification tools, global collaborative capabilities, and an emerging understanding of how to design systems that support rather than undermine truth-seeking.

The key insight from research across multiple disciplines is that effective truth navigation requires intentional cultivation of both individual cognitive skills and collective social practices. This includes developing meta-cognitive awareness, practicing intellectual humility, building information literacy skills, fostering epistemic communities, and creating technological and institutional systems aligned with truth-seeking rather than engagement maximization. Based on what we have seen so far, here are some practical strategies for information consumption in the digital age:

Table 13 – Practical Strategies for Information Consumption

Before Consuming:	Choose your information diet consciously (like food).
	Set boundaries on news and social media consumption.
	Seek out sources that challenge your existing views.
While Consuming:	Notice emotional reactions to information.
	Ask "Who benefits if I believe this?"
	Look for primary sources and original research.
	Check publication dates (old information presented as new).
After Consuming:	Pause before sharing emotional content.
	Fact-check before forming strong opinions.
	Discuss with people who might see things differently.
	Focus on actionable information over anxiety-inducing content.

Ultimately, truth in the digital age requires the same fundamental virtues that have always supported human knowledge: curiosity, humility, careful observation, logical reasoning, and commitment to evidence over convenience. What has changed is the scale, speed, and complexity of the information environment, requiring new applications of these timeless principles supported by a modern understanding of cognition, technology, and social systems.

The future of truth-seeking will likely depend on <u>our collective ability to create information environments that support human flourishing rather than merely capturing attention</u>, and on developing educational and cultural practices that prepare people for the cognitive demands of life in an information-rich world. This represents both a technical challenge and a moral imperative for how we structure the systems that shape human knowledge and understanding.

Chapter 6 Summary: Key Insights

The intersection of individual Bayesian cognition and social-reality construction creates both our greatest opportunities for collective wisdom and our greatest vulnerabilities to shared delusion. Understanding this dynamic is essential for navigating truth in the modern world. Here are some essential takeaways:

1. **Social Reality Construction**:

    Individual Bayesian brains, when networked together, create shared realities that can be either more accurate or more distorted than individual perceptions.

2. **Collective Illusion Mechanisms**:

    False consensus emerges when vocal minorities are mistaken for silent majorities, creating self-perpetuating cycles reinforced by social conformity pressures.

3. **Digital Amplification**:

    Modern information technologies dramatically accelerate both collective wisdom and collective illusion formation, making critical evaluation skills more crucial than ever.

4. **Three Basic Truth Types**:

    Objective facts, subjective meanings, and pragmatic effectiveness serve different purposes and require different evaluation methods.

5. **Practical Navigation**:

    Effective truth-seeking requires combining scientific rigor with philosophical wisdom, individual critical thinking with collective verification processes.

    The frameworks we've explored (from Bayesian reasoning to Socratic questioning to digital literacy) provide tools for distinguishing reliable knowledge from convincing illusion. But applying these tools effectively requires more than intellectual understanding; it demands awareness of how our embodied, physical state influences our capacity for clear thinking and accurate perception. This brings us to a crucial insight often overlooked in discussions of truth and reality: Our minds are not disembodied reasoning machines; they emerge from complex biological systems whose health and balance directly impact our cognitive capabilities.

    Truth isn't a single concept but a family of related approaches that serve different purposes. Understanding these differences enables more effective navigation of reality while maintaining appropriate humility about the limits of knowledge. These approaches are not necessarily incompatible or contradictory, but are instead complementary and interrelated. They can enrich and challenge each other and help us to achieve a more comprehensive and balanced understanding of ourselves, the world, and our role in it. This can help us make better decisions, communicate more effectively, and avoid errors and deception. However, this may not come easily. The search for truth can also be challenging, elusive, controversial, and sometimes unwelcome. But it can also be worth it if we seek with curiosity, honesty, openness, courage, humility, and vulnerability.

Scientists will defend objective truths, and thinkers will defend subjective truths. The turbulent convergence of these two seemingly opposing concepts may be where we need to spend more time as we seek balance for the world around us and the universe within each of us. I invite you to observe the world through both lenses. Let's be humble, open, and vulnerable. And let's give ourselves the opportunity to experience what happens when we open our minds to the possibilities that may be so easily dismissed by preconceived notions of truth.

The next chapter explores an entirely different type of truth: Our minds are not confined to our brains, and our most important inferences involve signals from throughout our entire body. Why is this a different type of truth? Because in spite of decades of research that back this up, most of us still struggle and, at times, fight with this concept of an embodied mind.

We'll discover how our gut produces neurotransmitters that influence decision-making, how sleep quality affects the accuracy of our Bayesian computations, and how nutrition directly impacts our brain's ability to generate reliable predictions about reality. This exploration of the embodied mind will show that optimal inference requires more than good mathematical reasoning and clarity on objective and subjective truths. It also demands caring for the entire biological system that generates consciousness.

The journey from truth frameworks to embodied cognition will reveal that our best decisions emerge not from pure rational analysis but from the integration of sophisticated reasoning with wisdom signals from our entire organism.

CHAPTER 7
THE EMBODIED MIND

Our model of the world emerges not just from cognitive processes but from the entire body as an integrated system of perception

Audrey sits in her third meeting of the morning, struggling to focus. Her stomach is rumbling because she skipped breakfast. Her shoulders are tense from sleeping poorly because her child who woke up sick at 3 a.m. She had wine with dinner last night, disrupting her few deep-sleep cycles. The coffee she's relying on is creating jittery anxiety rather than clear alertness. As her colleague presents quarterly numbers, Audrey finds herself inexplicably irritated by her tone of voice. She's having difficulty processing the information and feels like she's thinking through fog. She assumes this is just "one of those days" and pushes through with willpower.

What Audrey doesn't realize is that her brain, that remarkable prediction machine we've been exploring, isn't operating in isolation. Every thought, emotion, and decision is profoundly influenced by signals throughout her body. Her hungry gut is producing stress hormones that affect her mood. Her disrupted sleep has impaired her prefrontal cortex's ability to regulate emotions. Her tense muscles are sending signals that prime her brain for threat detection rather than creative problem-solving. Audrey isn't having a "bad day"; she's experiencing the embodied nature of consciousness. Her mind isn't confined to her skull but emerges from the integrated functioning of her entire biological system.

This might sound mystical, but it's hard neuroscience. Every component in our complex biological ecosystem influences the quality of inference and decision-making:

- The gut produces more serotonin than the brain.

- Sleep quality directly affects learning and memory formation.
- Posture influences confidence and decision-making.
- Inflammation from poor diet literally clouds thinking.

Understanding this embodied nature of cognition isn't just academically interesting; it's essential for optimizing our mental performance and overall well-being in this modern world. When we recognize how our physical state shapes our mental experience, we gain powerful tools for optimizing both our thinking and our well-being.

Let's journey through the surprising ways our body influences our mind. From the "second brain" in our gut to the critical role of sleep in reality construction. We'll discover how physical factors that seem unrelated to thinking (nutrition, inflammation, circadian rhythms) directly impact your ability to learn, remember, and make good decisions. We'll also explore practical strategies for optimizing this mind-body system.

Our Second Brain: Our Gut's Role in Reality Perception

The Buddhist concept of dependent origination or interconnectedness (Pratitya Samutpada) and Kant's understanding of how our minds structure perception find a surprising parallel in an unexpected place: the relationship between our digestive system and brain. Just as quantum physics revealed that seemingly separate phenomena are fundamentally connected, neuroscience has discovered that our perception of reality is intimately tied to systems throughout our body, not just our brain.

This isn't just a catchy metaphor. Our "gut-brain" produces many of the same neurotransmitters as our "head-brain." In fact, a large percentage of your body's serotonin (the "happiness chemical") is primarily manufactured in our intestines, not our brain. Our mood, our ability to focus, and our personality are all influenced by the microbial ecosystem living in our digestive system. Think about the language we already use: "gut feelings," "butterflies in your stomach," and "going with your gut." These aren't just colorful expressions; they're accurate descriptions of how our enteric nervous system influences our thoughts, decisions, and how we experience reality.

The Enteric Nervous System (ENS)

In chapter 2, we introduced the central nervous system (CNS) and the peripheral nervous system (PNS) as the main subdivisions of the human nervous system. We also introduced the somatic nervous system (SoNS) and the autonomic nervous system (ANS) as the main subsystems of the PNS. Diving deeper into the various subsystems of the human nervous system, we find the Enteric Nervous System (ENS). To show the ENS relationship to the rest of the nervous system, we've added to the table we presented in chapter 2:

Table 14 – The Human Nervous System Expanded

Central Nervous System (CNS)	Brain	
	Spinal Cord	
	Retina, optic nerve, olfactory nerves and olfactory epithelium (according to some scientists).	
Peripheral Nervous System (PNS)	**Somatic Nervous System (SoNS)** - *controls voluntary movements (motor neurons to skeletal muscles) and carries sensory information*	
	Autonomic Nervous System (ANS) - *controls involuntary functions like heart rate, digestion, breathing*	**Sympathetic Nervous System (SNS)** – *"Fight or flight" responses - increases heart rate, dilates pupils, inhibits digestion*
		Parasympathetic Nervous System (PSNS) – *"Rest and digest" responses - slows heart rate, constricts pupils, stimulates digestion*
		Enteric Nervous System (ENS) – *Controls the gastrointestinal tract and can function independently of the CNS*

The ENS is a complex network of neurons embedded in the lining of the gastrointestinal tract. Often called the "second brain," the ENS contains approximately 500 million neurons (more than in the spinal cord) and can operate somewhat independently of the Central Nervous System (CNS).

The ENS communicates bidirectionally with the brain through multiple pathways, including the Vagus nerve, immune system signaling, and the production of neurotransmitters and neuromodulators. This communication network allows gut function to influence brain activity and vice versa.

Michael Gershon, professor of pathology and cell biology at Columbia University and author of "**The Second Brain**," explains:

"The second brain doesn't help with the great thoughts of life. It's not going to help you write a book or solve a math equation. But it's in charge of your gut feelings."

While Gershon clarifies that "the second brain doesn't help with the great thoughts of life" but "it's in charge of our gut feelings," emerging research increasingly suggests its profound influence on aspects of higher-order thinking indirectly, through its direct impact on mood, motivation, and cognitive clarity.

Microbiome Health and Cognitive Function

The gut microbiome (the community of trillions of microorganisms living in our digestive tract) plays a crucial role in the gut-brain communication pathways. These microorganisms influence brain function through multiple mechanisms:

- **Neurotransmitter Production**:

    Gut bacteria produce neurotransmitters such as serotonin (approximately 90% of the body's serotonin is produced in the gut), dopamine, and Gamma-Aminobutyric Acid (GABA), which regulate mood, cognition, and perception.

- **Immune System Modulation**:

    The microbiome influences immune system function, affecting inflammation levels throughout the body, including the brain. Chronic inflammation has been linked to cognitive impairment and mood disorders.

- **Vagus Nerve Signaling**:

    Certain gut bacteria can directly activate the Vagus nerve, a major communication pathway between the gut and brain.

- **Stress Response Regulation**:

    Gut bacteria influence cortisol and other stress hormones.

- **Blood-Brain Barrier Effects**:

    Microbial compounds can alter the permeability of the barrier protecting our brain.

One of the most surprising discoveries in neuroscience is that our gut produces many of the same neurotransmitters that regulate mood and cognition in our brain. Research has shown associations between microbiome composition and various aspects of cognition and mental health. For example, a 2019 study published in Nature Microbiology found correlations between specific gut bacteria and quality of life and depression. Another Frontiers in Aging Neuroscience study found associations between microbiome composition and cognitive function in older adults. Here are the key gut-produced neurotransmitters:

- **Serotonin (90% produced in gut)**: Mood regulation, sleep, appetite, decision-making.
- **Dopamine**: Motivation, reward processing, attention, motor control.
- **GABA**: Anxiety reduction, relaxation, cognitive flexibility.
- **Acetylcholine**: Learning, memory, attention, muscle control.
- **Norepinephrine**: Alertness, arousal, stress response.

Scientific breakthroughs are often amazing; however, they are also difficult for the average person to benefit from right away. That is not the case with this Gut-Brain Axis breakthrough. Our brain influences our gut (stress can cause digestive problems), and our gut influences our brain (digestive health affects mood and cognition). This bidirectional communication means that caring for your digestive system directly impacts your mental performance. Improving our diet will have a direct impact on our neurotransmitter production, which will have a direct impact on our cognitive well-being. And we can do this TODAY. Here is an example of a Probiotic Depression Study:

> *A 2013 study by Tillisch et al. published in Gastroenterology gave women probiotic yogurt for <u>four weeks</u> while monitoring their brain activity with fMRI scans. Compared to controls, women consuming probiotics showed altered activity in brain regions controlling emotion and sensation, demonstrating that changing gut bacteria can directly influence brain function.*

This groundbreaking research was among the first to show in humans that dietary changes affecting gut bacteria can directly influence brain activity and, by extension, <u>how we perceive and respond to our environment</u>.

Our gut hosts trillions of microorganisms (bacteria, viruses, fungi, and other microbes) that collectively weigh about 2-3 pounds and contain more genetic material than our human cells. This microbiome functions as a crucial component of our extended nervous system. Some research findings include:

- People with depression often have less diverse gut microbiomes.
- Specific bacterial strains correlate with different personality traits and cognitive abilities.
- Antibiotic treatment can temporarily alter mood and cognitive function.
- Fecal microbiota transplants (used to treat infections) sometimes produce unexpected mood changes.

Nutritional Deficiencies and Their Impact on Brain Processing

We learned from our discussion on our evolutionary heritage that our brain is metabolically expensive. Recall that despite representing around 2% of our body weight, our brain consumes around 20% of our daily caloric intake. This massive energy requirement means that nutritional status directly impacts cognitive function in ways that are often underappreciated. Specific nutritional deficiencies can significantly impair brain function and alter perception. Here is a summary of what our brains need as a minimum:

Table 15 – Example of Our Brain's Nutritional Needs

Human Brain Nutritional Needs	
Glucose	Primary fuel source, requiring steady blood sugar levels.
Omega-3 Fatty Acids	Essential for neuron membrane structure and function.
B Vitamins	Critical for energy metabolism and neurotransmitter synthesis.
Antioxidants	Protection against oxidative stress and inflammation.
Minerals	Iron, magnesium, zinc for various neural processes.
Vitamin D	Low levels are associated with cognitive impairment and mood disorders.
Amino Acids	Building blocks for neurotransmitters and proteins.

Each one of these has a direct impact on our cognitive and mental performance. Let's zoom in on a handful of these for more details:

Table 16 – How the Brain Benefits from Omega-3, B Complex and Iron

Omega-3 Fatty Acids (DHA and EPA)	
Essential for brain cell membrane structure and function. Deficiency has been linked to cognitive decline, depression, and impaired learning.	
Brain Structure	DHA comprises 30% of brain gray matter.

Neuroplasticity	Essential for forming new neural connections.
Inflammation	EPA reduces neuroinflammation that impairs cognition.
Mood Regulation	Deficiency linked to depression and anxiety.
Sources	Fatty fish, algae supplements, walnuts, flaxseeds.

B Vitamins Complex	
Critical for energy metabolism in brain cells and neurotransmitter synthesis. Deficiencies in B12 and folate can cause cognitive impairment, psychosis, and depression.	
B1 (Thiamine)	Glucose metabolism and neural energy production.
B6 (Pyridoxine)	Neurotransmitter synthesis (serotonin, dopamine, GABA).
B12 (Cobalamin)	Myelin formation and neural communication.
Folate	DNA synthesis and neural development.
Deficiency Effects	Cognitive decline, depression, anxiety, memory problems.

Iron and Cognitive Performance	
Iron deficiency is the most common nutritional deficiency worldwide and significantly impacts cognitive function even before anemia develops.	
Oxygen Transport	Hemoglobin carries oxygen to brain tissue.
Neurotransmitter Synthesis	Required for dopamine and serotonin production.
Energy Metabolism	Essential for cellular energy production.
Attention and Focus	Iron deficiency strongly correlates with attention problems.

This is just a sample of the key nutritional requirements for improved brain processing, but this is not an exhaustive list. For example, Magnesium is also important because it is required for over 300 enzymatic reactions, many in the brain. Magnesium deficiency can cause irritability, fatigue, and cognitive problems. These nutritional factors don't just affect cognitive performance; they can fundamentally alter how we perceive and interpret the world around us.

Gut Inflammation, Hormone Regulation, and Mood Alterations

Chronic low-grade inflammation, often stemming from poor diet, can disrupt brain function through multiple pathways. The inflammatory cytokines produced during gut inflammation can cross the blood-brain barrier and activate microglia (the brain's immune cells), leading to neuroinflammation. This neuroinflammation has been linked to mood disorders, cognitive impairment, and altered perception. For instance, patients with inflammatory bowel diseases have higher rates of anxiety and depression, and improvements in gut health often correlate with improvements in mood and cognitive function. Inflammation can affect the brain in many ways:

- **Blood-Brain Barrier Disruption**:

    Inflammation increases permeability, allowing toxins to enter brain tissue.

- **Microglial Activation**:

    Brain immune cells become hyperactive, damaging neurons.

- **Neurotransmitter Disruption**:

    Inflammation interferes with serotonin, dopamine, and other signaling molecules.

- **Neuroplasticity Impairment**:

    Chronic inflammation reduces the brain's ability to form new connections.

- **Stress Response Dysregulation**:

    Inflammatory processes interfere with cortisol and other stress hormones.

Table 17 – Examples of Inflammatory and Anti-inflammatory Foods

Pro-Inflammatory Foods	Anti-Inflammatory Foods
Processed foods high in sugar and trans fats	Fatty fish rich in omega-3s.

Refined carbohydrates and high-glycemic foods	Colorful fruits and vegetables (antioxidants).
Excessive omega-6 fatty acids (vegetable oils)	Nuts, seeds and dark chocolate.
Food additives and preservatives	Olive oil and avocados.
Alcohol in excess	Turmeric, ginger, and other spices.

The gut also influences hormone regulation, including stress hormones like cortisol. Chronic stress can alter gut permeability ("leaky gut"), allowing bacterial components to trigger immune responses that further affect brain function and perception.

The Cycle of Poor Nutrition, Cognitive Impairment, and Distorted Reality Perception

A concerning feedback loop can develop between poor nutrition, cognitive impairment, and distorted reality perception:

1. Poor dietary choices (high in processed foods, sugar, and unhealthy fats) can disrupt the gut microbiome and cause inflammation.
2. This disruption impairs cognitive function, including decision-making and impulse control.
3. Impaired cognitive function leads to further poor dietary choices and difficulty breaking unhealthy patterns.
4. The resulting nutritional deficiencies and gut dysfunction further distort perception and cognition.

This cycle helps explain why dietary changes can be so difficult to maintain and why nutrition plays such a fundamental role in mental health and cognitive function.

Why Does This Matter to Your Daily Life?

Your gut microbiome influences your mental state in real-time:

Signs of an unhappy gut-brain:

- Afternoon energy crashes - Difficulty concentrating after meals - Mood swings related to eating patterns - Cravings for sugar and processed foods - Digestive issues coinciding with stress.

Supporting your second brain:

- Eat fermented foods (yogurt, kimchi, sauerkraut) to feed beneficial bacteria - Include fiber-rich foods to nourish your microbiome - Notice how different foods affect your mood and energy - Consider how stress affects your digestion (and vice versa).

Bottom Line: Pay attention to how you feel 30 minutes after eating. Your gut-brain is giving you constant feedback – start listening to it.

Supporting your second brain through nutrition creates the foundation for the next crucial element of embodied cognition: the nightly maintenance program your brain desperately needs to function optimally.

Sleep Deficit and Reality Processing

What if I told you there's a single intervention that could improve your memory, boost your creativity, regulate your emotions, strengthen your immune system, and help you make better decisions? You'd probably assume it's some expensive supplement or complicated procedure. Well, maybe there is a supplement in the market that makes all those claims, but I am not talking about that. I am talking about **sleep**, and most people are chronically and intentionally depriving themselves of it.

In his book "**Why We Sleep**," **Dr Matthew Walker** emphasizes that both the **quantity** and **quality** of sleep are non-negotiable biological necessities crucial for physical health, mental well-being, and cognitive function. Just as Plato's cave dwellers mistook shadows for reality, sleep-deprived individuals experience a distorted perception, but through a physiological rather than philosophical mechanism.

The predictive processing framework discussed earlier becomes particularly relevant when examining sleep's impact on reality perception. When sleep-deprived, the brain's ability to generate accurate predictions and incorporate sensory evidence becomes impaired, shifting the balance toward reliance on prior beliefs and resulting in a less accurate model of reality. This provides a concrete example of how physical states directly influence our construction of reality, bridging theoretical concepts with embodied experience. Some of the critical functions that take place during quality sleep are:

- **Memory Consolidation**: Transfer of information from short-term to long-term memory.
- **Toxin Clearance**: Removal of metabolic waste products, including amyloid plaques associated with Alzheimer's.

- **Neural Repair**: Restoration of damaged neurons and synaptic connections.
- **Hormone Regulation**: Production and regulation of growth hormone, cortisol, and other crucial compounds.
- **Immune System Maintenance**: Enhanced immune function and inflammation resolution.
- **Integrating learning**: Connecting new information with existing knowledge.
- **Regulating emotions**: Processing the day's experiences and preparing for tomorrow's challenges.

During deep sleep, our brain's **glymphatic system** becomes highly active, flushing out toxins that accumulate during waking hours. This process is so important that sleep deprivation is associated with accelerated cognitive aging and increased risk of neurodegenerative disease. In other words, sleep is not merely rest for the body but an active process essential for brain function, accurate reality processing, and maintenance functions that are crucial for learning, memory, decision-making, and emotional regulation. Sleep deprivation will significantly alter how we perceive and interact with the world.

How Sleep Quantity and Quality Affect Cognitive Function

Both sleep quantity (duration) and quality (architecture) profoundly impact cognitive function. The American Academy of Sleep Medicine recommends 7-9 hours of sleep for adults, yet about one-third of Americans regularly get less than this amount. Then again, this is just a baseline recommendation. We all know high-performing individuals who claim to sleep a lot less than the suggested guidelines. The important point to make here is that you need the quantity and quality of sleep your body demands, independent of who you are. It is up to us as individuals to do our due diligence to find out what the optimal numbers are for our body type because sleep deprivation does impair various cognitive functions. Some of them are:

- **Visual Misperceptions**:

    Misinterpreting visual stimuli or experiencing visual illusions.

- **Microsleeps**:

    Brief episodes of sleep intrusion into wakefulness, lasting seconds to minutes, during which awareness and responsiveness are impaired.

- **Time Distortion**:

    Altered perception of time passage, typically experienced as time slowing down.

- **Sensory Integration Problems**:

    Difficulty integrating information across sensory modalities.

    These impairments occur even with moderate sleep restriction. Research published in the journal *Sleep* by **Hans Van Dongen** et al. found that restricting sleep to 6 hours per night for 14 consecutive days produced cognitive deficits equivalent to two nights of total sleep deprivation. The cognitive impacts of sleep loss progress in severity with increasing duration of wakefulness.

    Other studies, such as one by **Drew Dawson and Kathryn Reid** published in *Nature*, have shown that after 17 to 19 hours of wakefulness, cognitive performance declines to a level equivalent to having a blood alcohol concentration of 0.05%. With continued wakefulness, microsleeps become frequent and unpredictable, and the ability to perform even simple cognitive tasks becomes severely impaired. These effects demonstrate how fundamentally sleep affects our ability to process reality accurately.

Sleep Deprivation, Perceptual Distortions, and Reality Construction

Since our brain constructs reality through Bayesian inference processes, sleep quality directly affects the accuracy of these constructions. Sleep-deprived brains make systematically different inferences about reality compared to well-rested ones. Sleep deprivation can cause significant perceptual distortions that alter our experience of reality. These include:

- **Visual Misperceptions**:

    Misinterpreting visual stimuli or experiencing visual illusions.

- **Increased Negativity Bias**:

    Sleep-deprived brains give disproportionate weight to negative information.

- **Time Distortion**:

    Altered perception of time passage, typically experienced as time slowing down.

- **Emotional Dysregulation**:

    Heightened amygdala activity with reduced prefrontal control.

- **Attention Deficits**:

    Difficulty maintaining focus and filtering irrelevant information.

With severe sleep deprivation, these perceptual distortions can progress to hallucinations and delusions. In the famous 1964 study supervised by Stanford researcher **William Dement**, high school student Randy Gardner stayed awake for a record-breaking 264 hours (11 days and 25 minutes). Within a few days of sleep deprivation, Gardner began to experience significant cognitive deficits and perceptual distortions, which progressed to complex hallucinations and paranoia. This demonstrated the profound impact a lack of sleep has on our perception of reality.

Memory Formation and Consolidation

Sleep plays a crucial role in memory processes that are fundamental to our construction of reality:

- **Memory Encoding**:

    Sleep deprivation impairs the ability to form new memories, particularly declarative memories (facts and experiences).

- **Memory Consolidation**:

    During sleep, especially deep slow-wave sleep and REM sleep, the brain consolidates memories, transferring information from short-term to long-term storage and integrating new memories with existing knowledge.

- **Memory Reconsolidation**:

    When memories are recalled, they become temporarily unstable and must be reconsolidated. Sleep facilitates this process, which is essential for maintaining accurate memories.

These memory processes are not just about remembering past events but are fundamental to how we construct our understanding of reality. Our sense of self, our understanding of cause and effect, and our ability to predict future events all depend on accurate memory formation and consolidation.

The Impact of Chronic Sleep Deficit on Decision-Making and Judgment

Chronic sleep deficit significantly impairs decision-making and judgment, further distorting our interaction with reality:

- **Risk Assessment**:

    Sleep-deprived individuals tend to make riskier decisions and underestimate the potential negative consequences of their choices.

- **Ethical Judgment**:

    Sleep deprivation has been shown to compromise ethical decision-making and moral judgment.

- **Optimism Bias**:

    Sleep-deprived people often show increased optimism bias, overestimating positive outcomes and underestimating negative ones.

- **Susceptibility to Suggestion**:

    Sleep deficit increases suggestibility and vulnerability to misinformation.

A landmark study published in **The New England Journal of Medicine** found that medical residents made **36% more serious medical errors** when working extended shifts compared to shorter shifts. This is because the cumulative effect of chronic sleep deprivation creates a distorted perception of reality characterized by impaired attention, memory problems, emotional dysregulation, and compromised decision-making, all of which affect how we construct and interact with our model of reality.

Why Does This Matter to Your Daily Life?

Sleep quality directly affects next-day performance:

- One night of poor sleep:

    40% reduction in ability to form new memories - Increased emotional reactivity (everything feels more intense) - Impaired decision-making (you're more likely to choose immediate gratification) - Reduced creativity and problem-solving ability.

- Sleep optimization basics:

    Keep your bedroom cool (65-68°F) and dark - Stop screens 1 hour before bed (blue light disrupts melatonin) - Keep consistent sleep/wake times (even on weekends) - If you can't sleep, get up and read until drowsy (don't lie awake anxious).

Bottom Line: Try one sleep improvement technique, and notice how it affects your thinking tomorrow.

When you're well-rested, your brain can handle stress more skillfully. But when sleep-deprived, even minor stressors can trigger the inflammatory cascade that clouds thinking and impairs decision-making.

Stress, Inflammation, and Cognitive Performance

Imagine your brain as a sophisticated orchestra. When you're calm and well-rested, different sections work together harmoniously. Here, the logical prefrontal cortex guides decisions while the emotional-limbic system provides valuable intuition. But when stress floods your system with cortisol and adrenaline, it's like someone suddenly cranked the volume on the percussion section while muting the strings.

This isn't a design flaw; it's a feature. Our stress response system evolved to help our ancestors survive immediate physical threats. We don't need careful analysis or creative problem-solving when facing an imminent physical threat. We need fast reflexes and intense focus on escape.

Stress profoundly affects cognitive function through multiple biological pathways, and its impact is intimately linked to how our brains construct reality. While acute stress (short-term, like facing an immediate physical threat) can temporarily enhance performance by sharpening focus and speeding decision-making, chronic stress (prolonged exposure to stressors) consistently impairs learning, memory, and rational judgment. The table below highlights some of the differences between short and long-term stress:

Table 18 – Acute vs Chronic Stress Effects

\	Acute Stress – Short Term
Enhanced Focus	Increased norepinephrine improves attention.
Memory Formation	Moderate stress hormones enhance memory consolidation.
Decision Speed	Faster processing for immediate threats.
Physical Performance	Increased strength and reaction time.

Chronic Stress – Long Term	
Hippocampal Damage	Prolonged cortisol exposure shrinks memory centers.
Prefrontal Impairment	Reduced executive function and decision-making.
Inflammation	Chronic stress triggers systemic inflammatory responses.
Neuroplasticity Reduction	Decreased ability to form new neural connections.
Immune Suppression	Increased susceptibility to illness and infection.

The **hypothalamic-pituitary-adrenal (HPA) axis** is our body's primary stress response system. It is a complex neuroendocrine pathway that orchestrates our physiological response to perceived threats, and its regulation directly impacts cognitive performance. Here are some of its functions:

1. **Stressor Detection:** The hypothalamus perceives a threat (whether real or imagined, physical or psychological).
2. **Hormone Release:** This triggers the release of Corticotropin-Releasing Hormone (CRH), which in turn stimulates the pituitary gland to release Adrenocorticotropic Hormone (ACTH).
3. **Cortisol Production:** ACTH signals the adrenal glands to produce cortisol and other stress hormones.
4. **Systemic Effects:** These stress hormones flood the body, affecting virtually every organ system to prepare for "fight or flight."
5. **Feedback Regulation:** Under normal circumstances, cortisol levels rise, then provide negative feedback to the hypothalamus and pituitary, suppressing further HPA axis activation and allowing the body to return to baseline.

However, when stress becomes toxic and chronic, this finely tuned system breaks down and can lead to:

- **Chronic Activation:** The HPA axis remains hyperactive due to ongoing perceived threats, unable to return to a calm baseline.
- **Dysregulated Feedback:** The system loses its ability to effectively shut down the stress response, leading to a vicious cycle.
- **Elevated Baseline:** Cortisol and other stress hormones remain chronically high, putting a constant strain on the body.

- **Multi-System Damage:** Prolonged stress affects the brain, immune, cardiovascular, and digestive systems, contributing to chronic inflammation and metabolic dysfunction.

The Role of Nervous System Dysregulation

Beyond the hormonal cascade of the HPA axis, chronic stress profoundly impacts the **Sympathetic Nervous System (SNS)**, responsible for "fight or flight" responses, and the **Parasympathetic Nervous System (PSNS)**, which governs "rest and digest" functions. In a healthy state, these two systems work in dynamic balance, allowing the body to adapt efficiently to demands and then return to a calm baseline. However, prolonged exposure to modern stressors often leads to **ANS dysregulation**, characterized by chronic sympathetic overactivity and/or parasympathetic underactivity. This imbalance has significant consequences for both physical and mental health:

- **Fueling Chronic Inflammation:**

    Sustained SNS activation releases pro-inflammatory cytokines, directly contributing to the systemic inflammation you described. Conversely, the PSNS, particularly through the vagus nerve, plays a crucial anti-inflammatory role. When the PSNS is suppressed due to chronic stress, the body's ability to dampen inflammation is compromised, leading to a persistent inflammatory state that impacts all organ systems, including the brain.

- **Impacting Cognitive Function:**

    This dysregulation directly impairs the brain's ability to function optimally. Chronic SNS arousal diverts resources away from higher-order cognitive processes (like those in the prefrontal cortex responsible for planning, decision-making, and emotional regulation) towards survival-oriented responses. It can disrupt neurotransmitter balance, alter cerebral blood flow, and interfere with neuroplasticity, making it harder for the brain to learn, remember, and adapt. The constant state of alert also exhausts the system, leading to fatigue, reduced attention, and difficulty concentrating.

- **Distorting Reality Perception:**

    A dysregulated nervous system can skew our brain's predictive models. When the body is constantly signaling "threat" (due to SNS overactivity), the brain's priors become biased towards danger. This can lead to increased negativity bias, hyper-vigilance, misinterpretation of ambiguous social cues as threatening, and a reduced capacity for nuanced emotional processing. The world literally appears more dangerous and less manageable to a dysregulated nervous system, further entrenching a distorted reality model.

Understanding this interplay highlights that our capacity for clear thinking and accurate reality perception is not just a function of our brain's computational power, but is deeply dependent on the physiological balance and health of our entire nervous system. Therefore, practices that promote ANS balance, such as mindfulness, deep breathing, and regular exercise, become crucial tools for optimizing cognitive performance and fostering a more adaptive model of reality.

Beyond these systemic effects, chronic stress profoundly impacts the very neural architecture responsible for constructing our reality. Elevated cortisol levels can lead to **atrophy in the hippocampus**, a region critical for memory formation and learning, thus compromising the brain's ability to accurately *update* its models with new data.

The **prefrontal cortex**, vital for executive functions like rational decision-making, planning, and emotional regulation, also becomes impaired. Meanwhile, the **amygdala**, our brain's threat detection center, becomes sensitized and hyperactive, pushing the brain to prioritize potential dangers. This neurological remodeling means a chronically stressed brain is inherently a **hyper-vigilant and biased brain**. It tends to:

- **Filter reality through a negativity bias:**

    Overweighing negative information, interpreting ambiguous cues as threatening, and struggling to recognize positive outcomes.

- **Impair learning and adaptation:**

    Reduced neuroplasticity and compromised memory systems make it harder to update internal models, leading to rigidity in thought and behavior.

- **Distort emotional landscape:**

    Increased amygdala activity coupled with reduced prefrontal control can lead to heightened anxiety, fear, and impaired emotional regulation, causing "emotional illusions" to become more prevalent and persistent.

Unlike our ancestors, who primarily faced acute physical threats with clear resolutions (e.g., escape a predator), modern humans often experience **multidimensional, chronic psychological stress** that keeps the HPA axis constantly activated without providing a natural outlet for fight or flight.

Work pressures, financial concerns, social media comparisons, constant information overload, misinformation, relationship conflicts, and political and environmental uncertainty – these abstract, unresolved stressors bombard us daily. Our ancient biology, evolved to manage short bursts of danger, is simply not equipped for this sustained volume of stimuli. This leads to a persistent state of low-grade physiological arousal, chronic inflammation, and neurological wear-and-tear that fundamentally compromises our brain's ability to construct a calm, coherent, and accurate model of reality. Our collective stress levels are at an all-time high, not because of a lack of effort, but because our biological systems are constantly struggling to keep pace with an environment they were not designed for.

It is important to note that every one of us is a different sentient being, and as such, we all react differently to nervous-system dysregulation, poor nutrition, and lack of sleep. Why is this important? When having discussions about what can be done to improve our health, it is not uncommon to hear comments like "my grandfather lived to be 100 years old, smoked his entire life, drank every weekend, never meditated, and was just fine." How your grandparent, uncle, or neighbor lived their life does very little, if anything, for you. His body was a different arrangement of atoms; he lived in a different time and in an entirely different environment.

The point here is not to draw comparisons with anyone older or current but instead to create a more conscious and sustainable way of being and living. This is hard because we are not very good at understanding how far we have deviated from our optimal self, or how much better we could be with respect to our own biology. Many of us are taught to react to the world around us, and that after a certain age, we just decay and become useless. That is not necessarily true. Death and aging are inevitable, but we can choose to build a mental and physical ecosystem that gives us a better chance to be active longer and not lose cognitive and physical function so dramatically.

Regarding stress, inflammation, and cognitive performance, it is key that we make time to understand our nervous system and how to regulate it. Being cognizant that stress itself is a nervous system response rather than a character weakness opens up powerful optimization possibilities. Instead of trying to eliminate stress through willpower, we can work with our autonomic nervous system to restore balance.

Chapter 7 Summary: Key Insights

Our mind isn't confined to our brain but emerges from the integrated functioning of our entire body. Optimizing cognitive performance requires understanding and caring for the biological systems that support consciousness, from gut bacteria to sleep architecture to inflammatory processes. Here are some essential takeaways

1. **The Second Brain**:

    Our gut contains 500 million neurons and produces neurotransmitters that directly influence mood, decision-making, and cognitive function.

2. **Nutrition as Information**:

    What we eat directly affects brain structure and function, with anti-inflammatory foods supporting optimal cognitive performance and processed foods promoting neuroinflammation.

3. **Sleep as Active Maintenance**:

    Sleep isn't rest but active brain maintenance, including memory consolidation, toxin clearance, and neural repair, essential for accurate reality construction.

4. **Stress-Cognition Integration**:

    While acute stress can enhance performance, chronic stress physically changes brain structure and systematically impairs learning, memory, and decision-making.

5. **Immediate Impact**:

    Unlike many health interventions, improvements in sleep, nutrition, and stress management often produce noticeable cognitive benefits within days.

6. **Systems Approach**:

    Optimal cognitive function emerges from the integrated optimization of sleep, nutrition, stress management, and gut health rather than addressing these areas separately.

Understanding your mind as embodied reveals that optimal cognitive function requires caring for your entire biological system. This foundation of physical well-being creates the conditions for the sophisticated mental training we'll explore next: the art of balanced self-examination that leads to authentic growth.

The embodied mind reveals why traditional approaches to personal development often fail. We can't think our way out of problems that have physical roots. But mental and emotional improvements follow naturally when we address the biological foundations of consciousness. Understanding our mind as embodied creates the stable foundation necessary for the sophisticated psychological work of balanced self-examination.

With our biological system optimized, we're ready to develop the metacognitive awareness that allows conscious evolution throughout life.

In the next chapter, we'll discover how to observe yourself with both honesty and compassion, developing the metacognitive awareness that allows conscious evolution. We'll explore techniques for recognizing limiting patterns, building evidence-based confidence, and maintaining the delicate balance between self-improvement and self-acceptance. This journey from embodied mind to self-scrutiny will reveal how physical optimization creates the stable foundation necessary for the psychological flexibility and emotional intelligence that characterize mature human development.

PART 2 CONCLUSIONS: TOWARD A UNIFIED MODEL OF REALITY

*"All models are of course wrong...
some are simply more wrong than others."*
Albert Einstein – paraphrasing

Throughout Part 2, we've embarked on a fascinating exploration of reality, moving from the conceptual landscapes of ancient philosophy to the perplexing insights of quantum physics and the empirical discoveries of modern neuroscience. While these perspectives originate from vastly different methodologies and historical contexts, they converge on several profound insights that point toward a more unified and dynamic understanding of what is "real." As neuroscientist **Jeff Beck** (Faculty Network Member of the Duke Institute for Brain Sciences) suggests, all knowledge is conditional, constrained by the data we acquire and the models we consider. Our brains constantly strive to build the best possible model based on available information. This integrative approach offers a promising path forward, one that honors the wisdom of diverse traditions while remaining open to new discoveries and perspectives. By recognizing both the constructed nature of our experience and the possibility of refining our models through various practices, we can develop a more nuanced, flexible, and empowering relationship with reality.

First, **reality as we experience it is not a simple, objective given.** Instead, it emerges from a dynamic and intricate interaction between an external world and our perceiving minds. This core insight is a powerful thread connecting all three domains:

- **Ancient Philosophy** (Chapter 4): Traditions like Hinduism's Maya and Buddhism's emphasis on the mind's role have long posited that our everyday perception is an illusory construction, veiling a deeper truth.

- **Quantum Physics** (Chapter 4): The **measurement-dependent nature of quantum phenomena** radically challenges classical objectivity, demonstrating that fundamental properties don't exist in a definite state independent of physical interaction; instead, our methods of inquiry play an active role in actualizing reality from a probabilistic superposition.
- **Neuroscience** (Chapter 5): The **brain's predictive processing model** reveals that what we experience as "reality" is a sophisticated, active construction based on sensory input, prior beliefs (Bayesian priors), and predictions geared for survival, not a passive, objective readout of the external world.

Second, our **models of reality are inherently limited and selective**, shaped by both cognitive and physiological constraints.

- **Philosophical insights** (Chapter 4): From Plato's allegory of the cave to Kant's distinction between phenomenal and noumenal worlds, ancient thinkers understood that our perception is filtered and structured by our minds.
- **Neuroscience of Perception** (Chapter 5): The brain's **cognitive biases and attentional bottlenecks** demonstrate that we are not wired to perceive every detail, leading to phenomena like change blindness and sensory illusions.
- **The Embodied Mind** (Chapter 7): Critically, our physiological state (including **gut health, nutritional status, sleep quality, and stress levels**) profoundly shapes the accuracy and coherence of our brain's reality-modeling processes. These biological factors are not merely peripheral influences but fundamental determinants of our capacity to perceive reality accurately and make optimal inferences.

Third, despite these limitations, our models of reality are **dynamic and can be continuously refined** through disciplined practices.

- **Ancient Wisdom** (Chapter 4): Contemplative traditions (like meditation in Hinduism and Buddhism) have long offered practices for transcending ordinary perception and accessing deeper truths, emphasizing direct, non-conceptual experience.
- **Quantum Physics** (Chapter 4): The scientific method itself, with its commitment to **falsifiability** and continuous questioning, embodies a relentless pursuit of deeper understanding through iterative experimentation.
- **The Bayesian Brain** (Chapter 5): This neuroscientific model provides a mathematical framework for how our brains *naturally* update beliefs based on new evidence. By consciously applying **Bayesian thinking**

(identifying priors, gathering evidence, weighing likelihoods, and updating posteriors), we can intentionally refine our personal models of the world. This active process allows us to overcome cognitive biases and adapt our beliefs for personal growth.

Fourth, our models of reality are **not merely theoretical constructs but have profound practical consequences** for how we live and interact with the world.

- **Philosophical traditions** (Chapters 4 & 6): From linking understanding reality with liberation from suffering (Buddhism) to emphasizing virtue and self-examination (Socrates), ancient wisdom offers frameworks for a flourishing life based on truth.
- **Neuroscience** (Chapters 5 & 7): Our brain's construction of reality directly impacts our emotional experiences (emotional illusions), social interactions (collective illusions), and physical well-being (via the embodied mind). Understanding these mechanisms provides actionable strategies for managing stress, improving decision-making, and enhancing overall health.
- **The Concept of Truth** (Chapter 6): Distinguishing between objective, subjective, and pragmatic truths enables us to navigate complex information environments and make more informed decisions, whether in personal life or the digital age.

Finally, the most comprehensive understanding of reality emerges not from choosing one perspective over others, but from **integrating insights across diverse traditions and scientific disciplines.** The striking parallels between ancient wisdom and modern scientific discoveries suggest that different approaches to understanding reality may be complementary rather than contradictory, each illuminating different facets of our relationship with the world. By recognizing both the embodied, physiological foundations of perception and the powerful cognitive and conceptual frameworks that give meaning to experience, we can develop a more complete and empowering model of how humans construct and interact with reality.

PART 3

A PRACTICAL TRANSFORMATION

CHAPTER 8
THE ART OF SELF SCRUTINY

*"The mind is not a vessel to be filled,
but a fire to be kindled."*
Plutarch

Alex stares at his reflection in the bathroom mirror after another difficult conversation with his partner. The same argument pattern happened again: a minor disagreement escalated into hurt feelings and defensive reactions. As the familiar spiral of self-criticism begins, "why do I always do this? what's wrong with me?," Alex feels stuck in a loop he can't seem to break.

Sound familiar? Most of us have been there. We know we have patterns that don't serve us, but we don't know how to change them. We want to grow and improve, but we're either too hard on ourselves (creating shame that paralyzes) or too easy on ourselves (avoiding the honest reflection that enables change). But what if there was a different way? What if self-examination could feel more like curiosity than criticism, more like detective work than self-attack?

The capacity for clear self-observation is one of your most powerful tools for growth. When we can see our patterns without being overwhelmed by them, when we can notice our reactions without being controlled by them, we can gain the following:

- The space between trigger and response, where conscious choice becomes possible.
- The possibility of intentional growth and learning how to see ourselves with greater clarity.

This isn't about becoming perfect or eliminating all our human quirks. It's about developing what psychologists call "metacognitive awareness," which is the ability to observe our thinking and emotional processes with clarity and compassion. It's like becoming the scientist of our own experience. In our exploration of reality models and how they shape our perceptions, we've established that our understanding of the world is neither fixed nor absolute. If our mental frameworks are malleable, then we possess the capacity to refine them, expand them, and ultimately transform how we navigate our experience of life. This isn't about harsh self-criticism but about developing the sophisticated skill of balanced self-examination that leads to genuine growth.

The embodied mind we explored in Chapter 7 provided the stable biological platform necessary for this psychological work. When our brain is well-nourished, adequately rested, and not overwhelmed by chronic stress, we can engage in the delicate process of honest self-reflection without becoming destabilized or defensive. Self-scrutiny is an art because it requires an exquisite balance of the following:

- Honesty to see our limitations clearly;
- Compassion to remain motivated for growth;
- Objectivity to recognize patterns; and
- Flexibility to adapt when circumstances change.

Mastering this balance gives us the opportunity to unlock our capacity for continuous evolution throughout life. In this chapter, we'll explore the sophisticated dance between self-examination and self-assurance, learning to recognize cognitive biases in our self-assessment while building evidence-based confidence. We'll learn about the type of metacognitive awareness that allows us to observe our mental processes rather than being unconsciously controlled by them. Let's explore how to become your own wise, kind, and discerning observer.

Developing Balanced Self-Awareness for Authentic Growth

The path of personal growth begins with a paradox: We must simultaneously question ourselves deeply and believe in our capacity to improve. We need to see ourselves clearly enough to grow, but not so harshly that we lose motivation to try. Too little self-examination and we stay stuck in unconscious patterns. Too much self-criticism and we create shame spirals that make change even harder. Finding the balance between these poles represents one of the fundamental challenges of mindful development.

Think of it like learning to drive. We need honest feedback about our mistakes (braking too late, taking corners too fast), but if an instructor constantly berates us ("You're terrible! You'll never learn!"), we would probably give up. The most effective learning happens in what we might call the "Goldilocks zone": honest enough to be useful, gentle enough to be sustainable.

The Balance Between Self-Examination and Self-Assurance

Self-examination without self-compassion can lead to a destructive spiral of criticism. Conversely, self-assurance without honest reflection can result in stagnation or delusional thinking. Research in positive psychology suggests that growth occurs most effectively in a mental environment that combines realistic assessment with fundamental self-acceptance. **Dr. Kristin Neff**, a pioneer in self-compassion research, distinguishes between self-esteem (which often depends on external validation and comparison to others) and self-compassion (which acknowledges our humanity and treats ourselves with the same kindness we would offer a friend). In her book **"Self-Compassion: The Proven Power of Being Kind to Yourself"** she indicates that self-compassion correlates more strongly with psychological well-being and resilience than self-esteem does. Neff tells us that:

> *"Self-compassion provides an island of calm, a refuge from the stormy seas of endless positive and negative self-judgment."*

This calm creates the psychological safety necessary for honest self-examination.

Table 19 – Self-Criticism vs Self-Comparison

	Self-Criticism Approach	Self-Compassion Approach
Motivation	Fear of inadequacy and social rejection	Genuine desire for well-being and growth
Emotional State	Shame, anxiety, defensiveness	Acceptance, curiosity, resilience
Response to Setbacks	Self-attack and rumination	Learning orientation and adaptive action
Long-term Outcomes	Decreased motivation, increased avoidance, mental health problems	Sustained motivation, increased resilience, better mental health

Dr. Neff identifies three essential elements of self-compassion that work together to create the psychological safety necessary for honest self-examination:

1. **Self-Kindness vs. Self-Judgment**

   Treat yourself with the same kindness you would offer a good friend who is struggling, rather than harsh internal criticism.

2. **Common Humanity vs. Isolation**

   Recognize that struggle, failure, and imperfection are part of the shared human experience rather than evidence of personal inadequacy.

3. **Mindfulness vs. Over-Identification**

   Hold painful thoughts and feelings in balanced awareness rather than being swept away by them or suppressing them entirely.

While self-compassion provides the emotional foundation for growth, evidence-based confidence provides the factual foundation. This type of confidence differs fundamentally from empty positive thinking or delusional self-regard; instead, it's grounded in accumulated evidence of your actual capabilities and resilience.

Table 20 – Components of Evidence-Based Confidence

Mastery Experiences	Successfully completing challenging tasks.
Vicarious Experiences	Observing others similar to yourself succeed.
Social Persuasion	Receiving credible encouragement and constructive feedback.
Physiological States	Managing stress responses and emotional reactions effectively.

These components were identified by psychologist **Albert Bandura**, whom we mentioned at the end of chapter 5 for his work on moral agency. In his self-efficacy research, these components of evidence-based confidence work together to create realistic confidence that can withstand setbacks and challenges. These components are far more than just vague affirmations. Evidence-based confidence develops through systematic documentation of actual achievements, problem-solving successes, and resilience demonstrations. But what happens when we struggle to believe in our abilities? What happens when, despite clear and verifiable evidence of competence, we experience a persistent feeling of being a fraud? This is referred to as Impostor Syndrome. **Dr Valerie Young**, co-founder of the impostor syndrome institute, worked with a group of high-achieving professionals experiencing impostor syndrome. Participants who maintained success journals for three months showed:

- 40% reduction in impostor feelings;
- Increased willingness to take on challenging assignments;
- Improved performance reviews;
- Better ability to internalize positive feedback; and
- Reduced anxiety about being "found out."

The key was helping participants see their accumulated evidence of competence rather than dismissing achievements as luck or external factors. So maybe keeping a journal should be something to consider.

Why Does This Matter to Your Daily Life?

What is your self-talk when you make a mistake?

Self-Critical Response:

- "I'm so stupid, I always do this" - Shame spiral that leads to avoidance - Motivation decreases over time - Creates anxiety about future challenges.

Self-Compassionate Response:

- "That didn't go well. What can I learn from this?" - Curiosity that leads to understanding - Motivation increases through safety - Builds resilience for future challenges.

Bottom Line: Studies show self-compassion leads to greater motivation for improvement, better emotional regulation, and increased willingness to try challenging tasks.

Recognizing Cognitive Biases in Self-Assessment

Despite the efficacy and sophistication of our brain's Bayesian inference processes, it has a fascinating quirk: It's much better at seeing other people's biases than its own. This isn't a design flaw; it's a feature that helped our ancestors survive by maintaining confidence and group cohesion. But in modern life, these blind spots can keep us stuck. Therefore, understanding these biases helps us develop more realistic self-perceptions and realistic goal setting. Here are some of the major self-assessment biases:

Table 21 – Examples of Self-Assessment Biases

Confirmation Bias in Self-Assessment	*We tend to seek information that confirms our existing beliefs about ourselves while ignoring contradictory evidence.*
Mechanism	Selective attention to self-confirming information.
Example	Noticing compliments that fit your self-image while dismissing those that don't.
Implications	Can maintain both overly positive and overly negative self-concepts.

Dunning-Kruger Effect	*Those with limited knowledge or skill in a domain tend to overestimate their abilities, while experts often underestimate theirs.*
Mechanism	Insufficient knowledge to recognize one's own incompetence.
Example	New drivers feeling overly confident; experienced drivers being overly cautious.
Implications	Can lead to taking on challenges you're not ready for or avoiding challenges you could handle.

Self-Serving Bias	*We attribute successes to our internal qualities and failures to external circumstances.*
Mechanism	Protects self-esteem but impairs learning from experience.
Example	"I got the promotion because I work hard" vs. "I didn't get promoted because of office politics."
Implications	Can prevent learning from failures and lead to overconfidence.

Availability Heuristic	*Recent or emotionally charged memories disproportionately influence our self-assessment.*
Mechanism	Easy-to-recall events seem more representative than they actually are.

Example	One bad presentation making you feel like a terrible public speaker.
Implications	Can lead to dramatic over- or under-estimation of abilities based on recent events.

Bias Detection Exercise:

Take five minutes to reflect on a recent success and a recent failure. For each:

1. Write down your initial explanation for why it happened.
2. Identify which biases might be influencing your explanation.
3. Challenge yourself to generate an alternative explanation that considers different factors.

   For example, if you succeeded on a project and immediately thought "I'm naturally talented at this," consider whether you're overlooking the role of preparation, support from others, or favorable circumstances.

Consider how these biases might be operating in your own self-evaluation. When you succeed at something, do you automatically attribute it to your "innate and natural" talent? If so, then you may want to consider whether you're overlooking the role of preparation, support from others, or favorable circumstances. Please understand that the intent is NOT to minimize our skills or talents. Instead, the goal is to seek balance between any hard work you can take credit for AND the role the environment and others have played in that success.

What about when the opposite takes place? When you fail, do you blame circumstances? Or maybe blame others? Blame is one of those things that many mental health experts recommend we eliminate from our minds and vocabulary. An old Chinese proverb comes to mind:

"He who blames others has a long way to go. He who blames himself is halfway there. He who blames no one has arrived."

The proverb clearly highlights the journey of self-awareness and personal growth. Awareness of these tendencies doesn't eliminate our biases but creates space for more nuanced self-understanding.

Developing Healthy Self-Criticism

Healthy self-criticism differs fundamentally from self-deprecation or harsh inner dialogue. It's characterized by:

- Specificity rather than generalization ("I could improve my presentation skills" versus "I'm terrible at communication");
- Focus on changeable behaviors rather than fixed traits;
- Constructive orientation toward improvement rather than punishment; and
- Balanced perspective that acknowledges strengths alongside areas for growth.

Recall research by psychologist **Albert Ellis** we introduced in chapter 5. Ellis is the founder of Rational Emotive Behavior Therapy (REBT)**,** which demonstrated that self-criticism becomes destructive when it involves "catastrophizing" (exaggerating the significance of mistakes) or "overgeneralizing" (applying specific failures to one's entire identity).

The Three-Column Technique Exercise:

Draw three columns on a page:

- In the first column, write down a self-critical thought.
- In the second, identify the cognitive distortion (e.g., catastrophizing, black-and-white thinking).
- In the third, write a more balanced perspective.

Example:

Column 1: "I completely failed that presentation."

Column 2: "Overgeneralization"

Column 3: "Some parts went well, and I can improve specific aspects next time."

Healthy self-criticism reframes your internal dialogue. Recall that reframing is a key element of upgrading the model of the world and ourselves that we host in our brains. Reframing will not deliver immediate results, just like going to the gym once will deliver immediate results. The idea is engaging in a disciplined process that teaches our brain how to predict better in the future instead of predicting the same old way it has in the past. So, instead of allowing yourself to think "I'm so disorganized, I'll never get anything done," teach yourself to say "I notice I'm struggling with organization in this particular project. What specific strategies might help me improve?"

Genuine confidence isn't about positive thinking or affirmations disconnected from reality. Rather, it emerges from accumulated evidence of our capabilities and resilience. For those who enjoy writing things down, consider maintaining a "success journal" documenting challenges conquered, skills developed, and positive feedback received. Follow Bandura's Evidence-Based Confidence components while documenting in the journal, especially when facing new challenges. This is a great way to begin the process of building up genuine confidence. Here is an example:

Success Journal Template Exercise:

Create a dedicated notebook or digital document with these sections:

1. **Achievements**: Record specific accomplishments, both large and small.
2. **Challenges Overcome**: Document obstacles you've navigated successfully.
3. **Skills Developed**: Track abilities you've improved over time.
4. **Positive Feedback**: Note constructive comments from others.
5. **Lessons Learned**: Capture insights gained from both successes and setbacks.

Spend 5 minutes at the end of each week adding to your journal, and review it monthly. This practice grounds your confidence in reality rather than wishful thinking.

To build evidence-based confidence, we have to put ourselves in a position where we will have experiences. We have to get up and "Do Something". Sometimes those experiences will lead to desired outcomes, and sometimes they won't. Both scenarios will position us to build confidence.

Practices for Balanced Self-Reflection

Developing the capacity for balanced self-reflection requires intentional practice. Consider incorporating these approaches:

1. **Structured reflection**:

    Set aside regular time (daily, weekly, or monthly) for deliberate self-assessment. Use prompts like "What went well this week and why?" and "What challenges did I face, and what can I learn from them?"

2. **Third-person perspective**:

    When evaluating yourself, try adopting the perspective of a wise, compassionate mentor. What would they notice about your progress and challenges?

3. **Feedback integration**:

   Actively seek feedback from trusted others, noting patterns across different sources while recognizing that all feedback is filtered through others' biases.

4. **Values alignment check**:

   Regularly assess whether your actions align with your core values, focusing less on achievement and more on consistency with what matters most to you.

5. **Meditation practices**:

   Mindfulness meditation cultivates the capacity to observe thoughts non-judgmentally, creating space between observation and reaction.

5-Minute Self-Reflection Exercise:

Take five minutes at the end of your day to answer these specific questions:

1. What went well today, and what personal strengths did I utilize?
2. What challenged me today, and how did I respond?
3. What would I do differently if I could revisit one interaction from today?
4. What am I grateful for in this moment?

These practices help develop what psychologists call "psychological flexibility," which is the ability to contact the present moment fully while changing or persisting in behavior that serves valued ends. Understanding our cognitive biases reveals why developing the capacity to observe our thinking process (rather than being completely identified with it) is such a powerful tool for growth and freedom.

Metacognition

Right now, as you read this sentence, something remarkable is happening: part of your mind is observing another part of your mind reading. This ability to think about thinking (called metacognition) is one of our most uniquely human capacities. While self-scrutiny focuses on what we think about ourselves, metacognition addresses how we think about thinking itself. This higher-order awareness of our cognitive processes represents a crucial capacity for mindful growth. We can begin explaining this concept with a very simple example. Pause right now and ask yourself the following questions:

1. What was I thinking about as I read the previous section?

2. Was I fully engaged, or was my mind wandering?
3. What assumptions am I making about this material?
4. How does this connect to what I already know?

Notice how this brief exercise shifts your awareness from the content to your own thinking process. Be honest with yourself and notice your thoughts and how you "feel" about those thoughts. Did you think that the previous section felt irrelevant or perhaps entirely aligned with your existing views? It turns out that in either case, there may be inherent biases that need to be observed, questioned, and optimized, and that is why we engage in this self-scrutiny process. We do this to question our Bayesian model in order to teach it to predict better in the future, so that our future is better than our past.

Understanding "Thinking About Thinking"

Metacognition involves monitoring and controlling our cognitive processes to become aware of our mental operations and learn to direct them more effectively. It encompasses:

- **Metacognitive knowledge**:

    Understanding our own cognitive strengths, weaknesses, and strategies

- **Metacognitive regulation**:

    Planning, monitoring, and evaluating our thinking processes

- **Metacognitive experiences**:

    The conscious experiences that accompany cognitive activities

Here is an example to ponder on: When reading this chapter, metacognitive knowledge might involve recognizing that you tend to understand concepts better when you relate them to personal experiences. Metacognitive regulation might include deciding to pause after each section to summarize key points. A metacognitive experience might be the sudden awareness that your mind has wandered from the text.

This capacity isn't merely academic; <u>it fundamentally shapes how we learn, make decisions, solve problems, and relate to others.</u>

Everyday Metacognitive Failures and Their Consequences:

Consider these common scenarios:

1. **The Email Misunderstanding**:

   Sarah drafted an email while feeling frustrated. She sent it immediately without pausing to review how her tone might be perceived. The recipient interpreted her directness as hostility, damaging their working relationship and requiring several follow-up conversations to repair.

2. **The Impulse Purchase**:

   Michael bought an expensive gadget during a flash sale, convinced it was exactly what he needed. He failed to question his excitement or consider his actual usage patterns. Three months later, the device sits unused in a drawer, which is a costly reminder of unexamined thinking.

3. **The Misplaced Certainty**:

   Jamie confidently presented a solution based on her expertise during a team meeting. When colleagues raised questions, she dismissed them, not recognizing her overconfidence bias. The implemented solution failed because of factors she hadn't considered, but others had tried to raise.

The Neuroscience of Metacognitive Awareness

Neuroscientific research has begun to illuminate the brain mechanisms underlying metacognition. Studies using functional magnetic resonance imaging (fMRI) have identified several brain regions associated with metacognitive processes, particularly the prefrontal cortex and anterior cingulate cortex.

The prefrontal cortex (especially its anterior regions) appears crucial for monitoring our thoughts and evaluating our performance. This area develops relatively late in human evolution and continues maturing well into early adulthood, which may explain why metacognitive abilities typically strengthen with age and experience.

Interestingly, research by neuroscientist **Stephen Fleming** suggests that metacognitive abilities vary independently of cognitive abilities themselves. Someone might perform well on cognitive tasks but have poor insight into their performance, or vice versa. This finding underscores that metacognition is a distinct capacity that can be specifically cultivated.

Metacognitive Strategies for Daily Life

Metacognition isn't confined to formal learning environments; it applies to virtually every domain of life. Here are specific strategies for enhancing metacognitive awareness in different contexts:

Reflection Techniques

- **Thought journaling**: Regularly document not just what you think, but how you think. Note patterns in your reasoning, emotional influences on your thinking, and moments of insight or confusion.
- **Decision post-mortems**: After making significant decisions, analyze your decision-making process. What information did you consider? What assumptions influenced you? What cognitive shortcuts did you take?
- **Cognitive labeling**: Practice identifying specific thinking patterns as they occur. For example, "I notice I'm catastrophizing right now" or "I'm using black-and-white thinking in this situation."

Decision-Making Frameworks

- **Pre-mortem analysis**: Before finalizing important decisions, imagine that your choice led to failure, then work backward to identify what might have gone wrong. This counters optimism bias and reveals potential blind spots.
- **Decision journals**: Document important decisions, including the context, your reasoning, expected outcomes, and uncertainties. Review these periodically to improve your decision-making process.
- **Multiple-models approach**: Deliberately apply different mental models to the same situation. How would an economist view this problem versus a psychologist? What would a historical perspective reveal versus a systems-thinking approach?

Pre-mortem and Pre-parade Analysis Exercise:

When making an important decision, create both a "pre-mortem" and "pre-parade" analysis:

1. Imagine it's one year later, and your decision led to complete failure. Write a detailed narrative describing what went wrong and why.
2. Now imagine it's one year later and your decision led to remarkable success. Write a detailed account of what went right and why.
3. Compare both scenarios to identify hidden assumptions, potential blind spots, and critical factors you might have overlooked.

For example, if you're considering a career change, your pre-mortem might reveal concerns about financial stability you hadn't fully acknowledged, while your pre-parade might highlight the importance of mentorship to your success.

Table 22 – Troubleshooting Common Metacognitive Obstacles

Obstacle	Symptom	Solution
Cognitive overload	Mind feels scattered, difficulty focusing on thinking processes.	Simplify tasks, use external memory aids, practice single-tasking.
Emotional reactivity	Strong emotions override metacognitive awareness.	Implement the 5-second pause, name emotions explicitly, practice self-compassion.
Habitual autopilot	Acting without awareness, falling into routine patterns.	Create environmental triggers (colored dots), schedule regular check-ins, vary routines.
Social pressure	Conforming to group thinking without examination.	Prepare independent thoughts before group discussions, assign a "devil's advocate" role.
Time pressure	Rushing decisions without metacognitive review.	Build in mandatory reflection periods, use simple heuristics like "If rushed, pause."

Learning to Recognize Mental Patterns

- **Cognitive distortion identification**: Familiarize yourself with common cognitive distortions (catastrophizing, mind-reading, overgeneralization, etc.) and practice spotting them in your thinking.
- **Emotional awareness**: Notice how different emotional states influence your thinking patterns. Anxiety might trigger excessive focus on risks, while excitement might lead to overlooking potential obstacles.
- **Belief examination**: Periodically question your fundamental assumptions about yourself, others, and how the world works. What evidence supports these beliefs? What contradicts them?

Developing Metacognitive Skills

Like any complex ability, metacognition develops through deliberate practice. Research suggests several approaches for strengthening this capacity:

1. **Explicit instruction**:

   Learning about cognitive processes and biases provides a vocabulary and framework for metacognitive awareness.

2. **Regular self-questioning**:

   Developing the habit of asking questions like "How do I know this?" "What assumptions am I making?" and "What alternative explanations exist?"

3. **Collaborative dialogue**:

   Discussing your thinking processes with others often reveals blind spots and alternative perspectives.

4. **Mindfulness practices**:

   Meditation and other mindfulness techniques strengthen the capacity to observe thoughts non-judgmentally.

5. **Challenging cognitive tasks**:

   Engaging with problems that stretch your cognitive abilities creates opportunities to observe your thinking under pressure.

Something to consider – Meditation and modern science:

Neuroscientist Richard Davidson has demonstrated that mindfulness meditation can produce measurable changes in brain structure and function. Regular meditators show increased gray matter density in areas associated with attention and emotional regulation, while showing decreased activity in the default mode network associated with self-referential thinking.

Tibetan monks with over 10,000 hours of meditation practice showed gamma wave activity (associated with heightened awareness) up to 700% above baseline, which are levels never before recorded in neuroscience research. This suggests that systematic contemplative practice can produce extraordinary states of consciousness measurable through scientific instruments

Thought Diffusion Exercise:

When caught in repetitive or unhelpful thinking, practice labeling thoughts as thoughts rather than facts by using the phrase *"I'm having the thought that..."* before the content. For example, transform *"I'm not good enough"* to *"I'm having the thought that I'm not good enough."* This creates psychological distance from thoughts and reduces their emotional impact. Try this right now with a recurring thought that troubles you:

1. Notice the thought in its usual form.
2. Restate it beginning with *"I'm having the thought that..."*
3. Notice any shift in how you relate to the thought.

Viewing intelligence and cognitive abilities as malleable rather than fixed creates motivation to develop metacognitive skills.

Metacognition's Role in Developing a Personal Philosophy

Effective self-scrutiny requires a coherent framework that guides how we approach self-examination, learning, and growth. This personal philosophy should be explicit rather than unconscious, adaptable rather than rigid, and grounded in evidence rather than wishful thinking. Metacognition serves as a cornerstone to this process for several reasons:

- It enables us to identify and modify limiting thought patterns.
- It helps us transfer learning across different domains and contexts.
- It facilitates adaptation to new situations and challenges.
- It supports emotional regulation by creating space between stimulus and response.
- It fosters intellectual humility by highlighting the limitations of our thinking.

As philosopher and psychologist **William James** noted:

> *"The greatest discovery of my generation is that human beings can alter their lives by altering their attitudes of mind."*

Table 23 – Examples Personal Development Philosophy Components

Growth Orientation	
Fundamental Belief	Abilities and traits are developable through effort and learning.
Mistake Reframe	Errors are information for improvement rather than evidence of inadequacy.
Challenge Embrace	Difficult situations are opportunities for growth rather than threats to avoid.

Process Focus	Success is measured by learning and improvement rather than just outcomes.

Evidence-Based Approach	
Data Gathering	Decisions about self-improvement based on reliable information.
Hypothesis Testing	Treating changes as experiments to be evaluated.
Feedback Integration	Actively seeking and learning from input from others.
Measurement Focus	Tracking progress through observable indicators.

Balanced Perspective	
Strength Recognition	Acknowledging existing capabilities and resources.
Limitation Acceptance	Honestly recognizing areas needing development.
Context Awareness	Understanding how situations influence performance.
Timeline Realism	Accepting that meaningful change takes time and patience.

Self-Compassion Integration	
Kindness Principle	Treating yourself with the same care you'd offer a good friend.
Common Humanity	Recognizing that struggle and imperfection are universal.
Mindful Awareness	Observing difficulties without being overwhelmed by them.
Sustainable Motivation	Maintaining energy for long-term development.

Metacognition, in essence, provides the mechanism for this alteration, the means by which we can observe, evaluate, and redirect our mental processes toward greater wisdom and effectiveness.

These insights about balanced self-awareness, cognitive biases, and metacognition aren't just intellectually interesting; they are skills you can develop through specific practices that create lasting changes in how you experience and navigate life.

Chapter 8 Summary: Key Insights

The ability to see ourselves clearly without losing motivation or self-worth is a learnable skill that forms the foundation for continuous growth throughout life. This sophisticated skill allows us to see patterns clearly enough to change them while maintaining the emotional safety necessary for sustained motivation and learning. However, this requires integrating self-compassion with honest assessment, developing metacognitive awareness, and creating systematic approaches to self-examination. Here are some essential takeaways of this chapter:

1. **Self-Compassion Foundation**:

    Honest self-examination requires the psychological safety created by treating yourself with kindness, recognizing common humanity in struggle, and maintaining mindful awareness of difficulties.

2. **Evidence-Based Confidence**:

    Sustainable confidence comes from systematically documenting your actual achievements, capabilities, and resilience rather than empty positive thinking or harsh self-criticism.

3. **Bias Compensation**:

    Accurate self-assessment requires understanding and compensating for cognitive biases like the Dunning-Kruger effect (mentioned in chapters 5 and 8), self-serving bias, and confirmation bias through multiple data sources.

4. **Metacognitive Awareness**:

    The ability to observe your thinking processes rather than being completely absorbed in them transforms your relationship to thoughts and emotions, creating space for conscious choice.

5. **Constructive Self-Evaluation**:

    Healthy self-criticism focuses on specific behaviors rather than global character, emphasizes learning over punishment, and maintains a balanced perspective on both strengths and growth areas.

The self-awareness and metacognitive skills developed through a balanced self-scrutiny process create the foundation for the next crucial aspect of human development: authentic, effective connection and communication with others. When we can observe our own thoughts and emotions with clarity and compassion, we're ready to engage in genuine dialogue rather than unconscious reactivity.

In the next chapter, we'll explore how the classical principles of communication – ethos, pathos, and logos – remain as relevant today as they were in ancient Greece. We'll discover how self-awareness transforms our ability to listen deeply, express ourselves clearly, and navigate disagreement constructively. We'll also learn how authentic communication serves not just external relationships but continues the internal development work we've been exploring.

The journey from self-scrutiny to communication mastery will reveal how individual awareness and interpersonal skill reinforce each other in a continuous cycle of growth and connection.

CHAPTER 9
COMMUNICATING BETTER

"Effective communication is the bridge between inner awareness and outer connection"

David sits across from his wife at the dinner table, feeling the familiar knot in his stomach. They need to talk about money again. Last time this conversation ended with her in tears and him sleeping on the couch. He has facts, spreadsheets, and logical arguments about why they need to cut spending. She gets emotional and says he doesn't understand what matters to her. David's approach is always the same: present the data, explain the logic, and wait for her to see reason. When that doesn't work, he gets frustrated and speaks louder, as if volume could somehow make truth more convincing. She retreats, he feels unheard, and nothing gets resolved.

What David doesn't realize is that he's trying to play a symphony using only one instrument. Communication isn't just about transferring information from one brain to another. Communication is a complex dance involving logic, emotion, identity, relationship dynamics, and shared meaning-making. He's been speaking in pure "logos" (logic) to someone who also needs "ethos" (trust) and "pathos" (emotional connection) before she can truly hear him.

Meanwhile, David's wife has been doing the same thing but in reverse order: She leads with emotion and values, hoping he'll understand what money means to her beyond mere numbers. She wants to feel heard and valued before diving into spreadsheets. She needs to know they're partners, not adversaries, before she can engage with his logical concerns. Neither of them is wrong. They're just operating on different communication dimensions simultaneously, like two radios tuned to different frequencies, each broadcasting clearly but neither able to receive the other's signal.

Communication is the bridge between our internal reality and the external world. It's through communication that we express our thoughts, understand others' perspectives, and collectively construct shared meaning. Enhancing this capacity is essential for personal growth and effective engagement with others. Yet despite its central importance to human life, most of us received little formal training in this crucial skill beyond basic grammar and vocabulary.

The good news is that the self-awareness we've explored through balanced self-scrutiny and self-observation in chapter 8 creates the foundation for truly effective communication. When we can observe our own thoughts and emotions with clarity and compassion, we're prepared to engage authentically with others rather than communicating from unconscious reactivity or defensive positioning. Additional good news is that the basic principles of effective communication aren't mysterious. They were figured out over 2,000 years ago by the ancient Greeks, validated by modern psychology, are completely learnable, and have proven remarkably durable across cultures and centuries.

Great communication isn't just about transmitting information clearly; it's about creating connection, facilitating understanding, and enabling collaborative problem-solving. By understanding and applying these principles, we can transform not just our conversations, but also our relationships, our capacity for learning from others, and our ability to consume information responsibly.

Let's explore how ancient wisdom and modern science can help you become the kind of communicator you've always wanted to be.

Beyond Information Exchange: The Multi-Dimensional Nature of Communication

Most people think of communication as information transfer: transmitting thoughts from our mind into someone else's mind as accurately and expediently as possible. This, however, is only the tip of the iceberg. While clarity is important, this mechanical view misses the profound richness of human interaction. Every conversation operates simultaneously across multiple dimensions, each influencing the overall effectiveness and meaning of the exchange. Every conversation should include at least the following dimensions:

- **Informational or Content Dimension**: These are the facts, ideas, or data being shared. It is important to be clear, accurate, and relevant.
- **Emotional Dimension**: This includes the feelings we convey and perceive, and builds rapport and psychological safety. It is important to focus on emotional attunement, mood creation, and emotional safety.
- **Identity Dimension**: This is the way we communicate who we are and what we value, which allows us to validate each other's sense of self and authenticity.
- **Relationship Dimension**: This provides the context for how the content should be interpreted. Important elements are trust development, conflict navigation, and mutual support.
- **Cultural Dimension**: This includes the cultural unspoken rules, values, and assumptions that shape how we interact. Important elements are communication styles, group belonging, and tradition navigation.

Research in communication theory suggests that misunderstandings often arise not from information gaps but from failing to recognize these multiple dimensions. For instance, what appears to be a disagreement about facts might actually reflect a clash of identities or a breakdown of trust. This is why purely logical arguments often fail to persuade, why technically accurate information can damage relationships, and why well-intentioned conversations sometimes go wrong. Effective communication requires awareness of these dimensions and the ability to navigate them all. Here are some common communication failures to watch out for:

Table 24 – Some Common Communication Failures

Information-Only Focus	Emotional Overwhelm	Identity Conflicts
Providing data without considering emotional impact.	Letting feelings dominate without including necessary facts.	Threatening others' sense of self through criticism.
Overwhelming others with details they don't need.	Making others responsible for managing your emotions.	Demanding that others change fundamental aspects of who they are.
Ignoring whether people are ready to receive information.	Assuming others share your emotional experience.	Failing to acknowledge others' values and perspectives.

Failing to connect information to what others care about	Using emotions to manipulate rather than communicate	Communicating in ways that feel inauthentic to yourself

Effective communicators recognize which dimensions are most relevant in a given interaction and adjust their approach accordingly. Sometimes clarity of information is paramount; other times, emotional attunement takes precedence. The magic happens when all dimensions align: people feel heard, understood, and respected, which creates the psychological safety necessary for productive dialogue even when discussing difficult topics.

Learning from Ancient Argumentation Wisdom

Over 2,300 years ago, the Greeks (specifically Aristotle) developed a sophisticated understanding of persuasion and dialogue that remains remarkably relevant today. He developed a framework for effective communication centered on three core elements: **Ethos** (Credibility), **Pathos** (Emotion), and **Logos** (Logic/Reason), along with considerations of timing (**Kairos**) and purpose (**Telos**). Before diving into Aristotle's framework, we must take a moment to clarify two words that, although popular in today's language, were used differently in ancient Greece.

Argumentation and Persuasion in Ancient Greece vs Today

There's a significant difference in the connotation and scope of "argumentation" as it was understood by the ancient Greeks, and how it's often perceived in today's modern discourse. The ancient Greek understanding of the word and process of argumentation, particularly through Aristotle's lens, was far more expansive, ethically grounded, and deeply integrated into the fabric of a functioning society. It was a high art aimed at effective persuasion for the common good and the pursuit of reasoned decision-making. Today, the term is often narrowed to denote conflictual exchanges, losing much of its original richness and positive implications. Here is some background:

Table 25 – Argumentation in Ancient Greece vs Today

Argumentation in Ancient Greece	
Holistic and Constructive	Argumentation wasn't merely about winning a dispute but about finding the available means of persuasion in any given situation. The goal was often to lead an audience to a more informed or virtuous understanding, or to make the best decision for the city-state or polis.
Emphasis on Truth and Probability	While persuasion was key, the underlying assumption was often that reasoned argument would lead closer to truth or the most probable and sensible course of action. It was a method for exploring ideas, testing propositions, and arriving at well-considered conclusions.
Focus on Civic Duty	Engaging in effective argumentation was seen as a civic responsibility, essential for democratic deliberation, legal proceedings, and public discourse. In essence, it was a positive force for societal progress.

Argumentation Today	
Conflict and Disagreement	In contemporary usage, "argument" or "argumentation" often conjures images of heated disputes, shouting matches, or simply people disagreeing vehemently. It's frequently associated with conflict and a desire to "win" at all costs.
Negative Emotions	The word itself can evoke feelings of stress, confrontation, and even anger. People often say things like, "I don't want to argue" to avoid conflict.
Lack of Productiveness	While formal debate still exists, everyday "arguments" are often perceived as unproductive, leading to stalemates rather than genuine understanding or resolution.

Focus on Opposition	The emphasis tends to be on opposing viewpoints rather than a collaborative search for truth or common ground.
Misconception of "Manipulation"	Aristotle's use of emotion (pathos) framework is often misinterpreted today as solely a tool for manipulative emotional appeals, rather than a legitimate aspect of human communication.

Just like argumentation, the word "persuasion" has also lost much of its classical gravitas and positive association. For Aristotle, persuasion was a vital, multi-faceted art that, when practiced ethically, was <u>essential for civic life, the pursuit of truth, and collective well-being</u>. Today, it's often viewed through a more cynical lens, frequently linked to manipulation, self-serving interests, and emotional rather than rational influence. Aristotle's views on persuasion can be summarized as follows:

- **A Natural and Necessary Human Faculty:**

    For Aristotle, persuasion was not inherently good or bad; it was a "faculty of observing in any given case the available means of persuasion." It was a neutral tool, like a knife, that could be used for good (e.g., upholding justice, guiding public policy) or ill (e.g., misleading the populace).

- **Integral to Deliberative Democracy:**

    In the Athenian democracy, the ability to persuade was paramount. Citizens had to be able to speak effectively in the assembly, advocate for their positions, and convince their peers. Persuasion was the engine of public discourse and decision-making.

- **Connected to Truth and Virtue (Ideally):**

    While Aristotle acknowledged that rhetoric could be used for unethical purposes, his ideal was that true and just arguments would, by their nature, be easier to persuade with. The *Rhetoric* aimed to equip speakers with the tools to defend truth and good, and to counter fallacious or harmful arguments. The integration of *ethos* (character, trustworthiness, credibility) into the means of persuasion highlights this ethical dimension. In the Aristotelian sense, a truly persuasive speaker would ideally be someone of good character and sound judgment.

- **A Means to Social Harmony and Progress:**

    Effective persuasion, by allowing for the free exchange of ideas and reasoned debate, was seen as contributing to the welfare and "good life" (eudaimonia) of the citizens and the polis (city-state). It was a way to resolve disputes, make collective decisions, and advance society.

We can clearly see the difference in how the term persuasion is used today in day-to-day conversations:

- **Manipulation and Self-Interest:**

    The most common negative association with "persuasion" today is that it's a technique used to subtly or overtly manipulate someone into doing or believing something that primarily benefits the persuader, not necessarily the persuaded. Think of "sales tactics," "spin," or "propaganda."

- **Emotional Appeals Over Reason:**

    While Aristotle explicitly included *pathos*, modern perceptions often see emotional appeals as inherently less legitimate or even deceptive compared to logical arguments. If someone is "persuading" you, there's often an underlying suspicion that they're trying to play on your emotions rather than engage your intellect.

- **Marketing and Advertising:**

    A huge chunk of modern persuasion occurs in the commercial realm. Advertising often employs highly sophisticated persuasive techniques, which, while effective, can contribute to the idea that persuasion is about getting people to buy things they don't need or want.

- **Distrust of "Rhetoric":**

    The word "rhetoric" itself, which is essentially the art of persuasion, has largely taken on a negative connotation, often implying empty words, insincere promises, or political posturing. This reflects the broader distrust of persuasion.

- **The "Zero-Sum" Game:**

    Modern persuasion is often framed as a contest where one side wins and the other loses, rather than a process of shared exploration or building consensus.

Aristotle's classical connotation for both Argumentation and Persuasion is far more useful than the current meaning. With this in mind, we can now dive into his fundamental elements of persuasive communications.

The Classical Foundation: Ethos, Pathos and Logos

- **Ethos**

    This concerns the credibility and character of the communicator. It asks: Do others trust what you're saying <u>based on who you are and what you've demonstrated over time</u>? Ethos isn't just about credentials; it's about demonstrating that you've done your homework, that you have relevant experience, and that you approach conversations with integrity.

    Modern Example of Ethos: *When Malala Yousafzai speaks about girls' education, her ethos comes from her lived experience as someone who risked her life for education, not just from her Nobel Prize or academic credentials.*

    Table 26 – Components of Ethos

Components of Ethos	
Competence	Do you know what you're talking about?
Character	Do others trust your intentions and integrity?
Connection	Do people feel you understand and care about their concerns?
Consistency	Does your communication align with your actions?

Building Ethos in Modern Context	
Do Your Homework	Research topics thoroughly before speaking about them.
Acknowledge Limitations	Be honest about what you don't know.
Share Your Sources	Help others understand how you developed your perspective.
Admit Mistakes	Correct errors promptly and openly when they occur.
Show Up Consistently	Let your actions align with your words over time.

- **Pathos**

    This involves the emotional dimension of communication. It recognizes that pure logic rarely persuades; people need to feel that you understand their emotional landscape and that your message resonates with their values and concerns. This is not manipulation through emotion, but authentic recognition that humans are feeling beings who need emotional connection to fully engage with ideas.

    Modern Example of Pathos: *Climate activists who share stories of specific communities affected by environmental changes often connect more effectively than those who only present statistical data, even when both are communicating the same core message.*

    Table 27 – Components of Pathos

Components of Pathos	
Emotional Attunement	Sensing and responding to others' emotional states.
Shared Values	Connecting ideas to what people genuinely care about.
Story and Metaphor	Using narrative to make abstract concepts personally meaningful.
Empathic Listening	Understanding others' emotional experience before trying to influence it.

- **Logos**

    This represents the logical structure of your argument. It's about evidence, reasoning, and helping others follow your thinking step by step. But effective logos isn't about overwhelming people with data; instead, it's about how well your ideas fit together, how solid your evidence is, and how clearly you help others follow your reasoning.

    Modern Example of Logos: *When explaining complex medical decisions, effective doctors don't just list statistics but create clear cause-and-effect explanations that patients can follow, often using visual aids or analogies.*

    Table 28 – Components of Logos

Components of Logos	
Clear Structure	Ideas organized in logical sequence

Quality Evidence	Reliable information that supports your points
Sound Reasoning	Logical connections between ideas
Consideration of Alternatives	Acknowledging different perspectives and potential objections

Aristotle's approach provides us with a solid foundation to improve the way we communicate across the various facets of daily life. Being credible, having positive emotion, and using logic and reason are three key elements for all our important conversations. Great things can happen when these three elements work together harmoniously. Pure logic (logos) without credibility (ethos) or emotional connection (pathos) feels cold and abstract. Emotional appeal (pathos) without logical foundation (logos) or credibility (ethos) seems manipulative. Credibility (ethos) without logical content (logos) or emotional resonance (pathos) appears authoritarian. But that is not all. In addition to Ethos, Pathos, and Logos, Aristotle also introduced Kairos and Telos:

- **Kairos**

    This addresses timing and context. Even the most well-crafted message can fall flat if delivered at the wrong moment or in inappropriate circumstances. Masterful communicators develop sensitivity to when others are ready to hear certain ideas.

    Modern Example: *A company CEO who waits until after a successful quarter to announce organizational changes, rather than during a period of uncertainty, demonstrates an understanding of Kairos.*

- **Telos**

    This focuses on purpose and goals. Before entering important conversations, skilled communicators clarify what they're trying to accomplish: Are they seeking to learn, to persuade, to solve a problem, or to strengthen a relationship?

    Modern Example: *A parent discussing screen time with a teenager will communicate differently depending on whether their goal is to establish firm rules, understand their child's perspective, or collaboratively develop solutions.*

Conversation Script Template: Applying Ethos-Pathos-Logos

Here's how we can structure a difficult conversation using the classical framework:

- **Opening (Ethos + Relationship Building):**

    "I wanted to talk with you about [topic]. I've been thinking about this carefully and have done some research/reflection. I value our relationship and want to understand your perspective as well."

- **Understanding (Pathos + Active Listening):**

    "Before I share my thoughts, I'd like to understand how you see this situation. What matters most to you about this?"

    [Listen actively, then acknowledge their perspective] "I can see why you feel that way, especially given [reference something specific they shared]."

- **Your Perspective (Logos + Clear Structure):**

    "From my perspective, there are three key aspects to consider:

    1. First, [your initial point with supporting evidence]
    2. Second, [your next point with reasoning]
    3. Finally, [your concluding point with implications]"

- **Finding Common Ground (Integration):**

    "It seems we both care about [shared value or concern]. Could we start by focusing on that area of agreement?"

- **Next Steps (Practical Application):**

    "What do you think would be a good way forward? I'd suggest [specific, reasonable action]."

The Greeks understood something we often forget: Persuasion isn't about winning; it's about creating the conditions where people can think together effectively. When Ethos, Pathos, and Logos work together, and when Kairos and Telos complement them, you're not manipulating someone into agreement; you're creating space for genuine, timely, and purposeful understanding and collaborative problem-solving.

Internal Communication: Dialoguing with Yourself

Before we can communicate effectively with others, we must establish clear and compassionate communication with ourselves. The quality of our internal dialogue directly influences our external expression; harsh self-criticism creates defensive communication, while balanced self-awareness enables authentic connection. Internal dialogue shapes our thinking, emotional responses, and subsequent external communication.

In chapter 3, we introduced the work of psychologist **Lev Vygotsky** on thought and language. He proposed that our internal speech develops from the internalization of social dialogue. Initially, children speak aloud to themselves (private speech), gradually transitioning to inner speech. This suggests that the quality of our self-talk reflects, in part, the communication patterns we've experienced with others. Improving internal communication involves:

- **Developing precise language for thoughts and feelings**:

    At the end of chapter 3, we shared that language shapes our thoughts, giving us new ways to conceptualize and understand the world. We established then that our level of awareness of the world around us is in part determined by the richness of our vocabulary. It turns out that this doesn't only apply to our external world but also to our internal world. Expanding your emotional vocabulary beyond basic terms like "good" or "bad" to more nuanced descriptors is a key element of creating a healthy internal communication practice. Below is a table with useful emotional language terms:

    Table 29 – Examples of Useful Emotional Language Terms

Basic words	Examples of more precise words
Anxious	Worried, concerned, apprehensive, panicked, overwhelmed
Sad	Disappointed, melancholy, grief-stricken, despairing
Angry	Irritated, frustrated, furious, outraged, resentful
Joyful	Content, pleased, delighted, ecstatic, euphoric

- **Questioning internal narratives**:

    Examine the stories you tell yourself about events, relationships, and your own capabilities. Recall that this is a core technique in Cognitive Behavioral Therapy (CBT) introduced in chapter 5.

- **Cultivating compassionate self-talk**:

    Address yourself with the same kindness and respect you would offer a valued friend.

- **Clarifying values and priorities**:

Revisit regularly what matters most to you, especially when facing difficult decisions. This is a key component of therapies like **Acceptance and Commitment Therapy (ACT)**, which helps individuals find clarity and direction in their lives.

Self-Talk Transformation Scripts:

Here are some examples of how to transform negative internal dialogue into constructive self-talk:

Scenario 1: After a Mistake

- Negative: "I'm such an idiot. I always mess things up."
- Constructive: "I made a mistake, which is something all humans do. What can I learn from this situation, and how can I address it effectively?"

Scenario 2: Facing a Challenge

- Negative: "This is too hard. I'll never be able to do this."
- Constructive: "This is challenging for me right now. What specific aspects am I struggling with, and what resources might help me develop in those areas?"

Scenario 3: Receiving Criticism

- Negative: "They think I'm incompetent. I should just give up."
- Constructive: "This feedback points to specific areas where I can improve. It doesn't define my worth or overall abilities."

In his book "**Chatter: The Voice in Our Head, Why it Matters and How to Harness It**," psychologist **Ethan Kross** suggests that using third-person language in self-talk (referring to yourself by name rather than as "I") can create psychological distance that enhances perspective and reduces emotional reactivity. For instance, in Scenario 2, the thought "I'll never be able to do this" could become "Leo, you're struggling right now, but you can find a way forward." This simple shift can make challenging thoughts feel more manageable and less personal. Practicing these deliberate shifts in your internal dialogue is the first step toward reclaiming agency over your inner world.

Advanced Interpersonal Communication Skills

In an increasingly interconnected yet often polarized world, the quality of our interactions and conversations dictates the success of our relationships, organizations, and societies. While basic communication allows us to exchange information, it is the mastery of *advanced interpersonal communication skills* that truly enables us to bridge divides, foster deep understanding, and collaboratively address complex challenges.

In this section, we dive into three fundamental pillars of an elevated style of communication:

- The art of truly hearing others through advanced listening;
- The precision of articulating complex thoughts; and
- The crucial ability to navigate disagreement productively.

By exploring the scientific underpinnings and practical applications of these skills, we aim to illuminate a path towards more effective, empathetic, and impactful human connections. This approach helps us balance self-expression with receptivity to others, which in turn presents us with the opportunity to mitigate many of the problems we experience at home, at work, in the community, and globally.

Advanced Listening: Fostering Connection and Understanding

Advanced listening is an active, sophisticated skill that goes far beyond simply waiting for your turn to speak. It involves multiple levels of attention and creates the psychological safety necessary for authentic communication. It is a profound and intentional process of fully attending to, understanding, and responding to a speaker, encompassing their explicit message, underlying emotions, and the broader context of their communication. This critical skill forms the bedrock of effective relationships, robust decision-making, and transformative change.

The scientific exploration of active listening began primarily with **Carl Rogers** and his colleagues in the mid-20th century. Arising from their work in **client-centered therapy**, Rogers emphasized that creating a therapeutic and growth-fostering environment hinged on three core conditions:

- **Empathy:** This is the genuine ability to understand and share the feelings of another from their unique perspective.
- **Unconditional Positive Regard:** This involves accepting and respecting the speaker without judgment, valuing their inherent worth.
- **Congruence (Genuineness):** This means being authentic and real in the interaction, fostering trust.

Advanced listening, within this framework, is a manifestation of these attitudes, crucial for establishing psychological safety and enabling deeper self-exploration and positive change.

Building on foundational active listening techniques, advanced listening ascends through deeper levels of engagement, as conceptualized by frameworks like **Otto Scharmer's Levels of Listening**, which illustrates the varying depths of our attention:

- **Downloading (Internal Listening):** Consider whether you listen primarily to confirm what you already know, reinforcing existing mental models and biases. While basic, recognizing this default mode is the first step towards deeper listening.

- **Factual Listening (Focused Listening):** Attend to external facts and objective data, and be open to new information that may contradict prior views. This is where traditional active listening techniques like **paraphrasing** ("So, what I hear you saying is...") and **clarifying questions** ("Could you explain what you mean by X?") are crucial for accurate comprehension.

- **Empathic Listening (Global/Intuitive Listening):** Move beyond words and facts to connect with the speaker's emotions, intentions, and underlying experiences. This involves:

    - **Reflecting Feelings:** Acknowledging and verbalizing the emotions expressed ("You seem frustrated by that")
    - **Attending to Non-Verbal Cues:** Interpreting body language, tone, and facial expressions (supported by research in non-verbal communication)
    - **Listening for the Unsaid:** Sensing what is implied, hinted at, or intentionally omitted.

- **Generative Listening (Systemic Listening):** The deepest level, involving listening for emergent possibilities, collective potential, and the dynamics of the broader system. It's about listening with an open mind and seeking insights that can transform the situation or relationship. This level often involves:

    - **Suspension of Judgment:** Consciously putting aside preconceptions
    - **Sensing the Whole:** Being aware of the interconnectedness of elements within a conversation or system

The profound impact and benefits of advanced listening are extensively documented across various disciplines:

- **Improved Relationships & Trust:** It creates deeper rapport, strengthens bonds, and fosters psychological safety, making individuals feel truly valued and understood.
- **Enhanced Problem-Solving & Innovation:** By truly comprehending diverse perspectives and underlying needs, individuals and groups can develop more comprehensive, creative, and robust solutions.
- **Increased Empathy & Emotional Intelligence:** Consistent practice cultivates a greater capacity to understand others' emotional states and enhances one's own emotional awareness and regulation.
- **Reduced Misunderstanding & Conflict:** Clearer, deeper communication inherently leads to fewer errors, less friction, and more constructive engagement during disagreements.
- **Neurological Correlates:** Emerging neuroimaging research suggests that deep, empathic listening activates reward systems in the listener's brain and can lead to "neural coupling" or synchronization between speaker and listener, indicating a profound, shared mental state.

Research by psychologist **John Gottman** found that successful relationships maintain a 5:1 ratio of positive to negative interactions, with active listening contributing significantly to the positive side of this equation.

Advanced listening is a sophisticated, learnable skill with a strong scientific basis. By consciously employing its techniques and cultivating its underlying attitudes of deep empathy and openness, individuals can significantly improve their relationships, foster profound understanding, and contribute to more effective, innovative, and harmonious interactions in every aspect of personal, professional, and societal life.

Articulating Complex Thoughts: Precision, Clarity, and Impact

The ability to articulate complex thoughts (to convey intricate ideas, nuanced perspectives, and multi-layered information clearly, concisely, and effectively) is a cornerstone of advanced interpersonal communication. This skill is paramount for leadership, problem-solving, collaboration, and bridging understanding gaps across diverse audiences in an increasingly complex world.

Cognitive Foundations: How Our Brains Process Information

Effective articulation is rooted in an understanding of human cognition. Scientific theories illuminate how we should structure communication to maximize comprehension:

- **Cognitive Load Theory (John Sweller):**

  This theory explains that our working memory has limited capacity. Effective articulation minimizes "extraneous cognitive load" (information irrelevant to learning), allowing the audience's limited resources to focus on essential information. Messages overloaded with jargon, disorganization, or unnecessary detail strain this capacity.

- **Schema Theory:**

  People understand new information by fitting it into existing mental frameworks or "schemas." Effective articulation either leverages familiar schemas or provides clear scaffolding to build new ones, making abstract concepts relatable.

- **Chunking:**

  Our brains process information in manageable "chunks." Presenting complex ideas in discrete, logically connected units helps with comprehension and retention.

  Research in cognitive psychology, educational psychology, and psycholinguistics consistently supports these principles, demonstrating how human information processing capabilities dictate optimal communication design.

Principles of Effective Articulation

Drawing from research in linguistics, communication science, and cognitive psychology, several empirically supported principles underpin impactful articulation:

- **Clarity and Simplicity:**

  - **Plain Language:** Use accessible vocabulary over specialized jargon, especially when communicating across disciplines. And define any necessary technical terms clearly.
  - **Directness:** Avoid overly convoluted sentences or the passive voice.

  Studies on readability (e.g., **Flesch-Kincaid**) and the "curse of knowledge" (**Pinker, Steven**, 2015) demonstrate that simpler, more direct language significantly enhances comprehension and recall across diverse audiences.

- **Structure and Organization:**

    - **Logical Flow:** Present ideas in a coherent, step-by-step manner (e.g., problem-solution, cause-effect, chronological, general-to-specific).
    - **Signposting:** Use clear transitions, introductory statements, and concise summaries to guide the audience through the thought process.
    - **Modularization:** Breaking down complex ideas into digestible, interconnected segments.

    Research in instructional design and rhetoric consistently shows that well-structured communication improves understanding, retention, and the ability to follow a complex argument.

- **Audience-Centricity (Empathic Adaptation):**

    - **Perspective-Taking:** Tailor content, examples, analogies, and language to the audience's existing knowledge, background, interests, and potential biases.
    - **Identifying Key Takeaways:** Focus on what the audience *needs* to know, *feels* about, or *needs to do* with the information.

    Communication Accommodation Theory (**Giles, Howard** 1973) and extensive research on persuasive communication emphasize the critical role of adapting messages to the audience's frame of reference for maximal impact.

- **Precision and Specificity:**

    - **Concrete Examples:** Use vivid examples, anecdotes, or analogies to illustrate abstract concepts.
    - **Data and Evidence:** Support claims with precise data, facts, or observations.
    - **Avoiding Ambiguity:** Choose words that convey exact meaning and minimize misinterpretation.

    Cognitive linguistics and communication studies highlight the power of specific, concrete language in creating clear mental models and reducing ambiguity.

- **Conciseness:**
  - **Efficiency:** Eliminate unnecessary words, redundant phrases, or extraneous details.
  - **Impact:** Get to the point efficiently without sacrificing clarity.

  Research on attention spans, information overload, and principles of effective writing consistently demonstrates that brevity enhances impact and message retention.

Delivery and Impact (Beyond Words)

Beyond verbal content, non-verbal cues significantly influence how complex thoughts are received:

- **Confident Delivery:** Appropriate posture, gestures, and eye contact enhance perceived credibility (ethos) and maintain audience engagement.
- **Voice Modulation:** Variation in pacing, tone, and volume can emphasize key points, manage cognitive load, and sustain interest.
- **Strategic Use of Visual Aids:** Well-designed diagrams, graphs, and images can simplify complex data, illustrate relationships, and leverage dual-coding theory (**Paivio, Allan** 1986) for better comprehension and memory.

Articulating complex thoughts is a highly advanced, learnable skill grounded in cognitive science and communication theory. By mastering the principles of clarity, structure, audience adaptation, and precise delivery, individuals can effectively convey their ideas, influence others, foster shared understanding, and drive innovation in an increasingly interconnected world.

Navigating Disagreement Productively: From Conflict to Collaboration

Disagreement is an inherent and inevitable aspect of human interaction, arising from the diverse perspectives, values, and goals that enrich our lives. The advanced communication skill lies not in avoiding conflict, but in transforming it into an opportunity for deeper understanding, creative problem-solving, stronger relationships, and collective progress.

Psychological Underpinnings of Conflict

Understanding the cognitive and emotional mechanisms that often derail disagreements is crucial for navigating them constructively:

- **Attribution Theory:** Individuals often attribute different causes to events or behaviors (e.g., internal character flaws vs. external situational factors), leading to misunderstandings and misjudgments of intent.
- **Confirmation Bias & Cognitive Dissonance:** People tend to seek out, interpret, and remember information that confirms their existing beliefs (confirmation bias) and experience discomfort when confronted with information that contradicts them (cognitive dissonance), making objective engagement challenging.
- **Emotional Contagion & Amygdala Hijack:** Stressful disagreements can trigger rapid, instinctive "fight-or-flight" responses (amygdala hijack), impairing rational thought, escalating emotional intensity, and hindering productive dialogue.

   Scientific Basis: Extensive research in social psychology, cognitive psychology, and neuroscience provides the foundation for these insights into human conflict behavior.

Principles of Productive Disagreement

Drawing from research in conflict resolution, negotiation, and communication studies, several strategies enable effective disagreement:

- **Emotional Regulation and Self-Awareness:**
    - **Pausing and De-escalation:** Recognizing personal emotional triggers and employing conscious strategies (e.g., deep breathing, taking a planned break, reframing thoughts) to calm physiological and psychological responses.
    - **Self-Awareness:** Understanding one's own underlying assumptions, biases, emotional state, and personal stakes in the disagreement.

   Research on emotional intelligence (**Goleman, Daniel**, 2005), mindfulness practices, and stress reduction techniques demonstrates the critical role of self-management in conflict.

- **Empathetic Understanding (Leveraging Advanced Listening) :**
    - **Perspective-Taking:** Actively and genuinely seek to understand the other person's viewpoint, their motivations, underlying inter-

ests, and concerns, even if you profoundly disagree with their conclusion. This involves listening for the "why" behind their "what."
- **Validation:** Acknowledge the legitimacy of the other's feelings or perspective, without necessarily agreeing with their stance ("I can see why you feel that way," "That's a valid concern to have").

Research in conflict mediation, Nonviolent Communication (**Rosenberg, Marshall**, 1999), and client-centered therapeutic principles (introduced in the section on advanced interpersonal communication skills) consistently shows that empathy and validation are powerful de-escalation tools that build rapport and openness.

- **Clear and Non-Blaming Articulation:**

  - **"I" Statements:** Express your own needs, feelings, and concerns from your personal perspective ("I feel concerned when X happens," "I need Y"), rather than making accusatory "you" statements ("You always do X").
  - **Focus on Behaviors, Not Character:** Critique specific actions, statements, or ideas, rather than attacking the other person's character, intelligence, or motives.
  - **Specific, Actionable Feedback:** Clearly state what the issue is and what kind of resolution or change is sought, avoiding vague complaints.

  Communication research on effective feedback delivery, de-escalation techniques, and relational communication highlights the importance of non-defensive and precise language.

- **Focus on Shared Goals and Interests (Beyond Positions):**

  - **Interest-Based Negotiation (Roger Fisher & William Ury – Getting to Yes):** Shift the dialogue from rigid positions ("I want X") to exploring underlying interests ("Why do I want X? What need does it fulfill?"), which often reveals common ground or alternative solutions that satisfy both parties' true needs.
  - **Collaborative Problem-Solving:** Frame the disagreement as a shared challenge to be solved together, fostering a "we against the problem" mentality rather than "me against you."

  Extensive research in negotiation theory, organizational psychology, and mediation practices demonstrates the superior outcomes of interest-based approaches over positional bargaining.

- **Establishing Rules of Engagement and Psychological Safety:**
    - **Agreed Ground Rules:** Set explicit norms for the discussion (e.g., no interruptions, listen to understand, one person speaks at a time, commit to seeking resolution).
    - **Creating a Safe Space:** Foster an environment where all parties feel psychologically safe to express their views, concerns, and vulnerabilities without fear of retaliation, ridicule, or humiliation.

Research on psychological safety in teams (**Edmondson, Amy**, 2018) and group dynamics underscores its critical role in enabling open dialogue, learning from mistakes, and constructive conflict.

Outcomes of Productive Disagreement

When disagreements are navigated skillfully, they yield significant benefits:

- Enhanced creativity and innovation (through the clash of ideas);
- Stronger, more resilient relationships built on mutual respect;
- Better, more robust decision-making (by rigorously challenging assumptions and exploring diverse alternatives);
- Increased understanding and empathy among all parties; and
- Sustainable resolutions that address underlying needs.

Productive disagreement is a highly sophisticated, learnable communication skill that transforms potential conflict into powerful opportunities for growth, fosters robust collaboration, and is essential for navigating the complexities of modern personal, professional, and societal life. Mastering it is not about avoiding friction, but about harnessing its energy for positive, collective progress.

The journey through advanced listening, the articulation of complex thoughts, and the productive navigation of disagreement reveals not just a set of techniques but a profound shift in how we engage with ourselves and others. These three areas, deeply rooted in psychological and communication science, are not merely "soft skills"; they are essential competencies for thriving in a world characterized by diversity and constant change. By cultivating the capacity to truly understand, to express ourselves with clarity and impact, and to transform conflict into constructive dialogue, we equip ourselves with the tools to build stronger relationships, foster innovation, and make more informed decisions. Ultimately, the widespread practice of these advanced interpersonal communication skills offers a powerful and tangible pathway toward a more collaborative, understanding, and harmonious future for all.

A Practical Framework for Communication Improvement

Drawing from these ancient principles and modern research, we can outline a systematic approach to improving our communication. This framework, tested across countless historical examples and applicable to daily conversations, provides a structured path for development.

Phase 1: Self-Assessment and Pattern Recognition

The journey begins with honest self-evaluation. Most of us have developed communication habits that may have served us in certain contexts but limit our effectiveness in others. Common patterns include:

- **The Reactor**: Responding immediately and emotionally, without pause for reflection
- **The Lecturer**: Dominating conversations with information rather than creating dialogue
- **The Avoider**: Sidestepping difficult conversations to maintain surface harmony
- **The Overwhelmer**: Providing too much information without a clear structure
- **The Rusher**: Seeking immediate resolution without allowing time for processing

  Recognizing your primary pattern isn't about self-judgment — it's about awareness that enables intentional change. For one week, track your significant conversations and note patterns in your listening-to-speaking ratio, emotional states, learning moments, and processing time.

Phase 2: Building the Foundation

Once you understand your current patterns, the next phase involves systematically developing the core elements of effective communication.

1. **Week 1 - Ethos (Credibility) :**

   Focus on building your credibility through preparation and authentic sharing. Before important conversations, ask yourself: Do I know enough about this topic to speak with authority? What's my track record on this subject? How can I demonstrate I've done my homework?

   Practice explicitly sharing your sources of knowledge: "I read this in...", "My experience with this was...", "I learned from..." This isn't about showing off; it's about helping others understand the foundation of your perspectives.

2. **Week 2 - Logos (Logic and Evidence) :**

   Concentrate on the logical structure of your communications. For each argument you make, identify your evidence, verify that your facts are current and accurate, and consider what others would need to know to understand your position.

   Practice using the phrase "Let me break this down" and actually provide 2 to 3 supporting points. This forces you to organize your thoughts and makes it easier for others to follow your reasoning.

3. **Week 3 - Pathos (Emotional Connection) :**

   Before responding emotionally, practice asking: What emotion am I feeling right now? What emotion is the other person experiencing? How can I acknowledge both while staying constructive?

   Use phrases like "I understand why you might feel..." before presenting your viewpoint. This doesn't mean agreeing with everything; it means recognizing the emotional reality that underlies different perspectives.

Phase 3: Advanced Integration

1. **Timing and Context (Kairos) :**

   Develop sensitivity to when and where conversations should happen. Before important discussions, ask: Is this the right time? What's the other person's current emotional and mental state? What external factors might affect this conversation?

   Practice delaying conversations when the timing isn't optimal. Use phrases like "Let me think about that" or "That's a good point, give me a moment to process."

2. **Purpose and Goals (Telos) :**

   Before each important conversation, clarify your intentions: What do I want to achieve? What would success look like? Am I trying to win, learn, solve problems, or build relationships?

   Start conversations with clarity about your goals: "My goal here is..." or "I'm hoping we can..."

Phase 4: The Three-Pillar Practice

Once you've developed familiarity with the individual elements, integrate them into what can be called the "Three-Pillar Practice": Listen + Speak + Process.

- **Advanced Listening (70/30 Rule):**

    Aim to listen 70% of the time and speak 30%. This isn't about being passive, it's about asking clarifying questions, summarizing what you've heard, and using phrases like "What I'm hearing is..." followed by "Is that accurate?"

- **Strategic Speaking (Quality Over Quantity):**

    Make your points in groups of three maximum. Use the Socratic method, ask two questions for every statement you make. Replace "I think..." with "What do you think about..."

- **Processing Integration:**

    Implement processing breaks in conversations. In heated discussions: "Let's both take 10 minutes to think about this." In complex decisions: "I'd like to sleep on this before we decide." In learning conversations: "That's interesting, let me process what you've shared."

Communication Across Worldviews

Perhaps the greatest communication challenge involves bridging fundamentally different ways of understanding reality. As explored in earlier chapters, people operate from diverse reality models that shape what they perceive as relevant, credible, and meaningful. In an increasingly diverse and politically polarized world, effective cross-worldview communication requires:

- **Epistemological humility**: Recognizing the limitations of your own knowledge framework
- **Conceptual translation**: Finding ways to express ideas in terms that resonate within different worldviews
- **Identifying shared reference points**: Establishing common ground through experiences or values that transcend worldview differences
- **Patience with misunderstanding**: Accepting that perfect understanding may not be immediately possible

Anthropologist **Wade Davis** notes that:

> *"The world in which you were born is just one model of reality. Other cultures are not failed attempts at being you; they are unique manifestations of the human spirit."*

This perspective fosters the openness necessary for genuine cross-worldview communication. Here are some communication strategies that might be useful when building a bridge of alternative ways to understand reality:

- **Find Shared Values:** Even when people disagree on specific policies or approaches, they often share underlying values like family well-being, community safety, or fairness. Starting with shared values creates common ground for productive dialogue.
- **Use Perspective-Taking:** Research by psychologist **Daniel Batson** shows that actively imagining others' experiences increases empathy and reduces prejudice, even across significant worldview differences.
- **Apply the Principle of Charity:** Give others the benefit of the doubt by assuming they have good reasons for their beliefs, even when you disagree with their conclusions.
- **Practice Intellectual Humility:** Acknowledge the limitations of your own knowledge and remain open to learning from those with different perspectives.

Advanced Techniques: Productive Concession and Strategic Patience

There are advanced skills that can transform how we navigate difficult conversations:

1. **Productive Concession**

    Involves finding valid points in every disagreement and acknowledging them. This isn't about surrendering your position – it's about demonstrating intellectual honesty and building credibility for your stronger arguments. Use phrases like "You're right about…" before presenting your counterpoint.

    Historical examples abound: Let's take the **Lincoln-Douglas debates**. These were a series of seven debates between the Democratic senator Stephen Douglas and Republican challenger Abraham Lincoln during the 1858 Illinois senatorial campaign, largely concerning the issue of slavery extension into the territories. Despite fundamental disagreements, Lincoln and Douglas treated each other with respect and made strategic concessions during their debates. When Douglas was forced to admit that territories could reject slavery under popular sovereignty, he conceded the point rather than dodging it. This honesty actually hurt him politically, but demonstrated intellectual integrity. In the Pulitzer-winning book **Battle Cry of Freedom**, **James M. McPherson** narrates some of the context behind this historical set of debates between Lincoln and Douglas.

2. **Strategic Patience**

   Means accepting partial progress rather than demanding immediate total agreement. Instead of seeking complete victory, look for areas of partial alignment. End conversations with "What can we agree on?" or "Where do we have common ground?"

   The Montreal Protocol provides a powerful example: The Montreal Protocol, an international treaty adopted on September 16, 1987, aimed to regulate the production and use of chemicals that contribute to the depletion of Earth's ozone layer. Initially signed by 46 countries, the treaty now has nearly 200 signatories. The agreement to ban CFCs started with only 40-50% scientific certainty about ozone depletion. Countries accepted partial progress rather than demanding 100% certainty. Through multiple iterations over several years, they achieved the consensus needed for effective action. Today, the ozone layer has largely recovered.

3. **Steelmanning Technique**

   Instead of attacking weak versions of others' arguments (known as strawmanning), steelmanning involves presenting others' viewpoints in their strongest, most compelling form before responding. This technique can build trust, demonstrate good faith, and reveal insights you might otherwise miss. The steelmanning process involves the following:

   1. **Listen Deeply**: Understand the other person's perspective as thoroughly as possible.
   2. **Strengthen Their Argument**: Present their viewpoint in its most compelling form.
   3. **Confirm Accuracy**: Check that they feel accurately represented.
   4. **Respond Thoughtfully**: Address the strong version of their argument rather than weak points.

   Although steelmanning fosters deeper understanding, promotes productive dialogue, and can lead to more robust solutions, it can be time-consuming, requires a degree of trust, and can potentially lead to over-generous interpretations. In his book **Intuition Pumps and Other Tools for Thinking**, philosopher **Daniel Dennett** offers a similar principle called the Principle of Charitable Interpretation. Dennett's principle is a philosophical guideline for interpreting someone's argument in the most rational and coherent way possible to avoid misinterpretations. In short, the Principle of Charity helps us understand our opponent's argument fairly. In contrast, steelmanning helps us strengthen our argument for the sake of a more productive and intellectually honest debate. Dennett himself, in his work, often moves from the principle of charity to a process that looks very much like steelmanning, demonstrating the close relationship between the two and the value they can both add to conversations.

Technology and the Evolution of Human Communication

hnologies have transformed how we connect, introducing new possibilities and challenges:

- **Global reach**: Digital platforms enable communication across vast distances and social boundaries
- **Persistence**: Digital communication creates permanent records that can be reviewed and shared
- **Information sharing**: Easily exchange documents, images, and complex data
- **Community building**: Find others with shared interests or experiences
- **Asynchronicity**: Communication across time zones and schedules
- **Multimodality**: Integration of text, audio, video, and interactive elements

However, these technologies also present challenges:

- **Reduced nonverbal cues**: Digital text communication eliminates facial expressions, tone of voice, and body language
- **Context collapse**: Messages intended for specific audiences reach unintended recipients
- **Attention fragmentation**: Multiple simultaneous conversations reduce the depth of engagement
- **Emotional Amplification**: Misunderstandings escalate more quickly without immediate feedback
- **Digital Disinhibition**: People say things online they wouldn't say face-to-face
- **Filter bubbles**: Algorithmic curation limits exposure to diverse perspectives

Fortunately, there are ways to make the most of digital communications. Here are some useful principles:

Compensate for Missing Cues	
Be more explicit	State intentions and emotions that would normally be conveyed nonverbally.
Use clarifying questions	Check understanding more frequently than in face-to-face communication.
Phone calls for complexity	Use voice or video for emotionally charged or complex topics.
Emoji judiciously	Use emotional indicators when appropriate, but don't rely on them exclusively.

Manage Attention Deliberately	
Single tasking	Focus on one conversation at a time rather than multitasking.
Response timing	Don't feel obligated to respond immediately; thoughtful responses are better than quick ones.
Notification management	Control when and how you receive digital interruptions.
Deep work protection	Create time blocks free from digital communication.

Practice Digital Empathy	
Assume positive intent	When messages seem harsh or unclear, consider benevolent interpretations.
Consider context	Remember that others may be dealing with stresses or circumstances you don't know about.
Private first	Address concerns privately before involving groups or public forums.
Repair quickly	If misunderstandings occur, clarify promptly rather than letting them fester.

Research by **Sherry Turkle** at MIT suggests that while digital communication offers connection, it may not provide the conversation necessary for developing empathy and deep understanding. Balancing technological convenience with intentional, present-focused interaction represents a crucial communication skill in the digital age.

Chapter 9 Summary: Key Insights

Masterful communication involves far more than information transmission – it requires conscious navigation of multiple dimensions, including emotion, identity, relationship, and culture. Integrating ancient wisdom with modern psychological insights allows you to develop communication skills that build authentic connections while facilitating collaborative problem-solving and mutual growth. Here are some essential takeaways:

1. **Multi-Dimensional Awareness**:

   Every conversation operates across informational, emotional, identity, relationship, power, and cultural dimensions simultaneously, requiring conscious attention to whichever dimensions are most relevant.

2. **Classical Integration**:

   The ancient framework of ethos (credibility), pathos (emotional connection), and logos (logical structure) remains powerful when integrated thoughtfully rather than used manipulatively.

3. **Internal Foundation**:

   Quality external communication depends on healthy internal dialogue characterized by self-compassion, precise emotional language, and curious self-inquiry rather than harsh self-judgment.

4. **Advanced Listening**:

   True listening involves multiple levels from basic content focus to intuitive understanding of unspoken needs, creating the psychological safety necessary for authentic expression.

5. **Constructive Disagreement**:

   Conflict becomes creative when you focus on underlying interests rather than surface positions, practice steelmanning others' arguments, and seek win-win solutions that honor everyone's values.

The communication mastery we've explored in this chapter (from deep listening to productive disagreement) creates the vital interpersonal foundation for your journey. This outward skill, deeply rooted in the **self-awareness and metacognition** cultivated through self-scrutiny (Chapter 8), and supported by the **embodied well-being** of your entire biological system (Chapter 7), now converges into the ultimate expression of mindful growth.

We've covered how our brain constructs reality, how beliefs shape perception, and how ancient wisdom resonates with modern science. The challenge now is to weave all these insights into the fabric of our daily existence, transforming knowledge into embodied wisdom and sustained action.

In our final chapter, we introduce **The 39-Minute Journey:** a practical, integrated daily framework designed to make continuous growth achievable and sustainable. This journey will show how individual development and authentic connection (fueled by everything we've discovered about our evolutionary heritage, predictive brains, and the nature of truth) can be systematically integrated into habits that truly transform your life, 39 minutes at a time. It's the culmination of our exploration: turning profound understanding into a powerful, personalized practice.

CHAPTER 10
YOUR DAILY PRACTICE: THE 39-MINUTE JOURNEY

"Everything we hear is an opinion, not a fact. Everything we see is a perspective, not the truth."
Marcus Aurelius

Transforming abstract principles into concrete growth requires structured processes. This might sound mechanical, but it reflects a profound truth about human development: insights without implementation remain mere intellectual entertainment, while implementation without systematic approaches rarely creates lasting change.

We've journeyed through our evolutionary heritage, the brain's predictive power, the constructed nature of reality, and the art of self-scrutiny. Now, the question isn't just 'what is real?' but 'how do I live optimally within that reality?'

The answer lies not in massive overhauls, but in consistent, intentional daily action. This chapter introduces a simple yet powerful framework: **The 39-Minute Journey.** Imagine dedicating just 13 minutes to nurture your **Body**, 13 minutes to cultivate your **Mind**, and 13 minutes to nourish your **Soul** each day. This short, sustainable investment (less than one hour) can fundamentally transform your well-being, deepen your awareness, and enhance your engagement with the world. It's a pragmatic, science-backed approach to integrate all the wisdom we've uncovered into the fabric of your daily life. It's designed to be achievable for everyone, because surely, we can all find 39 minutes in our day to invest in becoming our best selves. And if you have more than 39 minutes, then that is great... invest another 39.

The Science of Sustainable Change: Why 39 Minutes Works

Most approaches to personal development ignore crucial insights from neuroscience about how the brain works and how it changes. Understanding these mechanisms allows you to design growth processes that align with your natural learning systems rather than fighting against them. The consistent, intentional practice embedded in the 39-Minute Journey directly leverages the brain's natural mechanisms for learning and change, ensuring your efforts yield lasting results.

- **Neuroplasticity in Action:**

    Your brain is remarkably plastic, capable of reorganizing itself and forming new connections throughout your life. Every moment of **focused attention** and **repetitive practice** during your 39 minutes physically sculpts your neural pathways, strengthening desired behaviors and mental habits. This happens through molecular changes, enhanced neural communication (myelination), and the gradual shift from conscious effort to effortless automaticity. Just as exercise strengthens muscles, consistent mental and physical practices remodel your brain. This involves a neuroplasticity cycle where **intention setting** primes the brain for learning, **focused attention** strengthens neural connections, **repetitive practice** builds habits and myelinates pathways, and **rest and integration** solidify new learning during sleep.

- **Leveraging Prediction:**

    Your brain is a prediction machine, constantly updating its model of the world. Each deliberate practice in the 39-Minute Journey provides your brain with new, high-quality data to refine its predictions. When your predictions are successfully refined through these conscious efforts, your brain's reward systems are engaged, reinforcing the new patterns and encouraging continued learning. This is how you proactively teach your brain to predict better futures, moving beyond outdated models.

- **Optimizing the Growth Cycle:**

    Sustainable growth follows a cyclical pattern that honors both the need for new insights and the requirement for practical implementation. This cycle can be applied to any area of development, from professional skills to personal relationships to spiritual practice. Your daily 39 minutes actively engage all three phases. You gain **awareness** of patterns during reflection, **integrate** new insights into your mental models, and **apply** them through concrete actions. This continuous loop ensures that insights don't just stay in your head but become embodied wisdom.

Table 30 – Example of Sustainable Growth Cycle

Awareness
This is recognizing patterns, limitations, or opportunities for development. This might involve noticing recurring emotional reactions, identifying cognitive biases, or discovering new perspectives through reading or conversation.
Integration
This is processing new insights by connecting them to existing knowledge and experience. This phase involves reflection, journaling, discussion with others, or other forms of active engagement with new awareness.
Application
This is translating insights into concrete behavior changes. This might include practicing new communication techniques, implementing decision-making frameworks, or establishing habits that support continued growth.

Research on adult development by **Robert Kegan** and **Lisa Lahey** suggests that transformative learning requires not just cognitive understanding but also emotional processing and practical application. Their *Immunity to Change* framework demonstrates that awareness alone rarely produces lasting change without addressing the underlying adaptive challenges.

- **Working with Your Nature (The 50-40-10 Rule):**

    Sustainable change, as research suggests, relies significantly on intentional activities. The 39-Minute Journey places you firmly in control of your 40% of "intentional activities." By consistently engaging in these manageable practices, you work *with* your neurobiology and temperament, rather than fighting against them, creating supportive environments for lasting change. Research by psychologist **Sonja Lyubomirsky** suggests that sustainable change depends on three factors in roughly equal proportions.

Table 31 – The 50-40-10 Rule

50% Genetics and Temperament	
Personality Traits	Basic patterns of thinking, feeling, and being
Cognitive Style	How you naturally process information and make decisions
Emotional Reactivity	Your typical responses to stress, challenge, and opportunity
Physical Constitution	Energy levels, health patterns, and biological rhythms

40% Intentional Activities	
Conscious Practices	Meditation, exercise, journaling, skill development
Behavioral Choices	How you spend time, who you spend it with, what you focus on
Environmental Design	Creating contexts that support desired behaviors
Systematic Learning	Deliberate acquisition of new knowledge and capabilities

10% Life Circumstances	
External Conditions	Income, living situation, work environment, relationships
Life Events	Major changes, challenges, and opportunities
Cultural Context	Social norms, available resources, community support
Historical Moment	Technology, political climate, economic conditions

The 39-Minute Journey: Your Daily Practice

This framework offers a flexible template. Choose 1-2 activities for each segment, adapting them to your needs and energy levels. The key is consistency and intentionality, not rigid adherence.

13 Minutes for the Body: Nurturing Your Embodied Mind

(Drawing from Chapter 7: The Embodied Mind – Gut Health, Nutrition, Sleep, Stress Regulation)

This segment is about actively supporting your physical self, recognizing that your brain is deeply intertwined with your entire biological system. Optimal cognitive function, clear perception, and emotional resilience all depend on a well-cared-for body.

Choose 1-2 of these daily, for a total of 13 minutes:

- **Mindful Movement (e.g., 7-10 minutes):** Engage in stretching, mindful walking (even around your living space), light bodyweight exercises, Yoga, or Tai Chi. This supports neuroplasticity, reduces physical tension, and enhances blood flow to the brain. Connect with how your body feels, noticing sensations if you prefer more intense workouts, of course, that is fine too. The point is to move mindfully and intentionally.

- **Conscious Breathing (e.g., 5-7 minutes):** Practice diaphragmatic or box breathing. This directly regulates your **autonomic nervous system**, shifting it towards the "rest and digest" parasympathetic state, reducing the impact of chronic stress and fostering a calm foundation for clearer thinking. There are a variety of wonderful breathwork apps available online. Breathwork can prepare you at the beginning of the day, before an important meeting at work, before a conversation with a family member, or at the end of a long day.

- **Nutritional Check-in (e.g., 3-5 minutes):** Briefly reflect on your next meal or snack. Ask: "Am I choosing foods that support my brain and gut health?" Prioritize anti-inflammatory options (like fruits, vegetables, healthy fats) and recognize the profound impact of your **gut microbiome** on mood and cognition. This is not a one-way street: the brain and gut are in constant communication. Leading neurogastroenterologist **Emeran Mayer**, in his work at UCLA, has pioneered the research showing that the trillions of microbes in our gut profoundly influence our brain's function, affecting everything from our emotional responses to our cognitive performance. This isn't about rigid dieting, but conscious, supportive choices.

- **Hydration Moment (e.g., 1-2 minutes):** Simply drink a glass of water, fully present with the sensation. Proper hydration is fundamental for brain function and energy. Recall that it is important to stay hydrated throughout the day. The rule of thumb for daily intake is to take half your body weight and drink that amount in ounces.

13 Minutes for the Mind: Refining Your Reality Model

(Drawing from Chapters 3, 5, & 8: The Predictive Brain, Bayesian Inference, Self-Scrutiny, Metacognition)

This segment focuses on intentionally observing and refining your brain's internal model of reality, improving its predictions, and navigating cognitive biases. This is where you practice the "Art of Self-Scrutiny."

Choose 1-2 of these daily, for a total of 13 minutes:

- **Metacognitive Moment (e.g., 5-7 minutes):** Use an **Environmental Trigger** (like a colored dot on your phone or computer, as discussed in Chapter 8). When you see it, pause and ask: "What am I thinking/feeling right now? What assumptions am I making? What evidence supports or challenges this thought?" This helps you notice your brain's **predictive processing** and identify potential **cognitive biases**.

- **Prediction Error Reflection (e.g., 5-7 minutes):** Briefly recall a recent situation where your expectations didn't match reality. Ask: "What was my prediction? What actually happened? What can I learn to update my model for next time?" This is a quick daily application of **Bayesian thinking**, turning "prediction errors" into learning opportunities.

- **Belief Scrutiny (e.g., 5-7 minutes):** Briefly apply the **Three-Column Technique** (Chapter 8) mentally to a recurring limiting thought or judgment. Transform "I'm not good enough" into "I'm having the thought that I'm not good enough" (Thought Diffusion). This creates **psychological distance** and supports **belief updating**.

- **Values Alignment Check (e.g., 3-5 minutes):** Review one or two of your core values briefly. Ask: "Did my actions/decisions today align with this value? How can I embody it more fully tomorrow?" This connects your daily actions to your deepest sense of self and purpose.

13 Minutes for the Soul: Cultivating Meaning and Connection

(Drawing from Chapters 1, 2, 4, 6 & 9: Evolutionary Heritage, Social Brain, Philosophy, Truth, Communication)

This segment is about connecting with what truly gives your life meaning, fostering genuine connection, and nourishing your sense of purpose. This acknowledges the profound impact of our social and existential dimensions on our well-being.

Choose 1-2 of these daily, for a total of 13 minutes:

- **Gratitude Practice (e.g., 5-7 minutes):**

    Mentally (or briefly write) 3-5 things you are genuinely grateful for. This builds **positive neuroplasticity** and enhances your appreciation for the present moment, shifting your brain's focus from threat detection (negativity bias) to abundance.

- **Meaningful Connection (e.g., 5-7 minutes):**

    Intentionally reach out to one person (a short text, quick call, or thoughtful message) to express appreciation, share a positive thought, or simply check in. This directly nurtures your **social brain** and reinforces **interconnectedness**, fulfilling fundamental human needs for belonging.

- **Purpose Reflection (e.g., 3-5 minutes):**

    Briefly reflect on your deeper "why" or purpose in life. How does your day contribute to something larger than yourself? This can align with philosophical concepts like **Lila** (divine play) or your personal "mission," providing a sense of meaning.

- **Philosophical Reflection (e.g., 5-7 minutes):**

    Briefly ponder one of the "big questions" from chapters 4 or 6. For example: "Where did I experience the 'constructed nature of reality' today?" or "How did I engage with 'truth' in my interactions?" This fosters intellectual humility and continuous learning.

Adapting Your Journey: Flexibility, Assessment, and Growth

The 39-Minute Journey is a template, not a rigid prescription. Your commitment to consistency is far more important than perfect execution.

- **Be Flexible:**

    Life happens. If you miss a day, simply resume the next. If you only have 20 minutes, choose activities from the areas you need most. The intention is to create a sustainable habit, not a burden.

- **Personalize Your Practice:**

    Experiment with different activities within each 13-minute block. Some days you might need more Body focus, others more Mind or Soul. Tailor the content to your current challenges and goals.

- **Leverage Neuroplasticity:**

  Remember, every intentional minute builds new neural pathways. Small, consistent efforts compound over time into profound transformations.

- **Track Your Progress:**

  - Regularly assess your journey using insights from Chapter 8.
  - **The AAR (After-Action Review) Journal:** Use this weekly or monthly to reflect on your 39-minute practice. The AAR is a structured debriefing process originally developed by the U.S. Army to facilitate rapid learning from experience. It transforms a conversation or event into a valuable data source by moving beyond simple reflection.
  - **Qualitative & Quantitative Measures:** Note subjective shifts (e.g., "feeling calmer") and objective changes (e.g., "more consistent with daily breathing," "fewer emotional reactions").

- **Embrace Setbacks as Data:**

  Growth is rarely linear. If you hit resistance or skip days, view it as valuable information for refining your approach, not a failure. Apply **self-compassion** (Chapter 8) and revisit your motivation.

- **Specialized Programs as Supplements (in the Appendix):**

  For specific, deeper development in areas like communication, consider one of the following:

  - A detailed **24-Week Communication-Development Program** as a focused, supplementary initiative you undertake for a period; and
  - A condensed **7-day version** focusing on the most impactful principle: balancing listening and speaking.

Measuring Progress: Qualitative and Quantitative Approaches

Tracking development provides motivation and guides adjustments to your approach:

Quantitative measures include:

- Frequency counts (e.g., how often you practice a new communication technique);
- Rating scales (e.g., daily assessments of mindfulness and communication effectiveness on a 1-10 scale);

- Performance metrics (e.g., time spent in focused work, ratio of listening to speaking time);
- Physiological indicators (e.g., heart rate variability as a measure of stress regulation), and
- Relationship indicators (feedback from others on your communication improvements).

Qualitative measures include:

- Journal reflections documenting insights and experiences;
- Periodic narrative reviews of progress and challenges;
- Feedback from trusted others on observed changes; and
- Case studies of specific situations where you applied new approaches.

The AAR (After Action Review) Journal:

After important conversations or decisions, document four specific elements:

1. What was intended? (Your goals and expectations)
2. What actually happened? (Objective description of events)
3. Why did it happen that way? (Analysis of factors and dynamics)
4. What will I do differently next time? (Specific adjustments to approach)

This structured reflection, adapted from military debriefing protocols, accelerates learning from experience by creating a systematic way to extract insights from both successes and challenges.

Research on habit formation by psychologist **Phillippa Lally** suggests that tracking progress is most effective when it focuses on process rather than outcomes, emphasizing consistent practice rather than perfect performance.

Adapting to Setbacks and Resistance

Growth rarely follows a linear trajectory. Setbacks and resistance are not just inevitable but informative:

- **Normalizing setbacks**:

    Recognize that regression under stress is normal and doesn't negate progress. Neuroscience research indicates that we tend to revert to well-established neural pathways under pressure before newer patterns become fully consolidated.

- **Mining resistance for insight**:

    When you encounter internal resistance to change, explore it curiously rather than forcing your way through. Resistance often signals important values or concerns that need integration.

- **Adjusting approaches**:

    Use setbacks as data to refine your development strategy. Perhaps the pace is too ambitious, the approach doesn't match your learning style, or the goal needs recalibration.

- **Practicing self-compassion**:

    In chapter 8, we introduced **Kristin Neff's** research on self-compassion. We learned that self-compassion after setbacks leads to greater resilience and willingness to try again compared to self-criticism.

    Recall that **Carol Dweck's** research on mindset shows that viewing setbacks as learning opportunities rather than evidence of fixed limitations significantly impacts persistence and ultimate success.

Chapter 10 Summary: Key Insights

This chapter culminates our journey, transforming abstract insights into a concrete, sustainable path for daily growth: **The 39-Minute Journey.** This framework distills the profound lessons of our evolutionary heritage, brain science, and ancient wisdom into an achievable daily practice, showing that true transformation stems from consistent, intentional action.

The 39-Minute Journey offers a holistic approach to self-optimization:

1. **13 Minutes for the Body:** Rooted in the **Embodied Mind** (Chapter 7), these practices nurture your physiological foundations (gut health, nutrition, sleep, stress regulation, and, of course, movement). You optimize the biological platform for clear cognition and emotional resilience by consciously tending to your body.

2. **13 Minutes for the Mind:** Drawing from the **Predictive Brain** (Chapters 3 & 5) and the **Art of Self-Scrutiny** (Chapter 8), these minutes are dedicated to refining your internal model of reality. Through metacognition, belief examination, and reflection on prediction errors, you actively challenge biases, update your understanding, and sharpen your thinking.

3. **13 Minutes for the Soul:** Connecting to our **Evolutionary Heritage** (Chapters 1 & 2), **Philosophical Insights** (Chapters 4 & 6), and the **Social Brain** (Chapter 9), this segment nurtures your sense of purpose, meaning, and connection. Practices like gratitude, values alignment, and meaningful connection cultivate compassion, build stronger relationships, and ground you in a broader sense of self.

This journey is designed for **sustainable change**, leveraging neuroplasticity, working with your natural growth cycles, and recognizing that small, consistent efforts compound into profound transformation. It is a flexible template, inviting personalization and offering advanced resources for deeper dives when ready.

Ultimately, the 39-Minute Journey is an invitation to become the **conscious architect of your evolving self.** By consistently engaging in these practices, you actively participate in shaping your reality, moving beyond passive perception to a life of greater awareness, purpose, and well-being. This daily commitment enables you to truly live authentically from the human within.

CONCLUSION: RECLAIMING THE HUMAN INSIDE

"There is no truth... there is only perception"
Gustave Flaubert

We began this journey with a simple yet profound question: Who are we beneath the layers of social conditioning, external expectations, and automated responses that shape our daily existence? Throughout these pages, we've explored the intricate interplay between our brains, minds, and environments, examining how our perceptions form, how our beliefs take root, and how our sense of self emerges from this complex dance. Now, as we conclude, we return to that essential question with new insights, new tools, and perhaps most importantly, new possibilities for living authentically in a complex world.

Synthesis of Key Insights

The Human Condition: Brain, Mind, and Environment

Our exploration has revealed the remarkable three-way relationship between our physical brains, our subjective minds, and the environments in which we exist. This relationship isn't simply one of cause and effect but rather a continuous feedback loop of mutual influence and adaptation.

The human brain is not merely a passive receiver of information but an active participant in creating our experience. As neuroscientist **David Eagleman** notes, "The brain is a team of rivals," with different neural networks competing and collaborating to construct our moment-to-moment reality. This construction happens largely beneath our conscious awareness, with research suggesting that approximately 95% of brain activity occurs below the threshold of consciousness.

Yet the mind that emerges from this neural activity is not simply a by-product of electrochemical processes. It possesses qualities of awareness, intention, and meaning-making that transcend pure materialist explanations. The mind influences the brain just as the brain gives rise to the mind, a phenomenon increasingly recognized in fields from neuroplasticity to psychoneuroimmunology. Moreover, as we've explored, the mind extends beyond the confines of the skull, incorporating our bodies, environment, and social relationships into its cognitive processes.

And both brain and mind exist within environments (physical, social, cultural, and technological) that shape their development and functioning. As environmental psychologist **Roger Barker** observed through his pioneering "behavior setting" research, our actions are often more predictable based on our environment than on our personality traits or stated intentions.

What emerges from this synthesis is a view of human experience as neither purely determined nor completely free, but rather as a dynamic process of continuous co-creation between our biological inheritance, our conscious choices, and our contextual circumstances.

Reality as Construction: Perception, Belief, and Meaning

One of the most profound insights from our journey is the understanding that what we call "reality" is not something we passively perceive but something we actively construct. Our perceptual systems don't simply record the world like cameras or microphones; they selectively filter, organize, and interpret sensory data based on past experiences, current needs, and future expectations.

As cognitive scientist **Anil Seth** explains, "We don't just passively perceive the world; we actively generate it. The world we experience comes as much from the inside-out as from the outside-in." This process of construction happens at multiple levels:

- At the neurological level, our brains, through predictive processing, fill in gaps, make predictions, and create coherent narratives from incomplete information.
- At the psychological level, our beliefs and expectations shape what we notice, how we interpret events, and what we remember.
- At the social level, our shared languages, cultural frameworks, and collective agreements create consensual realities that feel objectively "true."

This constructive nature of perception explains why two people can witness the same event and come away with dramatically different experiences. It's not that one person is right and the other wrong; rather, each is constructing reality through different perceptual filters, different belief systems, and different meaning-making frameworks.

Understanding reality as construction doesn't mean embracing radical relativism where anything goes. Instead, it invites us to hold our constructions more lightly, to recognize their provisional nature, and to remain curious about alternative ways of seeing and being in the world.

The Growth Journey: Awareness, Communication, and Practice

How can we hope to change or grow if our experience is largely constructed through processes that operate below conscious awareness? Our exploration has revealed three essential elements of the human growth journey: expanding awareness, improving communication, and engaging in deliberate practice.

Awareness forms the foundation of all meaningful change. We cannot transform what we cannot see. Through practices like mindfulness meditation, somatic awareness, and reflective inquiry, we can gradually expand our capacity to notice the automatic patterns that shape our experience. As **Jon Kabat-Zinn** describes it, mindfulness involves:

> "...paying attention in a particular way: on purpose, in the present moment, and non-judgmentally."

This quality of attention allows us to observe the constructive processes of our minds rather than being completely identified with them.

Communication, both with ourselves and with others, builds upon this foundation of awareness. We make the implicit explicit through language, bringing unconscious patterns into conscious consideration. Dialogue with others provides essential feedback that helps us recognize our blind spots and expand our perspectives. Carol Dweck's research on growth mindset demonstrates that even subtle shifts in how we talk to ourselves about challenges and setbacks can dramatically impact our capacity for learning and resilience.

Practice transforms insights into embodied wisdom. Knowledge alone rarely changes behavior; we must repeatedly engage in new thinking, feeling, and acting patterns until they become integrated into our way of being. Neuroscientist **Donald Hebb's** famous axiom that "neurons that fire together, wire together" reminds us that practice literally reshapes our brains, creating new neural pathways that make desired behaviors increasingly automatic over time.

The journey of growth isn't linear or finite but cyclical and ongoing. Each expansion of awareness reveals new territories for exploration, each improvement in communication opens new possibilities for connection, and each practice creates the foundation for more refined and nuanced practices to follow.

Bridging Ancient Wisdom and Modern Science

Timeless Human Questions Through Contemporary Lenses

Throughout human history, people have grappled with fundamental questions about the nature of the mind, the relationship between the self and the other, and the possibility of personal transformation. While the language and conceptual frameworks have evolved, the essential inquiries remain remarkably consistent across cultures and eras.

Consider the ancient Greek aphorism "Know thyself," inscribed at the Temple of Apollo at Delphi. This simple directive has been echoed in wisdom traditions worldwide, from the Upanishads' teaching that "the self is the witness of the self" to the Confucian emphasis on self-cultivation through continuous reflection. Today, we might express this same fundamental insight through the language of metacognition, emotional intelligence, or self-awareness – but the core invitation to turn attention inward remains unchanged.

Similarly, the Buddhist concept of anatta (non-self) finds striking parallels in contemporary neuroscience's inability to locate a fixed, unchanging self within the brain. As neurologist **Mariano Sigman**' notes:

> "The brain does not contain one single area where the self-resides... rather, the self emerges from the coordinated activity of many brain regions working together."

What ancient contemplatives discovered through introspection, modern scientists are confirming through brain imaging and cognitive experiments.

Even the timeless question of free will versus determinism takes on new dimensions when viewed through contemporary understandings of neuroplasticity, epigenetics, and complex systems theory. Rather than seeing ourselves as either completely determined by biology and circumstance or entirely free to choose without constraint, we can recognize the complex interplay of conditions and choices that shape our lives moment by moment.

Where Philosophy, Neuroscience, and Personal Growth Converge

Perhaps the most exciting development in our understanding of human experience is the increasing convergence of previously separate domains of knowledge. Philosophy's conceptual clarity, neuroscience's empirical rigor, and personal growth practices' experiential wisdom are increasingly informing and enriching one another.

Consider the concept of attention. Philosophers have long explored attention as a fundamental aspect of consciousness and ethics. **William James** defined it as the active, selective focus of the mind, a conscious effort to deal with some things while withdrawing from others. In contrast, philosopher **Simone Weil** saw attention not as a willed effort, but as passive, selfless receptivity—an ethical act of emptying the self to truly see reality without preconceptions. Neuroscientists have since mapped the brain networks involved in these different forms of attention and documented how attention literally shapes neural activity. So, regardless of which definition of attention you gravitate toward, one thing is crystal clear: **Attention will physically change your brain**. And the good news is that contemplative traditions have developed sophisticated practices for training attention through meditation, mindfulness, and focused awareness exercises.

When these perspectives are brought together, we gain a richer understanding than any single approach could provide. We see that attention is simultaneously a neural process, a phenomenological experience, and a trainable skill, and that changes in any one of these dimensions affect the others.

Similar convergences are happening around concepts like empathy, resilience, and meaning-making. The philosopher's careful analysis of what these concepts entail, the neuroscientist's investigation of their biological underpinnings, and the practitioner's experiential knowledge of how to cultivate them are increasingly being recognized as complementary rather than competing approaches to understanding.

This convergence doesn't mean these fields are becoming indistinguishable. Each maintains its distinctive methods, standards of evidence, and areas of emphasis. But the boundaries between them are becoming more permeable, allowing insights to flow more freely across disciplinary lines.

Practical Wisdom for Modern Living

The true value of bridging ancient wisdom and modern science lies not in intellectual satisfaction but in practical application. How can these integrated insights help us navigate the unique challenges of contemporary life?

One area where this practical wisdom proves invaluable is in managing attention in an age of unprecedented distraction. Ancient contemplative practices like meditation provide time-tested methods for strengthening attention. At the same time, neuroscience offers evidence-based explanations for why these practices work and how they can be optimized for different purposes. Together, they offer a powerful toolkit for reclaiming our attention from the many forces competing for it in the digital age.

Another application lies in emotional regulation. Traditional wisdom traditions have long recognized the importance of understanding and working skillfully with emotions. Modern affective neuroscience has mapped the brain circuits involved in emotional processing and identified specific techniques for modulating emotional responses. When combined, these perspectives offer nuanced approaches to emotional well-being that honor both the biological reality of emotions and their subjective meaning in our lives.

Perhaps most importantly, this bridging of wisdom traditions and scientific understanding helps us navigate the tension between adaptation and authenticity that characterizes modern life. We need to adapt to rapidly changing social, technological, and environmental conditions while simultaneously maintaining a connection to our core values and sense of self. Ancient wisdom reminds us of the timeless human need for meaning, connection, and integrity. At the same time, contemporary science helps us understand how to meet these needs within the specific contexts we now inhabit.

Living Authentically in a Complex World

Navigating Social Pressures and External Expectations

We live in a world of unprecedented social complexity. Traditional societies offered relatively clear, stable roles and expectations; modern life presents us with a dizzying array of possible identities, values, and life paths. While this expansion of possibilities brings freedom, it also creates new forms of pressure and confusion.

Social media amplifies these pressures by creating continuous exposure to curated versions of others' lives, triggering what social psychologists call "social comparison" processes that can undermine contentment and authentic self-expression. Research by **Ethan Kross** at the University of Michigan demonstrates that passive consumption of social media correlates with decreased well-being and increased feelings of inadequacy, what he terms "social snacking without nutritional value."

Career expectations have similarly evolved from relatively straightforward paths to complex, shifting landscapes requiring continuous adaptation. As organizational psychologist **Adam Grant** observes, "The skills that made you successful yesterday will not make you successful tomorrow." This reality creates both opportunity and anxiety, as we must continuously reinvent ourselves while maintaining some sense of coherent identity.

Even our most intimate relationships exist within social contexts that shape expectations around partnership, parenting, friendship, and family life. These expectations often operate as invisible scripts, influencing our choices and judgments without our conscious awareness.

Navigating these pressures requires developing what sociologist **Arlie Hochschild** calls "emotion management strategies", ways of recognizing and responding to social expectations without being unconsciously controlled by them. These strategies include:

- Developing awareness of the specific social pressures and expectations that most strongly affect us.
- Distinguishing between external expectations that align with our values and those that don't.
- Creating supportive communities that validate authentic self-expression.
- Practicing compassionate boundary-setting when external demands conflict with internal needs.

The goal isn't to escape social influence (an impossible and ultimately undesirable aim) but rather to engage with it consciously, selectively incorporating external feedback while maintaining connection to our internal compass.

Cultivating Internal Awareness Amid External Noise

In a world of constant external stimulation, maintaining connection to our internal experience requires deliberate cultivation. The capacity to sense and respond to our own needs, values, emotions, and intuitions is not automatically maintained; it must be actively developed through regular practice.

Recall that Interoception is the ability to sense internal bodily states and forms the foundation of this internal awareness. Research by neuroscientist **A.D. Craig** has identified specific neural pathways that transmit information about our internal state to consciousness, creating what he calls "the material me" that grounds our sense of self. These pathways can be strengthened through practices like body scanning, breath awareness, and mindful movement.

Emotional literacy builds upon this interoceptive foundation, enabling us to recognize, name, and understand our emotional responses rather than being unconsciously driven by them. As psychologist **Lisa Feldman Barrett's** research demonstrates, the ability to make fine-grained distinctions between emotional states (what she calls "emotional granularity") correlates with greater psychological flexibility and well-being.

Values clarification takes internal awareness to a more conceptual level, helping us identify what matters most to us beneath the surface of habitual preferences and reactions. **Acceptance-and-Commitment Therapy (ACT)** offers structured processes for distinguishing between values (ongoing directions we want to move toward) and goals (specific outcomes we want to achieve), helping us make choices aligned with our deepest priorities.

Integrating these levels of internal awareness (physical, emotional, and values-based) creates what psychologist **Eugene Gendlin** called a "felt sense," an embodied knowing that can guide decision-making even in complex situations where purely analytical approaches fall short.

Finding Balance Between Adaptation and Authenticity

Perhaps the central challenge of modern life is finding a workable balance between adapting to external realities and remaining true to our internal values and needs. Lean too far toward adaptation, and we risk losing connection with our authentic selves; lean too far toward rigid authenticity, and we may struggle to function effectively in a complex, changing world.

This balance isn't achieved through a once-and-for-all decision but through an ongoing process of discernment and adjustment. Each situation presents unique considerations about when to adapt and when to stand firm, when to compromise, and when to maintain boundaries.

Psychologist **Robert Kegan's** constructive-developmental theory offers a helpful framework for understanding this balance. He describes human development as a progression through increasingly sophisticated ways of navigating the tension between autonomy and connection, independence and belonging. At more advanced stages of development, we become capable of "self-authorship," maintaining a coherent sense of self while flexibly engaging with diverse perspectives and contexts.

This capacity for self-authorship involves several key skills:

- Cognitive flexibility: The ability to hold multiple perspectives simultaneously without becoming rigidly identified with any single viewpoint
- Emotional resilience: The capacity to tolerate the discomfort that often accompanies authentic self-expression in the face of social pressure
- Ethical discernment: The wisdom to distinguish between beneficial adaptations that preserve integrity and harmful compromises that undermine core values
- Contextual awareness: The recognition that different situations may call for different balances between adaptation and authenticity

Ultimately, the balance between adaptation and authenticity isn't about finding a fixed middle point but about developing the capacity for dynamic, context-sensitive responses that honor both external realities and internal truths.

A Path Forward

Personal Transformation as Continuous Process

The journey of reclaiming The Human Inside is not a destination but a continuous process of unfolding. Like any complex skill or art form, it develops through cycles of practice, feedback, reflection, and refinement that continue throughout life.

This process isn't linear but spiral, revisiting similar themes at progressively deeper levels of understanding and integration. Issues we thought we had "solved" often reemerge in new forms, inviting us to engage with them from more nuanced perspectives. As psychologist **Carl Rogers** observed,

> *"The curious paradox is that when I accept myself just as I am, then I can change."*

Neuroscientist **Richard Davidson's** research on neuroplasticity confirms this view of transformation as an ongoing process rather than a one-time event. His studies demonstrate that while short-term practices produce temporary changes in brain activity, long-term, consistent engagement leads to structural changes in neural architecture. The brain remains plastic throughout life, continuously shaped by our experiences, attention, and practices.

This continuous nature of transformation has important implications for how we approach growth:

- It invites patience and persistence, recognizing that meaningful change typically happens gradually rather than overnight.
- It encourages us to focus on sustainable practices rather than intense but short-lived efforts.
- It reminds us to celebrate incremental progress rather than expecting perfection.
- It helps us recognize that setbacks and challenges are not failures but integral parts of the growth process.

By embracing transformation as a continuous process, we free ourselves from the pressure of arriving at some imagined state of completion and instead learn to find fulfillment in the journey itself.

Integrating New Understanding Into Daily Life

Theoretical understanding alone rarely produces lasting change. To truly reclaim **The Human Inside**, we must find ways to integrate our insights into the fabric of daily life, transforming abstract concepts into lived experiences.

This integration happens through what anthropologist **Gregory Bateson** called "deutero-learning" or "learning to learn", developing meta-cognitive frameworks that help us extract meaningful lessons from everyday experiences. Rather than compartmentalizing growth as something that happens in special contexts (therapy sessions, workshops, retreats), we learn to see each interaction, challenge, and routine activity as an opportunity for practice and refinement. Practical strategies for this integration include:

- Creating environmental cues that remind us of key insights and intentions (visual reminders, scheduled check-ins, physical objects that symbolize values);
- Establishing regular reflection practices that help us extract learning from daily experiences (journaling, contemplative walks, structured review processes);
- Developing implementation intentions that link specific situations to desired responses ("When X happens, I will practice Y"); and
- Building communities of practice that provide support, accountability, and shared learning.

Perhaps most importantly, integration involves bringing awareness to the small moments and mundane interactions that make up most of our lives. As Zen teacher **Thich Nhat Hanh** reminds us,

"The real miracle is not to walk on water or in thin air, but to walk on earth."

It's in these ordinary moments, preparing a meal, having a conversation, responding to an email, navigating a disagreement, that our understanding is truly tested and embodied.

Creating Communities of Growth and Awareness

While personal transformation involves internal work, it flourishes within supportive communities. As social beings, we develop relationships with others who reflect back our blind spots, celebrate our progress, challenge our limitations, and remind us of our capabilities when we forget.

Traditional communities of practice, religious congregations, artistic guilds, and scholarly traditions have historically provided structures for this kind of mutual growth. In today's more fragmented social landscape, we often need to intentionally create or seek out communities that can serve similar functions.

Effective communities of growth and awareness share several key characteristics:

- They balance challenge and support, providing both the safety needed for vulnerability and the stimulus needed for growth;
- They establish shared practices and languages while honoring individual differences in approach and expression.
- They create regular opportunities for both structured learning and spontaneous discovery; and
- They recognize and work skillfully with the interpersonal dynamics that inevitably arise in group settings.

Digital technologies offer new possibilities for creating these communities across geographic boundaries, connecting people with shared interests and commitments who might never otherwise meet. At the same time, research by social psychologist **Sherry Turkle** suggests that virtual connections cannot fully replace the embodied presence and non-verbal attunement that occur in physical gatherings.

The most effective approach may be what organizational theorist **Etienne Wenger** calls "communities of practice," groups that combine online and in-person interaction, structured activities and informal exchange, focused learning and social connection. These hybrid communities can provide the flexibility needed to fit into busy modern lives while still offering the depth of engagement that supports meaningful transformation.

Final Reflections: Returning to the Human Inside

The Journey From Who We Were Told to Be to Who We Are

At its heart, the journey we've explored throughout this book is about the movement from externally defined identity to internally generated authenticity, from who we were told to be to who we truly are. This movement isn't about rejecting all external influence or social learning; rather, it's about developing the discernment to recognize which external messages serve our growth and which constrain our potential.

For most of us, this journey begins with the recognition that aspects of our lives and identities have been shaped by forces outside our conscious awareness or choice. Family dynamics, educational systems, cultural messages, economic pressures, and technological environments have all contributed to our sense of self, often in ways we've never questioned or even noticed.

This recognition can initially be disorienting or even threatening, as it challenges the narrative of autonomous selfhood that pervades modern Western culture. If so much of who we are has been shaped by external forces, what does it mean to be "authentic"? Is there even a "real self" beneath these layers of social conditioning?

Our exploration suggests that authenticity isn't about discovering some pre-existing, unchanging core self that has been hidden by social influence. Rather, it's about developing the capacity to engage consciously with the ongoing process of self-creation that happens through our interactions with the world. As philosopher **Charles Taylor** puts it, authenticity involves "finding a way of being that is properly my own... in dialogue with others who matter to me."

This view of authenticity as dialogical rather than monological, emerging through relationship rather than in isolation, helps us navigate the journey from who we were told to be to who we are. It reminds us that becoming ourselves is not about escaping social influence but about engaging with it more consciously, selectively incorporating what resonates with our deepest values while compassionately releasing what doesn't.

Invitation to Ongoing Exploration

As we conclude this written journey, the real exploration is just beginning. The ideas, practices, and perspectives we've explored are not meant to be passively consumed but actively engaged with, questioned, tested in your own experience, and adapted to your unique circumstances.

This engagement might take many forms:

- Experimenting with the practices described throughout these pages, noticing which ones resonate with your learning style and current needs;
- Seeking out communities, teachers, or resources that can support your continued exploration of areas that particularly interest you;
- Keeping a journal of insights, questions, and experiences that arise as you integrate these ideas into your daily life;
- Engaging in dialogue with others about these concepts, recognizing that articulating ideas to someone else often clarifies your own understanding; and
- Periodically revisiting sections of this book as new life experiences create openings for deeper understanding.

Remember that exploration involves both structure and openness, the discipline to engage consistently with practices and ideas, combined with the receptivity to discover unexpected insights along the way. As Zen teacher **Shunryu Suzuki** famously advised,

> *"In the beginner's mind there are many possibilities, in the expert's mind there are few."*

Approach this ongoing exploration with compassion for yourself and others. Growth isn't linear, insights don't always translate immediately into changed behavior, and the journey involves setbacks as well as breakthroughs. What matters is not perfection but presence, showing up with sincerity and curiosity for each step of the path.

The Ever-Evolving Human Potential

We live in a time of both extraordinary challenge and unprecedented opportunity for human development. The complexity of modern life creates new forms of suffering and disconnection. Yet, it also provides access to wisdom traditions, scientific insights, and transformative practices that were previously available to only a select few.

This democratization of growth resources makes possible what psychologist **Abraham Maslow** called "full-humanness," the actualization of distinctly human capacities for self-awareness, meaning-making, creative expression, and compassionate connection. While earlier generations might have viewed such development as the province of saints, sages, or exceptional individuals, we now recognize it as a possibility available to anyone willing to engage in the necessary inner work.

At the same time, this potential for growth exists within a broader context of planetary challenges that require collective as well as individual transformation. Climate change, technological disruption, social inequality, and political polarization create conditions that both necessitate and complicate human development. Our individual journeys of reclaiming The Human Inside unfold within these larger systems, influenced by them and potentially influencing them in turn.

This recognition invites us to hold a both/and perspective: honoring the importance of personal growth while recognizing its interconnection with collective evolution. As **Gregory Bateson** observed:

"The major problems in the world are the result of the difference between how nature works and how people think."

By reclaiming the human inside, developing more integrated ways of thinking, feeling, and being, we contribute in some small way to addressing these larger misalignments.

The human potential continues to evolve, not toward some predetermined endpoint but toward ever-expanding possibilities for consciousness, connection, and contribution. By engaging wholeheartedly in our own development, we participate in this larger unfolding, becoming more fully ourselves while helping to shape what it means to be human in this pivotal moment of history.

As we close this exploration, let us return to where we began: the recognition that beneath all our social conditioning, beneath our habitual patterns of thought and behavior, beneath even our most cherished identities, there exists a capacity for presence, awareness, and choice that is our birthright as human beings. Reclaiming this capacity (moment by moment, day by day, through practices of awareness, communication, and embodied action) is the journey of a lifetime, available to each of us exactly where we are.

The Human Inside is not something to be constructed or achieved but something to be remembered and returned to, again and again, with patience, curiosity, and compassion. May your journey of remembering and returning bring you ever closer to the fullness of your humanity, in all its beautiful complexity.

APPENDIX

Creating a Generic and Structured Personal Development Plan

Effective growth benefits from intentional planning:

1. **Assessment**:

    Evaluate current strengths, challenges, and growth opportunities. Tools might include personality assessments, feedback from trusted others, or structured self-reflection exercises.

2. **Prioritization**:

    Identify high-leverage areas for development, those that will create the most significant positive impact across multiple domains of life.

3. **Goal setting**:

    Establish specific, measurable, achievable, relevant, and time-bound (SMART) development goals. Research by psychologist **Edwin Locke** indicates that specific, challenging goals lead to higher performance than vague or easy goals.

4. **Resource identification**:

    Determine what support, information, or tools you'll need. This might include books, courses, mentors, peer groups, or technological aids.

5. **Implementation planning**:

    Create detailed action steps, including when, where, and how you'll engage in development activities. Psychologist **Peter Gollwitzer's** research on implementation intentions shows that specifying exactly when and where you'll take action significantly increases follow-through.

6. **Obstacle anticipation**:

   Proactively identify potential barriers and develop strategies to overcome them. This "mental contrasting" approach, researched by psychologist **Gabriele Oettingen**, strengthens commitment and improves outcomes.

A Practical 24-Week Communication Development Program

Based on the ancient principles of effective communication, here's a structured approach to improving your conversational skills:

Weeks 1-2: Foundation Assessment

Begin with a comprehensive audit of your current communication patterns. Track 3-5 significant conversations daily, noting your listening-to-speaking ratio, emotional states, learning moments, and processing time. Identify whether you're primarily a Reactor, Lecturer, Avoider, Overwhelmer, or Rusher.

Weeks 3-6: Classical Foundation Building

- **Week 3 - Ethos (Credibility)**:

  Focus on building credibility through preparation and authentic sharing. Before important conversations, ask: Do I know enough about this topic? What's my track record? How can I demonstrate I've done my homework?

- **Week 4 - Logos (Logic/Evidence)**:

  Concentrate on logical structure. For each argument, identify your evidence, verify facts, and consider what others need to understand your position. Practice saying "Let me break this down" and provide 2-3 supporting points.

- **Week 5 - Pathos (Emotional Connection)**:

  Before responding emotionally, ask: What am I feeling? What is the other person experiencing? Use "I understand why you might feel..." before presenting your viewpoint.

- **Week 6 - Integration**:

  Consciously balance all three elements in important conversations. After each significant interaction, rate yourself 1-10 on Ethos, Pathos, and Logos, aiming for 7+ on each.

Weeks 7-10: Advanced Techniques

- **Week 7 - Kairos (Timing)**:

    Develop sensitivity to when conversations should happen. Ask: Is this the right time? What's their current emotional state? What external factors might affect this conversation?

- **Week 8 - Strategic Patience:**

    Practice delaying responses when you feel the urge to react immediately. Use phrases like "Let me think about that" or "That's a good point, give me a moment to process."

- **Week 9 - Telos (Purpose)**:

    Before important conversations, clarify your goals: What do I want to achieve? Am I trying to win, learn, solve problems, or build relationships? Start with "My goal here is…"

- **Week 10 - Integration**:

    Combine timing awareness with a clear purpose. Choose one difficult conversation you've been avoiding and apply the full framework.

Weeks 11-14: The Three-Pillar Practice

- **Week 11 - Advanced Listening**:

    Implement the 70/30 rule: Listen 70% of the time, speak 30%. Ask clarifying questions before making points, summarize what you heard, and use "What I'm hearing is…Is that accurate?"

- **Week 12 - Strategic Speaking**:

    Make points in groups of three maximum. Use the Socratic method: Ask two questions for every statement. Replace "I think…" with "What do you think about…"

- **Weeks 13-14 - Processing Integration**:

    Implement processing breaks. In heated discussions: "Let's take 10 minutes to think." In complex decisions: "I'd like to sleep on this." In learning conversations: "That's interesting, let me process what you've shared."

Weeks 15-18: Advanced Applications

- **Week 15 - Productive Concession:**

  Find one valid point in every disagreement and acknowledge it. Use "You're right about..." before presenting counterpoints. Aim to concede 2-3 minor points per significant conversation.

- **Week 16 - Small Wins Strategy:**

  Instead of seeking total agreement, look for partial alignment. End conversations with "What can we agree on?" or "Where do we have common ground?"

- **Week 17 - Question Integration:**

  Replace 50% of statements with questions. Instead of "That's wrong" → "Help me understand your thinking." Instead of "Here's what we should do" → "What do you think our options are?"

- **Week 18 - Emergency Protocols:**

  Practice responses for when conversations go wrong. If heated: "I can see we're both passionate. Should we take a break?" If you're wrong: "You know what, I think you're right. Let me reconsider."

Weeks 19-24: Mastery and Habit Formation

- **Week 19-20 - Context Adaptation:**

  Apply principles differently across contexts. Family conversations need higher Ethos thresholds and gentler Logos. Professional settings require preparation-based Ethos and strategic Pathos. Community engagement benefits from balanced approaches with emphasis on shared purpose.

- **Week 21-22 - Feedback Integration:**

  Conduct weekly reviews asking: Which conversations went well and why? Where did I struggle? What did I learn? How did I grow as a communicator?

- **Week 23-24 - Teaching Others:**

  The ultimate test of mastery is whether you can teach these principles to someone else. Choose one person to mentor in better communication, practice explaining the framework, and model the behavior you want to see.

7-Day Communication Starter Program

For those who find the 24-week program overwhelming, here's a condensed 7-day version focusing on the most impactful principle: balancing listening and speaking.

Day 1: Awareness

Track your listening-to-speaking ratio in conversations. Simply make a mental note: Are you speaking more than 50% of the time? Are you fully present when others speak?

Day 2: The 70/30 Practice

In every conversation today, aim to listen 70% and speak 30%. Set a silent intention before each interaction.

Day 3: Question Integration

Replace statements with questions whenever possible. Instead of "I disagree," try "What makes you see it that way?"

Day 4: The 5-Second Pause

Before responding to any question or statement, count silently to five. Notice how this changes your responses.

Day 5: Reflection Responses

Practice summarizing what others have said before adding your perspective: "So what you're saying is..."

Day 6: Curiosity Focus

Approach each conversation with genuine curiosity. What can you learn from this person that you didn't know before?

Day 7: Integration

Combine all practices, focusing on whichever element seems most needed in each conversation. Reflect on changes you've noticed in your interactions.

REFERENCES

Books

- **Allport, F. H.** (1924). *Social psychology*. Houghton Mifflin.
- **Aristotle** (4th BCE). *Rhetoric*. CreateSpace Independent Publishing Platform (2013 Edition)
- **Baggott, J.** (2013). *Farewell to reality: How modern physics has betrayed the search for scientific truth*. Oxford University Press.
- **Barker, R. G.,** (1968). *Ecological psychology; concepts and methods for studying the environment of human behavior*. Stanford University Press
- **Bartlett, F. C.** (1932). *Remembering: A study in experimental and social psychology*. Cambridge University Press.
- **Bateson, G.** (2000). *Steps to an Ecology of Mind: Collected Essays in Anthropology, Psychiatry, Evolution, and Epistemology*. University of Chicago Press.
- **Beck, A. T.** (1976). *Cognitive therapy and the emotional disorders*. International Universities Press.
- **Berger, P. L., & Luckmann, T.** (1966). *The social construction of reality: A treatise in the sociology of knowledge*. Doubleday.
- **Berkeley, G.** (1988, originally 1710 and 1713). *Principles of Human Knowledge/Three Dialogues*. Roger Woolhouse (ed.). London: Penguin Books.
- **Blackwell, A., Marriott, K., & Shimojima, A.** (Editors). (2004). *Diagrammatic Representation and Inference*. Springer.
- **Boyer, C. B., & Merzbach, U. C.** (2011). *A history of mathematics* (3rd ed.). John Wiley & Sons.
- **Brehm, J. W.** (1966). *A theory of psychological reactance*. Academic Press.
- **Brewer, J.** (2018). *A Craving Mind: From Cigarettes to Smartphones to Love – Why We Get Hooked and How We Can Break Bad Habits*. Yale University Press.
- **Brodie, R.** (2011). *Virus of the Mind: The new science of the meme*. Hay House.
- **Burton, D. M.** (2011). *The history of mathematics: An introduction* (7th ed.). McGraw-Hill Education.
- **Carroll, S.,** (2017). *The Big Picture: On the Origins of Life, Meaning, and the Universe Itself*. Dutton.
- **Chalmers, D. J.** (1996). *The conscious mind: In search of a fundamental theory*. Oxford University Press.
- **Chater, N., & Oaksford, M.** (Eds.). (2008). *The probabilistic mind: Prospects for Bayesian cognitive science*. Oxford University Press.

- **Clark, A.** (2013). *Mindware: An introduction to the philosophy of cognitive science.* Oxford University Press.
- **Clark, A.** (2024). *The Experience Machine: How Our Minds Predict and Shape Reality.* Vintage Books.
- **Cowen, T.** (2011). *The Great Stagnation: How America Ate All the Low-Hanging Fruit of Modern History, Got Sick, and Will (Eventually) Feel Better.* Dutton.
- **Cox, B., & Forshaw, J.** (2011). *The quantum universe: Everything that can happen does happen.* Da Capo Press.
- **Craig, A. D.** (2020). *How Do You Feel?: An Interoceptive Moment with Your Neurobiological Self.* Princeton University Press
- **Crease, R. P**. (2009). *The great experiments: The story of ancient to modern physics.* W. W. Norton & Company.
- **Crosby, A. W.** (1997). *The measure of reality: Quantification and Western society, 1250-1600.* Cambridge University Press.
- **Damasio, A.** (1994). *Descartes' Error: Emotion, Reason, and the Human Brain.* Putnam.
- **Danziger, K.** (1997). *Naming the Mind: How psychology found its language.* SAGE Publications, Limited
- **Darwin, C.** (2022, originally 1859). *On the Origin of Species.* Read & Co.Science.
- **Davidson, R. J., & Begley, S.** (2012). *The emotional life of your brain: How its unique patterns affect the way you think, feel, and live - and how you can change them.* Hudson Street Press.
- **Dawkins, R.** (1996). *Climbing Mount Improbable.* W. W. Norton & Company.
- **Dehaene, S.** (2011). *The number sense: How the mind creates mathematics* (Rev. and updated ed.). Oxford University Press.
- **Dement, W. C**. (2000). *The Promise of Sleep: A Pioneer in Sleep Medicine Explores the Vital Connection Between Health, Happiness, and a Good Night's Sleep.* Dell
- **Dennett, D. C.** (2014). *Intuition Pumps And Other Tools for Thinking.* W. W. Norton & Company.
- **Descartes, R**. (1998, originally 1638 and 1641) *Discourse on Method and Meditations on First Philosophy.* Donald A. Cress (trans.). Indianapolis: Hackett Publishing.
- **Dehaene, S**. (2011). *The number sense: How the mind creates mathematics* (Rev. and updated ed.). Oxford University Press.
- **Dweck, C. S.** (2006). *Mindset: The new psychology of success.* Random House.
- **Eagleman, D**. (2017). *The Brain: The story of you.* Vintage
- **Easwaran, E.** (Translator). (2007). *The Upanishads.* Nilgiri Press.
- **Edmonson, A.** (2018). *The Fearless Organization: Creating Psychological Safety in the Workplace for Learning, Innovation, and Growth.* Wiley.
- **Ellis, A.** (1962). *Reason and emotion in psychotherapy.* Birch Lane Pr (1994)
- **Everett, D. L.** (2008). *Don't sleep, there are snakes: Life and language in the Amazonian jungle.* Pantheon Books.
- **Feldman Barrett, L**. (2021). *7 ½ lessons about the brain.* Mariner Books
- **Festinger, L.** (1957). *A theory of cognitive dissonance.* Stanford University Press.
- **Feynman, R. P., Leighton, R. B., & Sands, M.** (2005). *The Feynman lectures on physics, Vol. III: Quantum mechanics.* Addison-Wesley. (Original work published 1965).

- **Fish, W.** (2009). *Philosophy of perception: A contemporary introduction.* Routledge.
- **Fisher, R. A.** (1925). *Statistical methods for research workers.* Oliver and Boyd.
- **Fisher, R., & Ury, W.** (2011). *Getting to Yes: Negotiating Agreement Without Giving In.* Penguin Books.
- **Fleming, S. M., & Frith, C. D.** (2014). *The cognitive neuroscience of metacognition.* Springer.
- **Fodor, J. A.** (1987). *Psychosemantics: The problem of meaning in the philosophy of mind.* MIT Press
- **Galef, J.** (2021). *The Scout Mindset: Why Some People See Things Clearly and Others Don't.* Portfolio.
- **Garfield, J., & Ben-Zvi, D.** (2007). *Developing students' statistical reasoning: Connecting research and teaching practice.* Springer Science & Business Media.
- **Gawdat, M.** (2017). *Solve for Happy: Engineer your path to joy.* Gallery Books.
- **Gigerenzer, G.** (2008). *Rationality for mortals: How people cope with uncertainty.* Oxford University Press.
- **Giles, H.** (2016). *Communication Accommodation Theory: Negotiating Personal Relationships and Social Identities across Contexts.* Cambridge University Press.
- **Goffman, E.** (1959). *The Presentation of Self in Everyday Life.* Anchor
- **Goleman, D.** (2005). Emotional Intelligence: Why It Can Matter More Than IQ. Bantam (2005 Edition).
- **Gottman, J.** (2015). *The Seven Principles for Making Marriage Work: A Practical Guide from the Country's Foremost Relationship Expert.* Harmony.
- **Gould, S. J.** (1996). *Full house: The spread of excellence from Plato to Darwin.*
- **Grant, A.** (2021). *Think Again: The Power of Knowing What You Don't Know.* Viking.
- **Greene, B.** (2004). *The fabric of the cosmos: Space, time, and the texture of reality.* Alfred A. Knopf.
- **Gregory, R. L.** (1970). *The intelligent eye.* Weidenfeld and Nicolson.
- **Griffiths, D. J.** (2018). *Introduction to quantum mechanics* (3rd ed.). Cambridge University Press.
- **Hacking, I.** (1990). *The taming of chance.* Cambridge University Press.
- **Haidt, J.** (2012). *The righteous mind: Why good people are divided by politics and religion.* Vintage.
- **Harari, Y. N.** (2015). *Sapiens: A brief history of humankind.* Harper.
- **Hawkins, J.** (2022). *A Thousand Brains: A new theory of intelligence.* Basic Books.
- **Hayes, S. C.,** (2025). *Get Out of Your Mind and Into Your Life: The New Acceptance and Commitment Therapy.* New Harbinger Publications.
- **Hayes, S. C., Strosahl, K. D., & Wilson, K. G.** (2012). *Acceptance and commitment therapy: The process and practice of mindful change* (2nd ed.). The Guilford Press.
- **Hebb, D. O.** (2012). *The Organization Of Behavior: A Neuropsychological Theory.* Psychology Press.
- **Heisenberg, W.** (1958). *Physics and philosophy: The revolution in modern science.* Harper & Row.
- **Hochschild, A. R.** (2012). *Managed Heart: Commercialization of Human Feeling.* University of California Press.

- **Hoffman, D. D.** (2022). *The case against reality: Why evolution hid the truth from our eyes.* W. W. Norton & Company.
- **Hohwy, J.** (2013). *The predictive mind.* Oxford University Press.
- **Jasanoff, A.** (2018). *The Biological Mind: How brain, body and environment collaborate to make us who we are.* Basic Books.
- **Johnson-Laird, P. N.** (1983). *Mental models: Towards a cognitive science of language, inference, and consciousness.* Harvard University Press.
- **Kabat-Zinn, J**. (2013). *Full Catastrophe Living (Revised Edition): Using the Wisdom of Your Body and Mind to Face Stress, Pain, and Illness.* Bantam.
- **Kahneman, D.** (2011). *Thinking, fast and slow.* Farrar, Straus and Giroux.
- **Kant, I.** (2001, originally 1783) *Prolegomena to Any Future Metaphysics.* James W. Ellington (trans. and ed.). Indianapolis: Hackett Publishing.
- **Kasser, T**. (2003). *The high price of materialism.* MIT Press. Bradford Books.
- **Kegan, R**. (1998). *In Over Our Heads: The Mental Demands of Modern Life.* Harvard University Press.
- **Kegan, R., & Lahey, L. L.** (2009). *Immunity to Change: How to Overcome It and Unlock the Potential in Yourself and Your Organization (Leadership for the Common Good).* Harvard Business Review Press.
- **Kierkegaard, S**. (2019). *Concluding Unscientific Postscript.* Princeton University Press.
- **Kline, M.** (1990). *Mathematical thought from ancient to modern times.* Oxford University Press.
- **Kross, E.** (2021). *Chatter: The Voice in Our Head, Why It Matters, and How to Harness It.* Crown.
- **Kruglanski, A. W.** (1989). *Lay epistemics and human knowledge: Cognitive and motivational bases.* Springer.
- **Lakoff, G., & Núñez, R. E.** (2000). *Where mathematics comes from: How the embodied mind brings mathematics into being.* Basic Books.
- **Lama, D., & Berzin, A.** (1997). *The Gelug/Kagyu tradition of Mahamudra.* Snow Lion.
- **Lao Tzu**. (2009). *Tao Te Ching* (S. Mitchell, Trans.). Harper Perennial. (Original work circa 4th-6th century BCE).
- **Levinson, S. C.** (2003). *Space in language and cognition: Explorations in linguistic relativity.* Cambridge University Press.
- **Levitin, D.** (2014). *The Organized Mind: Thinking in the Age of Information Overload.* Dutton.
- **Livio, M.** (2009). *Is God a mathematician?.* Simon & Schuster.
- **Lotto, B.** (2017). *Deviate: The Science of Seeing Differently.* Weidenfeld Nicolson.
- **Lyubomirsky, S.** (2008). *The How of Happiness: A New Approach to Getting the Life You Want.* Penguin Books.
- **Maslow, A**. (2011, 1962 Reprint). *Toward a Psychology of Being.* Martino Fine Books.
- **Mayer, E.** (2018). *The Mind-Gut Connection: How the Hidden Conversation Within Our Bodies Impacts Our Mood, Our Choices, and Our Overall Health.* Harper Paperbacks.
- **McKenna, T.** (1991). *The archaic revival: Speculations on psychedelic mushrooms, the Amazon, virtual reality, UFOs, evolution, shamanism, the rebirth of the Goddess, and the end of history.* Harper San Francisco.

- **McPherson, J.** (2013). *Battle Cry of Freedom: The Civil War Era*. Oxford University Press
- **National Academies of Sciences, Engineering, and Medicine.** (2008). *Science, evolution, and creationism*. National Academies Press.
- **Neff, K**. (2015). *Self-Compassion: The Proven Power of Being Kind to Yourself*. William Morrow Paperbacks.
- **Nguyen, J.** (2022). *Beyond Thoughts: An exploration of who we are beyond our minds*. One Satori Publishing.
- **Nguyen, J.** (2024). *Don't Believe Everything You Think: Why Your Thinking Is The Beginning & End Of Suffering*. Authors Equity.
- **Nin, A.** (1961). *Seduction of the minotaur*. Swallow Press.
- **Noelle-Neumann, E.** (1993). *The spiral of silence: Public opinion - our social skin* (2nd ed.). University of Chicago Press.
- **Paivio, A**. (2017). *Imagery and Verbal Processes*. Psychology Press.
- **Pariser, E.** (2011). *The filter bubble: What the Internet is hiding from you*. Penguin Press.
- **Paul, A. M.** (2022). *The Extended Mind*. Harper Collins Publ. USA.
- **Pearson, E. S**. (1938). *Karl Pearson: An appreciation of some aspects of his life and work*. Cambridge University Press.
- **Perlmutter, D., & Perlmutter, A.** (2021). *Brain Wash: Detox Your Mind for Clearer Thinking, Deeper Relationships, and Lasting Happiness*. Yellow Kite.
- **Pinker, S**. (2015). *The Sense of Style: The Thinking Person's Guide to Writing in the 21st Century*. Penguin Books.
- **Plack, C. J., Oxenham, W. J., & Fay, R. R.** (Eds.). (2005). *Pitch: Neural coding and perception*. Springer.
- **Plato**. (2004, originally around 380 B.C.E.) *The Republic*, C. D. C. Reeve (trans.). Indianapolis: Hackett Publishing.
- **Popper, K. R**. (2002). *The logic of scientific discovery*. Routledge. (Original work published 1959).
- **Porter, T. M.** (1986). *The rise of statistical thinking, 1820-1900*. Princeton University Press.
- **Potter, J., & Wetherell, M.** (1987). *Discourse and social psychology: Beyond attitudes and behaviour*. Sage Publications.
- **Quine, W. V. O., & Ullian, J. S.** (1978). *The web of belief* (2nd ed.). Random House.
- **Raese, J., Venturella, T.** (2024). *Our Shared Illusions: What Neuroscience Reveals About Our Minds, Our Planet, and Our Future*. Behavioral Health 2000, LLC.
- **Rogers, C.** (original 1951, new edition 2021). *Client-Centered Therapy: Its Current Practice, Implications, and Theory*. Robinson
- **Rose, T.** (2022). *Collective Illusions: Conformity, Complicity, and the Science of Why We Make Bad Decisions*. Hachette Book Group.
- **Rosenberg, M**. (2015). *Nonviolent Communication: A Language of Life: Life-Changing Tools for Healthy Relationships*. PuddleDancer Press
- **Rosenthal, R., & Jacobson, L.** (1968). *Pygmalion in the classroom: Teacher expectation and pupils' intellectual development*. Updated in 2003. Crown House Publishing.
- **Rowbottom, D.** (2010). *Popper's Critical Rationalism: A Philosophical Investigation*. (Routledge).

- **Rutherford, A.** (2024). *Neuroscience and Critical Thinking: Enhance Memory, Sharpen Decision-Making, Regulate Emotions, and Avoid Logical Fallacies.* (Independently Published).
- **Scharmer, O**. (2016). *Theory U: Leading from the Future as It Emerges* (original 2007). Berrett-Koehler Publishers
- **Schrödinger, E.** (1992). *Science and the human temperament* (J. Murphy, Trans.). W. W. Norton & Company. (Original essays published at various times).
- **Schwartz, B.** (2016). *The paradox of choice*. Ecco.
- **Seligman, M. E.P.** (1991). *Learned Optimism: How to Change Your Mind and Your Life.* New York, NY: Pocket Books.
- **Seth, A. K.** (2021). *Being You: A New Science of Consciousness.* Dutton.
- **Shubin, N.** (2008). *Your inner fish: A journey into the 3.5-billion-year history of the human body.* Pantheon.
- **Smil, V** (2022). *How the World Really Works: The Science Behind How We Got Here and Where We're Going.* Viking.
- **Siegel, D**. (2010). *Mindsight: The new science of personal transformation.* Bantam.
- **Sigman, M.** (2017). *The Secret Life of the Mind: How Your Brain Thinks, Feels, and Decides.* Little Brown Spark.
- **Stigler, S. M. (1986).** *The history of statistics: The measurement of uncertainty before 1900.* The Belknap Press of Harvard University Press.
- **Stringer, C. & Andrews, P.** (2012). *The complete world of human evolution (the complete series).* Thames & Hudson.
- **Stringer, C.** (2013). *Lone Survivors: How We Came to Be the Only Humans on Earth.* St. Martin's Griffin.
- **Suzuki, S.** (2020). *Zen mind, beginner's mind*. 50th anniversary edition (original version from 1970). Shambhala.
- **Sweller, J., Ayers, P., Kalyuga, S**. (2011). *Cognitive Load Theory*. Springer
- **Tattersall, I.** (2012). *Masters of the planet: The search for our human origins.* Palgrave Macmillan.
- **Taylor, C.** (2018). *The Ethics of Authenticity.* Harvard University Press.
- **Thich Nhat Hanh.** (1999). *The Heart of the Buddha's Teaching: Transforming Suffering into Peace, Joy, and Liberation.* Broadway Books.
- **Turkle, S.** (2015). *Reclaiming Conversation: The Power of Talk in a Digital Age.* Penguin Press.
- **Tyson, N. D.** (2022). *Starry Messenger: Cosmic perspectives on civilization.* Holt & Company, Henry.
- **Watts, A.** (1957). *The Way of Zen.* Pantheon Books.
- **Watzlawick, P., Bavelas, J. B., & Jackson, D. D.** (2011 Reprint). *Pragmatics of Human Communication: A Study of Interactional Patterns, Pathologies and Paradoxes.* W. W. Norton & Company
- **Wenger, E.** (1999). *Communities of Practice: Learning, Meaning, and Identity (Learning in Doing: Social, Cognitive and Computational Perspectives).* Cambridge University Press.
- **Wolfe, J. M., Kluender, K. R., Dennis, M. D., Bartoshuk, L. M., Greene, E., Klatzky, R. L., & Lederman, S. J**. (2018). *Sensation & perception* (5th ed.). Oxford University Press.

- **Woolley, S. C., & Howard, P. N.** (2019). *Computational propaganda: Political parties, politicians, and political manipulation on social media.* Oxford University Press.
- **Wrangham, R**. (2010). *Catching Fire: How cooking made us human.* Basic Books.
- **Vygotsky, L. S**. (1986). *Thought and language* (A. Kozulin, Trans.). MIT Press. (Original work published 1934)

Journal Articles

- **Alba, J. W., & Hasher, L.** (1983). Is memory schematic? *Psychological Bulletin, 93*(2), 203–231. https://doi.org/10.1037/0033-2909.93.2.203
- **Alger, I., Dridi, S., Stieglitz, J. & Wilson, M. L**. (2023). The evolution of early hominin food production and sharing, *Proc. Natl. Acad. Sci. U.S.A.* 120 (25) e2218096120, https://doi.org/10.1073/pnas.2218096120
- **Asch, S. E.** (1956). Studies of independence and conformity: I. A minority of one against a unanimous majority. *Psychological Monographs: General and Applied, 70*(9), 1–70. https://psycnet.apa.org/record/2011-16966-001
- **Andrews-Hanna, J. R.** (2012). The brain's default network and its adaptive role in internal mentation. *The Neuroscientist, 18*(3), 251–267. Doi: https://doi.org/10.1177/1073858411403316
- **Baddeley, A. D**. (2012). Working memory: Theories, models, and controversies. *Annual Review of Psychology, 63*, 1–29. Doi: https://doi.org/10.1146/annurev-psych-120710-100422
- **Barrett L. F.** (2017). The theory of constructed emotion: an active inference account of interoception and categorization. *Social cognitive and affective neuroscience, 12*(1), 1–23. https://doi.org/10.1093/scan/nsw154
- **Barrett, L. F., & Quigley, K. S.** (2021). Interoception: The Secret Ingredient. *Cerebrum: the Dana forum on brain science, 2021*, cer-06-21. https://pubmed.ncbi.nlm.nih.gov/34650672/
- **Barrett, L. F., Quigley, K. S., & Hamilton, P.** (2016). An active inference theory of allostasis and interoception in depression. *Philosophical Transactions of the Royal Society of London. Series B, Biological sciences, 371*(1708), 20160011. https://doi.org/10.1098/rstb.2016.0011
- **Baron J.** (2019). Actively open-minded thinking in politics. *Cognition.* 188:8-18. doi: https://doi.org/10.1016/j.cognition.2018.10.004
- **Barsalou L. W.** (2008). Grounded cognition. *Annual review of psychology, 59*, 617–645. https://doi.org/10.1146/annurev.psych.59.103006.093639
- **Bastiaanssen, T. F. S., Cowan, C. S. M., Van de Wouw, M., Quigley, E. M. M., Clarke, G., Dinan, T. G., & Cryan, J. F**. (2020). Gutted! Unraveling the Role of the Microbiome in Major Depressive Disorder. *Harvard Review of Psychiatry* 28(1), 26-39 doi: https://doi.org/10.1097/hrp.0000000000000243
- **Batson, D.,** (2017).The Empathy-Altruism Hypothesis: What and So What?', in Emma M. Seppälä, and others (eds), *The Oxford Handbook of Compassion Science*, Oxford Library of Psychology (2017; online edn, Oxford Academic, 5 Oct. 2017), https://doi.org/10.1093/oxfordhb/9780190464684.013.3.
- **Batra, O., McGuire, J. & Kable, J.** (2013). The valuation system: A coordinate-based meta-analysis of BOLD fMRI experiments examining neural correlates of subjective value. *NeuroImage,* 76: 412-427. https://doi.org/10.1016/j.neuroimage.2013.02.063

- **Bayes, T., & Price, R.** (1763). An essay towards solving a problem in the doctrine of chances. *Philosophical Transactions of the Royal Society of London*, 53, 370–418. Doi: https://doi.org/10.1098/rstl.1763.0053

- **Berger, L. R., Hawks, J., de Ruiter, D. J., Churchill, S. E., Schmid, P., Delezene, L. K., Kivell, T. L., Garvin, H. M., Williams, S. A., DeSilva, J. M., Skinner, M. M., Musiba, C. M., Cameron, N., Holliday, T. W., Harcourt-Smith, W., Ackermann, R. R., Bastir, M., Bogin, B., Bolter, D., Brophy, J., ... Zipfel, B.** (2015). Homo Naledi, a new species of the genus Homo from the Dinaledi Chamber, South Africa. *eLife*, 4, e09560. https://doi.org/10.7554/eLife.09560

- **Berlucchi, G., Buchtel, H. A.** (2009). Neuronal plasticity: historical roots and evolution of meaning. *Exp Brain Res*. 192(3):307-19. doi: 10.1007/s00221-008-1611-6. https://pubmed.ncbi.nlm.nih.gov/19002678/

- **Berna, F., Goldberg, P., Kolska Horowitz, L., Brink, J., Holt, S., Bamford, M., Chazan, M.** (2012, April 2). Microstratigraphic evidence of in situ fire in the Acheulean strata of Wonderwerk Cave, Northern Cape province, South Africa. *Proc Natl Acad Sci USA*, 109(20): 1215-1220. https://doi.org/10.1073/pnas.1117620109

- **Bogoshi, J., Naidoo, K., & Webb, P.** (1987). The oldest mathematical artifact. *The Mathematical Gazette*, 71(458), 294. Doi: https://doi.org/10.2307/3617049

- **Boroditsky, L.** (2011). How language shapes thought. *Scientific American*, 304(2), 62–65. https://www.scientificamerican.com/article/how-language-shapes-thought/

- **Braver, T. S., Lazar, S. W.,** (2025). Introduction to the Special Issue on Cognitive Neuroscience of Mindfulness. *Biol Psychiatry Cogn Neurosci Neuroimaging*. 2025 Apr;10(4):337-341. doi: https://doi.org/10.1016/j.bpsc.2025.02.009

- **Brewer, J. A., Worhunsky, P. D., Gray, J. R., Tang, Y. Y., Weber, J., & Kober, H.** (2011). Meditation experience is associated with differences in default mode network activity and connectivity. *Proceedings of the National Academy of Sciences*, 108(50), 20254–20259. Doi: https://doi.org/10.1073/pnas.1112029108

- **Buckner, R. L., Andrews-Hanna, J. R., & Schacter, D. L.** (2008). The brain's default network: Anatomy, function, and relevance to disease. *Annals of the New York Academy of Sciences*, 1124(1), 1–38. Doi: https://doi.org/10.1196/annals.1440.011

- **Carvalho, G. B., & Damasio, A.** (2021). Interoception and the origin of feelings: A new synthesis. *BioEssays*, 43(4), e2000261. Doi: https://doi.org/10.1002/bies.202000261

- **Cheong, H. J., Baksh, S. M., & Ju, I.** (2022). Spiral of Silence in an Algorithm-Driven Social Media Content Environment: Conceptual Framework and Research Propositions. *KOME – An International Journal of Pure Communication Inquiry*, 10(1), 114–132. https://komejournal.com/files/KOME_of_Bakshetal.pdf

- **Cialdini, R. B., & Goldstein, N. J.** (2004). Social influence: Compliance and conformity. *Annual Review of Psychology*, 55(1), 591–621. https://doi.org/10.1146/annurev.psych.55.090902.142015

- **Cinelli, M., Morales, G. D. F., Galeazzi, A., Quattrociocchi, W., & Starnini, M.** (2021). The echo chamber effect on social media. *Proceedings of the National Academy of Sciences*, 118(9), e2023301118. https://doi.org/10.1073/pnas.2023301118

- **Chalmers, D., & Clark, A.** (1998). The Extended Mind. *Analysis*, 58(1), 7-19. https://doi.org/10.1093/analys/58.1.7

- **Cross, I.** (2001). Music, cognition, culture, and evolution. *Annals of the New York Academy of Sciences*, 930(1), 177–187. Doi: https://doi.org/10.1111/j.1749-6632.2001.tb05723.x

- **Cosmides, L., & Tooby, J.** (1996). Are humans good intuitive statisticians after all? Rethinking some conclusions from the literature on judgment under uncertainty. *Cognition*, 58(1), 1–73. Doi: https://doi.org/10.1016/0010-0277(95)00664-8

- **Davidson, R. J.** (2004). Well-being and affective style: Neural substrates and biobehavioral correlates. *Philosophical Transactions of the Royal Society of London. Series B: Biological Sciences, 359*(1449), 1395–1411. Doi: https://doi.org/10.1098/rstb.2004.1510
- **Dawson, D., Reid, K.** (1997). Fatigue, alcohol, and performance impairment. *Nature* 388, 235. https://doi.org/10.1038/40775
- **De Lange, F. P., Heilbron, M., & Kok, P.** (2018). How expectations shape perception. *Trends in Cognitive Sciences, 21*(9), 764–779. Doi: https://doi.org/10.1016/j.tics.2018.06.002
- **den Ouden, H. E., Kok, P., & de Lange, F. P.** (2012). How prediction errors shape perception, attention, and motivation. *Frontiers in Psychology,* 3, 548. https://doi.org/10.3389/fpsyg.2012.00548
- **DeYoung, C. G., Hirsh, J. B., Shane, M. S., Papademetris, X., Rajeevan, N., & Gray, J. R.** (2010). Testing predictions from personality neuroscience. Brain structure and the big five. *Psychological Science, 21*(6), 820–828. https://doi.org/10.1177/0956797610370159
- **Donchin, E., & Coles, M. G. H.** (1988). Is the P300 component a manifestation of context updating? *Behavioral and Brain Sciences, 11*(3), 357-374. https://psycnet.apa.org/doi/10.1017/S0140525X00058027
- **Duhamel, J. R., Colby, C. L., & Goldberg, M. E.** (1992). The updating of the representation of visual space in parietal cortex by intended eye movements. *Science, 255*(5040), 90–92. Doi: https://doi.org/10.1126/science.1553535
- **Dunbar, R. M.**, (2009). The social brain hypothesis and its implications for social evolution. *Ann Hum Biol.* 36(5):562-72. doi: 10.1080/03014460902960289 https://pubmed.ncbi.nlm.nih.gov/19575315/
- **Ferrara, E., Varol, O., Davis, C., Flammini, A., & Menczer, F.** (2016). The rise of social bots. *Communications of the ACM, 59*(7), 96–104. https://doi.org/10.1145/2818717
- **Field, G. D., & Sampath, A. P.** (2017). Behavioural and physiological limits to vision in mammals. Philosophical *Transactions of the Royal Society B Biological Sciences.* https://doi.org/10.1098/rstb.2016.0072
- **Flesch, R.** (1948). A new readability yardstick. *Journal of Applied Psychology, 32*(3), 221–233. https://doi.org/10.1037/h0057532
- **Fonseca-Azevedo, K. & Herculano-Houzel, S.** (2012). Metabolic constraint imposes a tradeoff between body size and the number of brain neurons in human evolution. *Proceedings of the National Academy of Sciences, 109*(45), 18571–18576. Doi: https://doi.org/10.1073/pnas.1206390109
- **Frank, M. C., Everett, D. L., Fedorenko, S., & Gibson, E.** (2008). Number as a cognitive technology: Evidence from Pirahã language and cognition. *Cognition, 108*(3), 819–824. Doi: https://doi.org/10.1016/j.cognition.2008.04.007
- **Fredrickson B. L.** (2001). The role of positive emotions in positive psychology. The broaden-and-build theory of positive emotions. *The American psychologist, 56*(3), 218–226. https://doi.org/10.1037//0003-066x.56.3.218
- **Friston, K. J.** (2010). The free-energy principle: A unified brain theory? *Nature Reviews Neuroscience, 11*(2), 127–138. Doi: https://www.nature.com/articles/nrn2787
- **Furnham, A., & Marks, J.** (2013). Tolerance of ambiguity: A review of the recent literature. *Psychology, 4*(09), 717–728. http://dx.doi.org/10.4236/psych.2013.49102
- **Galinsky, A. D., & Moskowitz, G. B.** (2000). Perspective-taking: decreasing stereotype expression, stereotype accessibility, and in-group favoritism. *Journal of personality and social psychology, 78*(4), 708–724. https://doi.org/10.1037//0022-3514.78.4.708

- Garfinkel, S. N., Seth, A. K., Barrett, A. B., Suzuki, K., & Critchley, H. D. (2015). Knowing your own heart: Distinguishing interoceptive accuracy from interoceptive awareness. *Biological Psychology, 104*, 65-74. Doi: https://doi.org/10.1016/j.biopsycho.2014.11.004

- Gigerenzer, G., & Hoffrage, U. (1995). How to improve Bayesian reasoning without Instruction: Frequency Formats. *Psychological Review, 102*(4), 684–704. Doi: http://dx.doi.org/10.1037/0033-295X.102.4.684

- Gigerenzer, G., & Gaissmaier, R. (2011). Heuristic decision making. *Annual Review of Psychology, 62*, 451–482. Doi: https://doi.org/10.1146/annurev-psych-120709-145346

- Gordon, P. (2004). Numerical cognition without words: Evidence from Amazonia. *Science, 306*(5695), 496–499. Doi: https://doi.org/10.1126/science.1094492

- Gowlett, J.A.J. (2016). The discovery of fire by humans: A long and convoluted process. *Philosophical Transactions of the Royal Society of London. 371*(20150164). http://dx.doi.org/10.1098/rstb.2015.0164

- Graunt, J. (1662). *Natural and political observations mentioned in a following index, and made upon the bills of mortality.* https://archive.org/details/2356014R.nlm.nih.gov/page/n29/mode/2up

- Gregory, R. L. (1997). Knowledge in perception and illusion. *Philosophical Transactions of the Royal Society of London. Series B: Biological Sciences, 352*(1358), 1121–1127. Doi: https://doi.org/10.1098/rstb.1997.0095

- Gruber, M. J., Gelman, B. D., & Ranganath, C. (2014). States of curiosity modulate hippocampus-dependent learning via the dopaminergic circuit. *Neuron, 84*(2), 486–496. https://doi.org/10.1016/j.neuron.2014.08.060

- Herculano-Houzel, S. (2012). The remarkable, yet not extraordinary, human brain as a scaled-up primate brain and its associated cost. *Proceedings of the National Academy of Sciences, 109*(supplement_1), 10661–10668. Doi: https://doi.org/10.1073/pnas.1201895109

- Haug, M., Maier, C., Gewald, H., & Weitzel, T. (2025). Supporting opinions to fit in: a spiral of silence-theoretic explanation for establishing echo chambers and filter bubbles on social media. *Internet Research, 35*(7), 30-51. https://doi.org/10.1108/INTR-03-2024-0413

- Heffner, J., Son, J.-Y., & FeldmanHall, O. (2021). Emotion prediction errors guide socially adaptive behaviour. *Nature Human Behaviour, 5*(10), 1391-1401. https://doi.org/10.1038/s41562-021-01213-6

- Henshilwood, C. S., D'Errico, F., Van Niekerk, K. L., Coquinot, Y., Jacobs, Z., Lauritzen, S., Menu, M., & Garcia-Moreno, R. (2011). A 100,000-year-old ochre-processing workshop at Blombos Cave, South Africa. *Science, 334*(6053), 219–222. Doi: https://doi.org/10.1126/science.1211535

- Hoffrage, U., Lindsey, S., Hertwig, R., & Gigerenzer, G. (2000). Communicating statistical information. *Science, 290*(5500), 2261–2262. Doi: https://doi.org/10.1126/science.290.5500.2261

- Hsiang, S. M., Burke, M., & Miguel, E. (2013). Quantifying the influence of climate on human conflict. *Science, 341*(6151), 1235367. Doi: https://doi.org/10.1126/science.1235367

- Keller, G. B., & Mrsic-Flogel, T. D. (2018). Predictive Processing: A Canonical Cortical Computation. *Neuron, 100*(2), 424–435. Doi: https://doi.org/10.1016/j.neuron.2018.10.003

- Klayman, J., & Ha, Y.-w. (1987). Confirmation, disconfirmation, and information in hypothesis testing. *Psychological Review, 94*(2), 211–228. https://doi.org/10.1037/0033-295X.94.2.211

- Kleckner, I. R., Zhang, J., Touroutoglou, A., Chanes, L., Xia, C., Simmons, W. K., Quigley, K. S., Dickerson, B. C., & Barrett, L. F. (2017). Evidence for a Large-Scale Brain System Supporting Allostasis and Interoception in Humans. *Nature human behaviour, 1*, 0069. https://doi.org/10.1038/s41562-017-0069

- **Klucharev V, Hytönen K, Rijpkema M, Smidts A, & Fernández G.** Reinforcement learning signal predicts social conformity. *Neuron.* 2009 Jan 15;61(1):140-51. doi: https://doi.org/10.1016/j.neuron.2008.11.027
- **Kahan, D. M.** (2013). Ideology, motivated reasoning, and cognitive reflection. *Judgment and Decision Making, 8*(4), 407–424. http://dx.doi.org/10.1017/S1930297500005271
- **Kaplan, J., Gimbel, S. & Harris, S.** (2016). Neural correlates of maintaining one's political beliefs in the face of counterevidence. *Sci Rep* **6**, 39589. https://doi.org/10.1038/srep39589
- **Knill, D. C., & Pouget, A.** (2004). The Bayesian brain: the role of uncertainty in neural coding and computation. *Trends Neuroscience, 27*(12), 712–719. https://doi.org/10.1016/j.tins.2004.10.007
- **Kruger, J., & Dunning, D.** (1999). Unskilled and unaware of it: how difficulties in recognizing one's own incompetence lead to inflated self-assessments. *Journal of personality and social psychology, 77*(6), 1121–1134. https://doi.org/10.1037//0022-3514.77.6.1121
- **Kruglanski, A. W., & Webster, D. M.** (1996). Motivated closing of the mind: "Seizing" and "freezing." *Psychological Review, 103*(2), 263–283. https://doi.org/10.1037/0033-295X.103.2.263
- **Kunda Z.** (1990). The case for motivated reasoning. *Psychological Bulletin, 108*(3), 480–498. https://doi.org/10.1037/0033-2909.108.3.480
- **Leary, M. R., Diebels, K. J., Davisson, E. K., Jongman-Sereno, K. P., Isherwood, J. C., Raimi, K. T., Deffler, S. A., & Hoyle, R. H.** (2017). Cognitive and Interpersonal Features of Intellectual Humility. *Personality & social psychology bulletin, 43*(6), 793–813. https://doi.org/10.1177/0146167217697695
- **Lally, P., van Jaarsveld, C. H. M., Potts, H. W. W., & Wardle, J.** (2010). How are habits formed: Modelling habit formation in the real world. *European Journal of Social Psychology, 40*(6), 998–1009. https://doi.org/10.1002/ejsp.674
- **Linville P. W.** (1987). Self-complexity as a cognitive buffer against stress-related illness and depression. *Journal of personality and social psychology, 52*(4), 663–676. https://doi.org/10.1037//0022-3514.52.4.663
- **Lotto, B. R.** (2009). What are illusions, and why do we see them? *Journal of Vision.* 9(14): 7-7. http://dx.doi.org/10.1167/9.14.7
- **Lutz, A., Brefczynski-Lewis, J., Johnstone, T., & Davidson, R. J.** (2008). Regulation of the neural circuitry of emotion by compassion meditation: Effects of meditative expertise. *PLoS ONE, 3*(3), e1897. Doi: https://doi.org/10.1371/journal.pone.0001897
- **Lutz, A., Slagter, H. A., Dunne, J. D., & Davidson, R. J.** (2008). Attention regulation and monitoring in meditation. *Trends in Cognitive Sciences, 12*(4), 163–169. Doi: https://doi.org/10.1016/j.tics.2008.01.005
- **Maguire, E.A., Woollett, K., & Spiers, H. J.** (2006). London taxi drivers and bus drivers: A structural MRI and neuropsychological analysis. *Hippocampus,* 16(12), 1091-1101. https://doi.org/10.1002/hipo.20233
- **Markus, H., & Wurf, R.** (1987). The dynamic self-concept: A social psychological perspective. *Annual Review of Psychology, 38*(1), 299–337. https://doi.org/10.1146/annurev.ps.38.020187.001503
- **Martinón-Torres, M., Garate, D., Herries, A.I.R., & Petraglia, M.** (2024). No scientific evidence that Homo Naledi buried their dead and produced rock art. *Journal of Human Evolution, 195,* 103464. https://doi.org/10.1016/j.jhevol.2023.103464
- **Marzola, P., Melzer, T., Pavesi, E., Gil-Mohapel, J., & Brocardo, P. S.** (2023). Exploring the role of neuroplasticity in development, aging, and neurodegeneration. *Brain Sciences, 13*(12), 1610. https://doi.org/10.3390/brainsci13121610

- **Mayer E. A**. (2011). Gut feelings: the emerging biology of gut-brain communication. *Nature Reviews. Neuroscience*, *12*(8), 453–466. https://doi.org/10.1038/nrn3071
- **Menon, V**. (2023). 20 years of the default mode network: A review and synthesis. *Neuron*. *3*(16), 2469-2487. Doi: https://doi.org/10.1016/j.neuron.2023.04.023
- **Metcalfe, J., & Mischel, W**. (1999). A hot/cool-system analysis of delay of gratification: dynamics of willpower. *Psychological review*, *106*(1), 3–19. https://doi.org/10.1037/0033-295x.106.1.3
- **Meyers-Levy, J., & Zhu, R**. (2007). The influence of ceiling height: The effect of priming on the type of processing that people use. *Journal of Consumer Research*, *34*(2), 174–186. Dio: https://doi.org/10.1086/519146
- **Miller, D. T**. (2023*)*. A century of pluralistic ignorance: what we have learned about its origins, forms, and consequences. *Front. Soc. Psychol*. 1:1260896. https://doi.org/10.3389/frsps.2023.1260896
- **Miller, E. K., & Cohen, J. D**. (2001). An integrative theory of prefrontal cortex function. *Annual review of neuroscience*, *24*, 167–202. https://doi.org/10.1146/annurev.neuro.24.1.167
- **Miller, G. A**. (1956). The magical number seven, plus or minus two: Some limits on our capacity for processing information. *Psychological Review*, *63*(2), 81–97. Doi: https://psycnet.apa.org/doi/10.1037/h0043158
- **Miyake, A., Friedman, N. P., Emerson, M. J., Witzki, A. H., Howerter, A., & Wager, T. D**. (2000). The unity and diversity of executive functions and their contributions to complex "Frontal Lobe" tasks: a latent variable analysis. *Cognitive psychology*, *41*(1), 49–100. https://doi.org/10.1006/cogp.1999.0734
- **Moser, J. S., Schroder, H. S., Heeter, C., Moran, T. P., & Lee, Y. H**. (2011). Mind your errors: evidence for a neural mechanism linking growth mind-set to adaptive posterror adjustments. *Psychological Science*, *22*(12), 1484–1489. https://doi.org/10.1177/0956797611419520
- **Moyosore, A., Sturdee, M. & Rubegni, E**. (2022). A systematic survey on embodied cognition: 11 years of research in child–computer interaction. *International Journal for Child-Computer Interaction*, *33*, 100478. Doi: https://doi.org/10.1016/j.ijcci.2022.100478
- **Müller, E. J., Palesi, F., Hou, K. Y., Tan, J., Close, T., Wheeler-Kingshott, C. A. M. G., D'Angelo, E., Calamante, F., & Shine, J. M**. (2023). Parallel processing relies on a distributed, low-dimensional cortico-cerebellar architecture. *Network Neuroscience*, *7*(2), 844–863. https://doi.org/10.1162/netn_a_00308
- **Nickerson, R. S**. (1998). Confirmation bias: A ubiquitous phenomenon in many guises. *Review of General Psychology*, *2*(2), 175–220. https://psycnet.apa.org/doi/10.1037/1089-2680.2.2.175
- **Noelle-Neumann, E**. (1974). The spiral of silence: A theory of public opinion. *Journal of Communication, 24*(2), 43–51. https://doi.org/10.1111/j.1460-2466.1974.tb00367.x
- **Nord, C. L., & Garfinkel, S. N**. (2022). Interoceptive pathways to understand and treat mental health conditions. *Trends in Cognitive Sciences*, *26*(6), 499-513. Doi: https://doi.org/10.1016/j.tics.2022.03.004
- **Ochsner, K. N., & Gross, J. J**. (2005). The cognitive control of emotion. *Trends in Cognitive Sciences*, *9*(5), 242–249. Doi: https://doi.org/10.1016/j.tics.2005.03.010
- **Ochsner, K. N., Silvers, J. A., & Buhle, J. T**. (2012). Functional imaging studies of emotion regulation: a synthetic review and evolving model of the cognitive control of emotion. *Annals of the New York Academy of Sciences*, *1251*, E1–E24. https://doi.org/10.1111/j.1749-6632.2012.06751.x

- **Hong, L., & Page, S.** (2005). Groups of Diverse Problem Solvers Can Outperform Groups of High-Ability Problem Solvers. *Proceedings of the National Academy of Sciences, 101*, 16385-16389. https://ssrn.com/abstract=666281
- **Paluck, E. L., & Shepherd, H., & Aronow, P.** (2016). Changing climates of conflict: A social network experiment in 56 schools. *Proceedings of the National Academy of Sciences, 113*(3), 566–571. https://doi.org/10.1073/pnas.1514483113
- **Park, C. L.** (2010). Making sense of the meaning literature: An integrative review of meaning making and its effects on adjustment to stressful life events. *Psychological Bulletin, 136*(2), 257–301. https://doi.org/10.1037/a0018301
- **Perkins, H. W.** (2002). Social norms and the prevention of alcohol misuse in collegiate contexts. *Journal of Studies on Alcohol, Supplement,* (14), 164-172. https://doi.org/10.15288/jsas.2002.s14.164
- **Phelps, E. A.** (2005). Emotion and cognition: Insights from studies of the human amygdala. *Annual Review of Psychology, 56*, 27-53. https://doi.org/10.1146/annurev.psych.56.091103.070234
- **Phelps, E. A., & LeDoux, J. E.** (2005). Contributions of the amygdala to emotion processing: from animal models to human behavior. *Neuron, 48*(2), 175–187. https://doi.org/10.1016/j.neuron.2005.09.025
- **Polich, J.** (2007). Updating P300: An integrative theory of P3a and P3b. *Clinical Neurophysiology, 118*(10), 2128-2148. https://doi.org/10.1016/j.clinph.2007.04.019
- **Prentice, D. A., & Miller, D. T.** (1996). Pluralistic ignorance and the perpetuation of social norms by unwitting actors. *Advances in Experimental Social Psychology, 28*, 161–210. https://doi.org/10.1016/S0065-2601(08)60238-5
- **Raichle, M. E., MacLeod, A. M., Snyder, A. Z., Powers, W. J., Gusnard, D. A., & Shulman, G. L.** (2001). A default mode of brain function. *Proceedings of the National Academy of Sciences, 98*(2), 676–682. Doi: https://doi.org/10.1073/pnas.98.2.676
- **Ramachandran, V. S.** (1992). Blind spots. *Scientific American, 266*(5), 86–91. doi: https://doi.org/10.1038/scientificamerican0592-86
- **Ransom M, Fazelpour S, & Mole C.** (2017). Attention in the predictive mind. *Consciousness and Cognition*, 47:99-112. https://doi.org/10.1016/j.concog.2016.06.011
- **Rao, R., Ballard, D.** (1999). Predictive coding in the visual cortex: a functional interpretation of some extra-classical receptive-field effects. *Nat Neurosci* 2, 79–87. https://doi.org/10.1038/4580
- **Regier, T., & Kay, P.** (2009). Language, thought, and color: Whorf was Half Right. *Trends in Cognitive Sciences, 13*(9), 395-402. https://doi.org/10.1016/j.tics.2009.07.001
- **Reich, D., Green, R. E., Kircher, M., Krause, J., Patterson, N., Durand, E. Y., Viola, B., Briggs, A. W., Stenzel, U., Johnson, P. L., Maricic, T., Good, J. M., Marques-Bonet, T., Alkan, C., Fu, Q., Mallick, S., Li, H., Meyer, M., Eichler, E. E., Stoneking, M., ... Pääbo, S.** (2010). Genetic history of an archaic hominin group from Denisova Cave in Siberia. *Nature, 468*(7327), 1053–1060. https://doi.org/10.1038/nature09710
- **Roebroeks, W. & Billa, P.** (2011). On the earliest evidence for the habitual use of fire in Europe. *Proceedings of the National Academy of Sciences, 108*(113), 5209-5214. Doi: https://doi.org/10.1073/pnas.1018116108
- **Ross, L., Lepper, M. R., & Hubbard, M.** (1975). Perseverance in self-perception and social perception: biased attributional processes in the debriefing paradigm. *Journal of personality and social psychology, 32*(5), 880–892. https://doi.org/10.1037//0022-3514.32.5.880
- **Rouhani, N., & Niv, Y.** (2021). Signed and unsigned reward prediction errors dynamically enhance learning and memory. *eLife*, 10, e61077. https://doi.org/10.7554/elife.61077

- Rozenblit, L., & Keil, F. (2002). The misunderstood limits of folk science: an illusion of explanatory depth. *Cognitive Science, 26*(5), 521–562. https://doi.org/10.1207/s15516709cog2605_1
- Rozin, P., & Royzman, E. B. (2001). Negativity bias, negativity dominance, and contagion. *Personality and Social Psychology Review, 5*(4), 296–320. https://psycnet.apa.org/doi/10.1207/S15327957PSPR0504_2
- Seeley, W. W., Menon, V., Schatzberg, A. F., Keller, J., Glover, G. H., Kenna, H., Reiss, A. L., & Greicius, M. D. (2007). Dissociable intrinsic connectivity networks for salience processing and executive control. *The Journal of neuroscience: the official journal of the Society for Neuroscience, 27*(9), 2349–2356. https://doi.org/10.1523/JNEUROSCI.5587-06.2007
- Sel, A. (2014). Predictive codes of interoception, emotion, and the self. *Front. Psychol.* 5:189. doi: https://doi.org/10.3389/fpsyg.2014.00189
- Schanck, R. L. (1932). A study of a community and its groups and institutions conceived of as behaviors of individuals. *Psychological Monographs, 43*(2), 1–133. https://doi.org/10.1037/h0093296
- Schultz, W., Dayan, P., & Montague, P. R. (1997). A neural substrate of prediction and reward. *Science,* 275(5306), 1593-1599. https://doi.org/10.1126/science.275.5306.1593
- Schroder, H. S., Moran, T. P., Donnellan, M. B., & Moser, J. S. (2014). Mindset induction effects on cognitive control: a neurobehavioral investigation. *Biological psychology, 103*, 27–37. https://doi.org/10.1016/j.biopsycho.2014.08.004
- Schwartz, S. H. (1992). Universals in the content and structure of values: Theoretical advances and empirical tests in 20 countries. In M. P. Zanna (Ed.), *Advances in experimental social psychology,* Vol. 25, pp. 1–65). Academic Press. https://doi.org/10.1016/S0065-2601(08)60281-6
- Seitz, R. J., & Angel, H. F. (2020). Belief formation - A driving force for brain evolution. *Brain and cognition, 140*, 105548. https://doi.org/10.1016/j.bandc.2020.105548
- Seligman, M. E., & Schulman, P. (1986). Explanatory style as a predictor of productivity and quitting among life insurance sales agents. *Journal of Personality and Social Psychology,* 50(4), 832-838. https://psycnet.apa.org/doi/10.1037/0022-3514.50.4.832
- Shepard, R. N. (1964). Circularity in Judgements of Relative Pitch. *Journal of the Acoustical Society of America,* 36, 2346-2353. https://doi.org/10.1121/1.1919362
- Snyder, M., Tanke, E. D., & Berscheid, E. (1977). Social perception and interpersonal behavior: On the self-fulfilling nature of social stereotypes. *Journal of Personality and Social Psychology, 35*(9), 656–666. https://doi.org/10.1037/0022-3514.35.9.656
- Slovic, P., Finucane, M. L., Peters, E., & MacGregor, D. G. (2004). Risk as analysis and risk as feelings: Some thoughts about affect, reason, risk, and rationality. *Risk Analysis: An International Journal, 24*(2), 311–322. Doi: https://doi.org/10.1111/j.0272-4332.2004.00433.x
- Somerville, L. H., Heatherton, T. F., & Kelley, W. M. (2006). Dissociating neural systems supporting social rejection and social expectation violation. *Journal of Cognitive Neuroscience,* 18(9), 1515-1525. https://doi.org/10.1038/nn1728
- Stallen, M., & Sanfey, A. G. (2015). The neuroscience of social conformity: Implications for fundamental and applied research. *Frontiers in Neuroscience.* Frontiers Media S.A. https://doi.org/10.3389/fnins.2015.00337
- Sunstein, C. R. (2002). The law of group polarization. *Journal of Political Philosophy, 10*(2), 175–191. Doi: http://dx.doi.org/10.1111/1467-9760.00148
- Tajfel, H., & Turner, J. (2001). An integrative theory of intergroup conflict. In M. A. Hogg & D. Abrams (Eds.), *Intergroup relations: Essential readings* (pp. 94–109). Psychology

Press. https://www.scribd.com/document/414283115/Tajfel-Turner-1979-An-Integrative-Theory-of-Intergroup-Conflict-pdf

- **Tankard, M. E., & Paluck, E. L.** (2016). Norm perception and the formation of social norms. In *The Psychology of Social Change* (pp. 71-84). Cambridge University Press. **https://doi.org/10.1111/sipr.12022**

- **Tomasello, M., Melis, A. P., Tennie, C., Wyman, E., & Herrmann, E.** (2012). Two key steps in the evolution of human cooperation: The interdependence hypothesis. *Current Anthropology, 53*(5), 673–692. Doi: https://doi.org/10.1086/668207

- **Tversky, A., & Kahneman, D.** (1973). Availability: A heuristic for judging frequency and probability. *Cognitive Psychology, 5*(2), 207–232. Doi: https://doi.org/10.1016/0010-0285(73)90033-9

- **Tversky, A., & Kahneman, D.** (1974). Judgment under uncertainty: Heuristics and biases. *Science, 185*(4157), 1124–1131. https://www.science.org/doi/10.1126/science.185.4157.1124

- **Tversky, A., & Kahneman, D.** (1991). Loss aversion in riskless choice: A Reference-Dependent Model. *The Quarterly Journal of Economics, 106*(4), 1039–1061. https://doi.org/10.2307/2937956

- **Ulrich, R. S., Simons, R. F., Losito, B. D., Fiorito, E., Miles, M. A., & Zelson, M.** (1991). Stress recovery during exposure to natural and urban environments. *Journal of Environmental Psychology, 11*(3), 201–230. Doi: https://doi.org/10.1016/S0272-4944(05)80184-7

- **Van Dongen, H. P., Maislin, G., Mullington, J. M., & Dinges, D. F.** (2003). The cumulative cost of additional wakefulness: dose-response effects on neurobehavioral functions and sleep physiology from chronic sleep restriction and total sleep deprivation. *Sleep, 26*(2), 117–126. https://doi.org/10.1093/sleep/26.2.117

- **Van Grootel S., Van Laar C., Meeussen L., Schmader T. & Sczesny S.** (2018) Uncovering Pluralistic Ignorance to Change Men's Communal Self-descriptions, Attitudes, and Behavioral Intentions. *Front. Psychol.* 9:1344. doi: 10.3389/fpsyg.2018.01344

- **Van Veen, V., Krug, M. K., Schooler, J. W., & Carter, C. S.** (2009). Neural activity predicts attitude change in cognitive dissonance. *Nature Neuroscience, 12*(11), 1469–1474. https://doi.org/10.1038/nn.2413

- **Vernot, B., & Akey, J. M.** (2014). Resurrecting surviving Neandertal lineages from modern human genomes. *Science (New York, N.Y.), 343*(6174), 1017–1021. https://doi.org/10.1126/science.1245938

- **Vohs, K. D., Redden, J. P., & Rahinel, R.** (2013). Physical order produces healthy choices, generosity, and conventionality, whereas disorder produces creativity. *Psychological Science, 24*(9), 1860–1867. Doi: https://doi.org/10.1177/0956797613480186

- **Watson, J. M., & Strayer, D. L.** (2010). Supertaskers: Profiles in extraordinary multitasking ability. *Psychonomic bulletin & review, 17*(4), 479–485. https://doi.org/10.3758/PBR.17.4.479

- **Weng, H. Y., Fox, A. S., Shackman, N. R., Stodola, G. E., Caldwell, J. Z., Olson, M. C., Rogers, G. M., & Davidson, R. J.** (2020). Compassion training alters altruistic behavior and neural responses to suffering. *Psychological Science, 24*(7), 1171-1180. https://doi.org/10.1177/0956797612469537

- **Westen, D., Blagov, P. S., Harenski, K., Kilts, C., & Hamann, S.** (2006). Neural bases of motivated reasoning: an FMRI study of emotional constraints on partisan political judgment in the 2004 U.S. Presidential election. *Journal of cognitive neuroscience, 18*(11), 1947–1958. https://doi.org/10.1162/jocn.2006.18.11.1947

- **Wilson, T. D., & Brekke, N.** (1994). Mental contamination and mental correction: Unwanted influences on judgments and evaluations. *Psychological Bulletin, 116*(1), 117–142. https://doi.org/10.1037/0033-2909.116.1.117

- **Winawer, J., Witthoft, N., Frank, M. C., Wu, L., Wade, A. R., & Boroditsky, L.** (2007). Russian blues reveal effects of language on color discrimination. *Proceedings of the National Academy of Sciences, 104*(19), 7780-7785. https://www.pnas.org/doi/full/10.1073/pnas.0701644104
- **Young, T.** (1804). The Bakerian lecture. Experiments and calculations relative to physical optics. *Philosophical Transactions of the Royal Society of London*, https://doi.org/10.1098/rstl.1804.0001

Other Articles

- **Aiello, L. C., & Wheeler, P.** (1995). The Expensive-Tissue Hypothesis: *The Brain and the Digestive System in Human and Primate Evolution*. Current Anthropology, 36(2), 199–221. http://www.jstor.org/stable/2744104
- **Archie, L. C.** (206, June 30). *Søren Kierkegaard, 'Truth as Subjectivity*, Philosophy of Religion: Lander University. http://philosophy.lander.edu/intro/kierkegaard_phil.shtml
- **Arianrhod, R.** (2015, January 25). *Let There be Light! Celebrating the Theory of Electromagnetism*. The Conversation. https://theconversation.com/let-there-be-light-celebrating-the-theory-of-electromagnetism-35723
- **Belan, M.** (2023, July 5). *Infographic: Pathway of human evolution, from protocells to people*. Genetic Literacy Project – Science Not Ideology. https://geneticliteracyproject.org/2023/07/05/infographic-pathway-of-human-evolution-from-protocells-to-people/?
- **Belan, M.** (2023, June 9). *Visualized: The 4 Billion Year Path of Human Evolution*. Visual Capitalist. https://www.visualcapitalist.com/path-of-human-evolution/?
- **Berzin, A.** (2021, June). *The Buddhist Concept of Reality*. StudyBuddhism.com. https://studybuddhism.com/en/tibetan-buddhism/path-to-enlightenment/emptiness-voidness/the-buddhist-concept-of-reality#summary
- **Biology Notes Online** (2024, March 28). *Cyanobacteria - Definition, Characteristics, Structure, Functions, Examples* Biology Notes Online. https://biologynotesonline.com/cyanobacteria/
- **Blanshard, B.** (2025, July 3). *Rationalism*. Britannica. https://www.britannica.com/topic/rationalism/Religious-rationalism
- **Bolejko, K.** (2015, November 9). *From Newton to Einstein: The origins of general relativity*. The Conversation. https://theconversation.com/from-newton-to-einstein-the-origins-of-general-relativity-50013
- **Brain World.** (2021, May 6). *Fitting In: The Neuroscience of Conformity*. Brain World. https://brainworldmagazine.com/fitting-in-the-neuroscience-of-conformity/
- **Bohr, N.** (1949). Discussion with Einstein on Epistemological Problems in Atomic Physics. In P. A. Schilpp (Ed.), *Albert Einstein: Philosopher-Scientist* (pp. 199–241). Open Court.
- **Bryant KL, Hansen C, Hecht EE**. (2023, November 23). *Fermentation technology as a driver of human brain expansion*. Commun Biol. 6(1):1190. doi: 10.1038/s42003-023-05517-3. https://www.nature.com/articles/s42003-023-05517-3
- **Burini, R., Leonard, W.** (2018, August). *The evolutionary roles of nutrition selection and dietary quality in the human brain size and encephalization*. Nutrire 43(1):19. http://dx.doi.org/10.1186/s41110-018-0078-x
- **Capps, J.** (2023, May 22). *The Pragmatic Theory of Truth*, The Stanford Encyclopedia of Philosophy. https://plato.stanford.edu/archives/sum2023/entries/truth-pragmatic/ .

- **Cornelio, A., de Bittencourt-Navarrete, R., de Bittencourt Brum, R., Queiroz, C., & Costa, M.** (2016, April 25). *Human brain expansion during evolution is independent of fire control and cooking.* Frontiers in Neuroscience. 10:167 https://doi.org/10.3389/fnins.2016.00167

- **Dunbar, R.** (2021, August 28). *Dunbar's Number: Why the theory that humans can only maintain 150 friendships has withstood 30 years of scrutiny.* NeuroscienceNews.com. https://neurosciencenews.com/dunbars-number-social-brain-19210/

- **Duque, F.** (2022). *The probability of pluralistic ignorance.* Scholars at Harvard. https://scholar.harvard.edu/files/duque/files/the_probability_of_pluralistic_ignorance_long.pdf

- **Earth Now.** (n.d.). *Great Oxygenation Event: How Oxygen Filled the Atmosphere.* Earth Now. https://earthhow.com/great-oxygenation-event/?

- **Faye, J.** (2024, May 31). *Copenhagen Interpretation of Quantum Mechanics.* The Stanford Encyclopedia of Philosophy. https://plato.stanford.edu/archives/sum2024/entries/qm-copenhagen/

- **Fineman, M.** (1991, Jan 1). *Dalai Lama's Disciples Gather for Peace Prayer: Religion: About 150,000 participate in ceremony with the Peace Prize winner.* Los Angeles Times. https://www.latimes.com/archives/la-xpm-1991-01-01-mn-7464-story.html

- **Glaser, L.** (2016). *Understanding the Mind.* Cornell University: College of Arts and Sciences. https://as.cornell.edu/news/understanding-mind

- **Heath, S.** (2023, May 16). Medical TikTok Runs Rampant with Medical Misinformation. TechTarget.com https://www.techtarget.com/patientengagement/news/366584425/Medical-TikTok-Runs-Rampant-with-Medical-Misinformation

- **History.com Editors** (2017, October 6). *Hinduism.* History.com. https://www.history.com/articles/hinduism

- **Hofman, M.** (2019, May). *On the Nature and Evolution of the Human Mind.* Progress in Brain Research 250. http://dx.doi.org/10.1016/bs.pbr.2019.03.016

- **Ireland, C.** (2008, April 3). *Eating meat led to smaller stomachs, bigger brains.* Harvard Gazette. https://news.harvard.edu/gazette/story/2008/04/eating-meat-led-to-smaller-stomachs-bigger-brains/

- **Ivanova, A.** (2019, September 25). *Language is the Scaffold of the Mind.* Nautilus: Science Connected. https://nautil.us/language-is-the-scaffold-of-the-mind-237558/

- **Kartik, A.** (2022, February 18). *The Great Oxidation Event: How Cyanobacteria Changed Life.* American Society for Microbiology. https://asm.org/Articles/2022/February/The-Great-Oxidation-Event-How-Cyanobacteria-Change?

- **Kelly, M.** (2013, September 12). *Climate change and conflict: Scientists quantify warming's role in violence.* Princeton University News. https://www.princeton.edu/news/2013/09/12/climate-change-and-conflict-scientists-quantify-warmings-role-violence

- **Konopliov, A**. (2024, June 26). *Key Statistics on Fake News & Misinformation in Media in 2024.* Redline Digital. https://redline.digital/fake-news-statistics/

- **Leppert, R. & Matsa, K. E.** (2024, September 17). *More Americans – especially young adults – are regularly getting news on TikTok.* Pew Research Center, Short Reads. https://www.pewresearch.org/short-reads/2024/09/17/more-americans-regularly-get-news-on-tiktok-especially-young-adults/

- **Mastin, L.** (2009, October). *Important Scientists: Niels Bohr.* The Physics of the Universe. https://www.physicsoftheuniverse.com/scientists_bohr.html

- **Mastin, L.** (2009, October). *Important Scientists: Erwin Schrödinger.* The Physics of the Universe. https://www.physicsoftheuniverse.com/scientists_bohr.html

- **Matthias, A**. (2023, December 13). *Plato's Theory of Forms: Stepping out of the shadows and into the light.* Daily Philosophy. https://daily-philosophy.com/platos-theory-of-forms/
- **Morgan, K.** (2013, August 1). *Cool Heads Likely Won't Prevail in a Hotter, Wetter World.* Princeton University. https://as.cornell.edu/news/understanding-mind
- **Niels Bohr Institute.** (2012, July 18). *The Copenhagen Interpretation.* Niels Bohr Institute: University of Copenhagen. https://nbi.ku.dk/english/www/niels/bohr/koebenhavnerfortolkningen/
- **O'Gieblyn, M.** (2019, December 4). *Do We Have Minds of Our Own?* The New Yorker. https://www.newyorker.com/books/under-review/do-we-have-minds-of-our-own
- **Papin, E.** (2024, August 28). *The common ancestor of all present-day living organisms has been partly deciphered.* Le Monde. https://www.lemonde.fr/en/science/article/2024/08/28/the-common-ancestor-of-all-present-day-living-organisms-has-been-partly-deciphered_6722509_10.html?
- **Pearce, K.** (2017, December 19). *What Descartes Doubted, Berkeley Denied, and Kant Endorsed.* Cambridge University Press. https://plato.stanford.edu/archives/sum2024/entries/qm-copenhagen/
- **Perception, Problem of.** (2021). In E. N. Zalta (Ed.), *The Stanford Encyclopedia of Philosophy* (Winter 2021 ed.). Metaphysics Research Lab, Stanford University. https://plato.stanford.edu/entries/perception-problem/
- **Pipas, M. D.** (2024). *Social Influence and Groupthink.* RAIS Journal for Social Sciences. https://journal.rais.education/index.php/raiss/article/download/239/194/427
- **PlantPropagation.org** (n.d.). *Cyanobacteria: Architects of the Earth's Atmosphere – An In-Depth Exploration.* PlantPropagation.org. https://plantpropagation.org/cyanobacteria/?
- **Pobiner, B.** (2016, March). *Meat-Eating Among the Earliest Humans.* American Scientist, 104(2), 110. https://doi.org/10.1511/2016.119.110
- **Powder, J.** (2021, September 21). *The Gut Microbiome and the Brain.* John Hopkins University: Bloomberg School of Public Health. https://magazine.publichealth.jhu.edu/2021/gut-microbiome-and-brain
- **Quantum Entanglement.** (2020). In E. N. Zalta (Ed.), *The Stanford Encyclopedia of Philosophy* (Fall 2020 ed.). Metaphysics Research Lab, Stanford University. https://plato.stanford.edu/entries/qt-entangle/
- **Silverman, A.** (2014, July 14). *Plato's Middle Period Metaphysics and Epistemology.* The Stanford Encyclopedia of Philosophy. https://plato.stanford.edu/archives/fall2022/entries/plato-metaphysics/
- **Schwitzgebel, E**. (2024). Belief. In E. N. Zalta & U. Nodelman (Eds.), *The Stanford Encyclopedia of Philosophy* (Summer 2024 ed.). Metaphysics Research Lab, Stanford University. https://plato.stanford.edu/archives/spr2024/entries/belief/
- **Than, K.** (2010, May 14). *All Species Evolved From Single Cell, Study Finds.* National Geographic. https://www.nationalgeographic.com/adventure/article/100513-science-evolution-darwin-single-ancestor?
- **Tuttle, R. H.** (2025, June 27). *Human Evolution.* Britannica. https://www.britannica.com/science/human-evolution
- **Walter, C.** (2008, March 4). *Why Language is All Thumbs.* KurzweilAI.net Brain Archive. https://kurzweilai-brain.gothdyke.mom/articles/art0712.html
- **Walton, M.** (2022, May 26). *Sociologist Duncan Watts tackles misinformation and mistrust in science and society.* American Association for the Advancement of Science. https://www.aaas.org/membership/member-spotlight/sociologist-duncan-watts-tack-

- *les-misinformation-and-mistrust-science#:~:text=Watts%20studies%20the%20misinformation%20that,opinion%20about%20what%20is%20important*.
- **Whitesides, G.** (2020, August 10). Learning from Success: Lessons in Science and Diplomacy from the Montreal Protocol. Science & Diplomacy. https://www.sciencediplomacy.org/article/2020/learning-success-lessons-in-science-and-diplomacy-montreal-protocol
- **Wurtz, R. H.** (2008). Neuronal mechanisms of visual stability. *Vision Research*, *48*(19), 2070–2089. https://doi.org/10.1016/j.visres.2008.03.021

Online Videos

- **Boroditsky, L.** (May 2018). How language shapes the way we think [Video]. TED Conferences. https://www.youtube.com/watch?v=RKK7wGAYP6k
- **Harris, S.** (March 2010). *Science can answer moral questions* [Video]. TED Conferences. https://youtu.be/Hj9oB4zpHww
- **Herculano-Houzel, S.** (June 2013). *What is so special about the human brain?* [Video]. TED Conferences. https://www.ted.com/talks/suzana_herculano_houzel_what_is_so_special_about_the_human_brain
- **Lazar, S.** (January 2012). *How meditation can reshape our brains* [Video]. TEDxCambridge 2011. https://youtu.be/m8rRzTtP7Tc?si=ILbhmSOipGF26FuW
- **Levitin, D.** (August, 2014). *The Organized Mind: Thinking Straight in the Age of Information Overload* [Video]. Talks at Google. https://www.youtube.com/watch?v=aR1TNEHRY-U
- **Lotto, B.** (July 2009). *Optical Illusions show how we see*. [Video]. TED Conferences. https://www.ted.com/talks/beau_lotto_optical_illusions_show_how_we_see?utm_campaign=tedspread&utm_medium=referral&utm_source=tedcomshare
- **Rosenblum, L.** (October 2010). The McGurk Effect – Demonstrated and Explained. [Video]. YouTube - https://youtu.be/l_QI7y5aQqo
- **Schwartz, B**. (July 2005). The paradox of choice [Video]. TEDGlobal 2005. https://www.ted.com/talks/barry_schwartz_the_paradox_of_choice?utm_campaign=tedspread&utm_medium=referral&utm_source=tedcomshare
- **Wolpert, D.** (July 2011). *The real reason for brains* [Video]. TED Conferences. https://www.ted.com/talks/daniel_wolpert_the_real_reason_for_brains

Websites/Webpages

- **Auditory Neuroscience** (n. d.). Auditory Neuroscience – Making sense of sound. https://auditoryneuroscience.com/pitch/missing-fundamental-stimuli
- **Boston University Today** (February 9, 2024). POV: Health Misinformation is Rampant on Social Media. https://www.bu.edu/articles/2024/health-misinformation-rampant-on-social-media/
- **Brookings** (November 7, 2024). How Disinformation Defined the 2024 Election Narrative. https://www.brookings.edu/articles/how-disinformation-defined-the-2024-election-narrative/
- **Chandaria, S.** (n.d.). *Dr. Shamil Chandaria*. YouTube. Retrieved September 5, 2024, from https://www.youtube.com/@ShamilChandaria (The Bayesian Brain and the Ultimate Nature of Reality)

- **Cleveland Clinic (n.**d.).*The nervous system*. https://my.clevelandclinic.org/health/body/21202-nervous-system
- **Cypers Kamen, L.** (March 30, 2022). *Get Smart: Intellectual Humility and Critical Thinking with Mark Leary, PhD & Lee McIntyre, PhD*. Harvesting Happiness Podcast. https://podcasts.apple.com/us/podcast/get-smart-intellectual-humility-and-critical-thinking/id405336362?i=1000555662286
- **Cromie, W**. (October 28, 2004). *Overworked Interns Prone to Medical Errors*. The Harvard Gazette. https://news.harvard.edu/gazette/story/2004/10/overworked-interns-prone-to-medical-errors/
- **Harris, S.** (May 18, 2020). A conversation with Jonathan Haidt (No. 204) [Audio podcast]. Making Sense Podcast, Sam Harris. https://www.samharris.org/podcasts/making-sense-episodes/204-may-18-2020
- **Harris, S.** (May 22, 2023). *Constructing self and world* (No. 320) [Audio podcast episode]. *Making Sense Podcast*. Sam Harris. https://www.samharris.org/podcasts/making-sense-episodes/320-constructing-self-and-world
- **John Hopkins Medicine** (n.d.). *Brain Anatomy and How the Brain Works*. https://www.hopkinsmedicine.org/health/conditions-and-diseases/anatomy-of-the-brain
- **Martin, L., Hammond, N.** (July 22, 2025). *What We Know About the Brain*. Medical News Today. https://www.medicalnewstoday.com/articles/brain
- **McCarthy, G.** (2024). The Human Brain – Yale University Lecture. https://campuspress.yale.edu/humanbrain/lecture-notes2024/lecture2024-01/
- **Merzenich, M**. (2023). Dr Michael Merzenich Web Page. https://www.michaelmerzenich.com/
- **Misinformation Review** (2023). Who Knowingly shares false political information online? Harvard Kennedy School. https://misinforeview.hks.harvard.edu/article/who-knowingly-shares-false-political-information-online/
- **National Institute of Neurological Disorders and Stroke**. (n.d.) *Brains Basics: Know Your Brain*. National Institutes of Health. https://www.ninds.nih.gov/health-information/patient-caregiver-education/brain-basics-know-your-brain
- **Pang, D.** (September 2, 2023). *The Staggering Complexity of the Human Brain*. Psychology Today. https://www.psychologytoday.com/us/blog/consciousness-and-beyond/202309/the-staggering-complexity-of-the-human-brain
- **Pavlico, A.** (September 17, 2018). *Simone Weil on Attention, Learning, and Compassion*. 3 Quarks Daily. https://3quarksdaily.com/3quarksdaily/2018/09/simone-weil-on-attention-learning-and-compassion.html
- **Ponce de León, M., & Zollikofer, C**. (2021, October 26). *Inferring brain and cognitive evolution from fossil human endocasts*. University of Zurich. https://www.comparativelinguistics.uzh.ch/en/colloquium/past-isle-colloquium/Fall-Term-2021/Abstracts/2021-10-26.html
- **Sanders, R**. (2002). UC Berkeley scientists detail neural circuit that lets eye detect directional motion. UC Berkeley News. https://newsarchive.berkeley.edu/news/media/releases/2002/11/27_motion.html
- **World Health Organization.** (May 20, 2022). *World Health Statistics 2022*. World Health Organization News. https://www.who.int/news/item/20-05-2022-world-health-statistics-2022
- **Young, V.** (n.d.). Impostor Syndrome Institute. https://impostorsyndrome.com/valerie-young/

INDEX

A

acceptance and commitment therapy - ACT, 277, 316
adaptation, 282, 316, 326
advanced listening, 278, 279, 280, 284, 289, 294, 325
aerobic respiration, 28
affective-prediction errors
    P3b, 161

Aiello, Leslie
    expensive tissue hypothesis, 49

allostasis, 53
amphioxi, 28, 29, 51
anxiety, 64, 67, 76, 85, 217, 224, 234, 249, 258, 315
    shaping neural connections, 21

Aristotle, 192, 271
    argumentation and persuasion, 268
    ethos, 268, 272, 287
    kairos, 268, 274, 288
    logos, 268, 273, 288
    pathos, 268, 270, 273, 288
    telos, 268, 274, 288

australopithecines, 44

B

Bandura, Albert
    moral agency, 179, 248

Barker, Roger
    Ecological Psychology, 310

Barlow, Horace, 83
Baron, Jonathan
    active open-mindedness, 204

Bastiaanssen, Thomaz, 84
Baston, Daniel
    The Empathy-Altruism Hypothesis - What and so What?, 290

Bateson, Gregory
    deutero-learning, 318

Bayes, Thomas
    Bayes theorem, 134

Bayesian inference, 133, 136, 137, 138, 180, 181, 182, 184, 228, 249
    Bayesian priors, 137

Beck, Jeff
    Duke Institute for Brain Sciences, 239

behavioral confirmation
    Snyder, Mark, 171

belief perseverance
    Ross, Lepper, 171

beliefs, 134, 169, 179
    adaptive, 179
    Bayesian beliefs
        priors and posteriors, 136
    belief-dependent identity
        Kasser, Tim, 176
    conviction, 136
    definition
        Seitz, Rüdiger J., 168
    Fodor, Jerry, 167
    identity, 177
        Tajfel, Henri & Turner, Jonathan, 170
    Knill, David & Pouget, Alexandre, 168
    meaning
        Park, Crystal, 169
    Metcalfe, Janet & Mischel, Walter, 168
    perceptual filling-in
        Rao, Rajesh & Ballard, Dana, 171
    Quine, Willard & Ullian, Joe, 168
    Schwitzgebel, Eric, 167
    social coordination
        Tomasello, Michael, 170
    values, 178

Berkeley, George
    idealism, 107, 108, 111, 128

Berzin, Alexander
    Buddhism, 115

Blake, William, 198
Bohr, Neils, 105, 106, 112, 121, 123, 124
brain networks
    default mode network, 79, 101, 207
        Buckner, Randy, 169
    executive control network, 79
        Miller, Earl & Cohen, Jonathan, 169
    neural networks, 79, 100, 137, 151, 168, 309
    salience network, 79
        Seely, William, 169

Brewer, Judson
    A Craving Mind, 104, 207

Brodie, Richard
    Virus of the Mind, 89

Bryant, Kelsey
    fermentation hypothesis, 49

Buddhism, 99, 102, 105, 115, 117, 119, 121, 239, 240, 241
    Anatta – non-self, 116
    Anicca - impermanence, 116
    Dukkha - suffering, 116, 117
    four noble truths, 117
    Nirvana – ultimate truth, 118
    Pratitya Samutpada – dependent origination, 116, 128, 218

C

Chalmers, David & Clark, Andy
    The Extended Mind, 82, 84

Chandaria, Shamil
    Center for Eudaimonia and Human Flourishing, 19

Clark, Andy
    predictive processing framework, 169

cognitive behavioral therapy - CBT, 276
    Beck, Aaron & Ellis, Albert, 172, 173

cognitive biases, 142, 148
    anchoring bias, 142, 210
    availability heuristic, 146, 209, 250
    confirmation bias, 148, 205, 250, 262, 284
        Nickerson, Raymond, 170, 210
    conjunction fallacy, 143
    Dunning-Kruger effect, 149, 250, 262
    negativity bias, 64, 149, 228, 233, 234, 303
    recognizing, 249
    representative heuristic, 143, 144, 209
    the Linda problem, 143

cognitive dissonance, 204, 284
    Festinger, Leon, 171, 175

common ancestor, 31
conscious awareness, 20, 53, 63, 72, 131, 136, 138, 139, 168, 204, 309, 311, 315, 320
controlled hallucination
    affective experiences, 159
    Bayesian inference, 180
    reality, 150, 161

cooking, 17, 26, 41, 43, 44, 47, 49, 50, 95
Cowen, Tyler
    The Great Stagnation, 209

critical rationalism
    Popper, Karl, 177, 194

cyanobacteria, 26, 28, 29

D

Dalai Lama, 79, 115
Darwin, Charles, 31, 33, 37
Davidson, Richard
    neuroplasticity, 317
    The Emotional Life of Your Brain, 104
    The Emotional Life of Your Brain, 207

Davis, Wade
    The Wayfinders – Why Ancient Wisdom Matters in the Modern World, 289

Dawkins, Richard
    meme, 89

deGrasse Tyson, Neil
    The Starry Messenger, 192

Dement, William
    The Promise of Sleep, 229

denisovans, 30, 35, 36
Dennett, Daniel
    Intuition Pumps and Other Tools for Thinking, 291

Descartes, Rene, 83, 140
    Meditations on First Philosophy, 200

DeYoung, Colin
    personality neuroscience, 174

disinformation, 189
Dunbar, Robin
    Dunbar's number, 60, 209
    social brain hypothesis, 50, 60

Dweck, Carol
    Mindset, 173, 306

E

Eagleman, David
The Brain - The Story of You, 68, 309
unfinished brain, 70

echo chambers
Pariser, Eli
The Filter Bubble, 171
Pariser, Eli & Sunstein, Cass, 210

Edmonson, Amy
The Fearless Organization, 286

Einstein, Albert, 122, 123, 193, 194, 239
embodied cognition
Moyosore, Ale, Sturdee, Miriam & Rubegni, Elisa, 173

energy budget, 62
energy conversion, 26, 37, 39, 59, 65
extrasomatic, 42, 43
somatic, 42

environmental cognition, 86
ceiling height effects
Meyers-Levy, Joan, 86
Zhu, Rui, 86
natural elements
Ulrich, Roger, 87
spatial organization
Vohs, Kathleen, 87
the influence of climate in human conflict
Hsiang, Burke, Miguel & Kelly, 87

epistemology, 149, 162, 176, 180, 212
epistemic communities, 212
epistemic humility, 203, 289
epistemic pluralism, 213

Euclid, 140
event-related potentials (ERP), 161
evolution, 27, 28, 29, 30, 31, 33, 35, 36, 37, 38, 41, 42, 43, 45, 46, 47, 48, 50, 52, 57, 59, 60, 64, 66, 89, 90, 92, 95, 112, 129, 139, 140, 194, 206, 237, 246, 256, 322
adaptation, 38
convergent evolution, 33
negativity bias, 57

exteroceptive affective cues, 159, 160

F

Feldman Barrett, Lisa
7½ Lessons About the Brain, 19, 52, 103, 316

Fibonacci, 140
Fisher, Roger, & Ury, William
Getting to Yes, 285

G

Gautama, Siddhartha
Buddha, 115

Gawdat, Mo
Solve for Happy - Engineering Your Path to Joy, 150

Gershon, Michael
The Second Brain, 219

Giles, Howard
communication accommodation theory, 282

glymphatic system, 227
Goleman, Daniel
emotional intelligence, 284

Gottman, John
client-centered therapy, 280

Gould, Stephen Jay, 144
Grant, Adam, 315
perspective-taking, 204

great oxygenation event, 27
growth mindset
Dweck, Carol, 167, 177, 311

H

habilines, 44
Haidt, Jonathan
motivated reasoning, 176

Hanh, Thich Nhat, 319
Hansen, Corinna
fermentation hypothesis, 49

Harari, Yuval Noah
Sapiens, 90

Harris, Sam, 19, 199
Hawkins, Jeff, 18
A Thousand Brains, 53, 71

Hebb, Donald
neurons that fire together wire together, 311

Hecht, Erin
fermentation hypothesis, 49

Heisenberg, Werner, 105, 121, 123
Herculano-Houzel, Suzana, 48
neurogenetic trade-off, 45

Hinduism, 102, 105, 112, 114, 115, 119, 120, 121, 239, 240
- Advaita Vedanta, 114
- Atman, 113, 114
- Brahman, 112, 114, 128
- Lila, 113
- Maya, 113, 114, 126
- Upanishads, 106, 112, 114, 312
- Vedantas, 114

Hoffman, Donald
- *The Case Against Reality – Why Evolution Hid the Truth From our Eyes*, 150

homo erectus, 29, 35, 42, 44
homo naledi, 30, 35, 36
homo sapiens, 30, 35, 36, 90
Hume, David, 195
hypothalamic-pituitary-adrenal axis (HPA), 232, 233, 234
hypothesis
- brain expansion
  - expensive tissue, 49
  - fermentation, 49
  - metabolic constraint, 47
  - social brain, 50, 60, 61
- Sapir-Whorf, 88
- somatic marker, 85

I

identity diversification, 177
illusions
- change blindness, 74, 75, 103, 240
- collective, 183, 185, 186, 187, 188, 189, 195, 241
- color, 152
- Deutsch's tritone
  - **Deutsch, Diana**, 155
- emotional, 158, 159, 161, 185, 234, 241
- emotional illusions, 156
- figure-ground, 152
- McGurk effect, 155
- missing-fundamental, 155
- optical, 151
- pareidolia, 151
- phantom limb sensations, 151
- pluralistic ignorance
  - **Allport, Floyd & Katz, Daniel**, 185, 186
- ponzo, 153
- rotating-snakes, 154
  - **Kitaoka, Akiyoshi**, 153
- rubin vase, 152
- sensory, 157, 158, 240
- Shepard-tone
  - **Shepard, Roger**, 156

inflammation
- chronic, 224, 233, 235
- chronic stress, 232
- neuro, 224, 236
- poor diet, 225
- sleep, 227

intellectual humility, 182, 204, 205, 212, 260, 290, 303
- **Leary, Mark**, 177

interoception, 83, 158
- **Craig, A. D.**, 315
- **Damasio, Antonio**
  - somatic marker hypothesis, 85
- **Garfinkel, Sarah**, 85

interpretation bias
- **Gregory, Richard**, 170

J

Jassanoff, Alan, 83
- *The Biological Mind*, 82

K

Kabat-Zinn, Jon
- *Full Catastrophe Living*, 311

Kahan, Dan
- identity-protective cognition, 175

Kahneman, Daniel, 142, 168, 169, 209, 210
Kant, Immanuel, 104, 107, 110, 111, 128, 129, 218
- noumenal world, 104, 110, 240
- phenomenal world, 20, 104, 110, 113, 116, 240

Kasser, Tim
- belief-dependent identity, 176

Kavanagh, Jennifer
- truth decay, 210

Kegan, Robert
- *Immunity to Change – How to Overcome it and Unlock the Potential in Yourself and Your Organization*, 299
- *In Over Our Heads – The Mental Demands of Modern Life*, 316

Kierkegaard, Søren
- existentialism
  - subjective truths, 196

Konorski, Jerzy, 77
Kross, Ethan
- self talk, 277
- social media, 315

Kruglanski, Arie
cognitive closure, 177
Kuhn, Thomas
normal science, 179

L

Lahey, Lisa L.
Immunity to Change – How to Overcome it and Unlock the Potential in Yourself and Your Organization, 299
Lally, Phillippa
How Habits are Formed, 305
language, 37, 41, 50, 57, 89, 91, 101, 120, 276
  clarity and simplicity
    Flesch-Kincaid readability tests, 281
  cultural symbols
    Vygotsky, Lev & Blackwell, Alan, 88
  FOXP2 gene, 90
  influence cognition
    Boroditsky, Lera, 88
    Levinson, Stephen, 88
  language of mathematics, 140
  linguistic diversity
    Everett, Daniel, Gordon, Peter & Frank, Michael, 91
  linguistic equivalency
    Richards, I.A. & Tzu, Meng, 90
  Linguistic Society of America
    Jackendoff, Ray, 90
  McKenna, Terrence, 90
  Naming the Mind
    Danziger, Kurt, 90
  neuroplasticity, 21
  non-verbal, 279, 292
  Why Language is All Thumbs
    Walter, Chip, 90

Laplace, Pierre-Simon, 162, 163
Lazar, Sara
direct experience vs conceptual knowledge, 207

Lebombo bone, 140
Levitin, Daniel
The Organized Mind – Thinking Straight in the Age of Information Overload, 209

Lincoln-Douglas debates, 290
Lotto, Beau, 150
Lyubomirsky, Sonja
The How of Happiness – A New Approach to Getting the Life You Want, 299

M

Macknik, Stephen
Barrow Neurological Institute, 153
Maslow, Abraham
Toward a Psychology of Being, 322
Maxwell, James Clerk
electromagnetism, 193
Mayer, Emeran
The Mind-Gut Connection, 301
McPherson, James M.
Battle Cry of Freedom – The Civil War Era, 290

meditation, 80, 254, 259, 300
Mednick, Martha
Remote Associates Tests - RAT, 205

memory, 218, 221
  capacity, 281
  consolidation, 226, 229
  default mode network, 79
  formation, 59
  schema theory
    Alba, Joseph & Hasher, Lynn, 170
    Bartlett, Frederic, 170
  sleep, 226, 230
  spatial, 88

Merzenich, Michael
neuroplasticity, 20, 77

metacognition, 255
  eastern ancient wisdom, 206
  Fleming, Stephen, 149, 256
  metacognitive awareness, 205, 212, 237, 245, 256, 259
  metacognitive failures, 255
  metacognitive obstacles, 258
  Wilson, Timothy & Brekke, Nancy
    mental contamination and mental correction, 172

Metzger, Miriam
source-credibility crisis, 210

microbiome, 84, 220, 221, 225, 301
microsaccades, 103, 153
mind, 39, 41, 68, 73, 85, 87, 115, 117, 118, 124, 131, 133, 134, 149, 152, 165, 178, 184, 193, 196,

201, 216, 217, 235, 236, 237, 239, 241, 246, 251, 266, 279, 310, 312
misinformation, 189
model of the world, 19, 20, 21, 22, 53, 89, 94, 129, 136, 252, 298
Montreal protocol, 291
multitasking
    Watson, Jason & Strayer, David, 148

Murphy Paul, Annie
    The Extended Mind, 83

N

neanderthals, 30, 35, 36, 44
Neff, Kristin, 306
    Self-Compassion – The Proven Power of Being Kind to Yourself, 247

neocortex, 18, 52
nervous system, 20, 45
    autonomic nervous system - ANS, 51, 219, 234, 301
    central nervous system - CNS, 51, 219
    enteric nervous system - ENS, 218
    gut microbiome, 221
    nervous system dysregulation, 233
    parasympathetic nervous system - PSNS, 219, 233
    primitive organisms, 28, 51
    somatic nervous system - SoNS, 51, 219
    sympathetic nervous system - SNS, 219, 233

neural pruning, 69
neural regions
    amygdala, 21, 157, 161, 168, 172, 229, 234, 284
    anterior cingulate cortex, 157, 175, 256
    hippocampus, 157, 232, 234
        BDNF, 80
        computational aids, 88
        spatial memory, 78
        spatial relationships, 72
    insula, 157, 158
    prefrontal cortex, 21, 73, 85, 157, 173, 205, 217, 231, 233, 256

neurons, 43, 45, 46, 47, 48, 49, 50, 51, 69, 76, 77, 81, 84, 154, 219, 224, 227, 236, 335
neuroplasticity, 20, 21, 22, 59, 66, 68, 77, 78, 79, 80, 93, 95, 101, 129, 233, 234, 298, 301, 303, 307, 310, 312
    London taxi drivers, 78

neurotransmitter, 20, 220, 222, 224, 233
    acetylcholine, 221
    dopamine, 221
    GABA - Gamma-Aminobutyric Acid, 220, 221, 223
    norepinephrine, 221
    serotonin, 84, 218, 221

Newton, Isaac, 122, 140, 162, 193
Nin, Anaïs, 101
Nisbett, Richard & Miyamoto, Yuri
    the influence of culture in perception, 174

O

O'Gieblyn, Meghan
    Do we have minds of our own?, 83

P

Page, Scott
    collaborative truth-seeking, 212

Paivio, Allan
    dual-coding theory, 283

pattern recognition, 54, 59, 73, 287
Perlmutter, David and Austin
    Brain Wash, 20, 77

perspective-taking
    Galinsky, Adam & Moskowitz, Gordon, 172

Pinker, Steven
    The Sense of Style, 281

Plato, 107, 192
    allegory of the cave, 107

Ponce de León, Marcia, 57
pragmatists
    James, William, 77, 192, 197, 260, 313
    Sanders Pierce, Charles, 197

prediction error, 19, 71, 74, 157, 189
predictive processing, 71, 74, 128, 158, 163, 186, 226, 240, 302
    Andy Clark, Jakob Hohwy & Anil Seth, 72
    Georg Keller & Thomas Mrsic-Flogel, 104

primates, 30, 31, 32, 33, 42, 46, 48, 49
psychological flexibility, 180
pygmalion in the classroom study
    Rosenthal, Robert & Jacobson, Lenore, 171

Pythagoras, 140

Q

quantum theory, 105
    complementarity principle, 125
    consciousness, 127
    Heisenberg's uncertainty principle, 126
    measurement vs observation, 122
    parallels with ancient wisdom, 106, 109, 119
    quantum entanglement, 126
    superposition, 125
    wave-particle duality, 125

R

rational emotive behavior therapy - REBT
    Ellis, Albert, 174, 252
reality, 100
    Bayesian model of reality, 134
    Berkeley, George
        esse est percipi, 108
    Buddhism, 115
    constructed self, 101
    hallucinations, 149, 151
    Hinduism, 112
    Kant, Immanuel
        constructed reality, 110
    naive realism, 103, 111, 128
    Plato
        the realm of forms, 107
    quantum reality, 105, 122, 125
    quantum theory, 127
reality testing
    Klayman, Joshua & Ha, Young-won, 171
Rising Star cave, 35
Rogers, Carl, 317
    client-centered therapy, 278
Rose, Todd
    Collective Illusions, 184, 186
Rosenberg, Marshall
    Nonviolent Communication, 285

S

Sandberg, Sheryl, 22
Scharmer, Otto
    levels of listening, 279
Schrödinger, Erwin, 106, 121, 123
Schwartz, Barry
    paradox of choice, 208

second brain, 218, 219, 226, 236
    gut-brain axis, 84, 221
self-awareness, 18, 21, 59, 65, 85, 149, 251, 262, 275, 284, 294
self-criticism, 246, 247, 251, 262, 275, 306
self-fulfilling prophecies, 171
self-serving bias, 250
Seligman, Martin
    explanatory style, 206
sensory inputs, 19, 20, 58, 59, 71, 157
Seth, Anil
    predictive processing framework, 310
Shannon, Claude
    information theory, 208
Siegel, Dan
    Mindsight, 82
Sigman, Mariano
    The Secret Life of the Mind, 312
sleep, 80, 218, 226, 227, 229, 230, 236, 301
    depravation, 228
    quantity & quality, 227
Smil, Vaclav
    How the World Really Works, 26
social conformity
    Klucharev, Vasily, 187
    neurobiology, 189
    Stallen, Mirre & Sanfey, Alan, 188
Socrates
    self-examination, 241
    the good life, 203
    the Socratic method, 204
    truth, 192
somatic, 173
speciation, 31, 33
statistical reasoning paradox, 138, 145, 147
statistics, 17, 18, 141, 142, 143, 144, 147, 162, 273
    Achenwall, Gottfried, 142
    Fisher, Ronald A., 142
    frequency effect, 146
    Galton, Francis, 142
    Graunt, John
        Natural and Political Observations Made upon the Bills of Mortality, 141
    Pearson, Karl, 142
    statistical inference, 145
steelmanning, 291
stress
    ancient response to modern triggers, 39
    belief systems, 204
    cardiovascular awareness, 85

chronic, 232
cortisol, 224, 231
digestive problems, 221
hormone release, 58
hyper-vigilant brain, 234
management, 58
nervous system dysregulation, 233
oxidative, 222
reduction techniques, 284
response regulation, 220
short-term vs long-term, 231
sleep depravation, 231
survival, 231

Suzuki, Shunryu
Zen Mind, Beginner's Mind, 321

Sweller, John
cognitive load theory, 281

T

Tajfel, Henri
social identity dependence, 176

Tao Te Ching, 120

Taylor, Charles
The Ethics of Authenticity, 320

Thales of Miletus, 140
theory of evolution, 34, 35
theory of mind, 60, 102
truth, 191
    Buddhism
        impermanence, 206
        interdependence, 207
        non-duality, 207
    cognitive fusion, 206
    eastern ancient wisdom, 206
    objective truths, 192, 202
    pragmatic truths, 197, 202
    subjective truths, 195, 202
    truth-seeking, 212, 214

Turkle, Sherry
Reclaiming Conversation – The Power of Talk in a Digital Age, 293, 319

Tversky, Amos, 142, 169

U

universal values
    Schwartz, Shalom, 178

V

vagus nerve, 219, 220, 233
Varian, Hal, 209
Vasavada, Kashyap, 105
visual perception
    de Lange, Floris, Heilbron, Micha, & Kok, Peter, 103
Vygotsky, Lev
Thought and Language, 276

W

Walker, Matthew
Why We Sleep, 226

Watts, Duncan
misinformation, 209

Weil, Simone
attention, 313

Wenger, Etienne
Communities of Practice - Learning, Meaning, and Identity, 320

Wheeler, Peter
expensive tissue hypothesis, 49

Wrangham, Richard, 44, 50
Catching Fire, 44

Y

Young, Thomas, 122
Young, Valerie
impostor syndrome, 248

Z

Zollikofer, Christoph, 57

www.ingramcontent.com/pod-product-compliance
Lightning Source LLC
Chambersburg PA
CBHW071147070526
44584CB00019B/2693